Fire see page 288
First aid see page 291

GOOD HOUSEKEEPING
The Home Book

GOOD HOUSEKEEPING

Compiled by

The Home Book

Good Housekeeping Institute

Ebury Press : London

Published in Great Britain by Ebury Press
Chestergate House, Vauxhall Bridge Road
London SW1V 1HF

First impression 1978

ISBN 0 85223 128 8

Editor: Gill Edden
Research: Gillian Smedley, Jack Smith
Text: Josephine Dew
Illustrations: C. R. Evans
Designer: Derek Morrison

Printed and bound in Spain by
Novograph S.A., Madrid
Dep. Legal: M-42107-1977

Contents

FOR DETAILED CONTENTS SEE FIRST PAGE
OF EACH SECTION

Acknowledgments

The following people and organisations gave valuable help providing and checking the information in this book:

Aeonics Ltd

Trevor M. Aldridge M.A. (Cantab.)

Armstrong Cork Co. Ltd

Banking Information Service

Bayer Fibres (UK) Ltd

Bissell Appliances Ltd

The Board of Inland Revenue

The Boots Company Ltd

Bostik Ltd

Braby Group Ltd

Brick Development Association

British Association of Removers

British Carpet Manufacturers' Association

The British Ceramic Research Association

British Gas Corporation

British Holloware Manufacturers' Association

British Insurance Association

British Nova Works Ltd

The British Red Cross Society

British Standards Institution

The Building Societies Association

Cement and Concrete Association

J. P. Coats Ltd

Connolly Bros (Curriers) Ltd

The Continental Quilt Association

Copydex Ltd

Courtaulds Ltd

Crown Decorative Products Ltd

Department of the Environment

Department of Health and Social Security

Department for National Savings

Department of Transport

The Direct Sales and Services Association

Dunlop Ltd

Eaton Ltd, Yale Security Products Division

The Electricity Council

Electrolux Ltd

Fire Protection Association

Angela Fishburn

Formica Ltd

Dr Susan Garth

GKN Ltd

Glass and Glazing Federation

Glass Manufacturers' Federation

The Hire Purchase Trade Association

Home Laundering Consultative Council

Home Office

Hoover Ltd

Imperial Chemical Industries Ltd

St John Ambulance

H. & R. Johnson

Johnson Wax Ltd

Kitchen Devils Ltd

The Law Society

Leifheit International UK

The John Lewis Partnership

The Life Offices Association

Lord Chancellor's Office

The Mail Order Traders' Association of Great Britain

Metrication Board

Winifred M. Mitchell

F. E. Mostyn LL.B.

National Bedding Federation

National Fireplace Manufacturers' Association

National Water Council

The Newspaper Publishers' Association Ltd

Office of Fair Trading

Office of Population Censuses and Surveys

Passport Office

People's Dispensary for Sick Animals

Periodical Publishers Association Ltd

Post Office

Rentokil Ltd

Retail Trading Standards Association

Royal Society for the Prevention of Cruelty to Animals

Rufflette Ltd

Runnymede Rubber Co. Ltd

Arthur Sanderson & Sons Ltd

The Solid Fuel Advisory Service

Sterling Roncraft

The Stock Exchange

Sunbury Metal Pressings Ltd

Timber Research and Development Association

Trustee Savings Bank

Vitreous Enamel Development Council Ltd

Winsor and Newton Ltd

Foreword

Every household needs a ready reference book to solve the day-to-day problems that occur in the home – anything and everything from removing tea and coffee from the carpet to dealing with door-to-door sales or leaking gutters. Old fashioned remedies and methods won't do any more. For man made fibres, furniture with modern finishes and sophisticated kitchen and household equipment up-to-date products are needed. This is where the expertise of GOOD HOUSEKEEPING INSTITUTE comes in. The information in this book has been taken from the wealth of knowledge and research accumulated by our experts. We have covered the cleaning problems that we know people have to cope with and we give sound but simple methods of dealing with them. We give instructions for DIY jobs from making curtains to building a garden wall. Repairs of course are included, with special emphasis on modern adhesives which can be chosen to stick almost anything.

Then there's the other side of running a home – how to save money for it, how to buy it, how to insure it and what is very important to today's householder, a knowledge of consumer law.

We hope you will find that GHI have supplied you with the most up-to-date answers to your household problems; if not write to us at GOOD HOUSEKEEPING INSTITUTE, Chestergate House, Vauxhall Bridge Road, London SW1V 1HF.

Carol Macartney
Director

1. Making and mending

Soft furnishing fabrics

There is more to choosing soft furnishing fabrics than selecting a pattern that you like and a colour that goes with your decor – the type of fabric is an all important factor. Covering furniture in fabric that is meant for curtains can be an expensive mistake; it just will not stand up to the wear and tear it has to take.

When you buy furnishing fabrics you should find that they are clearly labelled. In addition to the name, width and price, there should be details of fibre content and there may be an indication of whether they are suitable for upholstery and loose covers or just curtains and bedcovers. If there is no label on the fabric itself, ask about the fibre content and for care instructions (these are often available on a leaflet at the point of sale or, in certain cases, on a sew-in label provided with each length of fabric).

Where the fabric is washable, check whether it has been pre-shrunk or given a shrink-resistant treatment. Untreated natural fibre fabrics can shrink on washing by up to 15 per cent and there could be slight shrinkage on dry cleaning, so estimate your requirements accordingly and wash before you cut, or leave allowances for possible shrinkage. Never try to wash any fabric marked 'dry clean only'.

Colour fastness, too, is important, not only with regard to wear, laundering and dry cleaning, but for protection against fading in strong daylight, particularly sunlight. Some furnishing fabrics are guaranteed not to fade, and many woven types are marked as conforming with British Standard 2543 which, although a minimum requirement for colour fastness, is worth looking for.

Since the life of soft furnishings is prolonged by regular cleaning, it is only sensible to bear in mind care requirements when making your initial choice. Try to buy machine washable, easy care fabrics when you know the article will be suited to, and small enough for, your domestic laundering and drying facilities. It will save a lot of effort and money. But do remember that certain soft furnishings, such as curtains with attached linings and interlinings, are better dry cleaned and, even though they may be washable, it is practical to send large articles like loose settee covers for professional treatment.

FABRIC	USES	CARE
Brocade and **brocatelle** are richly patterned weaves, sometimes with a shallow relief, produced on a jacquard loom. Made from silk, cotton or man-made fibres.	Curtains, bedcovers and the heavier qualities for upholstery.	These are heavy fabrics and are normally best dry cleaned, though those made from cotton or man-made fibres may be washed if labelled accordingly.
Cambric is a light weight cotton fabric.	Linings. Downproof cambric is used in making down filled eiderdowns, duvets and cushions to prevent the filling working through. It is not featherproof.	Wash or dry clean, according to label and the type and size of article.
Chintz and **Cretonne** are closely woven printed cotton fabrics. Chintz has a characteristic glazed finish. Cretonne is similar, but without the glaze, and may also be made of linen or viscose.	Curtains, bedcovers, quilts and loose covers.	Dry clean or wash according to the label. Certain dry cleaners will re-glaze chintz if this becomes necessary.

FABRIC	USES	CARE
Corduroy is usually made from cotton, sometimes in a mixture with man-made fibres. It has a short cut pile and is a ribbed fabric with a one-way nap and must be cut to allow for this. Do not use dress weight corduroy for upholstery; it will not wear well enough.	Light upholstery, curtains, cushions and bedcovers.	Check care instructions. Some cotton corduroy can be washed but try to avoid crushing. Rinse well and drip dry. Large articles are best dry cleaned.
Denim is an extremely hard-wearing and fairly inexpensive coarse cotton twill fabric. It comes in different weights – so choose the heavier type for loose covers.	Loose covers, cushions and bedcovers.	Washable.
Dupion is a fine fabric, originally one woven from raw, rough silk, giving a slubbed finish. Today it is usually a mixture of man-made fibres such as viscose and acetate. It comes in a wide range of colours.	Curtains, cushions, bedcovers.	Dry cleaning is usually recommended because of the mixture of yarns.
Glass fibre fabrics are translucent, flame-retardant, crease resistant, shrink and moth proof. They split easily, though, if subjected to excessive handling or constant rubbing against a curtain pelmet or window sill; they are also inclined to become charged with static electricity and consequently attract dust.	Unlined curtains.	Hand wash in the bath to avoid twisting or crushing which could crack the fibres. Wear rubber gloves to prevent skin irritation. Drip-dry – do not use clothes pegs and fold as little as possible.
Linen is a plain or patterned woven fabric made from flax. It is a strong and hard-wearing but creases easily. More practical is **linen-union**, a mixture with cotton, usually with a printed design. A number of **'linen-look'** fabrics with slubbed weave are made from man-made fibres and mixtures with cotton.	Loose covers, upholstery and curtains.	Washable but large and lined curtains may be more easily dry cleaned.
Moiré is the name given to a characteristic watermarked effect applied to silk or viscose fabrics by a process of heat under pressure.	Curtains, cushions, bedcovers.	Dry clean. Washing removes the watermarked effect.
Moquette is a tough hard-wearing fabric with a short loop or cut pile or a combination of the two. It is made from wool or cotton, with a woven cotton or viscose backing. Choose a heavy, close weave for hard wear.	Upholstery.	Dry clean.

FABRIC	USES	CARE
Nets are made from man-made fibres or cotton and may be either plain or patterned. Modern nets have a greater resistance to sunlight which prevents them yellowing.	Screening curtains.	Wash and drip dry. Use a warm iron if necessary.
PVC or polyurethane coated fabrics include imitation leathers and can have a woven or knitted backing.	Upholstery.	Clean with a well wrung out soapy cloth. Wipe dry.
Repp is a hard-wearing, medium priced fabric with a ribbed surface. Usually made from cotton but also available in silk, wool and viscose. It comes in a wide range of colours.	Curtains and cushions. Heavier quality repps are suitable for loose covers.	Dry clean, or wash if pre-shrunk and labelled accordingly.
Satin is a lustrous fabric of silk, cotton or man-made fibres woven so most of the warp (lengthwise) thread shows on the surface, making the fabric glossy on one side.	Curtains, bedcovers, cushions.	Check labelling and treat accordingly. Both satin and sateen tend to show spills as watermarks – not ideal if you have a young family.
Sateen is made of cotton and similar to satin but with the weft threads giving the surface sheen.	Lining curtains.	Washable.
Sheers are lightweight open-weave fabrics made from man-made fibres, cotton and wool. They come in various colours and designs.	See-through curtains.	Man-made fibre and cotton sheers are usually washable. Wools should be dry cleaned.
Tapestry is made of wool or mixtures with coarse yarns. It is a figured fabric produced on a jacquard loom, usually in a variety of colours. Can be expensive but is very hard wearing.	Upholstery, bedspreads.	Dry clean.
Ticking is a strong twill weave fabric made of cotton and with feather-proof qualities	Primary covers for feather filled pillows and cushions (use cambric for soft feathers and down fillings).	Wash or dry clean as necessary.
Tweed is a twill weave fabric made in wool, man-made fibres and mixtures and priced according to the weight and fibre content. Check suitability for the article in question. (Make sure you know the fibre content so you can deal with spills and marks.)	Upholstery, curtains, bedcovers and loose covers.	Dry clean, or wash according to the manufacturer's instructions.
Velour is a heavy pile fabric made of cotton sometimes in a mixture with viscose.	Curtains (the pile should run downwards). Heavier qualities are available for upholstery.	Dry clean.

FABRIC	USES	CARE
Velvet is a fine pile fabric made of silk, cotton or man-made fibres. Acrylic velvet has a backing either of cotton or of cotton in a mixture with man-made fibres. It is particularly good for upholstery because the pile has a natural resistance to staining, ie low absorbency. It comes in a wide range of colours and textures.	Upholstery, cushions and curtains (these should be made with the pile running in a downwards direction but blemishes in inexpensive velvets will be less noticeable if the pile runs upwards).	Dry clean unless labelled otherwise; some velvets are machine washable.

Curtains

Curtains can do a lot more for a room than simply framing the view or shutting out the night. Well made and well hung they can give a room a touch of drama, even luxury. Your starting point is the curtain track.

CHOOSING TRACKS
Most curtain tracks fall into one of three categories:

Traditional pole and rings can be made of brass or with a brass-look finish, wood, or plastic with a white, coloured or wood finish. When you buy the rings you should allow about 12 rings per metre of pole.

A cheaper version of the pole and rings looks much the same, but in fact has a flattened back and half-ring gliders, so that it fits snugly against the wall. Other variations on the pole and rings can be flatter band-type tracks, often in a wood finish or with white and gold decoration.

Ornamental ends called 'finials' are available for most curtain poles and band tracks.

Tracks which do not show These are slender, unobtrusive strips which are seen only when the curtains are pulled back. When the curtains are closed, stand-up headings hide the tracks. The tracks can usually be wall or ceiling mounted, de-pending on the design of the window and the required position for the curtain.

Some modern tracks are flexible and can be used round shallow curve bay windows. Often the glider hooks clip over or slide on to the tracks and some can be attached directly to the curtain heading tape. It is still possible to get curtain tracks and gliders in metal, but most are now made in plastic or nylon which have the advantage they do not rust, rattle or stick as metal ones can. An overlap section is available with most tracks – this ensures that the curtains overlap a little when you pull them.

For windows where you need screening curtains in addition to the ordinary curtains it is possible to buy a curtain track designed to take long extension brackets which hold a second track. Otherwise, where screening curtains are to be used alone, the extra-slim tracks designed specially to take nets are unobtrusive and easy to put up with just a screw or two. They take more weight than you might think, so as well as nets they can often be used for sheers and other lightweight materials. However, to make sure you choose a track that will take the weight of the curtains you are planning to put up, it is as well to ask the retailer's advice.

Tracks for small windows Special lightweight spring-loaded rods for small windows fit into the window recess and need no additional fixing. Or

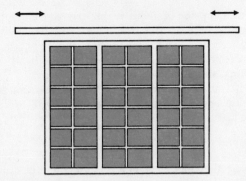

Allow enough track either side of the window to enable you to pull the curtains well back

you can hang the curtains on expanding curtain wire. This is the cheapest method of hanging curtains; you can buy the wire cut to fit your window, together with neat end pieces and plastic screw hooks to hold it in place.

Length of track
When buying a curtain track, remember that to avoid losing daylight it is important to choose one wide enough so the pulled-back curtains will clear, or almost clear, the window. How wide this is will depend in part on the weight of fabric and the type of heading that you choose, but as a general rule you should allow at least 15 cm of extra track on either side of small windows, 30 cm on either side of standard windows, and 45 cm extra track on either side of wide windows.

Cording sets
Cording sets make it possible to draw the curtains without handling the fabric. They are particularly useful for velvets, which otherwise fingermark, and for avoiding strain on the fabric when drawing heavy curtains. The sets are available for use with a number of the curtain tracks and some curtain poles.

CURTAIN HEADINGS
The heading tape you choose will depend on the effect you want to achieve. Most tapes are sold by the metre and the hooks can be bought separately; fixing instructions are usually available.

Gathered headings call for the least curtain material. You will need to allow a minimum of one-and-a-half times the width of your rail for both fabric and tape, plus extra for joins, side turnings and a curtain overlap if you want one. For a fuller, more generous look, allow double the width of your track.

Pinch-pleat headings This elegant style of heading is achieved with tapes which give groups of two- or three-fold french pleats that fan out slightly at the top of the curtain and leave spaces of smooth fabric between each group. It is possible to have either deep or shallow pleats. Different tapes are made for use with a concealed track or pole and rings. You will need to allow exactly double the width of your track when estimating for the fabric and the tape.

Pencil-pleat headings Pencil pleats are regular and close together, so for fabric and tape you will need to allow at least two-and-a-quarter times the width of your track – but two-and-a-half looks better, and for sheers three times the width is best.

This type of dense pleating is particularly suitable for sheers and nets which remain in position to give privacy or veil an unattractive view. A man-made fibre tape is available for use with fine fabrics. Heavier curtains that have been pencil-pleated make considerable bulk when you pull them back, so you will need to hang them on a track wide enough to allow them to be pulled back almost clear of the windows, otherwise they will cut out too much light. Pencil-pleat heading tape can usually be reversed so that the pockets for the hooks are near the lower edge for use with concealed track and near the top for the suspended style.

Detachable lining tapes Here the lining with its own tape is simply hooked on to the heading tape

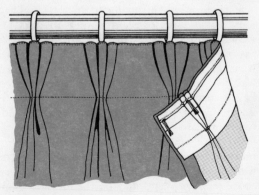

A pinch-pleat heading can be suspended on a pole and rings or used with concealed track

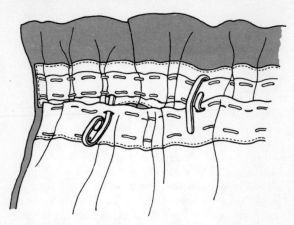

A separate lining tape hooks on to the main heading tape so that the lining can be detached

of the curtain and can be unhooked again for cleaning or washing. This is useful because the lining is on the window side and so is likely to get dirty sooner than the curtain itself.

CHOOSING A FABRIC

Before you make your final choice, it is a good idea to buy a metre of the fabric you are thinking of buying, take it home with you and live with it for a while. Look at it in daylight and in artificial light to see how the colour changes. See how it looks when it is bunched up and how it drapes. Finally try washing it (unless it is marked 'dry clean only') to see whether it shrinks and whether it runs.

Calculating the amount of fabric

How much fabric you will need depends first on the height and width of your curtain tracks. These must be in place before you measure up. The second consideration is the type of heading you have chosen. Curtain fabrics are usually 120–122 cm wide, so you may have to join widths and half widths to get the fullness you need. In your calculations, remember to add 8 cm to each width for turnings, plus 8 cm on each curtain if you want a centre overlap.

To work out the length of the material, first measure from the curtain rail to 1 cm above the window sill, 15 cm below the window sill or 2·5 cm above the floor, depending on the finished length of curtain required. Add 25 cm to this measurement for the heading and the hem. This will give a

hem allowance of about 15 cm, depending on the type of heading you use. There will be enough fabric to let down in case of slight shrinkage, but if you think the material is particularly likely to shrink, add about 5 cm to each curtain length.

If you are using a patterned fabric, measure the repeat and add this amount to each length except the first to allow for matching.

Lining fabric

Lining fabric is usually 120–122 cm wide. To calculate the amount of lining fabric you will need, take the total amount of fabric you have worked out for the curtains and deduct any allowance that you have made for pattern matching, then deduct a further 10 cm multiplied by the number of widths (because rather less fabric is required for the lining than for the curtain).

MAKING A LINED CURTAIN

1 Before cutting the first length of a patterned fabric, pin it up at the window to make sure the main repeat is attractively placed – at about eye level on full length curtains. Half repeats look best at the top and bottom.

2 When you have chosen a suitable part of the design for the top edge of the curtain, measure upwards from this point 1·3 to 1·5 cm for a pencil or pinch-pleat heading, or 3·5 cm above if you are going to use a gathering tape. Check these measurements against the recommendations of the heading tape manufacturer. Measure down to the curtain length you have calculated, add on the allowance for the hem and mark it with pins.

3 After you have cut the first length, lay it on top of the rest of the fabric and match the pattern exactly for each length – just as you would with wallpaper. The pattern level must correspond on all curtains in the same room. With velvets, make sure that the pile runs downwards on all the pieces.

4 Cut the number of lengths of curtain fabric that you need to give the desired total width. Join the widths if necessary using an open seam. Press flat carefully and, provided the fabric is not likely to fray badly, clip the selvedges diagonally at 8 cm intervals to prevent puckering. When pressing velvet, use a velvet pressing board and press from the wrong side.

5 Make a single turn of 4 cm down each edge of the curtain. For nets make a double turning totalling

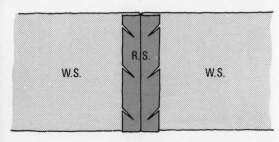

Clip tight selvedges on the seams to help them lie flat. Otherwise they tend to pull

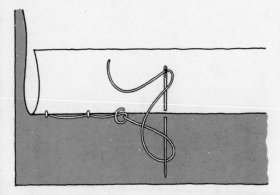

Lock stitch the lining invisibly to the curtain

4 cm. Tack, then sew the turnings into place with herringbone or slip hem stitch. Try to show as little thread as possible on the right side of the fabric (most automatic sewing machines have a blind hemming stitch which is ideal for sewing these side edges invisibly).

6 Join the widths of lining if necessary. Press the seams open and snip the selvedges diagonally as for curtains.

Attaching the lining
7 Lay the curtain on a flat surface, wrong side uppermost, and place the lining right side uppermost over it; the top edges of the lining and the curtain should meet and there should be an even overlap of lining at both sides.

8 Fold the lining back in half lengthwise so that its side edges meet. Pin the fold of the lining down the centre of the curtain and lockstitch the lining to the curtain using thread to match the curtain. (Lockstitch is a row of large loose stitches about 2·5 cm apart, which take up a single thread of the lining and then of the curtain so that the stitches do not show on the right side.) The stitching should come

to within 8 cm of the top and 25 cm of the lower edge of the curtain.

9 Work further lines of locking stitches either side of the centre about 38 cm apart.

10 Turn under the side edges of the lining leaving an even margin of 1–2 cm of curtain fabric. Pin the fold then trim off the excess lining leaving a 2 cm turning. Press along the fold. Pin the lining to the curtain and slip stitch in position.

11 Treating the curtain and lining as one fabric, attach the heading tape following the manufacturer's instructions. It is usual to turn over 1·3 to 1·5 cm for deep headings and 3·5 cm for gathered headings. If the lining is too bulky, trim off a bit from the top which will be covered by the curtain fabric or the tape. For deep headings, position the tape 3 mm below the fold line, for gathered headings 2·5 cm below the fold.

12 Knot the strings together securely at one end of the tape then tack the tapes into position and machine – taking care not to sew over the strings. The stitching at the top and bottom of the tape should both run in the same direction. Pull up the heading tape strings as tightly as you can then ease out the gathers or pleats until the curtain width is equal to half the width of the track, plus overlap if necessary. Tie the strings, but do not cut them off because you will need to untie them to flatten the curtains for washing or cleaning. It is possible to buy a plastic cord tidy, shaped so that the strings

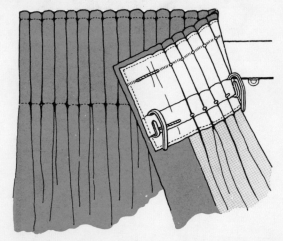

Secure tape firmly with machine stitching. Insert first hook as close to the end of the tape as possible
For pencil-pleat heading use standard hooks

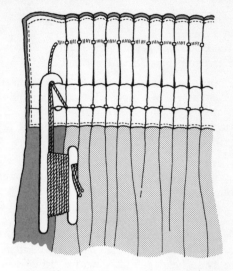

A cord tidy holds the strings out of sight

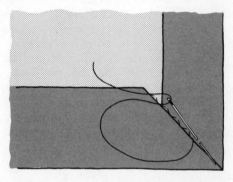

Neaten the lower corners with mitres and
slip stitch in place. Do not cut off the excess

can be wound round and held firmly in position.
This is hung out of sight at the back of the curtain.

Making the hem
13 Hang the curtains and, if they are heavy ones,
leave them to settle for a week or so before finishing
the hem. Then pin the hem into place – full length
curtains should just clear the floor. Double thickness hems improve the hang of most curtains but
use a single hem with bulky fabrics such as velvet.
Fold the corners into mitres but do not cut away
any excess fabric; you may need it later if the
curtain shrinks or you move to a house with a
deeper window. Tack and slip hem the top edge of
the hem in place and slip stitch the mitres.

14 On the lining, fold under a hem approximately
3 to 5 cm deep to finish 3 cm above the lower edge
of the curtain. Trim off any excess. Tack and slip
stitch the hem of the lining, but do not stitch the
lining to the curtain at the hem.

Weighting curtains
It is sometimes necessary to weight curtains to get
them to hang well. Use either flat, lead button
weights or string weights laid along the fold of the
hem, and in the case of string weights, attach them
to the side turnings. When making curtains from a
very loose-weave fabric, string weights should be
loosely stitched into position along the hem fold.

Loose linings
Where the lining is to be made separately from the
curtains, the side edges should be finished with a
double turn of fabric and a detachable curtain
lining tape attached along the top edge.

Roller blinds

Roller blinds are neat and attractive, space-making
in a small room and dramatic if you want a bold
focal point. Another great advantage is their cost.

Roller blinds need only enough fabric to cover the
window flat, so they are bound to be cheaper than
curtains, even allowing for the cost of the kit.

There are two types of roller blind kit that you can buy. One is a basic kit to which you add your own fabric; the other comes complete with the material.

Choosing a fabric

In theory, if you are going to make your blind from you own material, you can choose any fabric you like. In practice, though, it is best to go for a medium weight, closely woven fabric that does not fray easily. Cotton is ideal, as are linens, PVC and vinyl; or you could choose a special blind fabric such as holland, that will keep out the light. Be particularly careful when choosing patterned fabrics as they may not be printed on the straight grain and this could stop the blind rolling evenly. If the pattern is slightly off the straight you can probably stretch it diagonally to improve it; damping may help. If it is badly off the straight it is not a wise choice. Avoid nets and sheers, which are too light to roll well, and fabrics which are too thick and heavy to roll up. Plasticised and vinyl fabrics are particularly suitable for a kitchen or bathroom as they can be wiped clean.

Even if you do not want to cut the light completely, hold your chosen fabric up to natural light to check its translucence – some patterns lose definition. Then hold it against artificial light, looking at it from the wrong side, to find out how see-through it is and if you are likely to cast any interesting shadows after dusk.

If you are tempted to choose a dress fabric, consider the width. If the window is wider than 90 cm no matter how carefully you match and join the fabric you will still have a noticeable line against the light and the bulk of the seam could affect the roll-up action. If you cannot cut a blind from a single width, it is usually better to make two and stagger their positions so they overlap.

Equally, if your window is more than 2 m wide, unless it is a short drop, it is usually better to have two or more narrow blinds rather than one long one on which the spring mechanism might be overloaded.

Measuring up

You can hang a blind either inside the recess where it will be close to the glass or outside the recess; you may even like to have one translucent blind against the glass for daylight hours and hang another patterned blind in front of this to pull down after dark.

Once you decide where you want to put the blind, measure the window. This must be done accurately, because tiny errors add up to expensive mistakes. Use a wooden or metal rule as fabric tape measures tend to stretch.

Be sure to measure the window at the top, where the blind is going to be fixed, and not at the bottom. Windows are rarely square. If the blind is going to be outside the window recess allow for an overlap of 5 cm at each side and at the bottom, or the fabric may bunch awkwardly in the recess.

Choosing a kit

Kits are available in various widths. If the area of your window falls between two sizes, choose the larger one and cut the pole down as needed, allowing for the fact that the pole must be slightly longer than the finished width of the blind.

In the kit you will usually be provided with the roller, bottom bar, pullcord and acorn, glue and tacks for fixing the fabric to the roller, brackets and screws. Some kits also include a fabric stiffener, but where the fabric itself is included this will have been treated if necessary.

STEP-BY-STEP
GENERAL INSTRUCTIONS
(but check for special directions with your kit)

1 Fix the brackets in position either within the window recess or on the wall. The bracket for the square pin must always go on the left of the window as you face it; the bracket for the round pin then goes on the right. Measure the distance between the brackets and cut the wooden pole to length using a small saw, paying particular attention to the instructions given with the kit, eg in some cases you have to allow for the thickness of the metal end cap and deduct this measurement from the pole. Fit the metal cap firmly on to the cut end of the pole, first rubbing the wood down lightly with glasspaper to give a smooth finish.

Hammer the round pin through the hole in the cap into the end of the pole, but do not rest the spring end (square pin) of the pole on the floor as the vibration could damage the mechanism; balance the pole on a table or worktop and hammer sideways.

(cont'd overleaf)

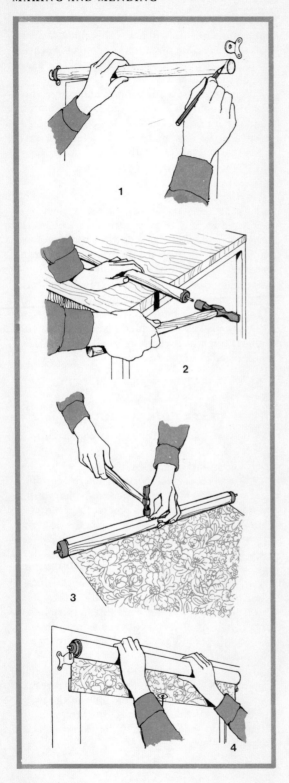

Fitting a roller blind. 1. Fix the brackets in position then mark and cut the pole to fit. Allow for the thickness of the end cap if necessary 2. Hammer the pin home, taking care not to damage the mechanism 3. Tack the fabric evenly to the pole, right side up 4. Hand-roll the blind to tension the spring

2 Pull a thread across the fabric to make sure that you are cutting absolutely square and cut the blind fabric width to the size of the wooden roller plus an allowance of 4 cm for side seams. Side seams may not be necessary on vinyl or plastics fabrics that are unlikely to fray. NB Patterned fabrics may not be printed exactly on the straight grain; cut these according to the pattern and not the grain.

The length should cover the required drop plus about 30 cm to allow for wrap-around at the top and the batten pocket at the bottom.

Turn under 2 cm each side (except on vinyl or plastics fabrics) and zigzag over the edge to prevent fraying and to hold the seam flat. If you do not have a swing needle machine use two rows of stitching close together. Snip the selvedges to help the blind hang flat. The batten pocket at the bottom is made by turning up 5 cm to the wrong side, enclosing the raw edge and machining or sticking the fabric near the edge. The material should now be ironed and a stiffener applied to both sides if the fabric has not been pre-stiffened. Pin the fabric on to a protected wall and spray with an aerosol fabric stiffener (have the window open, because the smell is pungent).

3 Lay the fabric out with the right side up and place the roller across near the top, about 4 cm down. Stick double-sided adhesive tape across the material to hold it temporarily and roll the roller on to it. This will get the roller fixed squarely and the blind will hang evenly. Then use either a staple gun or tacks at 5 cm intervals, working from the centre outwards, to hold the fabric permanently.

Cut the wooden bottom bar to length, 2·5 cm

shorter than the blind width, and insert it into the pocket at the bottom of the fabric; sew up the ends to neaten the pocket, if necessary. Fix the acorn to the end of the pullcord at the required length. Attach the pullcord on the right side in the middle of the batten, using the screws provided.

4 Roll up the blind by hand to 'tension' the spring and slot it into the fixing brackets. Pull down the blind, using the pullcord. If the blind fails to hold in the down position, or will not roll up when released, the spring is under-tensioned and you should repeat the hand roll-ing process. Hold the square pin between your fingers to prevent the spring from unwinding, and put the blind back on the brackets. If, when released, the blind springs up too quickly, the roller is over-tensioned and this may ulti-mately damage the mechanism. Solve this by removing the blind from the brackets, unrolling the fabric completely and then re-rolling by hand for about three-quarters of the length. Re-position and pull up as usual. It may take one or two attempts to get it exact. If the blind is still not working smoothly, check that the brackets are square.

Bedcovers

A THROW-OVER BEDSPREAD
This is the simplest bedcover to make and the most economical in terms of material.

Measuring
Measure the bed complete with bedclothes and pillow to make sure the cover will be large enough. Take the width measurement from the floor on one side, across the bed to the floor on the opposite side. Add 7 cm for side hems and 3 cm seam allowance for every join. The length should be taken from the top edge of the pillow, along the centre of the bed down to the floor at the foot of the bed. Add 7 cm for the hems and if you want to tuck the cover under the pillow, a further 30 cm. With patterned fabric, the pattern must be matched at the seams so, in the case of a large design, measure the repeat and add this to the length you buy.

Cutting the fabric
Furnishing fabrics come in different widths and you will get the neatest effect if you choose a fabric of an appropriate width, so that one width will give you a spread over the centre of the bed, and the second half of the fabric, cut lengthwise and joined selvedge to selvedge to the centre panel on either side, will make up the total width you need.

Try to arrange for the seams to fall along the side edges of the bed. In the case of a double bed, it may not always be possible to obtain a suitable width of fabric to achieve this, but follow the same procedure as seams a little way in from the edge look neater than a join down the centre.

Remember that if a patterned material is too wide for the bed, you may have to cut off equal pieces down either side rather than a single strip off one side so that you do not upset the balance of the pattern. If the side panels have to be cut nar-rower than half the width of the fabric, take the waste from the cut edges and leave the selvedges intact to facilitate pattern matching.

Making up
1 To join the side sections to the central panel, place the right sides of the fabric together, with any pattern matched and running in the same direction, and pin and tack plain seams 1·5 cm from the edges. Make sure you enclose the full width of the selvedges.

2 Machine the seams and remove the tacking. The

Throw-over bedspread. For a neat appearance have two seams, one either side of the bed, rather than a central seam. If possible retain selvedges to give a neat underside

stitching should run in the same direction for both seams (ie not up one side and down the other as this might cause slight distortion).

3 Clip tight selvedges diagonally every few centimetres to prevent puckering and press the seams open.

4 If the centre piece had to be cut narrower than a full width, neaten the raw seam turning by overcasting or machine zigzag.

5 To finish the hems with mitred corners, pin a

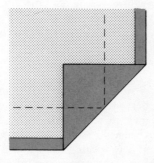

To mitre the corner press the hem lines in first. Open the second hem turning then fold the corner in, re-fold hem and stitch firmly in place

first fold of 1 cm on to the wrong side of the fabric, round all edges of the bedspread, then a second 2·5 cm deep. Tack the hem leaving 15 cm either side of each corner pinned only. Press the hem, including the pinned corners.

6 Remove the pins and open the second hem turning to expose the first. The pressing will have left a crease mark. To mitre the corners, take the point of one corner and fold in a triangle of fabric, putting the base line across the point where the creases meet. Refold the hem turning on both sides of the corner and complete the tacking. Repeat this on all corners then slip stitch the mitres. Slip stitch the hems round the bedspread or use a blind hemming stitch on your sewing machine.

7 To finish the hems with rounded corners, pin the curve with the bedspread in place. Place the bedspread on a level surface and mark an accurate curve along the pinned line. Leave a 3·5 cm hem allowance outside this line, and trim off excess fabric round the corner. Fold the bedspread in half lengthwise, with the curved edge on top and use this as a pattern for cutting the other curve at the foot of the bedspread.

To finish the hem, pin and tack a 1 cm turning on to the wrong side. Turn the bedspread to the

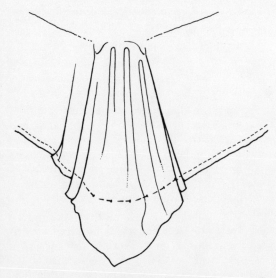

Pin the curve line with the bedspread in place.
Allow for turnings before cutting off the excess

right side and insert two rows of gathering stitches near to the folded edge around each of the curved sections. Draw up the gathering threads, securing them round a pin, to take up the excess fabric when making a second hem turning of 2·5 cm. Complete the hems, working out from the corners.

A QUILT

The stitching on a quilt must form a continuous design; any gaps in the stitching will allow the padding to bunch up unevenly in use. Machining straight lines to form squares or oblongs is one of the easiest ways of decorating the surface and anchoring the filling, particularly if you use a quilting attachment on the sewing machine foot to keep the lines evenly spaced. Alternatively you can outline linked motifs on a patterned fabric, but choose a motif that calls for straight lines as it is difficult to manipulate the thickness of a quilt to sew round curves.

The filling

Use a single layer of 270 g Terylene P3 wadding. It should be the width of the bed, although a little extra, if it avoids wastage, will not spoil the appearance. Measure the length from the foot of the bed to within 5 cm of the pillow.

If you cannot get the width you need, the wadding can be cut and pieced, but check your require-

ments carefully – it is an expensive filling to cut to waste.

The covering fabric

You will need two pieces of covering fabric, 5 cm wider and longer than the wadding. It may be more economical to use dress width fabric for wider beds, joining side pieces to the central panel and matching any pattern as for a throwover bedspread. If you coincide the joins with a line of quilting, they will be less visible.

Choose an easy care fabric for the top of the quilt to avoid the need for ironing when you launder it. Brushed nylon is a good choice for the reverse as it stops the quilt slipping off the bed.

Making the quilt

Try to work on a large surface, it makes the job much easier.

1 Make any seams necessary in the covering fabric and press them open.

2 Fold and pin a single turning of 2·5 cm on to the wrong side round the edges of both pieces of covering fabric. Press to mark the folds. Remove the pins.

3 Tack a line 3·5 cm in from the fold on each of the pieces to indicate the width of a plain border.

4 For straight line quilting, measure the area inside the border tacking line and work out to scale the size and shape of sections to give a balanced design. Between 11 and 13 cm is a good width for the

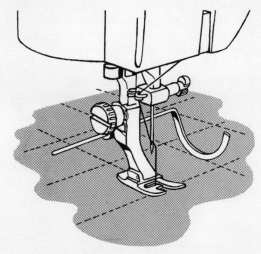

A quilting attachment on your machine helps to keep stitching lines evenly spaced

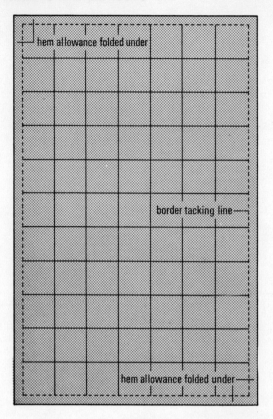

Mark the quilting lines with chalk on the right side of the top cover before starting to stitch

sections. Then use tailor's chalk and a straight edge or rule to mark the lines on the right side of the top cover.

You will need only one in each direction if you have a quilting attachment for your machine.

(Omit stage 4 if you are outlining motifs on a patterned fabric.)

5 Place the wadding on to the wrong side of the bottom cover, enclosing its edges in the edge turning of the fabric. Pin and tack the wadding in position through the fabric fold. Remove the pins.

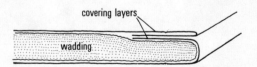

Enclose the wadding in the turning of the bottom cover and lay the top cover over; tack carefully in place along the folded edges

6 Lay the top cover, right side up, over the wadding and pin and tack the two covers together close to the folded edges. Remove the pins.

7 Pin and tack firmly through all thicknesses along the border lines, making sure you coincide the original tacking lines on top and bottom covers.

8 Pin and tack close to the chalked quilting lines through all thicknesses to stabilize the fabric and filling. Start with the lines nearest the centre and always work in the same direction. If you are using a quilting attachment or following pattern motifs, pin and tack lines approximately 15 cm apart in both directions. Remove all pins.

9 For the quilting, use a hinged sewing machine foot, Terylene thread and a stitch longer than that used for normal seaming. Work on the top side of the quilt, beginning with reverse stitches at the border, and machine slowly along each quilting line to the opposite side.

10 Complete the quilt with a line of machine stitching close to the outside edge, then a row of machining on either side of the border tacking line to neaten the start and finish of the quilting lines. Remove all tacking threads.

A DUVET (CONTINENTAL QUILT)

A duvet or continental quilt is simply a large bag filled with insulating material and stitched to stabilize the filling. The insulating material may be down, feathers, a mixture of the two or a synthetic fibre. A duvet takes the place of ordinary bedclothes on top of the bed and is very much lighter to sleep under.

Natural fillings

Down is the best and lightest filling for duvets but it is very expensive. Because of the difficulty of separating the down from the feathers, a down filling is allowed to contain a proportion (15 per cent) of fine, small fluffy feathers. In down and feather fillings, down predominates (51 per cent), whereas in feather and down fillings there are more feathers (85 per cent) than down, with a consequent increase in weight. All-feather fillings are also available.

Most of the down and feathers used are duck, although it is also possible to use goose down and feathers which are more expensive still. These have a natural curl which gives them more resilience than artificially curled poultry feathers, which are suitable only for upholstery cushions.

Buy loose duvet fillings from a reputable source and check that they comply with British Standard nos 1425 and 2005 and that they are certified as new.

Synthetic fillings

One of the main advantages of the synthetic fillings available is that they are non-allergenic and therefore suitable for people who suffer from feather or dust allergies. They are also washable (see page 191) so are a good choice for children's duvets. Synthetic fibre fillings, made by the reputable firms for this purpose, consist of continuous fibre filaments in a soft deep layer which ensures even warmth. However, it is important to check the cost of making a duvet with synthetic filling as it is often possible to buy the ready made version as cheaply.

Quantities of filling

Down – use approximately 142 g per 23 cm channelled section 2 m in length.

Down and feather Use approximately 170 g per 23 cm channelled section.

Feather and down Use approximately 200 g per 23 cm channelled section.

Synthetic Use 270 g Terylene P3 wadding, double.

Size

The size of a duvet is important; it should overlap on each side of the bed by at least 23 cm and it should be at least as long as the bed. For a person over 1·8 m in height, increase the length to 2·2 m.

Making a duvet with down and feather fillings

First, some hints to ensure good results.

Always make the primary cover of downproof cambric to prevent the filling from filtering through. Featherproof ticking will not do.

The right side of the cambric is the dull side.

Use a new, sharp, medium sized sewing machine needle so that perforations in the cambric are kept as small as possible.

Double stitch all seams to make them featherproof.

Allow plenty of space to work in – it is a good

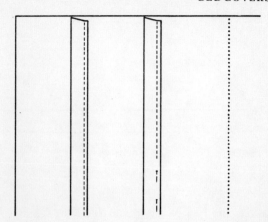

Mark stitching lines with chalk, then sew tapes 23–30 cm apart along the length of the quilt

idea to use a spare room so the work remains undisturbed. Close the windows and remove as much upholstered furniture as possible, as the filling will cling to it.

Cover your hair and your nose and mouth with a scarf as the filling is light and gets into everything.

1 Cut two rectangles of cambric the required size for the finished duvet, adding 4 cm on the length and width to allow for turnings. These will be the top and underside. You may need to join the fabric to get the required width.

2 Draw lines with tailor's chalk down the length of both pieces of fabric on the wrong side, spaced 23–30 cm apart. Cut 5 cm wide tapes, or strips of fabric, 4 cm shorter than the length of the fabric, one length of tape for each line drawn on one of the pieces of cambric.

3 Pin the tapes or strips along the chalk lines on the wrong side of one piece of cambric, positioning the tapes 2 cm from each end of the fabric. Sew in place 1 cm from the edge of the tapes.

4 With right sides together join the two rectangular pieces of cambric together down one side, using a fine stitch and two rows of stitching.

5 Now, working away from this side seam, join the top and bottom rectangular pieces together in sections; working on the inside, carefully pin, tack and machine stitch the loose edge of each tape along the appropriate chalk mark, sewing 1 cm from the edge of the tape.

6 Close the second side and the base seams by

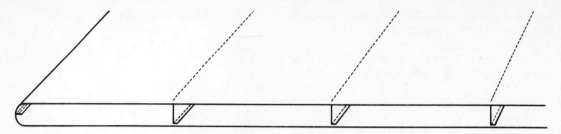

The tapes form walled channels to hold the filling evenly in place

turning in 1 cm of fabric and enclosing the raw edges (the raw edge of the base seam will meet the raw edge of the tapes), make a double row of top stitching around sides and base making sure that one row of stitching goes over the end of the tapes to close each channel. The best finish can be achieved by folding the vertical 'wall' at the centre so that the tapes lie flat and cause little extra bulk when sewing the end seams of the quilt.

7 The tapes will have formed walled channels. To fill the duvet, peg it along a line, open end at the top. Put a handful of filling into the first pocket, turn the top over and insert two pegs. Shake the filling down. Continue to work across the quilt – a handful in each pocket. Continue until the quilt is evenly filled.

8 Enclose the filling by making a double row of top stitching, with raw edges enclosed, across the top to close the channels. Flatten the tapes as for the base seam, ensuring that they are folded in the same direction. If desired, the seam round the quilt can then be bound.

Making a duvet with a synthetic fibre filling
1 Cut two rectangles of polyester/cotton fabric the required size of the finished duvet, adding 4 cm for turnings. Join the fabric if necessary to get the required width.

2 With right sides together, join the two pieces down the side seams, making a double row of stitching.

3 Turn right side out and draw lines with tailor's chalk equally spaced down the quilt length about 23–30 cm apart.

4 Place the filling inside, moving it about till it fits.

5 Sew the top and base seams, enclosing the raw edges and making a double row of top stitching.

6 Now stitch down the chalk lines to hold the filling in place. This can be done on a sewing machine but is easier by hand.

Lampshades

Many department stores and handicraft shops have a department where you can buy lampshade making materials and get expert advice on the subject at the same time.

Fabrics
Most lightweight fabrics can be used to cover a soft lampshade. The most important things to remember are that it must have good stretching qualities,

it must not fray easily and any pattern must be suited to the size and shape of the shade. Crepe backed satin, viscose dupions and silk shantungs are all suitable; cottons and other fabrics are worth experimenting with if they appear to have plenty of 'give'. For linings, crepe backed satin is the best choice as its shiny surface reflects the light.

Most lampshades can be washed if they are made in these fabrics – just swish them in a warm mild detergent solution, rinse and hang on the line to dry.

Heavy furnishing fabrics are not suitable for making lampshades as they are difficult to work. Nor should nylon be used as it could melt from the heat of the bulb.

Firm lampshades can be quickly and easily made using a fabric bonded to stiff card or a rigid translucent plastic sheet. All you have to do is cut it to size, attach it to the frame, glue the join and then trim as required. Alternatively buy bonding material or a translucent plastic film separately and press your own fabric on to the self-adhesive surface – you can even stiffen wallpaper provided you protect it with a sheet of tissue or kitchen paper to prevent the iron from scorching or smudging the pattern. Specially prepared parchments offer a further choice of lampshade material.

Do not use any material which masks too much light unless the lamp is for effect only. Test the material against a light bulb before you make it up.

Preparing the frame
You can buy frames ready treated with a white plastic coating, but ordinary metal frames will need painting or binding to protect them against rust.

Binding provides a good base for stitching on a non-removable shade and generally gives a more professional look.

Use a 1·3 cm wide lampshade tape for binding the rings and struts – it looks best if you dye the tape to match the inside or lining of the shade. For calculating length, allow about twice the total ring and strut measurement.

Apply the binding as follows:

1 Cut a piece of tape twice the length of a strut. Starting at the top, tuck the tape end under and wind the tape round.

2 Continue taping the strut just overlapping it so that there is no bulk. Wrap the tape tightly, otherwise any stitching later on will move and your lampshade will be loose and baggy.

3 At the bottom of the strut wind the tape round the bottom ring taking it first to the left and then to the right of the strut in a figure of eight, and finish off with a knot. Trim the tape off close to the bottom ring.

4 When each strut has been taped in this way, bind the top and the bottom rings, making a figure of eight twist round each join of ring and strut. Do not bind the section which attaches the shade to the actual light fitting. Your lampshade frame is now ready for covering.

If you are going to stick on the covering material, it is possible to use the white self-adhesive tape sold specially for binding lampshade frames, but this does tend to come unstuck eventually because it is folded over the wire rather than wound round it; and it is not such a good foundation as cotton tape.

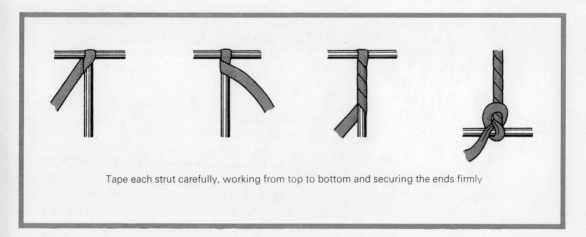

Tape each strut carefully, working from top to bottom and securing the ends firmly

Trimmings

Trimmings give a final decorative touch to a shade – as well as covering up any less than perfect stitching. Braid is a popular trim because it looks neat and is not difficult to apply, but all sorts of different trims are possible, from lace and velvet ribbons to plaited string. If you are skilled it can be creatively satisfying (as well as economical) to design and make your own trimmings. Again, most good lampshade departments and handicraft shops will be happy to advise.

A STRAIGHT-SIDED DRUM SHADE

An easy design for a firm shade is based on two rings of the same size – one with the lamp fitting, of course – instead of a strutted frame. This avoids having struts showing behind the shade. In the method given below the cover is sewn on to the frame, so choose a stiffened material which can be pierced by a needle. Both rings should be bound with a cotton tape (see page 27).

1 Draw and cut out a pattern on strong brown wrapping paper. The height should be the proposed height of the shade and the width the circumference of the ring plus a good overlap. Use paper clips or spring clothes pegs to fix the pattern to the outside of the rings so that you can see if the depth looks right when the shade is in position. Adjust the depth if necessary.

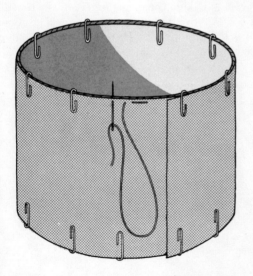

Clip the material to the rings before stitching to make the shade really taut and smooth

2 Transfer the pattern on to the lampshade material and carefully cut out.

3 Clip the material to the outside of the two rings. Be sure you get it really taut.

4 To attach the cover use a strong, double thread which matches the binding and a betweens needle, size 5 or 6. Begin on the top ring, 5 cm from the overlap, stitching from the outside, through the cover and lower edge of the binding where it goes under the ring, to within 5 cm of the join. Make sure the ring comes level with the edge of the cover – not above or below it, and keep the inside stitch small as it will not be hidden by the trimmings. Sew round the bottom ring, into the upper edge of the binding.

5 The overlap should now be trimmed back to 5 mm for a lightweight material, 1 cm for a heavier weight. Rule the line in pencil and cut with sharp, long bladed scissors. Glue down the overlap using a little clear adhesive applied with a cocktail stick or a sharpened matchstick. Sew the remaining sections.

6 Measure the trimmings and neaten the ends. Braid should have 5 mm turned under and glued or sewn down. Lightly glue the underside of the trimming, place one end to the join of the overlap on the top ring, and press it round with your fingers in a circle until the second end meets the first one exactly at the join. Repeat round the bottom ring. (If you wish, braid can be pulled really tightly as you are fixing it – it will then curl over the ring.)

A TIFFANY SHADE

Tiffany shades give a pretty, feminine effect; the frames are bow-shaped and have up to 12 struts. The instructions given below are for an easily made, unlined cover, with elastic top and bottom so it can be taken off for laundering – a style well suited to a lightweight, washable fabric.

1 Choose a tiffany frame with straight top and base rings, not scalloped. Unless it has a plastic coating, paint the frame with two coats of quick drying enamel paint and when it is completely dry, bind the two rings (see 'Preparing the frame').

2 The covering fabric should be cut on the straight grain in the form of a rectangle. For the width, measure the circumference of the widest part of the frame and add 5 cm to allow for the seam and a

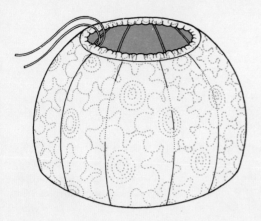

Gather up the cover evenly with strings and mark
the fitting line for the fringe

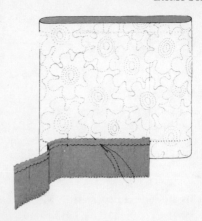

Hand sew the fringe in place, using the chalked
fitting line as a guide

little 'ease'. For the depth, measure the length of a
strut and add 10 cm for overlaps and hem turnings.

3 Fold the strip in half widthwise, right side to the
outside and join the short edges with a french seam.
Press the turning to one side.

4 Make double thickness hems on to the wrong
side along the other edges, turning in 1·5 cm with
each fold. Starting from the side seam, machine
stitch each hem to within 1·5 cm of the start to
form a casing, with opening, for the elastic insertion at the top and base of the cover.

5 Using a bodkin or hairgrip, thread strings
through both casings, then put the cover on the
frame and draw them up to gather even amounts of
fabric without strain. Mark the strings as a guide to
the lengths of elastic required.

6 Whilst the cover is still gathered on the frame,
use tailor's chalk to indicate the position of the
lower ring. This gives a fitting line for the fringe
trimming.

7 Remove the strings and take the cover off the
frame. Using a suitable length of fringe, neaten the
end by pinning under 1 cm then, starting at the
seam, pin it along the chalk fitting line. Hand sew
into position, using a matching thread and zigzag
stitch so that only small stitches are made on the
right side at the top and base of the fringe heading.
Fold under the end to make a butt join. Do not sew
the fringe on too tightly, otherwise it will not hang
properly.

8 Thread the correct length of elastic through each
casing and sew the ends firmly together. Carefully
ease the cover into position and space the gathers
evenly over the frame.

Needlework tools

NEEDLES AND PINS

There is a different design of needle to suit each type of sewing. Needles are numerically graded according to thickness to suit the fabric concerned: the higher the number, the finer the needle.

Sharps are oval-eyed needles, for general sewing.

Betweens are shorter than sharps, which makes for quicker sewing, and have a bevelled eye; larger betweens are used for tailoring, finer ones for delicate fabrics. Sharps and betweens come in sizes 1–10.

Ballpoint needles are for sewing knits and stretch fabrics; the round end pushes the threads aside rather than piercing them.

Self-threading needles are available for general sewing. The thread is pulled down through a sprung opening into the eye.

Darning needles are long so that the needle can be carried across a hole or along a row of stitches before the thread is pulled through. The long eye takes wool or thick thread. Darning needles come in sizes 1–9.

A bodkin is a large, blunt needle, round or flat, with a long or sometimes a round eye. It is used for threading elastic, tape, ribbon or cord through a casing or through holes for lacing.

Crewels or embroidery needles are similar in length to sharps but the eye is larger so it can take

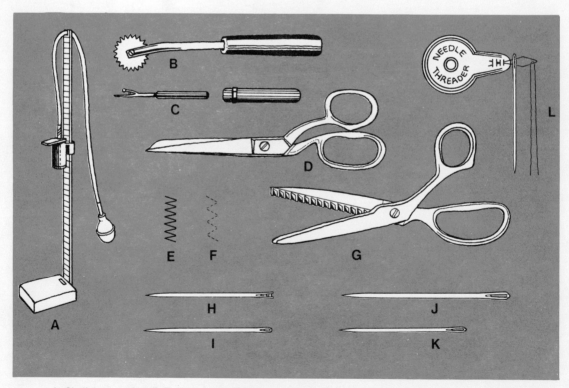

A. Chalk hem marker B. Tracing wheel C. Seam unpicker D. Dressmaking shears E. Two-step zigzag stitch F. Multi-stitch zigzag G. Pinking shears H. Self-threading needle I. 'Sharp' needle
J. Darning needle K. Crewel needle L. Needle threader

embroidery silks and wools. Available in sizes 1–10.

A needle threader can be used with most needles.

Pins Good quality fine steel pins come in assorted sizes and are usually 2·5 cm long. For fine fabrics and lampshade making there are very fine, 1·3 cm pins called lillikins. For lace and velvet, use Wedding Dress and Lace pins. These are fine like lillikins and 2·5 cm long. There are also fine pins 3·2 cm long, that are useful for pinning fur fabrics and thick tweeds.

Thimble
Choose a thimble with a good close fit to protect your needle-pushing middle finger. Steel is the strongest material; plastic and silver are not so durable.

SCISSORS
These should be of as good a quality as possible and used only for the purpose for which they are intended. Have them professionally sharpened as soon as they begin to lose their edge. An iron-monger usually operates a scissor sharpening service.

Dressmaking shears with long blades are the most efficient scissors for cutting out. They should have angled handles so that one edge of the lower blade rests on the surface of the table while you are cutting to give a steady, smooth, long cut.

Pointed scissors are for snipping threads, trimming turnings or clipping into corners. Blades are approximately 7·5 cm long.

Embroidery scissors have fine sharp points for embroidery work, cutting motifs, buttonholes etc.

Pinking shears give a zigzag cut and provide a quick method of neatening seam turnings on fabrics which do not fray.

A seam unpicker undoes machine-stitched seams quickly.

MARKING AIDS
Dressmaker's carbon paper is used with a **tracing wheel** with teeth to reproduce pattern markings on the fabric.

Tailor's chalk is used for transferring fitting lines from the paper pattern to the fabric or for marking alteration lines. It is available in white and other colours. Light markings can be brushed off.

MEASURING AIDS
Tape measure A strong, firm tape clearly marked on both sides in centimetres and inches and with metal ends is essential. Make sure the measurements come right to the end. Do not buy a cheap tape measure; it may stretch.

Hem gauge This is a good tool for making sure of an even hem – place it on the wrong side of the fabric, fold over the required depth and press with an iron to set it without marking the right side of the fabric.

Chalk hem marker With this you can mark your own hem without a friend crawling round you. Just puff on powdered tailor's chalk to make a line on the material after you have set the height on the measure.

Metre stick Used for checking the straight grain in pattern placing and taking hem lengths. Buy a smoothly finished one that will not snag on the fabric.

SEWING MACHINES
Straight stitch machines do straight stitching only, with a reverse for ending off seams. Included in the price you may get some basic attachments and you may be able to buy others.

Zigzag machines give you all that you get on the straight stitchers, together with an adjustable two-step zigzag stitch which can be used for neatening seams to stop fraying, mending tears, darning, making buttonholes and some simple embroidery for edge decoration. It can also be used for sewing stretch fabrics, provided the material is not too stretchy.

A semi-automatic machine will normally include the features of a zigzag machine with the addition of a multi-stitch zigzag (with variations). This gives a stitch range with greater elasticity than ordinary zigzag and so is better for jersey and other stretch fabrics – it also gives a greater choice of decorative stitches.

A fully automatic machine is capable of the stitching on all the other types of machine plus more complicated variations.

Basic needlework techniques and repairs

DARNING

1 Darning is done in the form of a small running stitch, the needle taking up half as much material as it passes over.

2 Use a thread as close as possible to the colour, thickness and texture of the threads of the material you are going to darn. It is sometimes possible to pull a thread from the seam turning or a spare piece of the fabric. (When a sweater is sold with a card of darning wool attached, always be sure and keep this in a safe place.)

3 Use the wool or thread single, unless it is thinner than the threads of the fabric being mended.

4 The darning needle should be long enough to pick up a complete row of stitches before pulling the thread through.

5 Work on the wrong side wherever possible, in the direction of the warp threads first.

6 When darning a hole, extend the darn well over the hole, so as to cover the surrounding thin areas. Use a darning mushroom so that you can see the worn sections and keep the darn even.

7 Leave small loops of thread (especially with wool or cotton) at the end of each row, to allow for tension in wear and possible shrinkage on laundering.

Place darns are for repairing thin, worn areas. For these it is only necessary to work in one direction. Start just beyond the worn area and work across to the same distance beyond. Turn and, picking up the stitches previously passed over, work back for the same number of stitches; this will bring you to one stitch beyond the start. Then take one stitch more on the next row, one stitch less on alternate rows. After several rows reverse the procedure to work the extra stitch at the opposite end. This gives a zigzag edge and spreads the strain over several threads.

Web darns are for repairing actual holes. Start by trimming off any loose threads (but not loops of knitted fabrics) round the edge of the hole. The first row of stitches should be made as long as the width of the hole and about 6 mm away from it. If it is surrounded by a thin area, start beyond this. Work each succeeding row close to the one before, increasing the length of each by one stitch till the hole is reached, and afterwards decrease again until the final row of stitches is 6 mm beyond the hole. When darning knitted fabric, catch in any loose loops to prevent laddering. Repeat the procedure in the opposite direction weaving the threads over and under the first set. In the completed darn, the hole

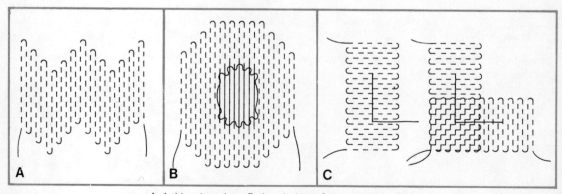

A. A thin-place darn B. A web darn C. A hedge-tear darn

should be filled, with no spaces. An octagonal shape is easier to work, shows less and wears better than a square or rectangular darn.

Hedge-tear darns are for L-shaped tears. To work a hedge-tear darn, draw the edges of the fabric together with a thread drawn from a seam turning and begin the darn about 1·5 cm above one side. Work across the tear, towards the corner, and to the same distance beyond, keeping the rows parallel and about 2 cm long. Turn and work across the second side, running the rows at right angles to the first half already done. This gives extra strengthening at the angle of the tear.

Darning by machine

If your machine has no special darning attachment, you can use the method below to darn holes or thin areas.

Tack a piece of suitable material under the part to be mended. Working on the right side, machine in rows 3 to 6 mm apart over the worn surface, keeping straight with the threads of the material. (On machine-knitted materials, stitch the rows on the bias, so that the material can still stretch). Trim the raw edges on the wrong side, close to the machining, or oversew them if you prefer. Press the repaired area.

PATCHING

1 Whenever possible, use a piece of the same material or match the article as closely as possible in texture even if, on a pair of jeans for instance, you choose a contrasting colour. If you are using new material for a patch, wash it first in order to shrink it, otherwise it may pucker when the garment is washed.

2 Cut the patch straight by the fabric threads and large enough to cover not only the hole, but also the thin area around it, allowing turnings according to the type of patch. Try to cut so that the threads of the patch will run in the same direction as those of the article.

3 Fold over, crease and tack the side turning allowances first, then top and bottom.

4 Place the patch in position. An easy way to centre it over the hole is to fold it in half both ways, on the straight grain, repeating the folds on the straight grain of the garment across the hole and matching the two sets of creases. If necessary, unpick a seam or hem to let the patch in. Keeping

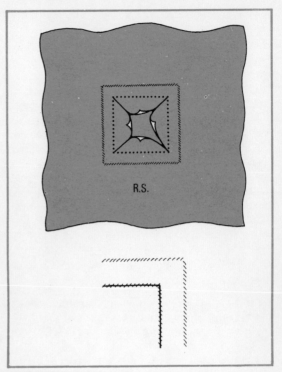

A calico' patch (*see page 34*)

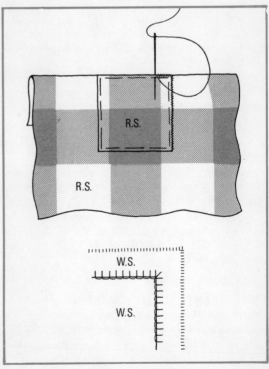

An overlaid patch (*see page 34*)

it absolutely flat, pin the corners diagonally and tack into position.

'Calico' patches are used for most cotton and linen household articles and unpatterned clothing in these fabrics.

Cut a patch either square or oblong allowing for 1 cm turnings. Turn in the edges on to the right side and tack them down. Centre the patch over the hole, right side to the wrong side of the article. Pin the corners diagonally, tack in position, then hem around the edges. Remove the pins and tacking stitches.

On the right side of the article, cut a diagonal line from the edge of the hole towards each corner, as far as the turning on the patch. Trim the edges of the hole straight to within 1·5 cm of the stitched line. The length of the corner cuts will enable you to turn the edges under to form a square. Tack and hem into position.

Overlaid patches should be made from the same fabric as the garment and are a neat way of repairing light and medium weight clothing fabrics, particularly patterned articles.

Cut the patch square. Turn in the edges 1 cm on to the wrong side and tack down. Pin the patch right side uppermost on to the right side of the garment, matching up any pattern. Tack into position. Fold the garment under along the edge of the patch and oversew each side of the patch to the fabric. Remove tacking.

Neaten the wrong side of the garment by trimming the worn section to match the patch turnings and loop-stitch the raw edges together.

'Woollen' patches are used on thick fabrics such as flannel, also blankets and baby clothes where it is important to avoid ridges.

Place the right side of the patch to the wrong side of the garment. Pin and tack in position without turnings and herringbone round the patch, making a square of stitches at the corners. On the right side, cut a diagonal line from the hole towards each corner. Trim the edges evenly and herringbone down the raw edges.

INSERTING A ZIP FASTENER

Where manufacturer's instructions are enclosed with the zip, follow these as to the method of insertion. If possible use a zipper foot on your sewing machine as this will make inserting a zip much easier.

Setting a zip into a slit opening

1 Indicate the position and length of the opening on the garment with a line of tacking, measuring the opening from the fitting line down. The zip length should be the length of the opening from the fitting line to the base, less about 1·5 cm.

2 Put rows of tacking either side and across the bottom of the opening and not less than 6 mm away from it.

3 Cut the opening along the first line of tacks until 6 mm from the base, then snip diagonally across to each corner.

4 Turn the seam allowance to the inside. Pin and tack down on the fold edge. Remove the pins. Press lightly and turn to the right side.

5 Place the zip under the opening with its slide upwards, 1·5 cm from the top fitting line. Check it is evenly placed all the way down. Pin and tack down.

6 Remove the pins and try the zip to ensure free movement, then stitch round 3 mm from the edge. Press.

Setting a zip into a seam

When a zip is concealed in a seam this means that the zip cannot be seen from the right side, although a row of stitching will be visible. This type of zip is often used for side, front or back openings, especially where there might be strain on the opening which could cause gaping. 'Invisible' zips look like a seam but for these it is essential to follow the maker's instructions.

To set a concealed zip:

1 Join the seam of the garment as far as the base of the opening. Press open the seam and press the turning under, to the fitting line, on the left hand side of the opening with the right side of the garment facing you. Tack.

2 Press the right hand seam turning under, almost to the fitting line, but leaving 3 mm extra all the way down.

3 Position the zip 1·5 cm from the top fitting line (or at the top of the opening if you are setting the zip into the side opening of a dress, etc). Place one side of the row of teeth almost to the fold on the right hand side. Pin and tack close to the edge all the way down.

4 Lay the left hand side over the zip. Pin and tack in place along the side and base just far enough from the folded edge to clear the teeth.

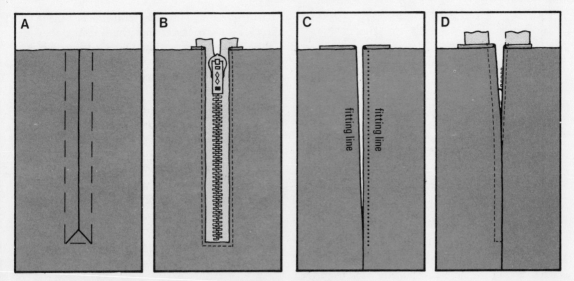

A. To set a zip into a slit opening first mark the position with tacking stitches then cut and press the turnings to the wrong side. B. Place the zip under the opening, pin, tack and stitch carefully in position. C. To set a zip into a seam, press the turnings under but allow a 3 mm overlap. D. Stitch close to the fold on the first edge, place the second edge to conceal zip and stitch just far enough away to clear the teeth

5 Remove the pins and check that the zip moves freely along its length. Machine along the tacks. Remove the tacks. Press.

BUTTONHOLES
Making a bound buttonhole

1 Mark the position of the buttonhole on the garment with tacking stitches, at least half the diameter of the button from the edge of the opening. Mark the buttonhole length – usually about 3 mm longer than the button diameter except on stretch fabrics and usually less than 6 mm wide, depending on the fabric thickness. Check that the holes are evenly spaced from each other and from the edge of the garment. Turn back any facing section on the garment so that it is not included in the sewing at this stage.

2 For the welt, cut a piece of fabric on the cross, 2·5 cm longer than the buttonhole and 5 cm wide. Mark the centre with tacking so you can centre the piece over the marked spot with right sides together. Tack it on and mark the buttonhole as before. Machine round the hole, the required depth of the binding (up to 3 mm) on either side of the button-hole line and the exact length of the hole,

checking that the number of stitches each end is equal. Remove the tacking.

3 Using a small sharp pair of scissors, or a seam unpicker, slit the actual buttonhole. Cut to within 6 mm of the ends and then carefully cut the corners diagonally, making sure you do not slit the stitching at any point, which would then make the hole too big.

4 Turn the top piece of fabric (the welt) through the slit to the back and press flat. Then fold the

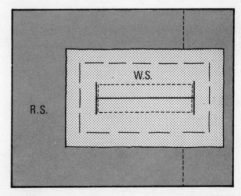

Machine round the marked buttonhole, keeping the ends absolutely square

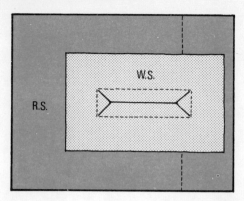

Cut the line of the buttonhole and diagonally into the corners of the machine stitching (*see page 35*)

welt so that the fold edges come together in the centre, filling the hole and looking neat from the right side. Overcast the fold edges together securely with temporary stitches.

5 On the wrong side of the garment, 'box pleat' the buttonhole ends and machine the ends of the pleats to strengthen them. Take care not to stitch through, which would show on the right side of the garment. Make sure all sections are lying flat.

6 Still on the wrong side of the garment, cover the buttonholes with the facing fabric and tack it round each individual hole. Mark out the buttonhole with pins at each corner, then cut it in the facing. Turn all the raw edges under and hem them neatly into position. Press carefully.

Hand-stitched buttonholes

Hand-stitched horizontal buttonholes, where the strain is taken across the buttonhole, are worked with one round end and one square. The rounded end holds the shank of the button and so is always on the outer edge of the garment. Vertical buttonholes are worked with two matching ends, either rounded or square. The buttonholes must always be cut straight to a thread and the same length as for a bound buttonhole.

It is best to interface the facing of the garment before making the buttonholes.

1 Mark the position of the buttonholes on the right side of the fabric and at least half the diameter of the button from the edge of the opening. Sew a rectangle 2 mm round each.

2 Slit along the marks, starting at the centre and cutting out towards the ends.

3 Cut off about 45 cm of buttonhole thread and begin with a backstitch on the wrong side of the fabric at the lower left hand corner. Work a line of buttonhole stitches to the other end of the opening. Work the stitches close together so the knots sit on the edge of the hole and just touch each other.

4 For a round end, overcast five or seven stitches in a fan shape (remember this is the end the shank of the button will go, and oversewing takes up less room than buttonhole stitch). Work along the top edge in buttonhole stitch as before.

5 For a straight end, make three backstitches full width across. Then work buttonhole stitches over this bar.

6 Finish on wrong side. For an extra strong finish, rub some beeswax over the stitches.

PUTTING IN A NEW TROUSER POCKET

1 First of all, turn the trousers inside out and cut off the old pocket. This must be cut in a straight line, but leaving at least 4 cm of the fabric of the old pocket still in place.

2 Turn the old pocket inside out, place it flat on a piece of paper, and draw a line round it allowing 1·5 cm for turnings round the curved edge and 2·5 cm along the straight edge. Cut out the pattern.

3 Pin the paper pattern on to a double thickness of strong fabric, making sure that the grain of the fabric is in the same direction as that of the old pocket. Cut round the pattern.

4 Make a french seam around the curved edge, but leave the straight side open. Press the seam. Turn the new pocket so that the right side is outside. Pull the remains of the old pocket through to the right side of the trousers. Pin the new pocket over the old remaining section with a 2·5 cm overlap.

5 Turn the visible raw edge of the new pocket under, tack and firmly and neatly sew the pocket into position.

6 Pull the pocket through to the inside of the trousers. Turn under the remaining raw edge; stitch down securely. Press the seams and edges to make a neat finish.

TURNING UP A HEM

The first step is to get the length of the garment right, and if you are working alone you will find a chalk hem marker useful (see page 31). Wear the garment, with fastenings and belt closed, plus shoes. Adjust the marker and, standing still, move it round you carefully. Take off the garment.

1 Pin at 2·5 cm intervals along the fitting line. Turn the hem in, folding along the pinned line and re-inserting the pins at right angles to the fold. Press up at right angles between the pins with an iron, matching up the seam lines. Tack the hem 1·5 cm away from the folded edge. Remove the pins.

2 The hem allowance should be 5–7·5 cm for a slim skirt, 2·5–5 cm for a full one. (Use a very narrow edge hem in the case of a circular skirt.) To measure the allowance accurately, make a hem gauge out of stiff card with a straight edge of the measured length. Trim off the excess fabric.

3 Neaten the raw edge either by turning in 6 mm and machining and pressing, or by using a zigzag machine stitch (multi-stitch zigzag for loosely woven fabrics, see page 31). Tack the hem firmly 2·5 cm from this edge and slipstitch it up evenly. Press.

4 For a fuller skirt, work to stage 2, then gather the raw edge evenly by hand or machine to fit the skirt circumference. Sew on bias tape, keeping the gathers in position. Finish by tacking and slip stitching the tape into position.

5 For a tailor's hem, work to stage 3, omitting the slipstitch. Fold the skirt back on the hem and finish with herringbone stitch between the hem and skirt, taking a few threads of the skirt with each stitch.

Sewing a false hem

1 Select a piece of fairly fine, closely woven fabric in a matching colour and cut a strip at least 6·5 cm deep and long enough to go round the hem plus 3 cm seam allowance. Use a straight grain strip for a straight hem; cut and join crossway strips for a flared hem; for a circular skirt, use a facing cut to the shape of the lower edge.

2 With the right sides together, carefully pin the strip to the garment and mark the ends where they will be joined together.

3 Unpin and stitch the ends of the strip together, making a plain seam with 1·5 cm turnings. Open out the seam and press. Press a 6 mm turning to the wrong side round one edge of the piece.

4 Pin and tack the right sides of the strip and the garment together, coinciding the join with a seam. Machine round, 1·5 cm from the raw edges.

5 Fold the strip inside the garment so the stitching line will not show on the right side and tack in position. Press the fold on the wrong side only. Then carefully slip hem the folded edge of the strip to the garment.

Upholstery tools and materials

Scissors Choose the largest and heaviest pair you can comfortably use; kitchen scissors with serrated blades can be used for cutting thin pieces of plastic foam.

Ripping chisel and mallet The ripping chisel is used when removing old covers to lift the heads of tacks which have become embedded in the frame.

The tip is blunt to prevent damage to the frame. An old screwdriver can be used as an alternative. The special mallet is used to prevent damage to the wooden handle of the chisel.

Tack lifter A wooden handled tool with a claw end for removing protruding tacks.

Cabriole hammer This usually has two small

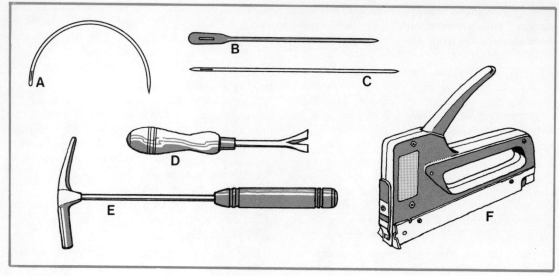

A. Slipping needle B. Regulator C. Upholsterer's needle D. Tack lifter E. Cabriole hammer F. Staple gun tacker

heads, 6 mm and 16 mm. The smaller head is usually magnetized for picking up tacks. Some cabriole hammers have a claw for lifting tacks in place of the larger hammer head.

Tack hammer Often referred to as a cross-pein hammer this has one head and one tapered, chisel-shaped end for initial tapping in until the tack is self-supporting. A cheaper alternative to the cabriole hammer.

Staple gun tacker An alternative method of fixing upholstery fabric, etc by driving in staples. It leaves you one hand free to position the work.

Tacks Use 13 mm or 16 mm improved tacks which have a large head for fixing webbing and hessian. Use 10 mm or 13 mm fine tacks for calico and final cover.

Webbing stretcher This is a block of wood about 15 × 5 × 2 cm which is used to keep webbing at tension while you fix it.

Webbing is strong herringbone-weave braid 5 cm wide, used to support springs and padding.

Rubber webbing is often used with latex foam, as an alternative to conventional springs rather than as a substitute for ordinary webbing. It consists of two layers of fabric, rubberized together and is made in various widths and degrees of elasticity.

Hessian is strong canvas for covering underneath a chair and to go over the webbing.

Scrim is a finer type of covering, often used over the stuffing.

Black linen or linenette is a closely woven, glazed fabric, sometimes used in place of hessian or scrim for the bottom of a chair, particularly where it is likely to show.

Upholsterer's calico is used between padding and the final cover.

Upholster's needles are 25–30 cm long and pointed at both ends so that they can be pushed completely into a thick stuffing at one point and withdrawn at another. Some upholster's needles are semi-circular for work on flat sections where you cannot use a straight needle, and there are curved needles for fastening springs to canvas. These are called slipping needles and spring needles respectively. Ordinary sewing needles are also required.

Stitching twine is strong, fine twine sold in balls and often rubbed with beeswax to strengthen it still further and prevent it fraying. Use the heavier spring twine for attaching springs.

Laid cord is used for lacing and lashing. It is a type of string, with fibres woven to create strength when you are forming the shape of a seat.

Gimp pins come in various colours and are sold in packets. They are used to attach **gimp and braid trimmings** or fine fabric covers where the fixing is visible.

Tape measure is vital, of course. Your needle-work tape measure will double for this.

Tailor's chalk for marking. A fibre-tipped pen is useful for marking foam.

Regulators have a pointed end for 'regulating' the distribution of stuffing and a blunt end for pushing fabric down round the seats of chairs, etc.

Stuffings include curled horsehair, flock (sold in rolls), synthetic fibre upholstery wadding (sold in rolls), linterfelt (a cotton waste product) and foam,

see below. Flock, which is used to cover springs, should be beaten with a pliable cane to make it light and fluffy. Horsehair should be teased and pulled well apart so that it is springy. Discard any lumps.

Plastic (polyether) foam is recommended for DIY work since it is easier to use than latex (natural rubber) foam which tends to tear with handling. Plastic foam comes in a wide range of depths and densities suited to different jobs. It is important to use a high density foam for seating.

A sewing machine is an essential time and labour saver for any serious upholstery work (see page 31). You may also find that **pincers** and a **screwdriver** from your household tool kit come in useful.

Simple upholstery techniques

If you plan to do a lot of upholstery, you would be wise to attend classes, or at least buy a really comprehensive handbook on the subject. To get you started, however, here are step-by-step instructions for two of the most commonly needed upholstery repairs around the house.

RE-WEBBING A SPRUNG DINING CHAIR

1 Turn the chair upside down on to the edge of a table or workbench and remove the old canvas, the webbing and all the old tacks using a ripping chisel, mallet and tack lifter and cutting the twine that binds the springs to the webbing. Clean the inside of any dust or shreds (a vacuum cleaner dusting attachment will do this well). If the frame is full of old tack holes fill these with plastic wood.

2 When fixing the webbing remember that each strip must fall across the centres of a line of springs.

Place the first strip of webbing on the back frame in the same position as the original webbing, leaving 2·5 cm of webbing overlapping the edge of the frame. Tap in two 13 mm or 16 mm tacks; fold the 2·5 cm flap over, and put in three more tacks. See these 'bite' well, and do not put them too near the edge of the frame.

3 Stretch the webbing across the frame to the front by folding it round the webbing stretcher and pressing this downwards against the frame so hard that the webbing is made absolutely taut – otherwise the seat will sag (see page 40). Still holding the stretcher, knock in two tacks where the webbing crosses the frame.

4 Cut off the webbing 2·5 cm beyond the tacks, fold over, and knock in another three tacks to hold the strip in place. Next attach a strip at right angles to the one you have fixed in place, using the same method, then do the next strip parallel to the original one and so on. Weave each strip in the

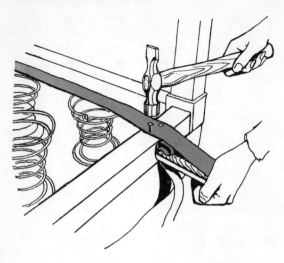

Stretch the webbing taut across the chair frame and tack securely in place (*see page 39*)

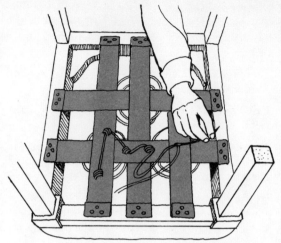

Sew each spring to a cross in the webbing to hold the spring in place (*see below left*)

opposite direction to the one next to it, as if you were darning. The webbing must fall across the centres of the springs.

5 At each point where the strips cross, sew the webbing to the rim of the spring the two strips are meant to support by making three stitches in each of three places round each spring to hold it firmly in place (above, right). Use a curved spring needle and double spring twine. Finally, cut a hessian cover for the base of the chair allowing 2·5 cm turnings all round and fix with small tacks at regular intervals.

RENOVATING A SPRUNG UPHOLSTERED ARMCHAIR

Unless you have carried out some previous upholstering, it is unwise to tackle a button-backed or leather covered chair.

Before you start, make sure you have plenty of time and somewhere to leave the chair at various stages of the work. A job like this makes a certain amount of mess, so if you can do it in a spare room or garage, so much the better.

Removing the old upholstery

Remove the old cover, using a blunt-tipped ripping chisel, plus mallet, and a tack lifter to extract the tacks. Keep the cover for use as a pattern for the calico lining later. If there are lots of tack holes, fill

these with plastic wood, leave to dry and sand smooth.

If the chair is an old one you will probably find there is a loose-laid soft padding over a coarser one, such as horsehair or coir fibre, probably enclosed in a hessian case and tacked to the top of the frame. Carefully lift off the loose soft padding, keeping it in its original shape if possible, and put it safely to one side. It is a good idea to pin a label on each piece of soft padding so you will know which part of the chair it came from when you want to put it back.

When all the loose padding has been removed, turn the chair over and look at the base. Remove the hessian cover then the webbing and free it from the springs by cutting the twine. Examine the springs to see if they have shifted out of place. They should be sewn to the hessian at the base of the padding in the same way as they were sewn to the webbing. If the twine has broken, or the springs have worked loose, you will have to remove the coarse padding in order to reposition them.

To do this, turn the chair the right way up again and remove the tacks holding the padding in place. Carefully lift off the padding from the seat so that the shape is not altered and put it to one side for the time being.

Replacing the hessian and webbing

1 Cut a new piece of hessian to cover the frame,

allowing for 2·5 cm turnings, and tack it in position. Leave the old piece in place as a guide to the correct position of the springs.

2 When the hessian is in place, sew the springs to it, using a curved spring needle and spring twine.

3 Turn the chair upside down again and position the new webbing. Tack into place in the same way as described in re-webbing a dining chair. Use a webbing stretcher to make sure it is really taut (see page 40).

4 Arrange the springs under the crosses of webbing and sew them firmly into place using the curved needle threaded with double twine.

5 Turn the chair right way up again and re-arrange the coarse padding on the hessian. If the padding is 'leaking', place a new piece of hessian over it, tucking it down round the sides and base as if you were making a bed. Tack the edges of the hessian to the frame in the same position as you found it in the first place.

6 If the chair has springs in the back, as well as the seat, they too will be held in place by webbing. Check that it is in good condition. If not, renew it in the same way as described for the seat of the chair.

Re-padding the back and arms
Work on the inside of the chair first.

7 After you have replaced the springs and coarse padding, carefully put back the soft padding as you originally found it.

8 This soft padding is then covered with synthetic fibre upholstery wadding to give the chair a firm but soft outline. Cut two pieces of wadding a little larger all round than the inside back of the chair, allowing extra for tucking down the back of the seat. The double thickness of wadding helps to ensure a smooth appearance. If the chair looks a bit thin on padding, cut a few smaller pieces of wadding to place under the main ones to help build up a rounded shape.

9 When the smaller pieces are in place, put the main layers on the back of the chair and trim them roughly to shape around the top and sides. Clip the wadding where the arms of the chair join the back. Tuck the wadding down the back of the seat and pull this out carefully at the outside back of the chair. Make sure the wadding is lying smoothly over the inside back of the chair.

10 Cut out calico to cover the inside back of the chair, using the old cover as a pattern, but allowing an extra 15 cm all round. This extra is to enable you to grasp the fabric and pull it taut before you tack it into place.

11 Place the calico over the wadding. Take the top edge of the calico over the top rail of the chair back and tack it temporarily to the underside of the top rail. Smooth the calico down over the inside of the chair back, clipping it above the arms as for the wadding. Clip diagonally into the lower corners of the calico so that it can be wrapped round the uprights of the back. Tuck the lower edge down the back of the seat and out at the back of the chair. Pull firmly, so that the calico is taut down the back of the chair. Temporarily tack the sides of the cover in place between the top and the arms.

Pleat the excess material at the curved top as shown (below). Pull the lower edge of the calico up

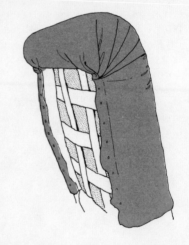

Pleat excess fabric round curves to neaten

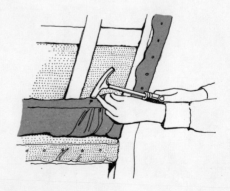

Tuck the cover down the seat and out at the back of the chair. Pull it taut and tack into place

around the horizontal rail at the bottom of the outside back of the chair and tack firmly into place. Adjust the tacks around the top and sides where necessary to make sure that the cover fits as smoothly as possible, and hammer them firmly into place. Trim off excess calico from the edges.

12 Repad and cover the inside arms of the chair using the same technique as for the back. Again, pleat the excess fabric at the curve of the arm. At the back of the arm take the calico through the chair to the outside, wrap it round the upright rail and tack it at the back of the armchair.

The seat of the chair
13 Replace the soft padding of the seat.

14 Cover the soft padding with layers of wadding, graduating their sizes to achieve a domed shape without hard ridges. To get a good front edge, allow the wadding to overlap the edge a little and fold under the lower layers along the front line of the seat. Now cover all the layers with one large piece. This should have a generous amount for tucking down the sides and back of the seat.

Clip the corners diagonally at the back to allow for the back uprights, and clip into the side edges to allow for the arm uprights. Continue the wadding down the front of the seat a little way before trimming it off. Mitre the excess wadding at the corners.

15 Place a large piece of calico over the wadding, clipping it to allow for the uprights. Push the

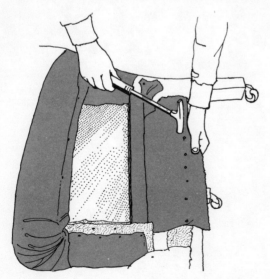

Tack the calico in place all round the front, sides and back of the seat

edges down the sides and back of the chair and then pull them through to the outside of the chair.

16 Temporarily tack the front into place, distributing any fullness of the fabric evenly. Then temporarily tack the sides and back of the calico piece in place.

17 Starting at the front and working down the sides to the back, adjust the tacks where necessary to ensure that the calico lies smoothly and taut across the seat. Hammer the tacks firmly in place.

When upholstering the chair directly, rather than making loose covers, there is no need to extend the calico cover any further.

The base of the chair
18 The base of the chair should now be covered to keep dust out, and black linenette is a good fabric to use. Cut a piece the size of the base of the chair allowing an extra 2 cm all round for turning. Stretch the fabric across the base of the chair with the extra fabric turned under all round, and tack in place

Covering the chair
19 Cover the inside of the chair back with furnishing fabric following the instructions given for the calico cover, but do not completely cover the side panel of the back – just overlap the fabric slightly as shown opposite, left, for the arms of the chair. Pleat the fabric to take up the excess where necessary, and tack it in place down the side panels of the chair, on to the top rail and on to the bottom rail.

20 Cover the inside arms of the chair as for the calico cover, but again do not completely cover the front panel. Pleat and tack the fabric as shown opposite, left, to take up any surplus.

21 Cover the seat of the chair following instructions given for the calico cover, but turning under the raw edge at the front of the chair.

22 Cut the outside side panels, allowing 8 cm for turning. Turn under the raw edges along the top and lower part of the front and tack into position. The lower front edge covers the raw side edge of the seat cover. The top front edge is wrapped around the upright and tacked in place as shown opposite, centre. The back edge is wrapped around the back upright and is tacked to the chair in the same way as the calico.

23 Cut the back panel allowing 8 cm for turning. Turn under the raw edge at the top and tack to the

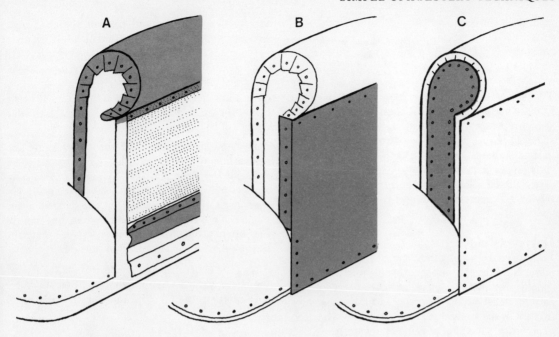

A. Cover the inside arms of the chair, pleating excess fabric and tacking it in place B. Tack the outside panel in place, turning in raw edges top and bottom C. Front panels are cut to shape

The finished chair

top horizontal rail. Wrap the side edges around the uprights as far down as the arms. Below there, turn under the raw edges and tack the fabric to the back of the uprights.

24 The front panels of the arms and the side panels of the back are covered with fabric cut to shape and size, with an allowance of 2·5 cm all round for turning. A layer of wadding will give extra shape to the arm panels. The panels are tacked in place on the arms and back as shown above, right.

25 Trim the panels with braid to give definition to the shape – and to hide the tacks. Braid should also be used to trim the bottom of the chair. Tack the braid in place with gimp pins or glue it in position with a fabric adhesive.

Loose covers

The secret of success for loose covers is good fitting, and to achieve this it is essential to have an accurate pattern. If you have furniture of a fairly standard shape, look in the pattern books at your nearest haberdashery counter – some manufacturers make patterns for loose covers and you will save yourself a lot of time and trouble if you can buy one. If necessary, though, you can make your own.

Making the pattern

You can make your pattern out of newspaper, but fabric is better. An old sheet would be ideal. You should still make the preliminary pieces of the pattern out of paper, however, and it is important to mark in the straight grain of the fabric while the paper is still pinned in position on the chair.

The instructions that follow are for making a loose cover for a Victorian type armchair. Alphabetical references refer to the diagram below.

1 Find the centre of the inside back and seat of the chair and draw with tailor's chalk or tack a line to mark this. In the diagram this is indicated by a dotted line. Make the pattern over one half of the chair and reverse it when you cut out for the other half of the chair. This means that both sides of your cover will be exactly the same.

2 Pin one straight edge of the paper along the centre line and trim the other edges to the exact shape of the back and seat (A and F). You may need to make darts so that the fabric fits smoothly over any rounded surfaces. Pin the darts in place while the paper is on the chair. When you remove the paper pattern trim away excess paper along the line of pins.

3 Lay the paper over the inside arm, taking it over the curve as far as the horizontal rail on the outer side of the arm (C). Pin and cut the pattern to shape.

4 Pin and cut paper to the shape of the front panel of the arm (E), the side panel of the back (B), the outside arm panel (D), front section (G), and back of chair. Label the pattern pieces. If your fabric has a very large motif it will be helpful, when you come to the cutting out stage, if you have indicated on the pattern the correct position of the largest motif.

5 Remove the paper pattern pieces and lay them

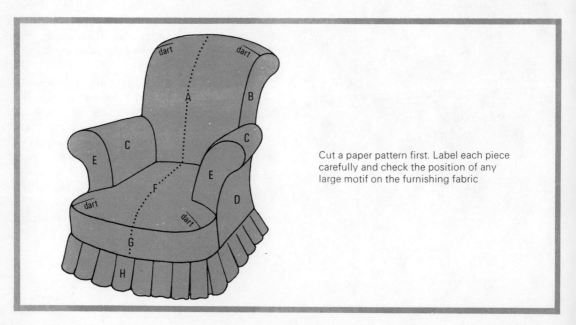

Cut a paper pattern first. Label each piece carefully and check the position of any large motif on the furnishing fabric

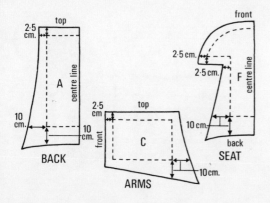

Allow extra fabric on pieces A, C and F as marked

on new sheets of paper or an old sheet. Add a seam allowance of 2·5 cm all round to pieces B, D, E and G and to the back piece. Add extra width to pieces A, C and F as shown above. This extra fabric, which includes a 2·5 cm seam allowance, enables you to tuck the cover securely down the sides of the armchair seat. Transfer any pattern markings.

6 Cut out the finished pattern pieces from fabric or paper.

NB Even if you are using a bought pattern, check and adjust the fit by laying the pieces over the chair.

Calculating quantities

When you are calculating how much fabric you will need, remember that pieces A, F, G and the back piece have to be cut from folded fabric, and that you need two each of B, C, D and E. The pleated frill round the bottom of the chair is three times the circumference of the chair base (plus seam allowances for any joins) times the distance between the chair base and the floor (plus a 2·5 cm seam allowance and a 2·5 cm allowance for the hem). Allow about 1 m extra for piping. As a rough guide to how much fabric is needed, the chair we illustrate used 6 m of 120 cm wide fabric. The frill was made by joining remnants after the main pieces were cut out.

If you choose fabric with a very large pattern, you may need extra in order to match the design where necessary.

Laying and cutting out

If you want a washable loose cover, check that the fabric is both washable and pre-shrunk before you

buy it. Even if the fabric is described as being pre-shrunk, it is a good idea to check before you start cutting. Pin out a square metre and press with a damp cloth. Then re-measure. If there is any shrinkage you will need to treat all the fabric in the same way before you start to cut it.

1 When the fabric is prepared, fold it in half lengthways, making sure that the pattern is placed centrally.

2 Place pieces A, F, G and the back section along the fold and arrange the other pieces to fit in with these. Make sure that the fabric design is running the right way for all pieces – the arrows on the diagram below show the direction of the fabric design.

3 Cut out the pattern shapes.

4 Leave the cutting out of the frill until you are fitting the made-up cover; it is easier to judge the correct length at that point. It can be made by joining left-over fabric, matching the design of the material where possible.

Checking the fit

This is very important and must be done before you join the sections together.

1 Stitch any necessary darts on the wrong side of the fabric, clip and press them open.

2 Arrange the fabric sections on the chair, right sides up. Tuck the pieces with the extra fabric allowance (A, C and F) firmly down the back and sides of the seat.

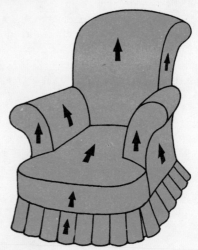

Any design on the fabric should follow the direction of the arrows

3 Pin the 2·5 cm seam allowances of the other pieces together. Keep adjusting the pins until the cover fits really smoothly – this takes quite a long time, but is well worth it for really good results.

4 Trim the excess fabric from the seam allowances so that once again they are 2·5 cm.

5 Notch the seam allowances so that you have no difficulty in matching up the sections when you come to sew them up. Remove the pins from the seam allowances, and take the fabric from the chair.

Piping

Piping always gives a professional touch to loose covers and, as well as being decorative, it helps to keep the cover in good shape. It is not necessary to pipe all the seams – only those that give definition to the shape, such as the front of the arms (E), the side panel of the back (B), and across the front of the seat (F). Measure the edges of the sections to be piped and add 5 cm to each measurement.

Cotton piping cord shrinks considerably on laundering, so boil and dry it twice before you use it to avoid problems when you wash your covers.

1 Fold over one corner of the fabric so that the weft threads run parallel to the selvedge. Crease and mark the line with tailor's chalk or pins.

2 Using a ruler, mark parallel lines from 4–5 cm apart, depending on the thickness of the cord.

3 Cut along these lines to give enough bias (cross-way) strips for the total length of piping required, measuring the length along the shorter edge and allowing extra for each join.

4 Cut the end of each strip parallel to the selvedge so the joins will run in the same direction (see below).

5 To join the strips, place two strips, right sides facing, selvedge edges together. Tack and machine.

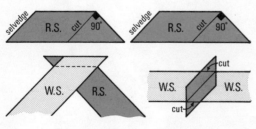

Cut and join bias strips for piping

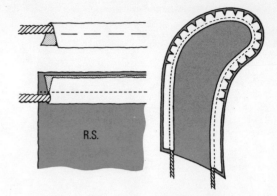

Enclose the cord in the bias strip then stitch the piping on to the cover before making up; clip the turnings so that it lies flat round curved sections

6 Remove tacking, press open the seam and trim off the corners.

7 Join the strips to give the necessary length for each section of piping and insert the cord.

8 Place cord in the centre and fold the strip over the cord, pinning it together close to the cord. Tack and machine as close to the cord as possible using a piping or zipper foot. Remove tacking thread.

9 Place the piping on right side of fabric section to be piped so that the machined line runs along the seam line and the cord lies towards the centre of the section.

10 Pin and tack the piping into place along the seam lines and as close to the cord as possible. For the side panels of the back (B) and the front panels of the arm (E) ease the piping round the curve, clipping the turning where necessary (see above, right).

11 Using a thread that matches the fabric, machine stitch the piping in place as close to the cord as possible.

Sewing the cover

The golden rule when sewing loose covers is to use a good strong thread – the seams have to take quite a lot of strain when you are pulling the cover over the chair. Use size 30s or 40s linen or polyester thread, depending on whether you are using a natural or man-made fabric.

1 Join the top of section A to the top of the outside back. Neaten the raw edges and press seam open.

2 Join the top of section C for the left side of the

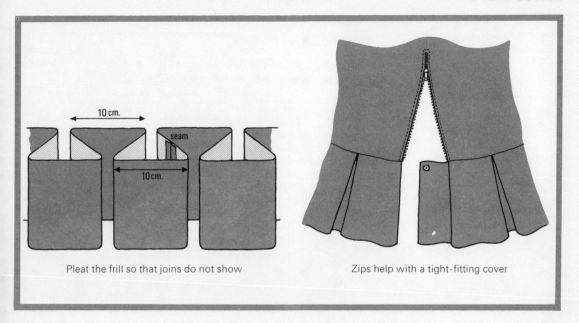

10 cm.

seam

10 cm.

Pleat the frill so that joins do not show

Zips help with a tight-fitting cover

chair to the top of D for the left side of the chair. Neaten the raw edges and press seam open.

3 Repeat step 2 for the right hand side of the chair.

4 Using a piping foot, insert piped section B between section A and the outside back matching the notches you made. Stitch as close to the cord as possible. Neaten the raw edges.

5 Insert piped sections E between C and D for both sides of the chair as in step 4.

6 Join the piped front edge of F to the top of G. Overcast the seam and press it down towards G.

7 Replace the ordinary foot and join the side edges of F to the lower edges of C and E. Neaten the raw edges and press open.

8 Join the side edges of G to lower side edges of sections D.

9 Join the lower edge of A to the back edge of F. Neaten raw edges and press seams open.

10 Join the back edges of C to the lower side edges of A and then to the bottom edges of section B.

11 Now try the cover on the chair to see whether you will need zips to make getting the loose cover on and off the chair easier.

12 If the cover goes on and comes off easily, join the back edges of sections D to the lower side edges

of the back piece. Neaten the raw edges and press seams open.

13 If the cover fits very tightly, insert zips upside down between sections D and the back. The length of the zip depends on how much you need to be able to open the cover. A strip of Velcro fastener is a neat and efficient alternative.

The frill

1 Put the cover on the chair and trim the lower edge level.

2 Place a pin 2·5 cm above the lower edge and measure the distance from the pin to the floor. Using tailor's chalk or pins, mark a line 1·5 cm above the pin and use this as the fitting line for attaching the frill. This will ensure that it clears the floor.

3 Cut the frill as described under **Calculating quantities**, page 45.

4 Turn up a 2·5 cm hem on the lower edge of the frill.

5 Pleat the frill, adjusting the pleats so that any joins are at the back.

6 Pin the frill to the cover, fitting lines together, again adjusting the pleats if necessary so that there

47

is a whole pleat at the centre front of the chair and at the back corners. Stitch frill to cover. Neaten the seam. Press upwards.

7 If you have inserted fastenings you will have to break the frill at the back corners. Keep the frill in place with press studs.

Keeping the cover in place
To prevent the cover from 'creeping' attach two tapes, each about 20 cm long, to the seam at the top of the frill at each corner of the chair. These tapes can be tied round the legs of the chair and will hold the cover securely in place.

Decorating tools

When you are decorating, having the right tools saves time and gives better results. Don't try to economise by buying cheap tools, for good tools well looked after will give you years of use. For larger items of equipment that you don't use often, such as trestles and scaffold boards, it is worth seeing if you can hire them from a local builder (look in the Yellow Pages).

LADDERS AND PLATFORMS
A sturdy **step ladder,** preferably one with a platform, is essential in decorating work. To reach the ceiling and other high places it is best to use two step ladders with a **scaffold board** between them. Use a board strong enough not to need any centre support.

For jobs lower down but still above comfortable reach from the floor, a **step stool** or **folding workbench** is ideal – just the right height for reaching low ceilings and hanging wall coverings For outdoor ladders and platforms, see page 57.

TOOLS FOR PREPARATION
For cleaning and making good you will need **brush, sponge, bucket, detergent, cloths** and **scraper** for scraping off paint and a **shave hook,** either triangular or multi-edged, when burning off or stripping mouldings.

To remove wallpaper you will need a **brush** for wetting and a **stripping knife** or **scraper.** For vinyl wall coverings, use a **wire brush** to score the surface so that water can penetrate. (Don't forget to wear protective **goggles** when using a wire brush or scraping loose materials.)

Plaster cracks can be filled in with a **filling knife,** and you will also need a **trowel** for large areas, 'wet or dry' waterproof **abrasive paper** and a **sanding block.**

Paint can be removed with a **blowlamp.** There are two types, running on either paraffin or bottled gas. The bottled gas type is easier for an amateur to handle, and has a flame adjustment which is important when working on moulded or carved places. Blowlamps should always be handled with care. **Chemical paint strippers,** though rather expensive, are effective for awkward areas such as around window frames.

PAINTING TOOLS
Paint in an open tin may be fouled and quickly forms a skin on top, so it is better to pour out the amount you need into some other container, such as a polythene **paint kettle** which has a handle and is light to carry.

A special **paint tin opener** is a good buy to make sure that you don't bend the lid of the tin when you open it, and so prevent it closing properly.

Masking tape, or small strips of aluminium or plastic held against the glass, will ensure a straight edge when you are painting window frames.

Brushes
You can cope with most painting jobs with brushes

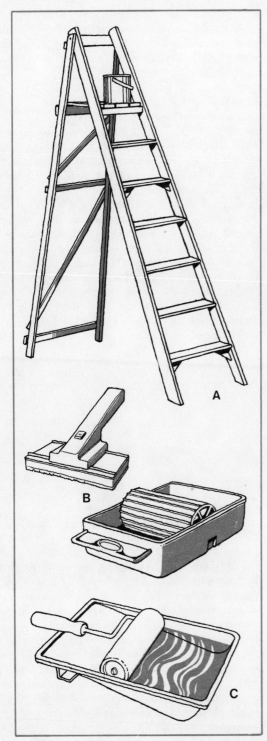

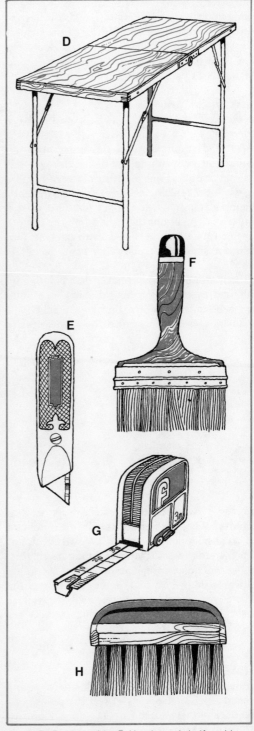

A. Step-ladder B. Painting pad and tray C. Roller and tray D. Pasting table E. Handyman's knife, with replaceable blade F. Pasting brush G. Retractable steel tape measure H. Paper hanger's brush in four sizes, starting with 12 mm for crevices and working up to 100 mm for walls. Good brushes are expensive because of the high price of the natural bristle they are made from. They are essential to give a good finish to your painting, though, and will last a long time given proper care.

Rollers and painting pads
The quickest and easiest way of covering large flat areas is with a **paint roller** – 17–18 cm, is a useful size. Nylon/lambswool rollers are probably best for emulsion painting and mohair for eggshell and sheen finishes; some mohair rollers are suitable for gloss. Foam rollers are also available, but they do tend to splash. With a roller you also need a **paint tray**. To cut out the tedious job of cleaning the paint tray after use, line it with cooking foil, which can simply be removed when the job is finished.

Painting pads are also quicker than painting by brush, and even though they may not give quite such a good finish as rollers, they are a good choice for the inexperienced because they are virtually drip-proof. They are available in a wide range of sizes and shapes for different jobs, and the replaceable ones are probably best. Painting pads come with a special type of paint tray.

WALLPAPERING TOOLS
Unless you are using ready-pasted paper you will need a **pasting table**. If you don't want to buy one, try and borrow or hire. If this fails, you can make do with a kitchen or dining table as long as you protect it really well with newspapers or a polythene sheet first.

You will also need a **metre rule** or **steel tape measure**, a **plumb-line**, a plastic **bucket**, long bladed **scissors**, a **pasting brush** (unless you're using ready-pasted paper) a **seam roller** and a handle-less **paper hanger's brush**.

A **T-square** is useful for getting a straight edge when you cut the paper, but if you haven't one, fold the paper back on itself with the edges in line and then cut with scissors or a **sharp knife**. Have a **cloth** handy for cleaning up spilt paste.

Paints

Paint has a dual purpose, protective as well as decorative. Whatever surface you are painting you need to consider not only the final, visual effect, but the preparatory work that goes underneath this. Without adequate preparation, often including painting with primer and undercoat before the finishing coat, any painted surface will deteriorate quickly. For details about preparing surfaces see pages 53–54.

PRIMERS
A primer is the first coat of paint that goes on to a bare surface. Its purpose is to seal the porosity of the surface so that subsequent coats form a protective layer over the surface instead of soaking into it. While an all-purpose primer will suit most surfaces it is always a good idea to take advice to find out if there is one specially suited to the job you have in mind.

For instance, wood primer, either white or pink, is the normal choice for priming softwoods (and thinned down is suitable for some hardwoods, such as oak); but aluminium primer is a better choice for very resinous wood, such as redwood, as well as being useful for priming copper pipes.

For pegboard and hardboard, use hardboard sealer or thinned down emulsion paint, both of which will prime the surface. Zinc chromate is the primer to choose to protect metals such as steel, iron and aluminium as it is anti-corrosive and heat resistant. A stabilizing primer should be used to prepare old flaking paint surfaces on brickwork and plaster. On surfaces such as new plaster, building boards and cement rendering use a primer with alkali resisting properties, if you are going to use an oil or resin based paint; priming is not necessary if you intend using emulsion paint.

In addition, because small children are likely to suck or chew painted wood, always make sure the primer you use is a leadless one when you are dealing with a cot or toys.

Knotting

Knotting is a solution of shellac in alcohol which is applied to knots in new wood to help prevent the natural resin bleeding through and spoiling the finished surface. It should be used only when needed, and then sparingly.

Fungicidal solutions

Fungicidal solutions are used for killing moulds and other organic growths both inside and outside the house. The surface can then be decorated without risk of further infection. Use with care; some types are poisonous.

UNDERCOATS

An undercoat is a heavily pigmented matt paint usually blended to go with the same maker's finishing coat. The purpose of an undercoat is to mask out any colour underneath and to provide a good foundation for the finish coat. Traditional undercoats are oil-based, but newer acrylic types make cleaning up easier because brushes can be washed out in water.

With modern paints it is not always necessary to use an undercoat but it helps, where you are making a strong colour change, to provide a solid finish.

FINISHING COATS

Never be tempted to use a paint that is not recommended for the purpose simply because you like the colour. Within a short time the paint will flake, fade, peel or blister and all your work will have been wasted.

Emulsion

Emulsion paints are tough, easy to apply and easy to clean. Inside the house emulsions can be used in any room, even kitchens and bathrooms provided you use the grade recommended, and on virtually any surface. Metal surfaces, such as kitchen and bathroom pipes, must first be primed with metal primer such as a chromate. Emulsion can be applied over a gloss painted surface provided it is well rubbed down first to provide a 'key'.

Until fairly recently emulsions were available only with a matt finish, but nowadays some give a glossy or 'silk' finish.

Emulsion paint is also available in a thixotropic, non-drip, form which is especially useful for painting ceilings. The important thing to remember when using a thixotropic paint is that unlike other paints it should not be stirred before use. Stirring converts the paint into a thin-flowing liquid and this is only necessary if you are using a paint roller.

Because emulsions are water thinned paints, you can clean your brushes simply by washing them under the tap.

Gloss paint

Gloss paint gives a durable finish and is still the favourite for woodwork because it resists scuffs and fingermarks wash off easily.

Polyurethane gloss has a really tough and long-lasting surface that is almost metal-like in its hardness. It is also available in a thixotropic, non-drip, form. With some types the brushes can be cleaned with a washing-up liquid solution.

As well as on woodwork, gloss paint can look good on walls and ceilings, but it is harder to apply to large areas than emulsion paint. Rolling helps to reduce the work involved but it is much more difficult to clean gloss paint from a roller than from a brush.

Don't use gloss to paint polystyrene sheets or tiles because the solvent it contains causes them to break down and dissolve.

Modern vinyl gloss paints have little or no smell, and brushes can be washed out in water. With ordinary gloss paints, the smell does tend to hang around and cleaning up can be rather a messy business. You will need plenty of white spirit, and this is flammable, so work with care.

Other oil paints

Eggshell paint has an attractive slight sheen, and is equally as tough as high gloss paint. Its main use is for inside walls and ceilings.

Flat 'matt' paint is a specially mixed oil-based paint that dries with no sheen or gloss. It will stand washing down and doesn't need an undercoat, although two finishing coats are recommended.

51

Special qualities are manufactured for exterior surfaces.

Leadless paints
Most paints have a low lead content these days but check with the manufacturer's literature before using anything on nursery furniture or toys.

Outdoor wall paints
Outdoor paints may be either emulsion, oil or resin based paints with various additives to improve their weather resistance and in some cases to give them texture. These additives may be crushed rock, mica and fine granite aggregate, reinforced mica or stone.

These paints are suitable for smooth walls or textured surfaces. The colour range is usually limited; deep colours stay brighter looking longer than white on town walls, a point to bear in mind since the paints are rather expensive.

Clean brushes either with water or white spirit, depending on whether the paint is water or oil based. Check the tin for instructions.

Distemper
Distemper is cheap but impermant and easily stained. It can also come off on you if you brush against it.

The original, non-washable distemper is a mixture of chalk, or some similar substance, and tint or stain, diluted with water. It needs to be scrubbed off completely before you can paint over it.

The formula for washable distemper is similar, but it also contains some oil emulsion. Distemper has been superseded by emulsion paint and is not now used to any great extent.

PAINT QUANTITIES
When you measure a room to estimate the amount of paint you will need, take the windows as flat areas. For example, a window 1 m by 2 m should be allowed for as $2 m^2$ of painted area. Staircases and banisters are estimated in the same way.

The chart opposite gives an approximate guide to the coverage of one coat of paint, but coverage will vary according to the type of paint and the surface

RECOMMENDED PAINTS

SURFACE	LOCATION	RECOMMENDED PAINT etc.
New woodwork	Indoors	Treat knots with knotting. Apply wood primer, undercoat and gloss or eggshell paint.
	Outdoors	Treat knots, apply wood primer and two coats of undercoat. Finish with gloss paint.
Previously painted woodwork	Indoors	Undercoat if doing extreme colour change, then gloss paint.
	Outdoors	Patch prime bare parts, two undercoats, gloss paint.
Ceilings and walls (new and untreated)	Any room	Use emulsion paint until the plaster has dried out. Then gloss or eggshell if preferred.
Ceilings and walls (emulsion paint)	Any room	Emulsion paint, gloss or eggshell.
Ceilings and walls (gloss paint)	Any room	Undercoat, then eggshell, gloss or emulsion paint.
Ceilings and walls (wallpaper)	Any room	Emulsion paint, matt or sheen.
Metal window frames	Any location	One coat of metal primer, undercoat, gloss paint.
Metal guttering and pipes	Outdoors	Prime with metal primer, undercoat, then gloss paint. Two coats of black bituminous paint inside the gutters give extra water resistance.

it is being applied to. So check on the tin or maker's literature.

Remember, too, that if you are covering a very dark background colour you may require two or more coats, again depending on the type of paint you use.

When you buy paint, try and get all you need from the same batch (usually marked on the tin) or you may find you get a slight colour variation. If you have to buy extra paint, start with the fresh batch from the corner of a wall, not in the middle; this normally prevents any slight colour difference being noticeable.

COVERAGE GUIDE	
1 *litre* of product . . .	. . . *covers up to given no. of sq metres*
Primer—wood	12
—metal	13
—plaster	15
Undercoating	15
Gloss paint	15
Eggshell and flat paint	15
Emulsion paint	11–15
Thixotropic paint	12–14
Exterior wall paint	6

Interior painting

The tools you are likely to need when painting a room are dealt with on pages 48–50. For which kind of paint you should use where, and how much of it you will need, see pages 50–53.

Before starting to paint a room, remove all the furniture and soft furnishings you can. Cover immovable furniture with cotton or polythene dust sheets and protect the floor with more dust sheets or old newspapers. You will also need a roll of kitchen paper or some rags to remove the inevitable splashes.

PREPARING THE SURFACE
Preparation is boring, but vital.

For walls, provided the existing paint is in good condition a thorough wash down should be all that is needed. Starting from the bottom up, wash over the area with either a special paint-cleaner or use a washing-up detergent. Rinse with clean water to remove the detergent (this is very important), this time working from the top down.

If the existing paint is powdery, blistered or flaking, however, it will need to be removed and the surface glasspapered.

Before painting over a wall-papered wall with emulsion paint, be sure the paper is firmly stuck to the wall, particularly at the edges, then wipe it over with a damp – not wet – cloth. If you get the paper too wet you will loosen it and it will come away from the wall, bringing your new paint with it. Certain papers cannot be painted – colours may bleed or the surface may be damaged by paint; if you are in any doubt, paint a small test area first, somewhere where it will not be noticeable.

If the wallpaper is in poor condition, or there are several layers of it, it should be wetted several times with warm water and washing-up liquid until loose, and then scraped off. Score vinyl wall coverings with a wire brush first (**wear protective goggles**) so the water can soak through and soften the paste below. After removing the paper, wash off all traces of paste and size.

Filling cracks Once the walls are clean, examine the plaster for any holes or cracks. To repair a crack successfully, first open it out with a scraper to make it wide and deep enough to provide a bed for the filler. Work away from you to protect your eyes. Dust out the opening with a stiff brush, press in the filler firmly and smooth it off slightly above the level of the surrounding plaster with a knife or small trowel.

When the filler has hardened, it may be necessary to wet the surface with a sponge and rub it down with wet abrasive paper. As soon as the surface is really dry, rub over again with a fine glass paper to give a smooth, even finish. Deep cracks or holes

53

may need two attempts at filling before they are properly smooth.

Damp patches Any damp patches on walls or ceilings should be treated at source (ie check guttering) and any stains left showing should be painted with a thin coat of damp sealer. If the walls are really badly stained, or in very poor condition, they may need to be lined with lining paper before you paint them (see page 59).

Preparing wood
Provided the woodwork you want to paint is already painted and in good condition it should only require washing and rubbing down with fine glasspaper to a smooth, matt finish. Any holes or cracks can be filled with a proprietary wood filler. However, if several layers of paint have been allowed to build up, or the paintwork is in bad condition the wisest course is to remove it.

Basically, there are three ways of removing paint from wood: sanding, using a chemical paint remover or a blowtorch.

Sanding, using a power tool and a sanding attachment with non-clog discs is probably the quickest way, but it does cause a considerable amount of dust. For small areas, mouldings and around window frames, a chemical paint remover is probably best. These chemical strippers can be expensive, though, and it is important to follow the

When using a blowtorch, work from the bottom up and remove the softened paint with a scraper

instructions carefully as they may damage skin and clothing.

To use a blowtorch, a certain amount of skill is necessary. So have a trial run outdoors first. Work from the bottom upwards, pre-heating first, and remove the softened paint with a 5 cm scraper. Once you have got the old paint off, rub down the bare wood with medium grade glasspaper, always working in the direction of the grain to avoid scratching. Treat any knots with shellac knotting and the wood is then ready for priming.

PAINTING TECHNIQUE
Emulsion paint is easy to put on (but if you are using a roller, do not get it too wet); gloss and eggshell paints need a bit more care. The first rule is never to dip the brush into the paint more than a third of the way up the bristles. Then, when you are painting, draw the brush first downwards, then up again over the same area. Next draw it across from left to right, and then back. Finally, very gently, run the very tip of the brush once more downwards, lift it off the wall, and then run it across. It is this final 'laying off' that gives you a smooth result because it evens out any obvious brushmarks.

PAINTING SEQUENCE
The sequence in which to paint a room is: first ceiling, second walls and then woodwork in the following order – doors, windows, picture rail and skirting board. Painting is always best done by daylight, and with the electricity mains switched off if you can. This is not always possible, but beware of paint seeping behind light fittings and switch panels and fusing the electricity supply.

Ceilings The quickest way to paint a ceiling is with a roller, using a 5 cm brush for the edges, corners and round light fittings. Start from the window and work back into the room in strips, taking care not to have the brush or roller over loaded.

Walls If you are using emulsion paint, start at the top right-hand corner (or the left one, if you are left-handed) and paint across in a horizontal strip. With gloss paint, work vertically in metre square patches. This way you make sure that the paint doesn't dry before you get to the next section so you will not get any hard lines.

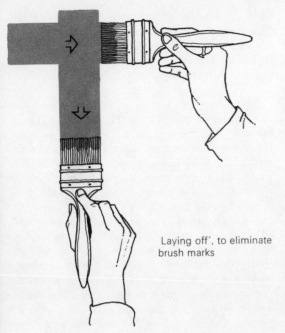

Laying off', to eliminate brush marks

Be careful when painting around light switches. Turn off the electricity and to avoid getting splashes on the plates remove them and put them back when the paint is dry.

Radiators Some radiators are designed to be detachable (or you could call in a plumber). If you don't want to move them, but still want to paint behind them, you can buy a specially angled brush or painting pad. Take care not to get paint into the airlock hole or the knobs for turning radiators on and off.

Doors If possible, paint the door surround and let it dry before you paint the door itself. Have the door open while you are painting, and leave it open till the paint is dry.

Take off all the door fittings before you start to paint, then start at the top right hand corner (left, if you are left-handed) and work down and across in squares. Panel doors are tricky to paint well, but if you follow the numerical sequence shown below the result should be satisfactory.

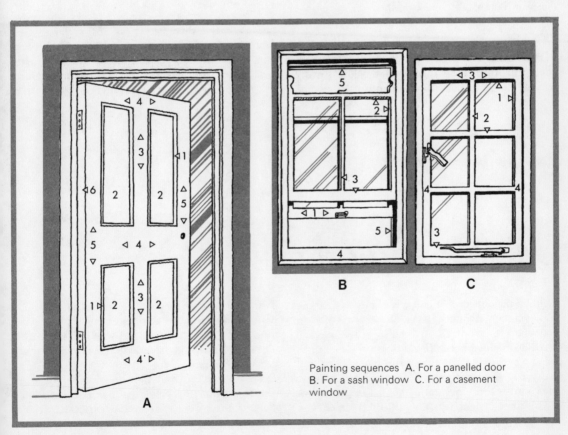

Painting sequences A. For a panelled door B. For a sash window C. For a casement window

For louvre doors, start by painting the inside of the slats. Then do the outside using up the paint you will find has trickled through. Next do the outside frame and finally the inside frame.

Provided you have removed the door furniture, you can paint a flush door just as you would a wall but take particular care 'laying off'.

Windows It is a good idea to paint the window as early in the day as possible, to give it time to dry so it can be closed at night. Again it helps to paint the outer framework first and let it dry before you start to paint the window.

Very few people have a really steady hand, so it is sensible to stick masking tape round the panes of glass just where the glass joins the frame. Once the paint is dry the tape can be removed leaving you with a nice, clean line.

For the painting sequence for either sash or casement windows, follow the numerical order shown in the diagrams on page 55.

When you have finished, wipe down any fittings you haven't been able to remove (catches, etc.) so the paint doesn't dry and clog them. Also remove any paint splashes from sashcords, or they will not run properly.

Picture rails Here, too, masking tape along both edges will protect the wall above and below. Picture rails are best painted with a 37 mm brush.

Skirting boards Lift the carpet if you can. Otherwise protect it with a sheet of stiff cardboard you can slide along with you as you paint. Use masking tape or a plastic shield where the upper edge of the skirting meets the wall.

LOOKING AFTER YOUR BRUSHES

Never allow paint to harden on your brushes. Use cold water to remove emulsion paint and white spirit or a branded brush cleaner to remove oil-based paints. Some modern oil-based paints can be removed with water and washing-up liquid; check the label on the tin.

If you are stopping work only for a short time (say to have lunch), wrap the bristles in cooking foil or in a plastic bag; for a limited period this will prevent oil-based paints from drying out, and save wasting cleaning products. When you stop work for the night, don't leave a brush standing on its bristles in a jar of cleaning fluid. Suspend it with a piece of string or a long nail or a stick tied across the handle.

After cleaning always hang brushes up to dry because letting them lie flat can distort the bristles. Once the brushes are thoroughly dry, flick them with your fingers to shake away any loose bristles, dust or dry paint flakes. Then wrap them carefully in clean paper and store them in a cool, airy place.

Outdoor painting

Painting the outside of a house is quite a task. Even with a certain amount of skill, and the weather on your side, to paint all four sides of an average three-bedroomed house (including walls as well as wood work) is likely to take a full month, working every day. For this reason most people who do their own exterior decorating spread out the work over a three or four year period. Alternatively you may prefer to employ professionals to paint walls

(which need doing every five to seven years, or when paint starts to deteriorate), so that you have time to concentrate on the rest yourself. Paintwork on wood and pipes should be renewed roughly every three years.

Autumn is the best time of year for outdoor painting, when the building fabric has had all summer to dry out. Try to avoid painting in rain or hot sun.

SCAFFOLDS AND LADDERS

The safest and most comfortable way of painting the higher parts of the outside of a house is with the help of portable scaffolding. This can be extended to the height you want and has a largish working platform on top. It takes apart for storage and some makes have locking wheels to push it around on when it is standing on a hard surface such as concrete. You will need to stand the legs on boards if you are working on a soft base, such as earth or tarmac. The disadvantage of portable scaffolding is the price. But it is worthwhile seeing if you can hire (look in the Yellow Pages).

Ladders come cheaper. Aluminium ones are lighter than wood to carry around. To raise an extension ladder, stand it a metre or so away from the wall. Put one foot on the bottom rung and hold the lower section of the ladder with one hand while with the other hand you push the upper section as far as you can reach. Then pull the bottom section out a bit further from the wall so you can push a bit higher, and continue until you reach the height you want. Some ladders are operated by side ropes, which help when you have to extend the ladder to its full height.

In its final position the distance of the foot of the ladder from the wall should be about a quarter of the extended height. Rest the feet on a plank if you are on soft ground or tarmac. Secure the ladder either by tying one of the lower rungs to a handy drainpipe, or by tying the bottom rung to a stake driven into the ground. Once you are up, tie one of the upper rungs to an eye screw let into the fascia board. Don't rest the ladder against the gutter itself if you can avoid it, especially if you have plastic guttering. **Never work on an unsecured ladder.** To reach dormer windows set in a steep tiled roof, use a roofing ladder or a scaffold. Do not rest the ladder on the tiles.

While you are working above the ground, carry the tools you need in a pocket in your overall or painting apron, not in your hands. Paint should be carried in a small plastic bucket, or better still, a paint kettle.

When you are ready to start painting, protect any paving beneath with old cotton sheets. Do not use polythene, because a ladder standing on polythene would be liable to slip.

ORDER OF PAINTING

Generally speaking, the order of painting the out-

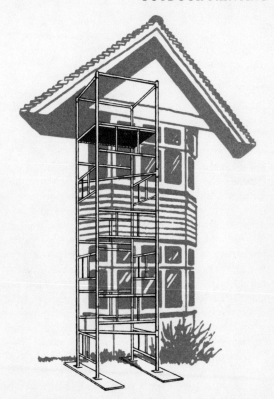

A work scaffold will enable you to reach high points with minimum danger

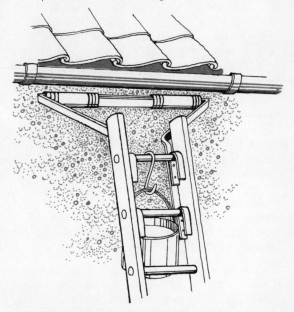

Use a ladder stay to improve your working position. Make some arrangement so you do not have to hold the paint tin while you work

side of a house is: start at the top and work down. Complete all preparation first, then paint the walls. After that go on to gutters and fascia boards, downpipes, top windows, then lower windows, doors and finally air brick grilles.

Make sure that all the surfaces you are going to paint are clean, dry and in good condition. It takes time but will certainly repay you.

PREPARATION AND PAINTING

Gutters Plastic gutters do not need painting, but do need cleaning out with a trowel and wet cloth (the debris will be rich in rotting leaves and bird droppings, so keep it for the compost heap). Clean out metal gutters with a trowel, then brush out the gutter with a wire brush (**wear protective goggles and gloves when you do this**). Scrape out any rusty patches. If the rusting is really bad, a wire brush attachment on a power drill will cut down the work and time involved – but be careful when using a power tool at the top of a ladder and remember to **protect your eyes and hands**.

Wipe or brush off all the loose dust from the surface of the metal. Once it is thoroughly clean and dry apply a good even coat of metal primer right away. (If more elaborate repairs are called for, see pages 144–6.)

The inside of the gutters should be given two coats of black bituminous paint. This is more water-resistant than oil paint and it won't be seen. Use a metal primer, undercoat and one or two coats of gloss paint for the outsides.

Fascia boards Fill in any holes and cracks using a hard stopping and sand down with fine abrasive paper, rubbing in the direction of the grain to prevent scratching. Scrape out any knots to remove exuded resin, then go over them with a patent knotting. Prime any bare patches and then apply an undercoat and one or two coats of gloss paint. With modern alkyd resin based paints you won't need to sand down between coats as long as the second coat is applied just a few days after the first is dry. Check on the paint tin and follow directions for the second (or third) coat application.

Rendered walls If a rendered wall shows cracks these should be repaired with either a branded cement-work filler, following the maker's instructions, or you can make your own mixture using six parts plasterer's sand to one part cement. Fill the cracks using a trowel or scraper.

Pebbledash walls Where the brick is exposed behind the pebbledash, brush out any loose particles, damp down and re-render with a mixture of one part cement to six parts plasterer's sand. When rendered level with the original coat, scratch and leave to dry. Next apply an alkali resisting solution to new work and a stabilizing primer to seal the surface.

Make up a branded stipple mixture, following the maker's instructions, and scrub the mixture on to the surface with a banister brush and 'stipple' to match the existing pebbledash. After 15 minutes brush over again with a partly loaded brush and beat back some of the sharpest stipple points. Leave to dry.

If your pebbledash wall needs painting but not first aid, brush it over with a stiff brush to get rid of all loose dust and grit. If you come across any signs of organic growth, scrub over with a fungicide and leave for a day to kill off any remaining spores. Next damp down the wall with a hose to neutralize the natural porosity of the coating under the pebbles.

For the paint to choose for exterior walls, see page 52. The paint will be best applied with either a 100 mm brush or with a roller (see pages 48–50).

The amount of paint you will need will vary according to the porosity of the wall surface, but for a guide see the chart on page 53.

Downpipes Clean or remove any rust in the same way as for gutters. To clean behind a downpipe insert a sheet of abrasive paper between the pipe and the wall and pull it backwards and forwards, then do the same with a clean rag. To paint the back of the pipe, use a piece of non-fluffy cloth dipped in paint and pull it backwards and forwards in the same way. Paint the front of the pipe as for gutters, using a 50 or 25 mm brush.

Windows and window frames Examine the windows and window frames and replace any broken sashcords and cracked panes of glass. Renew any decayed woodwork by cutting out the soft parts well into the good wood, and immediately coat with primer. If the frames are really rotted, have them replaced. Check underneath the sill to make sure the rain drip channel (the groove running along the length of the sill) hasn't become clogged with paint. Rake it out if it has, otherwise water may penetrate the wall. Do not paint behind the drip channel; this acts as a valve to keep the wood in equilibrium.

Have a look at the pointings – the little cement fillets joining the window frame to the masonry – and if they are cracked rake them out and replace them with a mastic compound, following the maker's instructions.

If you find any cracks in the putty around the glass, rake this out with a small wood chisel or an old kitchen knife with the blade snapped off at an angle, tapping gently with a light hammer on the back of the blade. Now clean the windows, using methylated spirit round the edges of the glass to provide a really clean surface for the new putty. Sand down the exposed wood of the rebate and paint with primer to stop the oil from the putty sinking into the bare wood. When the paint is dry, apply the new putty and level out with a putty knife.

If your windows have metal frames, and any patches of rust have developed, scrape thoroughly and brush with a wire brush (**wear goggles to protect your eyes**). When you have removed the rust and loose flaking paint, apply rust proofer following the maker's directions closely with respect to drying time and the application of the following paint coats. With some rust-proofing treatments primers are also necessary.

When painting window frames use a 50 mm and 25 mm brush and a cutting-in brush with angled bristles which make it easier to put the paint on without getting it on the glass. Follow the sequence illustrated on page 55 for interior windows. If you can't be bothered to use masking tape to protect the panes, and you haven't a cutting-in brush, an alternative is to use a small piece of sheet aluminium or plastic as a guide, held against the glass and butting up to the frame.

Doors Doors should have any blistered or defective paint removed either with a chemical stripper or a blowlamp (handle with care). Wipe the door down thoroughly and sand with glasspaper to give an even surface. Paint in reasonable condition will need only washing down and lightly sanding to produce a clean, smooth surface.

Doors should be painted with a 50 or 25 mm brush in the same numerical sequence as described on page 55 for inside doors. Be sure you work with clean brushes and either a new can of paint or paint from a part-used can strained through an old pair of tights into a clean container. The standard of the paintwork on doors will be much more noticeable than that on smaller areas such as window frames and sills.

Ventilation points Make sure all air bricks and wall vents are clear before you start painting. If the metal is rusty, rub off the rust with a wire brush in the same way as for gutters.

Wall coverings

What used to be called wallpaper is now a wall covering – due to the advances of technology which mean that you can now hang plastics, fabrics, cork and other fibres. Some of these materials are better than paper when it comes to resisting steam and staining; others just look nicer.

PAPERS
Wallpaper comes in an enormous range of patterns and colours in various qualities. Even the thinnest will go a long way towards covering a bad surface on a wall. For a plain colour cover on a wall that would look uneven if just painted, first hang a **lining paper** which can then be emulsion painted. Where a wall is painted and you want to put a pale paper over the paint, it is also sensible to line it first to prevent the colour showing through. If the paint is loose, or if you want to cover distemper, it must be removed before you hang the paper.

True professionals will line using the paper horizontally to prevent the joins of both papers coming on top of each other – beginners had best stick to vertical hanging. Putting up wallpaper is easy once you've practised a bit (see pages 62–66) though remember that very thin papers tear easily when wetted with paste.

Most papers are now sold ready-trimmed, though some of the more expensive hand-blocked varieties still need some trimming. This is very difficult to do well without a special trimming machine and takes a long time. So if the retailer won't do the trimming for you, you'd be wiser to settle on another wallpaper – or another retailer.

Hand-printed paper may be produced by block, silk-screen or stencil printing and because this takes longer than machine printing and the runs are smaller, it tends to be more expensive.

Flock paper is made by glueing silk, nylon or wool cuttings on to the surface of the paper to make up a three-dimensional design. Silk and wool flock papers should be handled with care when you hang them as they are very easy to mark. In fact they are best left to the professional.

Embossed papers are pressed between rollers after printing to make a relief design. Some manufacturers use cotton-based papers to give an even stronger, more heavily embossed design.

Woodchip papers get their grainy texture and resistance to scuffs from tiny woodchips and saw-dust which are added to the paper pulp; they come in medium and coarse textures. Woodchip papers need to be painted over after hanging.

VINYL
Vinyl wallcoverings come in masses of colours and patterns with the advantage of washability or scrubability according to the quality you pick. Vinyls are hung with a heavier duty paste than paper but the process is equally simple and good results are easily achieved.

With **ready-pasted vinyls** the job becomes even simpler as you just dunk the cut length of wall-covering in a trough of water (the cardboard trough is supplied when you buy the rolls) and this activates the paste and it is ready to hang after the required soaking time.

Vinyls with a difference include one with a raised nylon flock design on a vinyl backing. It is very tough and can be washed down in the same way as an ordinary vinyl. There is also a heavy grade vinyl specially designed for kitchens and

When hanging ready pasted paper, soak it first in the tray provided to activate the paste

bathrooms and particularly good for covering problem areas such as old tiles. It has a sculptured finish so that tile joins don't show through and is hung with heavy duty paste.

Self-adhesive vinyl just needs to be unrolled and have the backing paper stripped off before hanging. It works out expensive for large areas and is difficult to hang in long drops without help. Only choose it for wallcovering if you must have a particular pattern.

POLYETHYLENE
This is different from other wallcoverings in that when it comes to hanging you paste the wall then hang the cut length of paper to it, straight from the roll, and just trim the bottom. This is the easiest wallcovering for a beginner to use, though you must take care not to stretch it at the edges or the pattern won't match. It looks and feels like a fabric, and can be used anywhere, including over tiles, but must be hung with a special heavy duty paste.

ANAGLYPTA
Anaglypta comes in a wide range of embossed designs and is an ideal wallcovering for cracked walls and rough areas. When finished it is best

given two coats of emulsion paint. It needs to be handled with care otherwise stretching may occur and the embossing is easily pressed out.

A more durable embossed wallcovering is an anaglypta with a vinyl content. It can be left in its plain white finish or painted with emulsion using a soft lambswool roller.

HESSIAN

Hessian gives walls a fabric covered look, but tends to be pricey. Unless you are expert at hanging you should choose a paper-backed variety which will not shrink or stretch. Non-paper-backed hessians need to be over-lapped when hanging, allowed to shrink and then trimmed to a butt joint – no job for an amateur. Choose a paper-backed brand that is only 52 cm wide too; some hessians are only sold in one metre widths, which are difficult to handle.

Hessian should be hung using a heavy duty paste, and is not really suitable for kitchens and bath-rooms. If you specially want a hessian look in these rooms it is best to pick a hessian patterned vinyl wallcovering.

CORK

Cork for walls comes in tile form in various shades and patterns. You put them up with a contact adhesive. They give some degree of noise and heat insulation; the waxed variety will need an occasional rub over with wax polish to protect them.

FOILS

These are metallic foil designs on either a vinyl or a paper backing. The foil is used to enhance the design and give a depth to the pattern. Foils are

Measurement in metres round walls including doors and windows	WALLPAPER QUANTITIES							
	Height in metres from skirting							
	2·0 to 2·25	2·25 to 2·50	2·50 to 2·75	2·75 to 3·0	3·0 to 3·25	3·25 to 3·50	3·50 to 3·75	3·75 to 4·0
11·0	5	5	6	6	7	7	8	8
11·0	5	6	7	7	8	8	9	9
12·0	6	6	7	8	8	9	9	10
13·0	6	7	8	8	9	10	10	10
14·0	7	7	8	9	10	10	11	11
15·0	7	8	9	9	10	11	12	12
16·0	8	8	9	10	11	11	12	13
17·0	8	9	10	10	11	12	13	14
18·0	9	9	10	11	12	13	14	15
19·0	9	10	11	12	13	14	15	16
20·0	9	10	11	12	13	14	15	16
21·0	10	11	12	13	14	15	16	17
22·0	10	11	13	14	15	16	17	18
23·0	11	12	13	14	15	17	18	19
24·0	11	12	14	15	16	17	18	20
25·0	12	13	14	15	17	18	19	20
26·0	12	13	15	16	17	19	20	21
27·0	13	14	15	17	18	19	21	22
28·0	13	14	16	17	19	20	21	23
29·0	13	15	16	18	19	21	22	24
30·0	14	15	17	18	20	21	23	24
				Number of rolls required				

available ready-pasted or unpasted, and are hung in the same way as standard wallcoverings. See special note about hanging these on page 65.

EXOTICS

There are a number of specialist wallcoverings on the market which are not really suitable for an amateur to hang. They are generally expensive to buy and unless you are very sure of your skills it would be foolish to spoil them by inferior hanging.

Specialist wallcoverings we do not recommend you to hang yourself include **grasscloths** (where natural grasses are bonded to a paper backing), **silks** and other delicate fabrics laminated to a paper backing, **wall carpet, wall suede** and **cork veneer** (which is cork laminated to backing paper).

HOW MUCH TO BUY

Most wallpapers and other coverings are sold ready-trimmed in rolls 10 m × 520 mm and packed in polythene sleeves.

A fatal mistake beginners make is to work out the quantity of paper needed without allowing for the pattern drop and matching up, plus a bit extra at the top and bottom. The wisest course is to take the measurements of your room to the shop with you, and when you have chosen the wallpaper, get the salesman to do the estimating for you. While you are ordering, it is a good idea to buy an extra roll to allow for any mistakes.

Before you fall in love with a covering costing more than you can afford, however, the chart on page 61 will help to give you an idea of the quantities you may need.

Hanging wall coverings

PREPARATION

It is well worth preparing the walls thoroughly before you begin wallpapering. If the existing cover is paint and it is in a reasonable condition, a good wash down may well be enough (see page 195). If it is gloss paint, rub with coarse glasspaper to roughen the surface. But hanging new wallpaper over old is never a good idea. This is because moisture from the fresh paste can seep through the old paper and loosen the existing paste behind. Then shortly after, down will come old paper, new paper and all.

Many of the newer wallpapers and vinyl coverings are easy to remove as the top surface simply peels away leaving the backing paper ready to take the new covering. Other kinds of paper need a thorough wetting with a large brush, after which the paper can be peeled off with a stripping knife.

If the paper is a washable one, first score it with a wire brush or scraper to help the water get through and soften the paste behind. Washing-up liquid helps to soften the paste. **Wear protective goggles when doing this.**

Once all the old paper has been removed the walls should be washed down to get rid of old paste and odd strips of paper. If the wall has been sized, you will need to wash it off well and scrub hard to get back to a really clean surface. Fill in any cracks or holes as described on page 53 and finish with a light rub over with medium grade glasspaper.

SIZING

The walls should now be sized. Home decorators often skip this step, but sizing helps the paper slide to match up the pattern and stick better, and so makes it easier to put on. You can use a diluted solution of cellulose wallpaper adhesive or an ordinary glue size. Whichever you use follow the maker's directions on the packet regarding the correct amount of water needed to make the size. Cover the whole surface and let it dry (you'll know when it has, because the wall will glisten as if it were frosted with sugar).

FINDING THE VERTICAL

When you are papering a room, the best place to start is by the window. Paper as far as you can to the side of the room, away from the light, then go back to the other side of the window and start again. This way, by papering against the light, you avoid the shadows cast against the edges. It is important never to overlap wallcoverings, they must be butt joined.

Do not, however, be tempted to take the edge of

Match patterns carefully before cutting

Use a plumbline to find the vertical, and mark it on the wall. Hang the paper against this line

the window frame as a guide for a vertical line to work from. For this you will need a plumb-line. These are not expensive to buy, but if necessary it is quite easy to make your own by tying something small and heavy (like a small spanner or a key) to a long piece of string. Fix the free end of the string to a point at the top of the wall about 50 cm from one side of the window frame. The string will hang in a dead straight line, so mark its position either by chalking the string and twanging it against the wall to leave a vertical line, or marking alongside it in three or four places with a pencil. This is the plumb-line against which to place your first drop of paper.

CUTTING

Before cutting and pasting the wallpaper, unroll it and check it for any slight variation in colour or pattern. If the variation is really noticeable, return the roll to your supplier. But if the variation is only slight, put the roll aside to use in a corner or a part of the room that is away from the light.

When you are ready to cut the first length of paper, unroll it by drawing it over the edge of the table to help take out the curl, and to stop it springing back. Cut the length at least 10 cm longer than the height of the room as you have measured it against your plumbline. This first length will give you the guide for the other lengths, although there

Paste from the centre outwards, taking it right to the edge of the paper

Fold the paper paste to paste to carry it

are two points you should watch. First, you must have an exact pattern match (check the right-hand edge of the second roll against the left-hand edge of the first if you are papering to the left of the window). Second, be sure the ceiling height doesn't differ in other parts of the room. Take plumbline measurements to be sure.

PASTING

Use the type of paste recommended by the manufacturer of the wall covering if possible. Heavy vinyl coverings, for instance, need a much stronger paste than conventional papers. Make up the paste or adhesive following the maker's instructions carefully. Too thick a paste is not only difficult to work with, it can also mark through the paper. If the paste is too thin, the paper will not stick.

Put your first length of paper, pattern side down, on the pasting table and apply the paste with a wide 100 or 125 mm distemper brush working from the middle outwards. Take the paste right to the edges of the paper, but be careful it doesn't dribble over on to the printed side.

It is unlikely that you will have a table long enough to let you paste the whole ceiling-to-floor strip of paper all at once. As you go along, fold up the pasted section so it lies paste to paste and draw up the unpasted section on to the table. If you are using a heavy or very thick paper, you may need to let the paste soak in while you get on with the second sheet. In all cases, you should look at any directions given with the paper and follow them closely, because with some coverings, especially coated vinyls, you may have to hang them immediately after pasting. Always paste and hang the lengths in the order you have cut them.

HANGING

To hang the paper, pick up the first pasted length and when you are on top of the ladder, unfold the top half and put it in position against your plumbline mark with the bottom half still folded. Smooth the top of the paper on to the wall with a paper hanger's brush, allowing a 5 cm surplus at the top. Then let go of the rest of the paper, which will fall by its own weight. Slide it into position, then brush it down the centre and across from side to side, removing any blisters and creases and making sure it stays against the plumb-line mark. Trim the surplus paper from the top and bottom with scissors and dab off any paste drips before they have a chance to dry.

Now hang the second length in the same way, matching the pattern with the first length by butting one edge against the other. Try not to overlap, as this gives a bumpy finish. After the paper has been up about ten minutes, neaten the butt join by gently rolling it up and down with a seam roller. Remember though, never use a seam roller on embossed or raised design papers.

Go on as above till you come to a corner. Corners, unfortunately, are rarely square or plumb. For this reason, paper round a corner then trim the paper so that no more than 1 cm remains on the new wall. Now plumb the new wall with your line and use this as a guide to hang the next piece. Use the off-cuts in areas covered by curtains or behind doors. On this occasion you may need to overlap a bit, but make it as little as necessary.

Light switches

Before you start papering round light switches, turn off the electricity at the mains. If you have a modern switch take off the front plate and trim the paper to fit neatly under the plate. If you have an old fashioned switch that you cannot remove easily, hang the top half of the length of paper, mark the paper at the spot where the centre of the fitting comes and cut small slits radiating outwards. Gently brush the paper into position, letting the switch project through. Press the paper round the shape of the switch and trim off the ragged edges. Be particularly careful near electrical fittings if you are using a foil wall covering. The foil must not project into the switch box in case it makes an electrical contact.

Slide the paper gently into place against your vertical line, top half first, then brush it flat

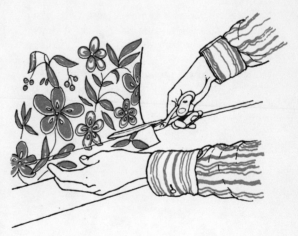

Use scissors to trim off the surplus

Round a switch that you can't remove, brush the paper gently into place and trim the ragged edges as close as possible with scissors

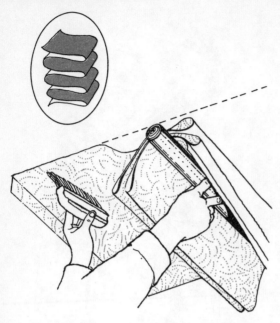

When papering a ceiling, concertina the lengths, paste surface to paste, and support the weight of the folded paper with a roll of lining paper

Ceilings

Basically, papering a ceiling is much the same as papering a wall. Having said that, it must be admitted it is also considerably more difficult and a project to which you should give a bit of serious thought, at least before attempting it on your own. The first time you paper a ceiling start by using a plain lining paper. This is an inexpensive way to gain experience and if the result is not too good you can always mask it with a coat of emulsion paint.

You cannot paper or paint a ceiling unless you can reach it. So you will need some sort of platform that allows you to walk across the room at a comfortable height. Two good solid step-ladders with a plank balanced between them around the third step work well, and you can probably hire if you don't want to buy.

To paper a ceiling the paper is hung across the width of the room not the length. As with walls, begin work at the end of the room nearest the window. Again, you will need a guide line to measure your first length of paper against. To get this, fix a piece of string rubbed in coloured chalk dust at a point 50 cm from, and parallel with, the window wall. Make it taught then pluck it smartly so it snaps back leaving a line of chalk dust to show the right position on the ceiling.

Measure the paper allowing a surplus of 5 or 6 cm at each end. As you paste the cut paper, fold it concertina-style. When the whole length is pasted try and get someone to carry the weight of the folded paper supported on a roll of lining paper or one of the DIY aids for holding the paper which look like a bricklayer's hawk. Position the first end against the wall and along the chalk mark. Brush the paper on the ceiling, moving gradually backwards along the plank so the concertina pleats in the paper unfold naturally as you go. Trim the paper at both ends and treat the second and following lengths of paper in the same way. It isn't easy to deal with the light fitting on a ceiling, so try and work it when measuring so that any fitting comes at the join between two lengths of paper. If this isn't possible then remove the light shade and bulb and deal with it in the same way as fixed light switches – cut star pattern and trim it. **Remember to turn the mains off first.**

Painting furniture

A fresh coat of paint can turn a second-hand piece of furniture into one you can take pride in. But as with most home-decorating, you usually need to 'off with the old' before you can 'on with the new'.

If the old finish is in reasonable condition – ie not chipped or cracked – you can lightly rub it down with fine glasspaper and wipe over with white spirit to remove any wax. Dry off thoroughly and paint with gloss paint. More often, though, you will need to strip the surface completely and start again.

STRIPPING
Protect the floor with newspaper, and remove any handles and fittings from the furniture. **Work with the window open because some strippers are flammable, and in any case the fumes should not be inhaled. Do not smoke when using paint strippers.**

Apply paint stripper evenly with a brush. After a few minutes, when the paint starts to soften, scrape it off gently and carefully with a wide-bladed scraper. Always work in the direction of the grain of the wood.

Next, **wearing goggles to protect your eyes,** use a stiff brush or a pad of steel wool to remove the softened paint from any carved or moulded sections. You may have to work quite hard to get at the fiddly corners. Neutralize the wood according to the directions on the paint stripper bottle. Then sand down the surface (by hand, or with an electric sander) until it is really smooth. Start with a medium grade glasspaper and work down to a fine grade for finishing.

Fill in the grain with grain filler and make good any holes or cracks. Then sand off again lightly. Vacuum off dust or use 'tacky' cloth (impregnated duster for decorators) before painting.

WHITEWOOD FURNITURE
New whitewood furniture is sold unpainted, but will still need a certain amount of preparation. Remove the drawers and unscrew the handles, replacing them only when the final coat of paint is dry. Using no. 1 or no. 0 grade glasspaper folded round a wood or cork block, smooth down all the surfaces. Take care round the edges of doors and drawers. Always rub in the direction of the grain, and dust off thoroughly afterwards.

Because whitewood furniture is made from deal or pine it sometimes has knots in it. These should be sealed with a coat of shellac-based knotting to stop the resin 'bleeding'. Whitewood also tends to swell when moistened so it can be a good idea to raise any uneven fibres deliberately; use a fine wood grain filler, the ready-mixed type is best, and spread it thinly across the surface. When this has dried, rub over with glasspaper and dust off carefully before painting.

PAINTING
For most wood furniture, the traditional three-coat method is best. First a priming coat to give adhesion and seal porosity; next the undercoat for a non-porous ground of dense, even colour; and finally a finishing coat of gloss or eggshell paint.

Allow the primer to dry, then rub it down with glasspaper, working along the grain of the wood. Wipe off the dust with a rag or use a tacky cloth. Apply an undercoat (for painting technique see page 54).

Allow the undercoat to dry, then lightly glasspaper and dust off. Apply the top coat, using the same brushwork technique as for the undercoat, and taking care that each new brushload trespasses into the previous wet edge while it is still wet to give you an even finish.

Gloss paint may feel dry to the touch after a few hours, but is best left alone for several days until the surface has hardened.

Doors and drawers
Doors and drawer fronts should be painted on both sides with an equal number of coats to prevent warping. Never paint the runners of drawers, or the drawers will not open. If you are painting furniture for the kitchen or bathroom, remember to paint the backs as well for protection against condensation.

COLOUR WITHOUT PAINT
Sometimes untreated wood furniture has such an attractive grain it seems a pity to cover it over with paint. An alternative is to use a transparent pigmented varnish which allows the grain of the wood to show through. Follow the maker's directions for applying.

The surface needs to be prepared in the same way as for painting so it is clean, dry, smooth and free from all old finishes. Then you apply the first coat of varnish with a cloth pad, and brush on subsequent ones until you get the colour you want. Allow six hours for each coat to dry, or as the manufacturer directs, and rub down in between with fine glasspaper or steel wool.

Wood can also be dyed, using a proprietary wood dye or stain. These come in a number of bright colours as well as traditional wood finishes. Some are ready-mixed liquids, others are powders to be mixed with water or methylated spirits. Apply to the bare wood with a sponge, brush or cloth working along the grain following the maker's instructions. To seal in the dye and protect the wood, finish with clear polyurethane wood seal.

WICKER AND CANE

Old wickerwork chairs are likely to have a considerable amount of dust in the weave, which you will need to remove with a stiff brush. Next scrub the chair over with soap and water or diluted washing-up liquid to get rid of any grease. Rinse with cold water. Do this outside on a dry day.

Let the chair dry for at least 24 hours before painting; check that the spaces are free from any dried-in soap. Painting cane is probably best done with an aerosol spray, although you can use a brush. But to get a first class finish in either case the sur-

face must be absolutely free from any traces of grease, dust or moisture. If you are brush painting rather than spraying, you will need to rub over with glasspaper first to give a smooth surface. Also, with brush painting, you may need to apply an undercoat before the finishing coat.

Spray paint gets everywhere, so work outside or in a garage or shed. Cover all working surfaces with newspaper and mask off any parts not to be included in the painting with masking tape. Then, shake the can well, and holding it about 15 cm from the object to be painted, start spraying. Use a steady, even movement and work in a small section at a time until you have covered the whole chair. Give it several light coats, leaving the paint to dry well in between; a heavy coat will probably result in unsightly 'runs'.

Finishes and seals

If wood is not to be painted, it still needs the application of a finish to keep the surface in good condition, whether it be french polish adding beauty to a fine piece of furniture, or a polyurethane seal protecting a parquet floor.

There is a wide range of finishes suitable for DIY application, but as these are not all applied in the same way it is important to study the manufacturer's instructions carefully in advance.

FINISHES FOR FURNITURE

Wax This was the first wood finish ever used. Wax brings out the colour and grain of the wood, but don't expect much of a shine at first as the initial coat of wax will soak into the pores of the wood. There may even be a slightly patchy appearance at first, but further waxing and rubbing up will eventually give the wood a beautiful mellow shine. You can speed up this process by giving the wood an initial sealing coat of shellac or button polish or polyurethane. This prevents the first coat of wax being completely absorbed.

Application A proprietary brand of wax polish can be used for waxing, or you can make up your own in this way:

Shred 50 g of beeswax into a jam jar and add 250 ml of turpentine or turps substitute. Stand the jar in hot water until the wax melts and mixes to form a paste of buttery consistency. This polish can be left in the jar with the top covered. **Warning: never try and melt the wax over a naked flame.** Turps and turps substitute are both flammable.

Use a non-fluffy rag to rub the wax generously over the whole surface of the wood as evenly as possible. Use a stiff brush for mouldings or carved sections.

Oiling This is suitable for most woods, especially teak, and gives a waxy sheen. Over-oiling often results in a sticky build up. One of the proprietary teak oils is best for the purpose; linseed oil is not now considered suitable because it takes a long time to dry and during this time dirt and dust are attracted to the sticky surface.

Application Rub the oil well into the wood and allow it to dry, then burnish with a coarse cloth or brush, finally finishing off with a duster. Several applications of oil may be necessary, depending on the nature of the wood.

Neither waxing nor oiling gives complete resistance to heat and water marking, though oil gives a little more protection than wax against water.

French polish This is the name given to types of polish which are made from shellac and methylated spirit. French polish brings out the beauty and depth of colour in good quality wood, such as oak and mahogany, in a way that is practically impossible with any other wood finish. Unfortunately the surface can be damaged by hot plates and is easily spoilt by water marking, so it needs to be treated with a certain amount of care.

Application French polishing is a slightly involved procedure and needs a lot of practice. Kits are available and your wisest course is to follow the maker's instructions, starting with a not-too-precious piece of furniture first.

Varnish Varnish is easy to apply by brush to any type of wood, and different grades are available which give either a brilliant, a semi-matt or matt finish. Varnish needs protecting from dust, as it is very slow drying.

Application Pour the varnish into a clean container. Use a good quality brush and apply the first coat evenly. Leave to dry for 24 hours, wipe down to get rid of any dust or grit, and apply a second coat. If a third coat is necessary, leave even longer before applying it and wait at least four days before you polish it. Use a liquid polish and buff up briskly with a soft cloth. Do not use the surface for at least a week.

Clear cellulose This is a special kind of transparent varnish which is usually found on TV sets, record players and the arms and legs of modern furniture. It is applied at the factory, and gives good protection against dust, grease and grime but can be damaged by hot plates.

SEALS

Seals are probably the easiest type of finish to apply and are suitable for most types of wood – as well as for cork, linoleum and other types of flooring (but check the maker's recommendation).

Seals are very durable and give a good resistance to heat and water marking. They will, however, wear eventually and it is worth remembering it.

Application Seals are usually applied with a brush or a cotton pad, according to the manufacturer's instructions. **You should always work in a well ventilated room** as the smell of most seals is overpowering and could be toxic. Some seals are not suitable for application in humid conditions, this prevents even drying and you will end up with a patchy effect. The type of surface will govern the number of coats needed; softwoods, for example, may need as many as three or four coats to give a completely sealed surface. Light sanding after each coat of seal, once the surface is dry and hard, will remove any slight unevenness and give a smooth finish.

Sealed finishes themselves vary, according to the product used:

Polyurethane gives an extremely durable surface and is available with a matt, satin or gloss finish. There may be a slight colour change, depending on the porosity of the wood and original colour of the surface. The seal takes from four to six hours to dry; the two-can type needs to be mixed just before application and must be used within the specified time otherwise it will harden.

Phenol urea gives a durable finish with a waxed appearance and is unlikely to cause any change in colour. It is slightly more difficult to apply than polyurethane, but dries faster.

Oleo-resinous seals give a durable matt finish with a slight colour change because it penetrates into the surface more than the other two types. Takes six hours or more to dry and harden.

Urea formaldehyde has very similar qualities to oleo-resinous seals, but tends to dry more rapidly and with a higher gloss.

Seals are now available in a number of bright colours and wood stain finishes (see page 67). Apart from being invaluable for floors they are also particularly suitable for light coloured or whitewood furniture, which might otherwise be painted, as they make the most of the natural beauty of the grain.

Maintenance is easy; a wipe over with a damp cloth or mop is all that is required, though an occasional polish with wax polish sparingly applied will give even greater durability, especially on wood floors where traffic is heavy.

Adhesives

Not all that many years ago, the only household glue available was a mixture made by boiling up animal and fish bones and skins. You did the best you could with it for everything from sticking in a photograph to mending a teacup. Now, literally hundreds of specialist products are available, so many it can be confusing. If in any doubt ask before you buy.

Buy small sizes even though in unit cost it works out more expensive. This is because adhesives can deteriorate after long periods of storage. When left around in near-freezing conditions in garages and toolsheds synthetic resin emulsions particularly can undergo changes that will make them useless by the time you want to use them again. All adhesives are best kept at temperatures between 10°C and 25°C and always away from damp and wet.

Be sure you always put the cap or lid back on the adhesive after using it. If it is left off essential ingredients evaporate quickly, and dust and dirt can get in and contaminate the glue.

Many adhesives contain solvents which give off flammable vapours, so try and work with the window open and never near naked lights. Inhaling adhesive is also dangerous.

Before you start
While nowadays almost anything can be stuck to anything else, you can't expect miracles. Even when you have picked the right type of adhesive for the job, you need to give it a chance to work properly. This means that first you must clean the surfaces you want to join, getting rid of every trace of dust, damp and grease. If both the surfaces are smooth, give them a rub over with glasspaper, emery board or a wire brush to give a good key for the adhesive to latch on to.

Remember that with the exception of 'contact' adhesives, glued surfaces usually need to be held together under pressure while they set. Anything that can be laid flat is simple enough; just put a suitable weight on top. With china, glass, wooden articles and many other things, however, you may have to invent your own clamps by using rubber bands, sticky tape and so on.

With some adhesives the instructions may tell you the glue should be applied and then left for 15 minutes or so before the surfaces are brought together. Never be tempted to hurry this step.

If you have any doubts that you have chosen the right adhesive for the job, or if you are using a glue you have had by you for some time, it may be worth your while having a trial run first. For instance, try sticking an old saucer together before you start on the wedding present vase.

Always read the manufacturer's instructions and follow them to the letter, including any warnings about getting adhesive on your skin or clothes.

CHOOSING ADHESIVES

USE	ADHESIVE	APPLICATION	REMOVAL
1 Paper, thin card, snapshots, cutting out games for children.	Use inexpensive thin glue or paste; many brands are sold at stationery shops.	Some brands squeeze out through a nozzle, others go on with a small brush. They dry quickly.	If still tacky, just wipe off. If the glue has dried, remove by soaking with warm water.

USE	ADHESIVE	APPLICATION	REMOVAL
2 Most china, glass pottery, earthenware, chunky jewellery, leather.	Use a clear adhesive; these are usually made from synthetic rubber in a petroleum-based solvent. Water resistance varies so check before you buy.	Apply with a spatula. All dry quickly.	Remove with acetone or nail polish remover.
3 Metal, china or glass, where a particularly strong water resistant and heat-proof bond is required.	Use an epoxy-resin adhesive. These are synthetic two-part adhesives that begin to set only when mixed.	Mix equal volumes of resin and hardener and coat one or both surfaces lightly before putting them together. The setting period for different epoxy resins varies; a quick version is available, sometimes referred to as '5-minute' or 'rapid', but the time can be up to six hours at room temperature. Bonding will be faster if you expose the article you have mended to a gentle heat. Mix the adhesive in a container, and with an implement, that you can throw away.	Wipe off extra adhesive with a cellulose thinner before it begins to set. When dry, epoxy-resin adhesives are almost impossible to remove.
4 Bonding laminated plastic to wood, sticking hardboard panelling etc. Any job where it is impossible to apply even pressure to hold the surfaces together while they bond.	Use a contact adhesive. Basically similar to clear adhesives these are sold in larger quantities for bigger jobs. They come in the form of thick liquids and give good water resistance. On jobs where it may be difficult to be exact use a type of contact adhesive that allows a small amount of initial movement for adjustment.	Apply to both surfaces with a spatula or knife and spread with a serrated comb to give even distribution. Some contact adhesives stick strongly the instant the two surfaces are brought together; as no adjustment is possible use some kind of location guide to make sure you get the position exactly right. **Use with care. The solvent is flammable and can be dangerous to inhale.**	Remove with acetone or a solvent cleaner supplied by the manufacturer of the adhesive.
5 Upholstery, carpets and rugs.	Use a latex adhesive, made from natural rubber in an emulsion with water. It comes as a thick, white liquid which dries to a translucent film giving strong, flexible joins.	Coat both surfaces and let them dry before pressing them together. Alternatively coat one surface only and put them together at once.	Remove any surplus with a damp cloth while the latex is still wet. Once dry, latex is difficult to remove. You can try with white spirit, but the fabric may well be left with a residual stain. It is best to use the maker's own solvent cleaner.

USE	ADHESIVE	APPLICATION	REMOVAL
6 General indoor woodwork jobs and repairs.	Use a PVA adhesive. These are based on polyvinyl acetate emulsions and are suitable for joining porous materials where a flexible join is unnecessary.	Spread the adhesive, which is originally white and dries clear, on to one surface only and assemble at once. Clamp joint until dry.	Wipe away all excess with a damp cloth while it is still tacky. PVA is difficult to remove when dry.
7 Outdoor woodwork and larger indoor jobs.	Several manufacturers make a higher strength PVA adhesive suitable for these jobs. For most outdoor woodwork, however, a urea-formaldehyde adhesive is recommended. These are usually synthetic resin powders that are mixed with water and undergo irreversible chemical changes on setting. The bond they form is heat resistant, waterproof and very strong.	Follow the directions carefully. Screw or clamp joints until dry.	Cannot be removed.
8 Plastics	Most plastics except polythene and polypropylene can be successfully repaired with either a clear or a contact adhesive. Some soft plastics such as PVC upholstery, aidbeds, paddling pools and so on can be difficult to mend. For these, vinyl adhesives have been formulated, usually designed to be used together with repair patches.	See above, under 2 and 4. Follow manufacturer's directions.	See above, under 2 and 4.
9 Fixing wall tiles.	Use a wall tile adhesive, choosing a water resistant one for shower cubicles and similar installations.	Spread on the wall or on the tile, using a serrated comb to give even distribution. Work on a small area at a time.	Remove surplus of the standard adhesive with a wet cloth. For the water-resistant type, use the manufacturer's own solvent.
10 Laying floor tiles.	Use the adhesive recommended by the manufacturer of the floor covering.	Spread with a knife or trowel and 'work' with a large serrated comb.	Excess adhesive can be easily removed while it is still wet, but taking tiles up once the adhesive has hardened is a job for a professional. Take care not to let it dry on clothes or carpets – permanent damage is likely.

Tiling walls and ceilings

Until fairly recently, ceramic tiling used to be considered a job for a professional, because the tiles were thick and had to be fixed with a sand and cement mortar. Today, due to ready mixed adhesives and smaller, thinner tiles that are easier to cut, it is reasonably simple to do the job yourself.

SHAPES OF TILES

Do-it-yourself ceramic wall tiles are usually bought in two sizes: $108 \times 108 \times 4$ mm and $152 \times 152 \times 6 \cdot 5$ mm.

The basic 'field' tile has four squared edges and, in most cases, small protrusions on each side, known as lugs. These make sure of even spacing between the tiles, ready for grouting. When tiles don't have these lugs, you need to remember to leave 1 mm spaces between the tiles by inserting small pieces of card or matchsticks.

Tiles marked RE have one rounded edge, and are for use around windows and for the final row of tiles. REX tiles have two adjoining round edges and are used for corners. Neither of these has spacer lugs. Border tiles are glazed on two adjacent edges.

You can also buy bath trims, which are ceramic strips with rounded edges to fill in the gap between the bath and the wall, both in the interest of neatness and to seal out the damp.

Where to buy tiles

Department and hardware stores usually stock the basic, plain-glazed DIY tiles. For something more imaginative it is worth going to a builders' merchant. If the ones you want are not in stock, you can probably order them. Some most attractive designs are available, and while hand-painted tiles can work out rather expensive, by mixing and matching them with cheaper tiles you can make them go further.

If you want to use tiles on a fireplace, or near anywhere that is likely to be hot, make sure you use special fireplace tiles which are thicker and stronger.

Suitable surfaces

Wall tiles can be fixed to almost any kind of surface, provided it is flat, firm and dry.

Paint should be wiped down to remove all traces of dirt and grease before you start tiling. Old emulsion paint or distemper tends to flake, so you should remove it. Newly plastered walls should be left for at least a month to let them dry out completely before you start. Plywood, hardboard and plasterboard must all be rigid, flat and adequately braced and primed before fixing (use water resistant or marine grade for bathrooms).

Wallpaper must be removed before you tile, because the wallpaper adhesive won't be strong enough to hold the tiles and will peel off, bringing the tiles with it. If the wall underneath the paper is crumbly, it will need re-plastering and then leaving to dry before you can use it as a base for your tiles.

If you have a room that is already tiled, it is quite simple to stick new tiles over old ones. If there are any odd loose tiles, remove and refix them and allow time for the adhesive to set before you re-tile (see also later in this section).

Marking out

Find the lowest point of the area you want to tile and at this point make a mark on the wall one tile high above the floor or skirting board. Use a spirit level to position a batten so the top edge is level with this mark. Take this as your base line and continue nailing battens all round the room to make sure that the tile joints will meet up accurately.

Mark the centre of the batten in the middle of the first wall, and then beginning from this mark go left and right marking out the tile units, including the spacer lugs, on the wood. You will find you have even spaces at each end, but if the spaces are so narrow that you would have to cut tiles to less than about 1 cm to fill them, move up your first tile so it goes over instead of alongside the centre mark, to make room for a wider cut tile at each end. This will look neater.

To cut a ceramic tile, measure the space to be

73

filled carefully and score the tile where it is to be cut, using a tile cutter and straight edge. Put a matchstick or a pencil under the scored line and press the outside edges of the tile down firmly. It will then break cleanly along the line. If you have to cut an awkward shape, cut the unwanted area away a little at a time with tile nippers or sharp pincers.

When you have marked out your first horizontal row of tiles, use a plumb line to make a true vertical line on the wall straight up from your first tile mark on the left hand side. Nail a batten up the wall against this line. The horizontal and vertical battens must form a true right angle.

HOW TO APPLY CERAMIC TILES

1 Read the instructions on the adhesive pack carefully. Work from the lower left hand corner, row by row, applying enough adhesive to stick about the first six tiles. Use a trowel or a broad knife, then 'comb' the surface with a serrated spreader to give a ribbed effect. This provides a better bond for the tiles. (When you come to stick cut tiles, spread the adhesive on the backs of them individually.)

2 Starting at the intersection of the horizontal and vertical battens, begin with the bottom row of tiles and work upwards. Check with your spirit level at the top of each row to make sure it is truly horizontal. Press each tile firmly into position; you'll find the spacer lugs keep the tiles an even distance apart. Try not to slide the tiles into place as that squeezes the adhesive up between them. Wipe off any surplus adhesive at once with a damp cloth.

3 On corners and windows use RE and REX tiles with rounded edges. These don't have spacer lugs so you will need to keep them apart with a matchstick or piece of card. To tile round a sink or some similar fitting, first nail a batten to the wall at the nearest tile's height from the top of the lowest point of the fitting. This batten will then provide a base for the tiling above.

4 After about 24 hours, when the adhesive has set, remove all the battens and fill in any cut tiles. These should be left for a further 24 hours to set. Then make up the grout according to the instructions on the packet. Using a sponge, push the grout well into all the joints, wiping off the excess with a damp cloth as you go. Finish by drawing down joints gently with your finger. When dry, polish with a soft cloth.

Tiling over old tiles

Provided the old tiles are firmly stuck to the wall, and free from dirt and grease, it is a reasonably simple job to retile over them using a suitable adhesive and following the manufacturer's instructions. Remember, though, that the adhesive may take longer to dry than on a porous surface, so wait to do the grouting for several days after you have fixed the tiles.

If a wall is only half-tiled and you want to extend the tiling higher up, the join where the double thickness of tiles meets the single thickness will be less noticeable if you cover the top row of the old tiles with round-edged new ones. Then smooth off the join with a proprietary filler or use a half-round or angle softwood moulding to neaten the edge.

CORK AND OTHER WALL TILES

Cork tiles make an attractive covering for a wall because they not only look good but make a worthwhile contribution to heat and noise insulation.

Because the adhesive used is a contact one, some of which give you at most three seconds grace before bonding, accurate positioning is vital. It is safer, therefore, to use one of the newer types of contact adhesive which give adjustment time. **Contact adhesives are flammable, so work with the windows open and avoid naked lights.**

Other tiles for walls are available in metal, plastic and even stone. The methods of fixing vary from make to make, so you should always follow the manufacturer's instructions.

CEILING TILES

Ceiling tiles look decorative and also avoid the nuisance of cracked ceilings and some give a degree of sound absorption. They also cut down heat loss and provide a substitute for loft insulation if you have no access to your loft, or if the house has a flat roof.

Ceiling tiles are made in a number of materials, some of which are pre-decorated. The best known and probably most readily available tiles are those made in expanded polystyrene; the fire resistant grade should be used, so check when buying. Don't use polystyrene tiles for the ceiling above a cooker where you could be in real trouble if, say, a chip pan caught fire; especially if the ceiling is lower than normal – about 2·4 m.

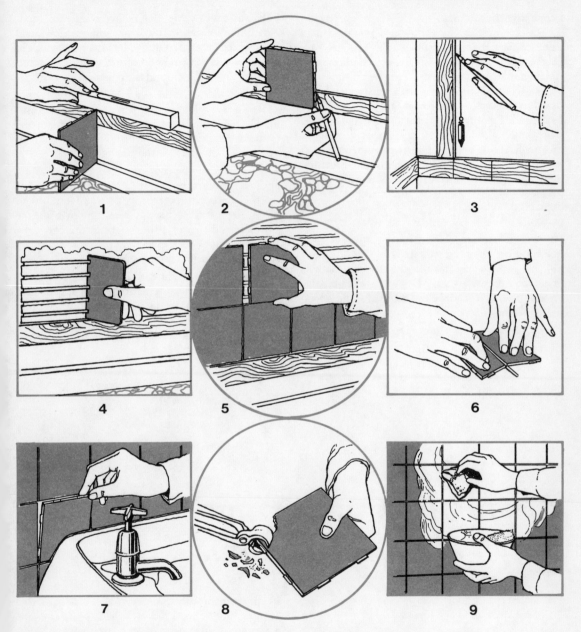

Tiling a wall. 1. Fix a batten with its top edge one tile high above floor or skirting board. Check the level with a spirit level **2.** Mark the batten from the centre outwards, allowing for tile and spacers **3.** Fix a vertical batten in line with the last mark on the left hand side. Check the perpendicular with a plumb line **4.** Spread enough adhesive for about six tiles at a time using a serrated spreader **5.** Work from the bottom upwards checking the line of each row with a spirit level **6.** To cut a tile, score it first, place it over a pencil and press the outside edges down firmly **7.** When tiling round fittings fit whole tiles first, leave cut tiles until last **8.** Cut awkward shapes a little at a time with tile nippers **9.** After 24 hours apply grout, using a sponge

Preparing the surface

The ceiling must be clean and dry. Rub down gloss paint with glasspaper to provide a key and size bare plaster. If the ceiling is really in poor condition it is worth employing a builder to remove all the existing plaster and laths and cover the joists with hardboard so you can fix the tiles on that.

Expanded polystyrene tiles can be cut with a sharp knife, although a battery operated cutter is more efficient on curves and irregular shapes, such as cutting out semi-circles to fit round a central light fitting. Remember to mark your cuts with a pencil first.

Fixing

Polystyrene tiles are fixed with special adhesives, but not all of these are suitable for every surface. So always read the manufacturer's instructions first. Don't press too hard when working with polystyrene or you will make a dent in the tile which will not come out.

1 Mark off the centre point of the ceiling by fixing chalked strings across it from the centres of the walls and plucking to give quartering lines. Count the number of tiles that will go along each line, and if the space left by the wall is less than the width of half a tile, mark a new line that will allow you a broader row of tiles round the edge.

2 Apply adhesive to the whole of the tile back – not in four or five blobs, which was at one time recommended – and position the first tile in one of the centre angles. Follow with three others to make up a square in the centre of the ceiling.

3 After making the centre square, continue tiling one quarter of the ceiling at a time up to the border. To fit a border tile correctly, place a loose tile on top of the last fixed tile and mark the overlap line with a pencil. Remove the loose tile and cut along the line. This will leave you with the correctly shaped piece to slip into position.

4 Finish off the edges with expanded polystyrene coving, fixing the corner mitres first. If you like, you can then decorate the tiles with a fire retarding grade of emulsion paint. Don't use gloss because the paint contains a solvent which will cause the tiles to break down.

Laying floor coverings: vinyl, wood and ceramic

Whatever type of floor covering you choose to lay, it will only look good and wear well if it is put down correctly. This means not only by the correct method, but also on a clean, even surface that is free from dirt and grease and, most important of all, from damp.

So as a first step, take a good look at the floor you plan to cover. Is it a solid floor? That is, one made of bricks, slabs or concrete laid either directly on the ground or over a damp-proof membrane. If it is a suspended wooden floor of boards laid over joists, is the ventilation satisfactory?

Preparing the sub-floor

Houses built since 1965 have had, by law, to incorporate a damp-proof membrane over solid floors, and if you live in an older type house it is worth putting one in. You may be able to do this yourself, using either a brush-on epoxy-pitch compound or a polyester resin, and following the manufacturer's instructions. If you have a bad case of damp, however, or a large area of floor to cover, it is better to call in an expert to deal with it for you.

To prepare a wooden floor, the surfaces must first be cleaned of dirt, dust, grease, built-up wax or old polish. The most effective way to do this is to scrub over the floor, section by section, with coarse grade steel wool and white spirit. (**The spirit is flammable, so keep the window open and don't have any naked lights.**) As you finish each section, dry it off with a clean rag. Once the floor is completely dry, fix any loose floorboards and pull out or punch down any projecting nails.

Then smooth down any rough patches with a plane, or if a large area needs to be treated, it will be worth your while to hire a sander (look in the Yellow Pages). Don't try to sand a floor with a small DIY sander; you will either burn out the motor or clog it with dust, or both. Follow the instructions that come with a hired sander, and when you have finished, sweep up the dust. You will find you have raised quite a bit if your sander has no vacuum attachment at the back.

Another effective treatment for a slightly uneven wooden floor is to cover it with 6 mm hardboard. The hardboard needs to be prepared a couple of days before you lay it by brushing the mesh side of the panels with water – about 500 ml to each 1·2 m square panel. Leave it to dry in the room in which it will be used.

Use special hardboard nails and lay the panels rough side up, starting from the centre of the floor and staggering the panels so you don't get continuous joins. Fasten down the panels with the nails at approximately 15 cm intervals. Remember, though, if you are going to lay hardboard, good underfloor ventilation is essential.

To level a slightly uneven solid floor, use a self-levelling compound that you spread over the floor and leave to settle and harden to its own level. A solid floor that is badly uneven may have to be professionally re-laid.

TYPES OF FLOORING AND HOW TO LAY THEM
Vinyl: sheet and tiles

As a floor covering vinyl is resistant to wear and grease, easy to clean and comfortable to walk on. As a general rule, the more expensive the vinyl the greater the thickness and so the longer the wear and greater the comfort. Vinyl comes in a wide range of colours and designs, everything from modern geometrics to traditional florals and mock stone or wood.

Vinyl sheet is also available with a needled-felt or foam backing which can be used successfully on

Many hired sanding machines have a vacuum attachment to collect the inevitable dust

a slightly uneven floor. The backing also helps to cut down noise and makes the surface warmer.

Vinyl sheet and tiles can be laid on either wood or solid floors.

Laying vinyl sheet

If you store the vinyl in a warm room for a day or so before laying it will become supple and so easier to handle.

First, decide which way the flooring is to run so you can best avoid having visible joins, especially at doorways. If the sub-floor is made of wood, ideally the vinyl should run across rather than along the floorboards. Before you start to lay the vinyl, check with the manufacturer's instructions. These usually suggest the type of adhesive to use and give tips on fitting.

With a strong pair of scissors or a knife cut lengths to fit the room, allowing a small overlap at

77

Double sided adhesive tape is the easiest method of seaming sheet vinyl floor covering

Cut each length a little oversize initially, to allow for shrinkage; trim to an exact fit with a sharp knife

both ends. If you have alcoves or other tricky shapes cut out a replica of the shape in paper first, then use this as a pattern for cutting out the flooring.

Some sheet vinyls tend to shrink, so you may need to leave the material creased up round the edges and walk about on it for a week or two to let it settle down before you trim it; the maker will advise on this.

Match the pattern carefully at the seams and secure these either with adhesive or a double-sided sticky tape. In most cases, the edges round the sides of the room don't need to be stuck down except at doorways, but some manufacturers recommend it; in this case you should not have to worry about shrinkage.

To fit vinyl sheeting into a corner, crease the material up against the skirting and snip a release cut in the form of a v, at first rather smaller than you guess to be necessary. Then trim this down, a little at a time, until the material fits exactly.

Laying vinyl tiles

If the tiles are the self-adhesive kind, all you need do is peel off the backing and press the tiles into place. Ordinary tiles are set in a bed of adhesive. Use a floor tiling adhesive, if possible one recommended by the manufacturer of the tiles.

To lay tiles to obtain the neatest effect, first divide the floor area into quarters with chalk guidelines. Put a nail in the centre point of each wall, stretch chalked strings across and pluck to mark the lines. Lay a row of loose tiles from the point where the guidelines cross in the centre of the room, working out to the edge in each direction. If when you get to the skirting you find you are left with a space of less than half a tile, move the whole row over until you have an even width at each end so the border tiles are equal. Redraw the guidelines.

Start tiling at the centre, working on one quarter of the floor at a time. Spread the adhesive evenly, using only enough for about 16 tiles at a time so it doesn't dry before you get them down. Keep on tiling as far as possible towards the wall, but leave the fitting of part tiles for the border until all four quarters are completed.

To cut a border tile to fill in the gap, balance a loose tile exactly over your last fixed one. Then hold a second loose tile over the first one, but with its edge against the wall. Score along where the second loose tile overlaps the first and cut. You will find the trimmed section will fit into the border.

Divide floor into quarters and start tiling from the centre; loose-lay tiles first to check fit

Lay border tiles last, cutting them to fit exactly into the space left along the wall

To fit tiles round door posts and awkward corners, make a template of thin card and transfer the shape on to the tile for cutting out. Alternatively you can buy a profile gauge which is made of moveable needles which you press into shape and then trace the result on the tile before cutting.

Vinyl asbestos tiles
Vinyl asbestos is probably the only floor covering that can tolerate a small amount of damp. The tiles have good wearing qualities but tend to scratch if something heavy – such as a washing machine – is pushed about on them.

The tiles should be laid in the same way as vinyl tiles but because they tend to be more brittle it is important to press – not slide – them into place.

Linoleum tiles and sheet
Linoleum is an old favourite but these days it is difficult to find in the shops – you may have to order it. Lino is relatively inexpensive, hard-wearing and stain resistant but, unlike vinyl, the colour range is limited.

Linoleum should be laid in the same way as vinyl, but because it tends to stretch you will need to leave it down for a while before cutting and fixing, unless it is to be stuck down all over. Cut with strong scissors or a sharp knife.

Cork
Cork provides an attractive floor covering and is also a good insulator, quiet and warm to walk on. Unfortunately it is expensive. It also dents easily and may be damaged if heavy furniture is dragged over the floor.

Most vinyl adhesives are suitable for cork, but some manufacturers recommend fixing cork tiles to wooden sub-floors with sprigs (small headless pins).

Quarry and ceramic tiles
These are also attractive and hard-wearing, although a bit cold and hard to walk on. They are usually laid only on solid floors, and it is advisable to have a professional to do the fixing.

Wood
Wood flooring has always been popular because of its warmth and natural look. Nowadays there is a wide choice of do-it-yourself wood flooring materials available, easier to lay and considerably cheaper than the traditional parquet. The simplest form of wood flooring consists of plywood squares with a hardwood surface already made up into panels – usually 16 squares to a panel, and set out in a basket-weave or chequerboard effect. These are easy to lay using the recommended adhesive on a solid floor, and either adhesive or panel pins on a wooden one.

Some wood blocks for home laying come ready-coated with contact adhesive – in which case you only need to remove the protective backing paper and press them in place on the prepared floor surface – with others you will need to use the adhesive recommended by the manufacturer.

To give a floorboard effect over a solid floor, you can get strips of plywood with a hardwood surface which interlock and are held in position without glueing, the advantages are obvious.

As with other types of flooring, however, wood floors can only be laid successfully if the sub-floor is in the right condition. So if you think you may have any problems – especially with damp or ventilation – it would be wise to consult a specialist before you start work.

Laying carpets

Choose a carpet of a quality suitable for the use it will get. Hall and living room carpets, for instance, need to be more hard-wearing than bedroom carpets if they are to last. As a general rule, the cost of a carpet will be a pretty good guide to its quality, but design and luxury finish may add to the expense without adding to the quality of the carpet in use. Many manufacturers use a labelling system which gives the fibre content of the carpet and its recommended use (the situation in which it will give its best performance). It is always worth studying these labels carefully, because you can't tell the grade of a carpet just by looking at it.

Carpet types and fibres
Carpets may be either woven or tufted. Woven carpets are the traditional type, and here the carpet fibres and the backing are woven together. Tufted carpets are made by a process in which the pile is tufted into a hessian or canvas backing, and then locked into position by a coating of latex adhesive. A fabric secondary backing or a foam backing is then applied.

Of the main carpet fibres available, wool makes a carpet that is warm, resilient and fairly fireproof – it only smoulders. Nylon is tough and is often blended with wool to give extra strength. Nylon alone soils easily – although it is not difficult to clean – and melts when it comes in touch with flame.

Acrylic fibres are the nearest to natural wool, but pick up the dirt more easily and are flammable. They are easy to clean, however, and strong. Polypropylene is another man-made fibre – tough and stain resistant, so a good choice if you have a young family. Rayon is used mainly in the cheaper grades of carpet, separately or as a blend with other fibres.

Sisal and coir make attractive inexpensive carpeting, but are difficult to clean; sisal can also fade in a strong light. Haircord is extremely hard wearing, doesn't attract dirt and is fire resistant.

Carpet widths
Any carpet over 1·8 m wide is termed broadloom; anything narrower is referred to as body-width or strip carpet. Of the traditional carpets, broadloom is the easier for a beginner to lay – preferably one with a foam or other non-fray secondary backing. Strip carpeting may work out less costly especially in an unusual shaped room; however, it is more difficult to lay than broadloom and it is best to employ a professional to do the job.

Most types of carpet are available in the form of tiles, either loose-laid or self-adhesive, as well as the traditional strip and broadloom carpeting. This has the advantage that if a tile becomes marked or damaged it is easy to take it out and replace it with a new one. You can also move the tiles around from time to time to give even wear.

Measuring
The best way to be sure of buying the correct

80

amount of carpeting is to draw an accurate floor plan of the room with the measurements marked in and to take it with you when you buy. Most good stores will then be able to work out for you exactly what you need.

If you are choosing a new carpet to go with existing furnishings, it helps to take along samples of other colours and fabrics in the room. Remember that colours change under different types of artificial lighting, so look at carpet samples in daylight too, and – if possible – try to borrow a sample to look at in your home under your own room lighting before you make your final choice.

If you are having the carpet laid professionally, they will usually measure up for you.

Preparing the floor
You should always do all in your power to deal with damp before laying a carpet, see page 150. Then make sure the carpeting is put down on a sound, even floor. If your floor is made of boards, old loose nails should be removed and replaced with new ones, their heads driven below the surface of the boards; uneven boards should be levelled out. Felt paper – even old newspapers – laid over the boards will stop dust coming through the planks and forming lines of dirt along the carpet. If the floor is in really poor condition, cover it completely with hardboard (see page 77).

Concrete or quarry tile floors should be covered with tarred paper, tar side down, to stop the dust coming through, or use grey paper felt, which comes in rolls 1 m wide. Uneven quarry tiles are best covered with hardboard – though in this case you may need a professional to fix it down for you.

Underlay
Underlay is essential with all but foam-backed carpets. It acts as a soundproofer and seals in warmth, gives a soft feel underfoot and, most important of all, extends the life of your carpet. Never be tempted to leave an old carpet down to act as an underlay; the worn sections will cause the new carpet to wear unevenly.

Basically, there is a choice of two types of carpet underlay: rubber and felt. Rubber, and this includes foam and sponge types, is helpful where floorboards are slightly uneven or over concrete floors; moths don't like it either. Don't use rubber underlay, though, in rooms with underfloor heating unless you check that it is suitable for the job (if it is, the label will say so). Ordinary rubber underlays

go hard in contact with heat, and anyway rubber doesn't conduct heat as well as underfelt.

Felt underlay is best for narrow width carpets as it is softer and the seams settle into it more easily than into rubber.

EQUIPMENT AND HOW TO USE IT

Double-sided adhesive tape Use this when you want to fix foam-backed carpet. First stick the tape to the floor, right up to the skirting board, then peel off the top backing and press the carpet on to it firmly, pushing it into the wall to get a good fit.

Grippers are for fixing any carpet; you need a special type for a foam-backed carpet. Tackless grippers are made in wood or metal – a common type is a strip of plywood about 2·5 cm wide with nails sticking out at intervals at an angle. Grippers can be nailed to the floor; hardened nails are used for concrete floors. In certain cases, especially with underfloor heating, the grippers are glued down. The nails must always face the wall so the carpet pulls tight on them when stretched in position.

Fix tackless grippers with the spikes facing into the wall so the carpet will grip firmly when stretched

Threshold strips These are metal strips which keep carpet joins neatly in place in doorways – can be used to join two carpets or a carpet to another type of flooring, such as vinyl sheet or tiles. The carpet fits under a lip and is pressed into a groove with a bolster chisel. Carefully work along the length of the strip; finish by tapping the lip downwards gently with a hammer and a wooden block to secure it firmly.

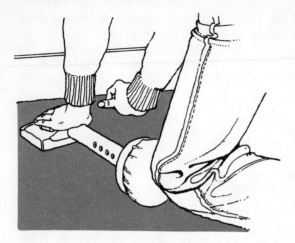

To stretch the carpet into place, hold the head of the knee-kicker down with one hand and kick the padded end with your knee

Knee-kicker This helps ensure that the carpet lies tight and flat to the floor. Practice using it on a spare piece of carpet first. Place the kicker a few centimetres away from the wall and hit it with your knee, square on, pressing the head part down with your hand. It is better to hit several times gently rather than to bang it really hard. (A knee-kicker is expensive to buy, but you can hire from hire service shops, look in the Yellow Pages.)

Staple gun This is useful for fixing foam-backed carpets and underlay. Hold the top of the gun down

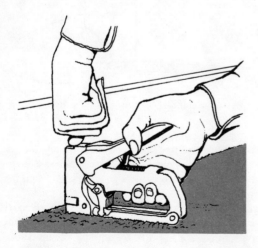

A staple gun is a useful tool for fixing foam-backed carpet and underlay

firmly as you shoot, otherwise the staples will not hold. This is an inexpensive tool useful for DIY jobs but it can be hired if necessary.

Carpet seaming tape This is a paper tape with a hessian strip running down the centre of one side. The tape is loose laid on the floor, hessian side up, and spread with adhesive under the carpet join, and the carpet is glued to it.

Bolster chisel is similar to a cold chisel with a wide 10 cm blade, used for pushing the edges of the carpet into the threshold strip and finishing off after fitting to tackless grippers.

You will also need strong **scissors** and a sharp **knife** for cutting and trimming.

FITTING THE CARPET

1 Cut paper underlay to cover the whole area. Butt join and leave loose laid. If using tackless grippers (see above) nail these about 5 mm from the skirting board, cutting small pieces to fit round corners and doorways. Remember – nails or spikes must face into the wall.

2 Loose lay strips of underlay and cut to fit the edges, making sure these meet but don't overlap. The underlay must fit right to the gripper, but not over it. On a wooden floor you can secure the underlay with a staple gun. On stone floors join rubber underlay with single-sided adhesive tape.

3 Fit threshold strips (see above). Start at doorway corner – lay carpet in one corner; always down the length of the room with the pile running away from the window. Tuck carpet under lip with a bolster chisel to grip on to spikes.

4 With your trimming knife cut carpet to fit round corners or doorway. Press into base of skirting board with your fingers, then cut slits down to this indent. Cut away excess and firmly press carpet on to gripper nails with a bolster chisel.

5 Press the carpet firmly into the skirting board then mark a chalk line slightly above this – it is better to trim later if necessary. Use sharp scissors to cut along the chalk line. Press the carpet on to the gripper with a bolster.

6 Fit two adjacent walls, then use a knee-kicker (see above) to stretch the carpet to fit the third and fourth walls. This is not absolutely necessary if the carpet has a pliable backing but does give a really professional finish.

7 To fit foam-backed carpet to wooden floors, cut

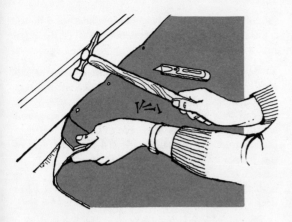

On a wooden floor, turn the edge of the carpet under and tack to the floor at 10 cm intervals

to fit flush with wall as step 5 (you won't need underlay) and secure with staples every 30 cm. Hammer in carpet tacks about the same distance apart, or use double-sided adhesive tape. Even easier is to loose lay the carpet, fixing only in doorways.

8 On wooden floors, the 'turn and tack' method is good for carpets that tend to fray. Cut the underlay to within 4 cm of the skirting. Allow enough carpet to turn under 4 cm on each edge and hammer carpet tacks in 10 cm apart. This is easy to do, but a tackless gripper gives a smoother, tighter finish.

Stair carpets

On staircases you need really tough carpeting, otherwise the front edges and treads of the stairs will wear and become dangerous. The carpet must also be fixed very taut, so unless you are an expert leave it to a professional.

The carpet should be laid so that the pile lies down the stairs and, when you are buying, always allow an extra 60 cm on the overall length so that the carpet can be moved at intervals. Ideally, it should be moved twice in the first year of a carpet's life, and once every following year.

Always put a good underlay on the stairs. Stair pads are best, and should overhang by about 5 cm over the nose of each tread.

PATCHING WORN CARPETS

Always keep any off-cuts when a new carpet has been laid so you can use them later to patch any worn areas. If, when the time comes, you don't have any spare bits, find a small area of carpet which is hidden by furniture – such as under a bed – and cut a piece from there.

Foam-backed carpets

Measure the widest and longest part of the worn or damaged area. Cut a patch slightly larger than these measurements.

Lay the patch over the worn area so that the pile goes the same way as the carpet beneath. Secure in place with a couple of carpet tacks. Using the edges of the patch as a guide, cut through the carpet below with a sharp knife. Pull out the tacks, remove the patch and lift out the damaged square, then check that your patch fits snugly. Then cut a strip of adhesive tape 5 cm longer than the hole. If you can, turn back the carpet so that the foam faces you. Stick on the strip to overlap the hole by half its width and at each end by 2·5 cm. Cut and fit three more strips in the same way to surround the square. Lay the carpet flat again and press the patch on to the tape edges and lightly hammer along the joins. The joins should be almost invisible.

If the hole is right in the middle of a fitted carpet, cut out the worn area as before and get someone to lift the carpet slightly so you can insert the tape. Try not to pull the edges too much or they will stretch and bag. Press down firmly and hammer gently into place.

Woven carpets

Untack and turn the carpet right back. Push in long pins to mark out a square slightly larger than the worn area. Mark the square on the back with a ruler and a felt tip pen. Apply latex adhesive generously round the square, extending it about 2·5 cm on each side – this stops the edges fraying.

Slide a piece of wood under the area then cut along the marked square with a knife. Use this piece of carpet as a template for cutting a patch – try to match pile and pattern.

Cut four strips of hessian tape (such as upholsterer's webbing), each 5 cm longer than the sides of the square, and coat with adhesive on one side. Stick the tapes on the edges at the back of the carpet, as described above under foam-backed carpets.

Dab adhesive on to the edges and sides of the patch (try to avoid getting it on the tufts) and rub in gently with a rag. Press the patch in place from the right side and hammer the edges gently to ensure good adhesion.

BINDING A CARPET

Latex adhesive can be used with binding tape to prevent a frayed carpet deteriorating further or for binding raw edges. Self-adhesive tapes for carpet binding are also available but are not as strong as the latex method.

To bind a woven carpet use 3·5–4 cm binding tape. Trim the frayed edge of the carpet and place it pile-side down. Apply a band of adhesive along the edge the same width as the binding tape and half way down the pile.
Cut the required length of binding tape and paste it all over. Leave to dry. Lay the pasted binding tape along the back of the carpet allowing 5 mm to protrude over the edge; fold this over and press into the pile. Hammer gently to help make a good bond, a piece of 25 × 50 mm softwood laid over the edge first will help to make a neat bond on the edges.

To bind sisal and cord carpets or mats you will need 7·5 cm wide tape to allow for 3·5 cm borders on each side of the carpet.

Trim the raw or frayed edge and cut the required length of tape. Apply adhesive to half the width of the tape, and an equally wide strip on one side of the carpet. When both are nearly dry, put the pasted surfaces together. Turn over, and repeat with the other half of the tape. When the tape has been doubled over so there is an equal width both sides, tap with a hammer to help adhesion. Use a piece of wood as described above.

Woodworking tools

When buying tools, choose the best you can afford; cheap tools make any job that much more difficult.

Tools are best kept indoors in a box with partitions to prevent them from being knocked against each other. Alternatively hang them on the wall on pegboard, which saves space and makes them easy to keep track of. Clean all tools (except those with a non-stick finish) with an oily rag from time to time.

SAWING

Handsaws have long, flexible blades and are used for cutting larger pieces of wood. There are three types of handsaw: the **panel saw** is for cross-cut and jointing work, also for cutting plywood and man-made boards; the **rip saw** is for cutting softwoods, working along the grain; and the **cross-cut saw** is for cutting across the grain of hardwoods and softwoods and with the grain of exceptionally hard woods.

Tenon saws have stiff backs and are used for cutting joints, boards and narrow battens. A tenon saw with a 25 cm blade is generally the most convenient to use.

Junior hacksaw This is a general purpose metal-cutting saw with a thin, straight, replaceable blade, used for cutting metal or plastics, eg sawing through screws or metal brackets.

Fretsaws are used for cutting patterns in thin wood and for model making. Blades can be replaced.

Keyhole saw (also known as padsaw) This is for cutting keyholes and other small patterns in wood. Available with wood or metal handles keyhole saws have replaceable blades which can be changed when blunt.

SMOOTHING

Planes are needed for levelling the edges of wood

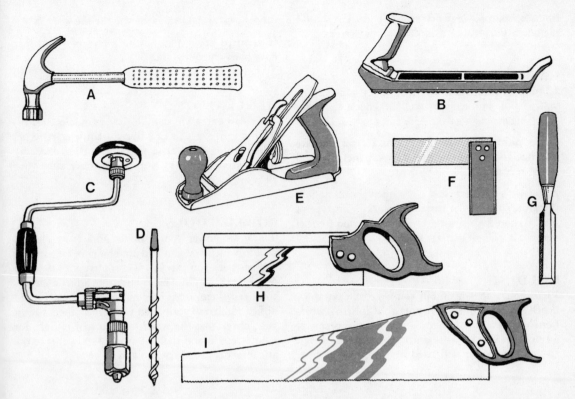

A. Claw hammer B. Surform C. Ratchet brace D. Wood auger bit E. Plane F. Try square G. Chisel
H. Tenon saw I. Rip saw

or reducing it in thickness. Special planes are available for different jobs, such as a **rebate plane** for cutting rebates in wood for glass or panelling. The **jack-plane** is best suited for general use and is large enough to cope with smoothing off lengths of wood.

Rasps come in different types for the general shaping of wood. The finish depends on the fineness of the teeth. **Surforms** work on the same principle as rasps. They have replaceable blades and come in various shapes, including round.

Oilstones are for sharpening planes and chisels. These come in coarse, medium and fine. A combination medium/fine stone is a good general purpose one.

A honing guide helps you get the correct angle for sharpening on the stone.

BORING

Chisels are necessary for making joints in wood. They come in several shapes and sizes; a set of three, 6 mm, 12 mm and 25 mm should serve for most home carpentry work.

Bradawl This is a chisel-pointed tool used for making screw holes so it is easy to drive in the screw.

Ratchet brace This has spring-loaded jaws and is designed for holding **wood auger bits**.

Screwdrivers Screwdrivers with long shafts are easier to work with, but a couple with very short handles will also come in useful where space is restricted. A ratchet screwdriver with detachable fittings that allows you to use the same screwdriver for various sizes of screw is a useful tool. There are also numerous jobs in carpentry which might call for a cross-top screwdriver, so your kit should include a Pozidriv or a Phillips screwdriver.

HAMMERING

Claw hammers have rounded forks which allow you to pull out nails as well as knock them in. Available in weights from 450–570 g.

Cross-pein hammer This is useful for delicate jobs like knocking in picture sprigs, panel pins and upholstery tacks.

A joiner's mallet has a wooden head and is therefore valuable for carpentry work. This type of mallet should always be used with a wood chisel because it will not damage the handle of the chisel.

HOLDING

Vices hold things firm, but you need a heavy work bench to mount one on. A **portable folding work bench** with a built-in vice is much more practical for DIY use. The light-weight version can be carried around the house and used on site, saving time running up and down to the shed or the workshop.

G-cramps apply pressure to pieces of wood that have been glued together.

GENERAL

Your carpentry kit should also include a **handyman's knife**, a pair of **pliers**, a **folding rule**, an **adjustable spanner**, a **spirit level** for checking horizontals and a **try square** to make sure your right angles are true.

POWER TOOLS

The basic power source of the tool is an electric drill to which you can add attachments for sanding and sawing. You can buy a complete kit (almost a home workshop in itself) or add the attachments as you need them, one at a time. Power tools are not difficult to handle provided you buy a model to suit you; check that the weight of the tool is right for your strength and that the chuck size will take the attachments you are most likely to need.

Fixing and fastening

NAILS

Whatever type of nail you are using, the length should be about twice that of the section of timber it has to hold (eg for 25 mm timber use a 50 mm nail), and the thinner material should be nailed to the thicker, rather than the other way round.

The french nail, also called the round wire nail. This is the most familiar kind of nail and is used for knocking things together without much regard for the final look.

An oval nail gives a neater finish because its head is smaller than the french nail and can be punched below the surface. This can be used for fixing floor boards.

The lost-head nail is neater still because it is designed to have its head punched home below the surface of the wood, after which the hole can be masked with filler.

The clout This usually comes in a galvanised

finish for use outdoors (such as fixing roofing felt to wood).

The masonry nail is used for securing building materials such as timber battens or plasterboard to masonry. You should always wear goggles when working with these to protect your eyes from flying chips of masonry.

The panel pin has a slim head and a fine body and is used for securing light pieces of wood, such as mouldings.

The tack Used for fixing carpets and upholstery.

The sprig has no head and is used for fixing some floor coverings, such as lino, and also in picture framing.

The cut floor nail is used for fixing floor boards.

The chair nail is also called the brass domed nail and is used primarily to cover the tacks round an upholstered edge. Comes in copper or chromed finish.

Corrugated fasteners are for holding butt joints together.

Staple This is for fixing fencing and trellis wires in the garden. There is also an insulated version for fixing electrical cables.

Some hints on nailing
You will get a stronger nailed joint if you drive the nails in at an angle, especially when driving into end grain wood. Nails should be staggered rather than driven in in a line along the grain of the wood. This guards against splitting.

SCREWS
Screws have several advantages over nails as a method of fixing. The shock is less when they are driven home, they are easier to remove and replace, and they also grip more firmly. To make sure of good grip, however, you should always first drill a pilot hole the same diameter as the central core of the screw, not including the thread.

The most common material for screws is steel, which may rust unless protected with a metal primer (rubbing over with a little wax or candle grease also helps). Even so, in damp conditions it is better to use zinc or chromium-plated screws.

Screw diameters are given by numbers ranging

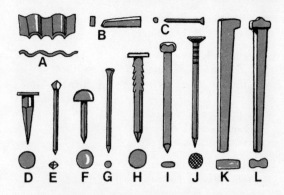

A. Corrugated fastener B. Sprig C. Panel pin
D. Tack E. Lost-head nail F. Chair nail
G. Masonry nail H. Clout I. Oval nail J. French nail K. Cut floor brad L. Cut floor nail

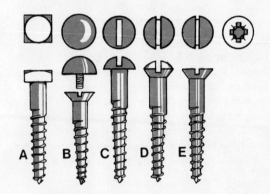

A. Coach screw B. Dome head screw
C. Round head screw D. Raised head screw
E. Countersunk head screw

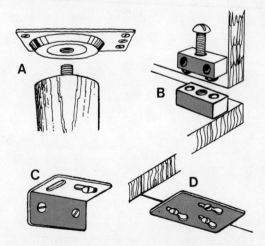

A. Leg fixing plate B. Corner block C. Angle plate D. Flat plate

from 0 (very small) up to 20 gauge. Lengths vary from 6 mm up to 152 mm.

Countersunk screw This is a flat-headed screw and comes in a wide range of sizes. Its head screws down flush with the surface or slightly below so the wood needs to be drilled with a countersink bit before the screw is driven in.

It is also possible to buy countersunk screws with a cross top head instead of a slot.

Raised head screw These are often nickel or chromium plated and are used to fix door-handle plates and so on. The screw is countersunk, leaving the upper part of the head raised above the rim.

Round head Here the whole head of the screw protrudes above the surface. These come in black enamel, chrome and brass finishes and are used mainly for fixing hardware fittings where the metal is too thin to countersink.

Dome head These are also known as mirror screws; their purpose is to give a decorative finish to screws which must remain accessible and cannot therefore be painted or plastered over. The screw part, which is countersunk, is used for fixing, after which the dome-shaped cap is threaded into the countersunk head to give a decorative finish. These are frequently used on mirrors and bath panels.

Coach screw This is an especially strong screw, available in lengths from 25 mm up to 150 mm. It has a square head and is turned with a spanner.

Screwdrivers
When choosing a screwdriver for a job, it is best to pick one that just fits the slot of the screw head. If it is too wide it can scratch the surface you are screwing into, and if it is too small it will jump out of the slot and you will not be able to apply enough pressure. The right size, as well as the right type, of screwdriver is equally important when you are using cross head screws.

WORK-SAVING FASTENINGS
These are the type of fastenings which are supplied with self-assembly furniture. You can also buy them separately. (For illustrations, see page 87.)

Leg fixing plates These are fixed to the table with screws and house a socket. You then fix a screw to the table leg and thread it into the socket.

Flat plates These are metal plates that you fix underneath a flat surface and which pull the wood together, edge to edge, so that joints are tightened between parallel boards.

Corner blocks These are two sets of plastic blocks which together form 90° joints for self-assembly furniture. The blocks are screwed to both pieces of wood and then bolted together.

Angle plates are right-angled to each other, one plate having screwholes, the other slots so that the screws can accommodate any movement of the timber. Any adjustment can be carried out while you are assembling.

Keyhole plates These are useful for wall units. The plate is screwed to the unit and the slot fitted over a screw projecting from the wall.

See also pages 95 and 110.

Door fittings

HINGES
Hinges come in a wide variety of materials: steel, cast iron, brass, aluminium, and even fibre-reinforced nylon (which has the advantage it never needs oiling); some come with chromium or nickel plated finish. There are also many different styles of hinge, so if you are making cabinets or cupboards, decide on the type of hinge you are going to

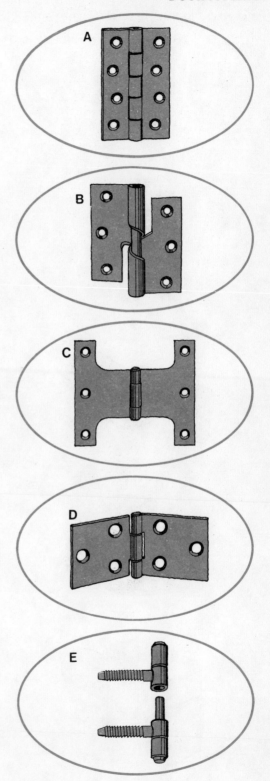

A. Butt hinge B. Rising butt hinge
C. Parliament hinge D. Back-flap
hinge E. Lift-off hinge

use before starting work. This way you can make allowance for the depth of the recesses you will need for fixing.

If an existing hinge needs replacing, take the old one with you to the shop so you can match it up exactly. Some specialist hinges may not be available from an ordinary DIY shop, in which case try an architectural ironmongers.

The drawings, right, show some of the most convenient and widely used hinges you may at some time need to fix around the house:

Butt hinge The most usual type of hinge for doors, windows and cupboards. You need to recess it into both the door and the frame, fixing it to the door first.

Rising butt hinge This causes the door to lift as it opens and so to clear the carpet. You will need to cut away a small section of the top of the door at the hinge end to allow the door to clear the frame.

Parliament hinge This lets a door fold back flat against a wall.

Back-flap hinge This is similar to a butt hinge, except that the countersinks for the screw heads are on the same side as the hinge knuckle. This hinge is most often used for table leaves, lids of boxes and bureau tops.

Lift-off hinge This makes it easy to lift off cupboard doors for cleaning or painting.

CATCHES
Most DIY shops carry a large range of catches which are sold together with fitting instructions, fitting templates and screws.

Magnetic catches are usually the easiest to fit. Some (as illustrated, page 90) have slotted holes

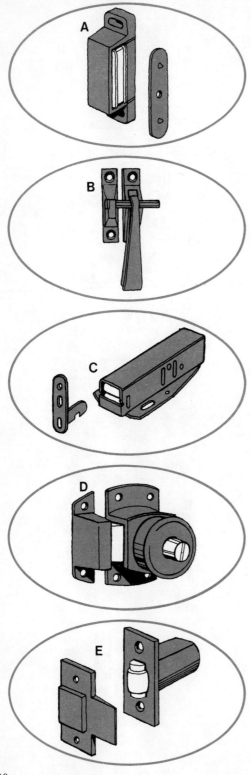

A. Magnetic catch B. Turn catch
C. Push catch D. Press-button catch
E. Roller catch

so you can align the plate with the magnet after fitting. Magnetic catches are available with different strengths of 'pull', usually 1·3 kg, 2·7 kg and 4 kg. You choose the pull to suit the size and weight of the door (for example, wardrobe doors will probably need a catch with a 4 kg pull).

Turn catches are also easy to fit, but are really suitable only for very small doors. They take the form of a hook fixed to the door frame and a tee-piece on a spindle which is fixed to the door.

Push catches are more sophisticated, with spring loaded jaws into which the hook, usually fixed to the door, connects. When the door is closed it is secured by the hook, and a push on the outside of the door makes it unclip and open. These are suitable for most cupboard and wardrobe doors, and are not difficult to fit provided you follow the instructions.

Press-button catch This is a popular type of cupboard catch (also often seen on motor cars) which is worked by pressing the button in the handle.

Roller catch These catches are available in a wide variety of styles and materials for either surface or mortise (as illustrated) fitting. Cupboard doors usually have surface fitting; large doors, such as wardrobe and room doors, are better with the catches mortised in. Some have an adjustable roller that can be strengthened to suit the weight of the door.

LOCKS
More information on locks is given on pages 159–162

Emergency release bathroom or lavatory lock These are an especially good idea if you have children or old people in the house. The lock can be opened from the outside by turning a coin in the release slot, should the need arise.

Glass sliding door lock Designed for patio doors,

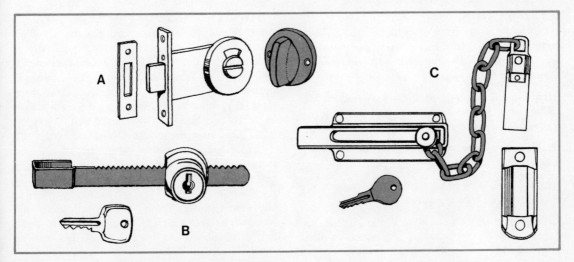

A. Emergency release lock B. Glass sliding door lock C. Chain door lock

these are simple to fit because they do not require any cutting. The ratchet clip wraps round the inside door and the lock slides on to the ratchet.

Chain door lock This is a sophisticated version of the standard security chain and has the advantage that it can be locked from either side of the door.

Magnetic door holder This comes in two parts, one of which you attach to the door and the other to the wall or floor. The magnetic pull then holds the door in the position you want it.

Buying timber for simple jobs

Woods are divided into two categories: softwoods and hardwoods. Most amateur carpenters work with softwoods because they are, as a general rule, easier to handle than hard. They are also cheaper, so it is less expensive should you make a mistake.

SOFTWOODS

Softwoods come from coniferous trees and are usually light in colour. Some of the most-used softwoods are:

Cedar Cedar varies in colour from pink to deep brown or 'red' and its resinous surface is particularly suitable for painting and clear finishes.

Red and white deal These are soft white or yellow resinous woods coming mainly from pine, spruce or fir trees. Deal is often used for kitchen furniture and is cheap, light and durable.

Douglas fir (also known as Columbian pine) This is a straight-grained, resilient wood which is also extremely strong.

Pitch pine Yellow to orange in colour, with dark brown knots. Pitch pine is very even in texture, and harder to work than other softwoods.

91

HARDWOODS

Hardwoods come from deciduous trees. These mature more slowly than conifers, so hardwoods are in less plentiful supply than soft. Some of the hundreds of hardwoods are:

Afrormosia A light brown wood, extremely hard and strong. Afrormosia makes a good substitute for teak and is less expensive.

Beech is non-resinous, light in colour, and often used for chair frames and for floorboards.

Birch is often used in Scandinavian furniture. It is easy to work and close-grained.

Chestnut Sweet chestnut is a good choice for palings and fences because it is resistant to damp and decay.

Elm is hard and dark and difficult to work, but is more resistant than most woods to water and therefore often used for garden furniture.

Mahogany is hard, strong and beautifully grained. It is easy to work and is used a lot for making furniture, where it is usually given a french polished finish.

Maple is also hard, strong and close-grained. Maple is difficult to nail but it takes paint well.

Oak is a light-coloured, hard, heavy and very durable wood which resists rot well. English oak is famous, and expensive. It is also possible to buy cheaper imported oak, notably Japanese.

Rosewood varies from chocolate brown to rich purple-brown striped with black.

Sapele is an African hardwood which can be used like mahogany. It needs careful working though, especially planing.

Sycamore is a very white, fine-grained hardwood which resists water well but is prone to cracking and warping.

Teak has a very even grain and is used for household furniture and garden chairs and tables. It is often used for flooring and other structural jobs in the house, eg stairs, panelling.

Walnut is another high quality wood used for furniture. It varies considerably in colour, and has a beautiful grain. Walnut veneer is sometimes superimposed on a foundation of cheaper wood to give an attractive and expensive-looking finish.

CHOOSING GOOD TIMBER

When buying timber make sure that the wood has been properly seasoned and stored. Wood with a high moisture content will feel cold to the touch and as well as being harder to work, is liable to warp and may even attract dry rot. Even if the wood seems dry, it is a good idea to store it for a few days in the room where it is to be used before starting work. This gives the moisture content of the wood a chance to come into balance with that in the atmosphere, especially important in a centrally heated house.

Defects to avoid

Naturally, you want the timber you buy to be as free as possible from defects. These are some to avoid if you can:

Shakes These show up in the form of splits or cracks across the board; they may be the result of too rapid drying or the 'shaking up' the tree got when it hit the ground.

Sapwood Look out for a board with a lighter coloured strip down the edge – a sign it comes from the outer wood of the tree and the timber will be softer.

Bark-edged boards (waney edges) Bark on the edge of a board makes it more liable to decay and insect attack.

Knots A large number of knots in a board can weaken the timber, a few do no great harm provided you treat them with shellac knotting (see page 51) to prevent the resin seeping out and breaking up a painted surface.

QUANTITIES

Timber is sold in a range of standard lengths and thicknesses. For both softwoods and hardwoods these begin at lengths of 1·8 m. Softwoods then increase in steps of 300 mm and hardwoods in steps of 100 mm.

When having timber cut for you, remember that the measurements the dealer will be quoting are the 'sawn' or 'nominal' sizes – ie the size of the board as he will cut it and before squaring off and planing which will reduce all the dimensions of the wood. So if the measurements you have taken are for the exact finished size, be sure and make this clear, or you may well end up with a board too small for the job.

BUILDING BOARDS

For some carpentry jobs – such as panelling – man-made building boards are usually a better choice than natural timber because they are less likely to warp or shrink. They are also more economical. Building boards are sold in standard sheet sizes, but if you need only a small amount, it is worth asking if off-cuts are available.

Hardboard is made from timber chipped into particles, ground into a fibre and mixed with water to form a porridge-like substance which is pressed into sheets at high temperature. Hardboard is easy to work with and comes in a number of decorative finishes as well as the standard type which has one face rough and the other smooth. It can be used for panelling, pelmets and to make an even surface under wood or vinyl floor coverings (see page 77). With timber framing it can also be used for shelves, table tops and doors.

Pegboard is perforated hardboard and is particularly handy for kitchen use.

Chipboard is made from wood chips bonded together with resin. It is available with either a plain or veneered surface with either a wood or a melamine finish. Chipboard is used in furniture making and for covering solid floors; it is rigid and inclined to be heavy to handle.

Blockboard is light to handle and consists of outer layers of ply and an inner core of wooden strips. Blockboard is stronger than chipboard, and also more expensive.

Plywood is made up of 'plies' (veneers) of wood laid at right angles to obtain the maximum stiffness and glued together – the thickness of the plywood depends on the number of plies. For outdoor use choose a plywood labelled WBP – water and boil-proof.

Making shelves

Even though several different kinds of ready-made shelving units are now available, there is still a lot to be said for making one's own shelves. Not only does it work out cheaper, but the arrangement can be more flexible, especially when it comes to fixing shelves in an alcove or an awkward space.

The shelving material you choose depends to an extent on the weight to be supported and the length of the span. As a general rule, timber makes the most attractive and strongest shelves, but width is limited to 150 mm to 225 mm. For wider shelves you will need to use chipboard, blockboard or plywood (see above). The best wood thickness for shelves is 18 mm but if the span of the shelf is longer than 1 m you will need to support it with a bearer along the back, or with a central support bracket; otherwise it will soon begin to sag in the middle.

Wood surfaces need some form of treatment both to protect them and to enhance their appearance. A coat of wood primer with an undercoat and gloss paint finish is traditional, but if the timber has an attractive grain you could use a clear polyurethane wood seal to retain the natural colour and grain of the wood.

FREE STANDING SHELVES

It takes only a little skill to build a strong, attractive bookcase working to a box design. This looks very good in pine, which is available in widths up to 225 mm. If you want wider shelves, use chipboard, plywood or blockboard. Use hardboard or thin plywood for the back. Timber must be cut accurately so, if you are cutting your own, use a carpenter's square to mark off the cutting lines.

First glue the lower shelf and then the top to the side uprights with a wood-working adhesive (an

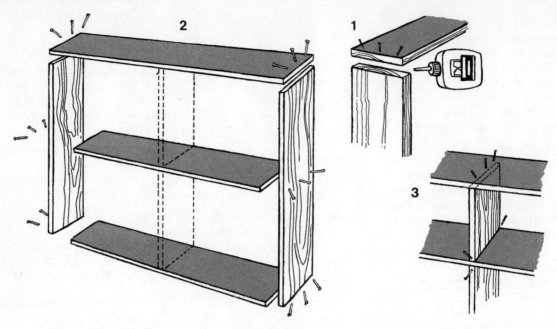

1. Glue and nail all joints, hammering the nails in at an angle for maximum grip 2. Fix lower shelf first, then the top one, centre shelf last. Add centre supports if the shelves are more than 1m long 3. The nails holding the centre supports should also be driven in at an angle

extra pair of hands will come in useful here). Fix the centre shelf in the same way.

Hammer oval nails in at a slight angle where the tops join the uprights, checking all the joints with the carpenter's square. Punch the nail heads below the surface of the wood with a nail punch and fill in the holes with plastic wood or filler.

If the bookcase is to be more than 1 m long, centre supports will be needed. The nails holding these should also be driven in at a slight angle.

Fix the hardboard to the back with glue and panel pins. Lightly rub down the wooden surfaces with fine grade glasspaper, paying particular attention to the edges. Wipe over to remove any dust and the bookcase will be ready for priming and painting or for sealing.

FIXED SHELVES

Fixing shelves to a wall is not really a difficult matter and success depends in the main on two factors: accurate level and a strong fixing. The first step is to drill holes in the wall and plug them to grip the screws firmly.

Basically walls are either hard and solid (brick, stone, concrete, building blocks) or soft and hollow (hardboard, plaster, lath-and-plaster, insulation board).

Solid walls

Solid walls are hard to drill into. A power tool running at its slowest speed and with a special tungsten tipped masonry drill is the easiest way to tackle the job. Do not try to use an ordinary woodworking drill; even if it does not break you will blunt it.

If you have no power tool, use a wheel brace to drill the hole or use a hand held impact punch which you hit with a hammer. Twist the punch as you go to release the dust from the hole and prevent it jamming up.

Once you have drilled the holes, the next step is to plug them to guard against ending up with a loose and wobbly fitting. Wallplugs are small hollow tubes of either fibre or plastic material which you push into the holes. As the thread of a screw is inserted, the walls of the plug expand and grip into the surrounding brickwork.

Hollow walls

The interior walls of many houses are made of soft materials such as lath-and-plaster or man-made

94

boards. These are not strong enough (even with wallplugs) to hold screws supporting a shelf, but several types of special fitting offer a solution.

A **toggle plug** is a screw-headed bolt with an alloy sheath lying along its length. The toggle is inserted with the bolt only just protruding beyond the sheath's pivot point. The sheath will then drop down with the pull of gravity and will lie behind the wall board when the bolt is tightened.

A **spring toggle** has a pair of folded wings attached to its bolt. They pass through the hole, then fly open on the other side and grip the back of the board. These are good for hollow walls like those made of lath-and-plaster.

The **anchor bolt** has a plastic sleeve lying along the bolt. When the screw is tightened the internal section is drawn up to give a compression fitting between the wall and the hardboard.

Fixing shelves in an alcove

The simplest place to put up shelves is in an alcove or recess. The best method is to support the shelves with wooden battens. If the recess is small you will need only two of these, one at each end, for each shelf. If the alcove is more than about a metre, however, it is safer to run a batten along the back wall as well.

Using a spirit level, mark off a line for each shelf at the required height along the wall. If you are planning to use the shelves for books you may like to allow for a deeper shelf at the bottom to take large, heavy volumes.

Cut wooden battens to the required length, using 16×38 mm timber. The battens should be 25 to 50 mm shorter than the depth of the shelf. Planing or sanding off any edges that will be visible when the shelf is up will make them look neater.

The size of screw needed for any fixing job depends on the thickness of the wood to be fixed and the surface it is being fixed to. As a general rule, the diameter of the screw should not be more than one-eighth of the width of the wood and the length of the screw should be about three times the thickness of the wood it is going through. So in this case, assuming the wall is firm and in good condition, use No 8 countersunk wood screws 38 mm long (a No 8 screw is 4·5 mm in diameter).

Using a 4·5 mm diameter drill bit, drill three holes in each piece of wood, one in the centre and one about 50 mm from each end. Hold the battens against the guide line marked on the wall and mark the positions for the screw holes. You can do this by putting the screws in the holes and gently tapping them with a hammer.

Using a No 8 or 4·5 mm masonry bit, drill holes in the wall making them deep enough for the length of the screw; plug the holes with No 8 fibre or plastic wallplugs. Screw the battens on to the wall.

Cut your shelves to length (if the timber merchant has not done this for you) and set in place on the battens.

One problem you may have to face is that very few walls are completely flat, so you may well find there is an uneven gap at the back between the shelf and the wall. This will not matter, of course, if you are going to use the shelf for books because it will be out of sight. If you are planning to use the shelf for ornaments, however, the best answer is to buy some quarter-round beading and fix it along the back of the shelf with panel pins, to hide the gaps.

Instead of using wooden bearers, you can also fix shelves in a recess by using angled aluminium or steel, but remember that metal is harder to drill than wood.

Divided shelves

Where you are planning to use shelves in a recess for more than one purpose it is a good idea to divide the shelf area into sections with slotted uprights.

Drill and fix the side battens as described above. Cut the middle shelf and the two upright dividers and mark the positions for slots that coincide exactly. Saw down both sides of each slot, then use a 6 mm chisel to cut out the sawn waste wood. Trim back the edges with a broad chisel. Glue the uprights and the centre shelf together. Use a woodwork adhesive carefully spread in the slots.

Cut the top and bottom shelves and set the bottom shelf in place on the end bearers. Slide the centre shelf and uprights into position, then place the top shelf on the end battens.

High level shelves

There are many cases when a shelf set high up on a wall and fixed with metal brackets can provide useful extra storage space, especially in work shops and garages.

First mark on the wall the height at which the shelf is required then, using a spirit level and a rule, draw a line parallel to the floor and the exact length of the shelf. Next draw two short lines

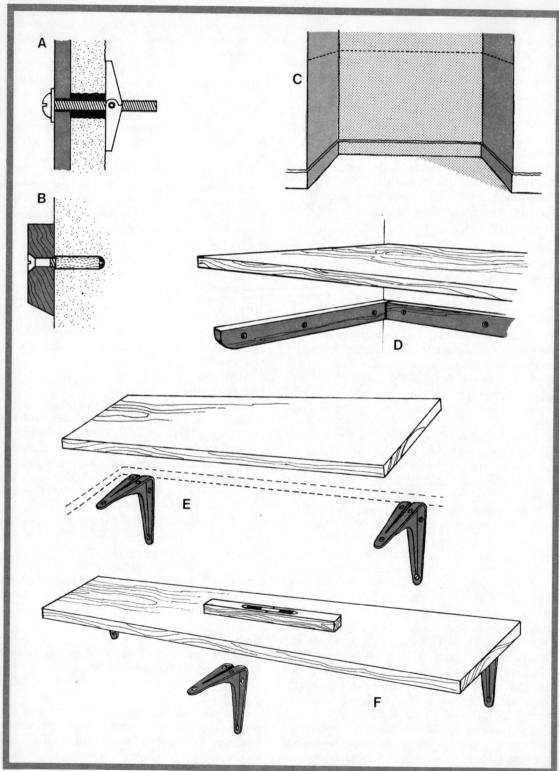

A. A spring toggle bolt gives a secure fixture on wallboards or lath and plaster B. With solid walls, drill and insert a wall plug to hold the screw C. Before fixing a shelf in an alcove mark a line at the required height D. Fix wooden battens on marked lines to support shelf E. A second line helps indicate thickness of shelf and position for brackets F. Use a spirit level to check level of shelf; a third bracket may be necessary if the shelf is more than 1 metre long

parallel with the ends of the first line and the exact thickness of the shelf you are going to use.

Get someone to help you hold the brackets in a vertical position 50–75 mm inside the ends of the shelf; with the tops of the brackets level with the lower guidelines mark the positions for the screw holes on the wall. Put up the two end brackets and lay the shelf across them, using a spirit level to check the level.

If the shelf is a long one, you will need extra brackets to support the centre section. Mark positions for these after you have put up the outer brackets and checked the level of the shelf.

The shelf can then be fixed in position by screwing through the brackets into the wood.

Corner shelves

A triangular shelf can be fixed in a corner by resting it on two bearers. Remember, though, that the corner is unlikely to be square. Cut a cardboard pattern of the angle and use this as a guide when you cut the wood.

If you want two straight shelves to meet in a corner, lay the first shelf in place on its bearer, then put the second shelf in position, laying it on top of the first one.

Draw a line on the upper shelf from the corner to the point where the two planks make the angle. Saw off the top plank along this line.

Then put the sawn plank back again and draw a line along the cut edge on to the lower plank. This will give you your second sawing line, and the planks should then join exactly.

UNIT SHELVING

There are a number of types of ready-made shelf units available. These are usually sold as uprights with brackets, so all you have to buy is the wood for the shelf. Sometimes shelves are also supplied, ready finished to a given length.

The uprights come in a variety of lengths and the shelf depth can be adjusted by moving the brackets in the slots to give you the depth of shelf you want. The main supports may be made of slotted aluminium, steel or wood and look quite decorative, as well as being strong.

The supports are reasonably simple to assemble. The uprights are fixed to the wall by screws and the main point to watch is that you get a true vertical between the supports when you fix them; remember to use a spirit level to check the horizontal lines. Drill and plug the wall as described under **Fixing shelves in an alcove**, page 95.

Laminating

Plastic laminate is extremely hard-wearing. It doesn't chip, warp or split, is easy to clean and can withstand temperatures up to about 155°C.

You can use a plastic laminate on almost any horizontal or vertical surface, provided the base is rigid, smooth and free from dirt and grease. An uneven surface should first be covered with resin-bonded plywood or tempered hardboard fixed face down on the top and nailed with panel pins every 10–15 cm. The laminate is then fixed to this new surface.

Laminate is sold either in sheet form in sizes

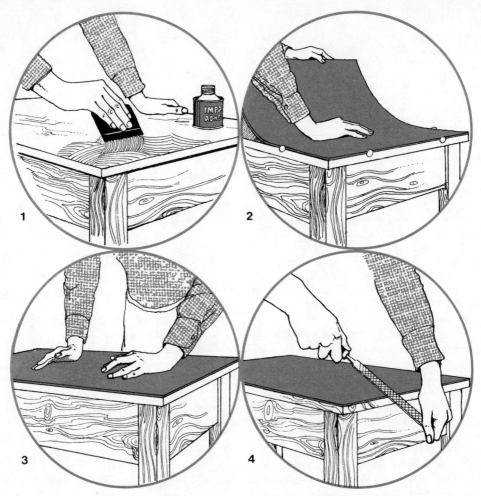

Laminating a table top. 1. Clean the surface to be covered and spread with contact adhesive, using a serrated spreader 2. Use drawing pins as a guide for accurate positioning 3. Press down firmly, working from the centre outwards 4. File off over hanging edges with downward strokes

from about $2 \cdot 4 \times 1 \cdot 2$ m up to $3 \cdot 6 \times 1 \cdot 2$ m or in handy sized stock panels. It is available in a wide range of colours and patterns, including woodgrains, marble and textured surfaces. It also comes in two finishes; satin, which is suitable for all working surfaces, and glossy, which is recommended for vertical surfaces only.

TABLE AND WORK SURFACES

Really awkward shaped surfaces are best left to an expert, but covering a table or work surface with laminate is one of the simpler, and most satisfactory, jobs round the house to do yourself. The easiest method is to glue on the new laminate surface and finish off with flexible plastic edging. The final effect will be neater and more professional, though, if you make your edging strip from the same laminate as the top surface. To do this, you will need to cut your edging strip from the laminate before the top is resurfaced.

First measure the area to be covered, add the width of the edging, then allow an extra 6 mm all round for wastage.

Cutting tools

Cutting laminate used to be something of a problem for all but the most patient and steady-handed. Nowadays a special, inexpensive laminate trimmer is available which can be used to cut the material exactly to shape, whether the edge is straight or curved. It consists of a rigid plastic guide arm shaped rather like a large comb, an adjustable stop and a hardened triangular cutter that can be replaced when you have worn it down.

To use the cutter, set the stop at the appropriate distance from the blade and then score along the laminate several times until you have cut it about half way through. You can then bend the loose edge upwards until it breaks off. There is a small groove at the end of the guide arm to help bend small strips.

The alternative tool to use for cutting laminate is a fine tooth saw or a tool rather like a knife with a special hardened blade.

Fixing the laminate

Use glasspaper or a plane to clean up the surface to be covered to make sure that the sheet will lie smoothly and there are no bumps or other irregularities to distort the laminate. If the surface is in poor condition, fill in any gaps or knotholes with filler and allow to dry before planing off. Dirt or grease should be wiped off with white spirit.

Once you have cut off your edging strips, apply contact adhesive to both the surface and the laminate. It is best to use one of the modern contact adhesives that allow you a few seconds' grace to make adjustments before final bonding. If you are using an ordinary contact adhesive, then put in a few drawing pins to act as position guides.

Spread the adhesive evenly using a serrated-edged spreader. The wood will need slightly more than the laminate. Leave it to dry till it feels tacky. This usually takes about 15 minutes, but could take longer on a cold day.

Remember when using this type of adhesive to have plenty of ventilation and keep it away from naked flame.

When both surfaces are ready, place – do not slide – the laminate in position and press it down firmly, working from the centre outwards and smoothing out any air bubbles as you go. Make sure that every part is bonded firmly to the surface.

After 30 minutes or so, remove any over-hanging edges with a flat, fine-cut file, using quick downward strokes. Upward strokes may lift the edge. If necessary, finish off with glasspaper on a block. Glue on the laminate or plastic edging strips. If you are using plastic strips, do not try to bend them around the corners. Cut off the ends with scissors and trim them flush with a plane or upward strokes of a fine file.

Woodworking repairs

CHAIRS

It can often be difficult to find someone who will do small furniture repairs, and even if you are lucky you may have to pay a good deal for the service. It is worth it, of course, if you are dealing with a valuable antique, but for something as ordinary as a rickety dining chair it is more practical to tackle the job yourself.

The first thing to try and find out is the cause of the problem, especially with an old chair, so you can decide whether or not it is worth the time and the trouble to repair it at all. So first, check the chair thoroughly for woodworm. Look particularly at the underside of the seat, which may be unvarnished and so more prone to attack than sealed areas. If the frame is really riddled with worm, then forget it, because even if you mend it the frame will probably have been too badly weakened to last for long.

If only a small area is affected by woodworm you can probably treat it successfully using a proprietary woodworm fluid, following the maker's instructions. For a chair that you are particularly anxious to save, perhaps because it is one of a set, it may be possible to cut out and replace worm-damaged wood, provided it is restricted to one section of the frame.

Loose joints

If the wood itself is sound but the chair is wobbly, try tightening the existing screws or brackets. If the screws no longer fit snugly it may be because the holes have become enlarged, in which case replace the original screws with some that are slightly thicker, or plug the holes to get a tighter fit.

If the chair is an old one, however, it may be that the original glue holding the joints in place has perished so the whole frame of the chair is loose. In this case, it should not be difficult to take the joints apart, unscrewing any corner blocks, scrape off the old glue and replace it with a modern woodworking adhesive. Put the frame together again while the glue is still wet and clamp it into position while it dries. Use woodworkers' sash cramps for large pieces of furniture and G cramps for smaller items.

If you have neither of these, make a tourniquet with strong cord and a stick. Use offcuts of timber

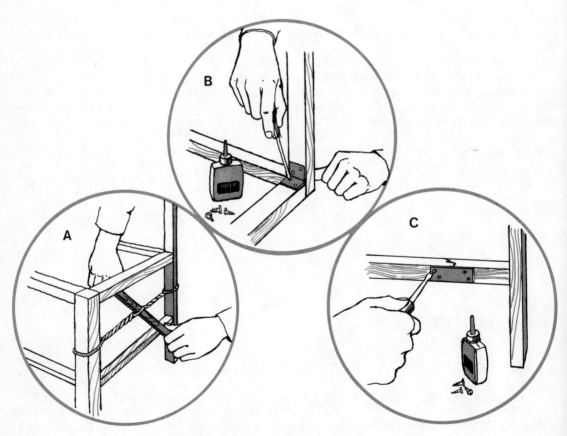

A. A tourniquet will hold the chair frame tightly until the glue dries B. An angle plate will hold a rail that snaps off near the leg C. A flat plate may hold a rail that snaps in the middle

100

or hardboard to prevent the cord chafing the frame, then tie the cord round the frame and twist the stick as in a tourniquet, to provide tension while the glue sets.

Rails

The most common problems with ordinary upright dining chairs are that over time the rails tend to work loose or break as a result of none-too-gentle handling.

If the sections of wood holding the seat come loose, lever them out and scrape off the old glue. Apply a fresh coat of woodworking adhesive and hold the chair under tension with a tourniquet, as described above, until the glue dries. A connecting rail that snaps near the leg of the chair can often be repaired with a small angle plate (see page 88). This should be screwed securely into the leg and the rail. Coat the joint with glue first, to give it extra strength.

When a connecting rail has snapped in the middle, apply glue to both surfaces, press them together and fix a flat metal plate (see page 88), screwed to the underside of the rail.

If a connecting rail has been badly splintered, you may need to replace it with a new piece of wood. In this case, saw off the old rail and prise out the old wood and glue from the recess with a small chisel. Then, using the old rail as a guide, cut a new rail, taper the ends and glue it into position.

Legs

If a chair rocks because its legs are uneven, do not try to cut down the legs to balance it. Instead, build up the short legs with thin slivers of wood just smaller than the shape of the leg, glueing them in place with woodworking adhesive. If necessary, secure the layers in place with a panel pin. Allow the glue to dry, then lightly smooth off with glass-paper.

DRAWERS

To ease a stiff or sticking drawer try giving the runners and the bottom of the drawer a thin coat of soap or candle grease, first rubbing over the surface with glasspaper if the wood is rough. If the drawer still sticks, it may be because condensation or some other form of damp has caused the wood to swell in places, in which case you will need to sand down the surface till it is true again.

If you buy an old chest at an auction or a second hand shop, you may find a drawer will not open smoothly because one of the runners is broken or missing. To replace it, plane down a piece of hard-wood to match the existing runner exactly, then fix the new runner in place with PVA adhesive and, if necessary, screws or panel pins.

Loose handles

To repair a loose or broken drawer handle, first see how the original handle was fixed. If the thread is worn at the point where the nut should grip, place a metal washer between the nut and the inside of the drawer so the nut will grip the thread at an unworn part. Handles which are held in place with wooden dowels or screwed directly into the wood may need the original hole packing with slivers of wood and woodworking adhesive.

HINGES

Creaking hinges can usually be cured with a few drops of oil. Do not over-lubricate and wipe off the surplus to stop it attracting dust.

If the wood round a hinge is broken or split, cut away the old piece with a tenon saw and sharp chisel and fit a new piece with adhesive and fine pins. Then choose a new position for the hinge, either above or below the new piece of wood. If necessary, turn the door upside down and use the opposite edge for the hinges. Remember if you do this you will have to move lock and door handle to the other side.

FLOORBOARDS

Hollow floors have timber floorboards laid across joists. When the fixing nails which hold the boards in place rust or become loose, this allows the boards to move up and down and rub against each other, which causes squeaking.

To cure a squeak, locate the position of the faulty floorboard and hammer down any loose nails, punching the nail heads down, or remove them with a claw hammer. Before fixing any new nails, check on the position of any gas and water pipes or electricity cables, any or all of which may be running in the cavity area under the floor.

Refix at the joists with cut floorboard nails (see page 87) hammered in at an angle; if the floor-boards are likely to be lifted at a later date, for re-wiring for instance, use countersunk wood screws for fixing instead.

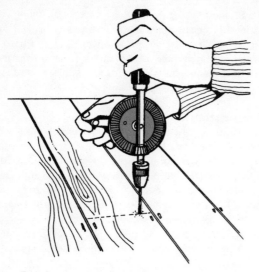

To remove a floorboard, drill a starter hole close to the joist large enough to insert the saw blade

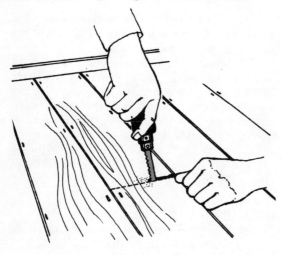

Cut through the board with a padsaw

Use a wedge of wood and a bolster chisel to prise up the board

Before laying the new board screw a timber support to the joist

If a board is cracked or split, you will need to cut out the damaged section and replace it with a new one. First look for the joists. These are usually placed about 40 cm apart and are about 5 cm thick; you will recognise them by the nail positions.

Drill a hole through the floorboard close to the joist and use a floorboard saw or a padsaw to cut across the board parallel to the joist. Then do the same at the other end of the damaged section.

If the board is a tongued and grooved one, cut down the edge of the board with the floorboard saw and prise it out. You cannot put tongued and grooved board back, so you will need to replace it with ordinary floorboard. Measure the length of new board required; if you cannot get the exact width to match, buy the next size up and sand or plane it to fit. It is important that the new board fits as tightly as possible.

Fasten a piece of timber at least 4 cm thick to the joist to support the new piece of board. Tap the board down on either side. Knock two nails into each new piece of timber to hold the board firmly in place. Nail down the ends of the existing board.

CREAKING STAIRS

Stairs quite often develop creaks and unfortunately they can be tricky to get at. The most likely cause is that the wedges and corner blocks have worked loose.

If the underside of your staircase is inaccessible, take up the stair carpet and nail through the front of the tread into the riser. Drive the nail in at an angle and punch the head under.

If it is possible to get at the underside of the staircase, hammer back the wedges into position and refix the corner blocks, making new ones from off-cuts of timber if necessary, or fit metal brackets.

Repairing veneer

Furniture is veneered by a process in which thin, flat strips or layers of well grained hardwood, often walnut or mahogany, are applied to the face of less expensive wood or man-made board. This makes it possible to produce expensive-looking furniture for a much lower price than if it were made of solid hardwood throughout.

The best veneered furniture is made by adding veneer to the basic wood before the furniture is cut and fixed together. Cheaper furniture may just have veneer stuck on the top surfaces and doors after the piece has been put together.

Veneer needs more care than other wood surfaces, because if a veneered surface, or even just a part of it, gets wet the adhesive is softened and the thin sheet of veneer may come away from the wood underneath.

Patching

When a strip of veneer has been damaged, you can buy a new strip to put in its place. If you only need a small section go to a DIY or art shop that sells marquetry kits; for a larger quantity look for a firm that specialises in veneers. If you are unable to buy a new piece of veneer that is an exact colour match, try bleaching it if it is too dark, or soaking it in wood dye if you want to make it darker.

Then put the new piece of veneer over the damaged area, matching up the grain, and cut out an oval shape slightly larger than the damaged area, through both pieces of veneer. Use a sharp knife – a modelling knife with a thin blade is ideal – but take care not to press too hard otherwise the cut marks will go deeply into the base wood and may show through the repaired section when the new veneer is dry.

To remove the damaged veneer, first clean off any old polish with white spirit. Then hold a pad of wet cotton wool over the damaged surface to melt the glue that is holding it in place. Take care not to over-wet otherwise the veneer on either side of the damaged piece may also lift away. When you have stripped off the old veneer, carefully scrape off any hard glue underneath with a narrow-bladed chisel, until the surface is smooth and clean.

Damp the new patch of veneer and apply a PVA adhesive to it and to the wood base surface. When the adhesive starts to dry, press the new patch firmly into place. Using a knife handle or a smooth piece of wood, stroke the veneer firmly across the surface until it is level with the existing veneer finish. Then clamp or weight down until the adhesive has set. Place a piece of greaseproof or brown paper between the veneer and the weights to prevent it sticking to them.

If you need to put in a new piece of veneer on a

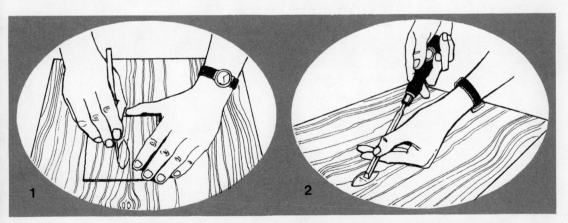

1. Match up the grain of the new veneer with the old and cut out a section through both thicknesses
2. After removing the damaged veneer, clean the surface thoroughly with a chisel

surface where you cannot apply pressure with cramps or weights, try holding the patch in position with sticky tape. If this does not work, use an instant-bonding contact adhesive in place of the PVA adhesive.

Once it has stuck firmly, the new veneer can be lightly sanded and waxed and polished to match the surrounding wood.

Blisters

It is sometimes possible to make good a blister on a veneered surface without cutting out the surrounding area. Incise the blister in the direction of the grain, then squeeze a little PVA adhesive down through the cut – you may need to work the adhesive into the crack with the blade of a knife. Then press the veneer back into place and wipe off any excess adhesive before it has a chance to dry. The cut should be concealed in the grain.

Scratches and burns

If veneer has been scratched, try sanding out the damage. For a deeper scratch, fill in with a matching wood filler, sand lightly and repolish. Cigarette burns can often be removed by rubbing over with a few drops of liquid metal polish on a soft cloth. A bad burn will need to be cut out and patched as described above.

Door repairs

A STICKING DOOR

The most common reason a door needs attention is because it is sticking. This can be caused by any number of things – even something as simple as the amount of humidity in the air, so a door that works perfectly well in summer may stick in winter. In this case, plane down the swollen door to an exact fit, then take off a further 3 mm, prime the bare surface and paint or varnish. Then fit a plastic weather strip. Because this is flexible it will shape itself to fill in the gap between the door and the frame, even when the door contracts again in summer.

If the door sticks in one place only, it is probably because it was made from badly seasoned wood. You will be able to spot the place where it is sticking because the paintwork will be worn. Plane away a sliver of wood at this point, working very carefully and testing often to be sure you are not taking off too much. Prime the wood and repaint.

Sometimes sticking is caused by the screws in the door hinges working loose. If the existing screws cannot be tightened further, replace them

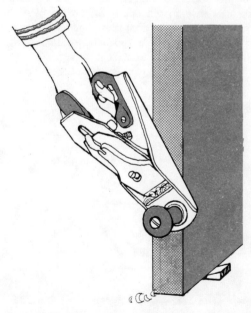

A swollen door can be planed to fit; a wedge underneath will hold it steady

with new ones. Fill the holes with plastic wood or a sliver of wood.

If the door not only sticks, but also gapes at another point, the trouble may be due to warping (perhaps through the use of unseasoned wood), or the door may have been badly made, or the frame may be faulty. This sort of defect is difficult to remedy yourself and is better left to a skilled carpenter.

Rising butt hinges

When you have laid a new carpet, because it is likely to be thicker than the old one, you may find there is no longer sufficient clearance at the bottom of the door. It is better not to plane off the bottom of the door, however, as this can be a cause of warping. Instead, fit rising butts (see page 89). These are spiral hinges that lift the door from the floor as it opens and closes, so that it clears the carpet. As the door will then rise slightly as it opens, a small section should be cut from the top of the door at the hinge end so it clears the door frame.

A SHRUNKEN DOOR

Old houses are sometimes draughty because a door has shrunk over the years. It may then be necessary to fit a new door, or it may be possible to fix on a lath to bring the door back to its original size. Take off the lock and plane down the edge of the door to give a level surface. Fix on the lath, using glue and panel pins, replace the lock in its new position, prime the new wood and paint it.

A RATTLING DOOR

To stop a door rattling, move the striker plate – the

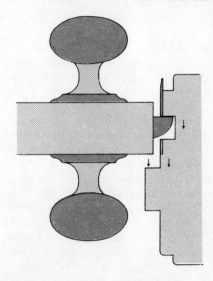

To stop a door rattling adjust the position of the striker plate as indicated by the arrows

part on the door frame where the latch fits. Unscrew it from the frame and cut the recess back slightly towards the door stop. Refit the striker plate and check the door. If it still rattles move the plate a bit more until the fault is remedied.

Door stops

A rubber or plastic door stop will prevent a door being flung open too widely and damaging the wall behind it. Screw the stop to the floor or skirting board at the back of the door with a round-headed screw. If it is the handle that hits the wall, use an extended stop that projects far enough to protect the wall.

Window repairs

FRAMES

Window frames may be made either of steel or aluminium, or of wood. Of these, only aluminium frames are virtually trouble free. Below we deal

with some of the more common window problems.

Rust

Not only ugly but destructive, rust can break down

steel frames completely if not dealt with in good time.

Remove any loose traces of rust round a window frame with steel wool, emery cloth or a wire brush (**wear protective goggles and gloves**). Clean the surface well then brush on a chemical rust remover. These contain acid, so work with care. Wash off the remover with water or spirit, according to the manufacturer's instructions. Allow the metal to dry thoroughly before applying a metal primer and a fresh coat of paint.

If rust has been neglected, the frame may be so badly damaged that it will be necessary to replace the window. This is a rather difficult job and it is probably advisable to call in an expert to do the job. A local builder will put in a single window for you, or you could get in touch with a specialist firm who will come and change all the windows to aluminium in single or double-glazed units.

Rot

Wooden window frames provide a breeding ground for wet rot. If only part of the frame is affected you may be able to treat it by cutting out the rotten wood well into the good timber and treating the bared surfaces with wood preservative before making good with new timber, also pre-treated with preservative.

If the wood is really rotten, the window is best replaced. Wooden and metal windows are available in the same standard range of sizes, so you may prefer to replace the wooden window frame with one made in aluminium if you can do so without spoiling the character of your property.

The best protection against rot in wooden windows is to keep them well painted and free from damp.

Jammed and twisted windows

Casement windows sometimes become stiff to open as a result of having been allowed to clog up with paint. At the first sign of jamming, it is wise to strip off the layers of old paint with a chemical paint stripper, prime and re-paint. If you just keep on thumping at the window to open it by force, if it is metal you will probably end up with a twisted frame. A wooden frame will break and so will the glass.

If a frame has become twisted and you want to have a go at repairing it yourself, find which part of the window is meeting the surround first and put in a wedge at this point. Then tap the window

gently shut. Take care, because the glass could break; and if tapping gently does not do the job **don't** try tapping harder – send for an expert.

If the window sticks because the wood has swollen, plane as for a sticking door, page 104.

Replacing a broken sash cord

Giving sash window grooves an occasional rub over with soap or a candle helps keep the windows running smoothly. But sooner or later a sash cord is bound to break. To put in a new cord, you will need a helper; sash windows can be heavy once you have removed the beads (the long strips of wood that form the grooves in which the windows slide).

To renew the cord that works a lower window, remove the beading strips by levering them off with a blunt chisel. Raise the window slightly and pull forward so that it comes away from the frame. Support the side with the broken cord by resting it on a table; remove the fillet of timber covering the weight compartment at the bottom of the frame on that side, so you can get out the weight.

Pull out the two pieces of broken cord and use them to measure off a new piece of cord exactly the same length. Fix one end of the new cord to the weight in the same way that the old one was secured.

Tie a small piece of chain or similar flexible weighting material to a length of string – this is often known as a 'mouse' – and insert the weighted end into the casing over the pulley and feed it down until it is visible at the bottom. Fasten the loose end of the string to stop it being drawn into the casing, then remove the mouse from the other end of the string and secure the string to the free end of the new sash cord.

The cord can then be drawn up and over the top of the pulley while the weight is put back in its place in the casing.

Now lift the window back close to the frame, but do not put it in until the cord has been secured in the same way as the old cord and at a similar distance along the groove. Test the window movement up and down to make sure the cord is the right length, then replace the fillet and beading strips.

A broken cord on a top window is dealt with in the same way, except that the lower sash must be drawn out of its frame first so that you can remove the parting beading between the two windows. The top sash can then be swung out of the frame.

GLAZING

Preparations

If you are putting new glass in a broken window, the first thing is to remove all the broken glass from the window frame. Wear heavy gloves and goggles to protect your hands and eyes and wrap the fragments of glass in several layers of newspaper before putting them in the dustbin. Start at the top of the pane and tap out the pieces with a small hammer. If it is an upstairs window, warn people below of the danger.

Once you have removed the glass, chip out all the old hardened putty from the rebates (the angles the glass fits in) by tapping along the edge with a wood chisel. Pull out the brads holding the glass in a wooden frame. If the window has a metal frame, you will find small metal clips at intervals around the rebate. Save these to use again when you are putting in the new pane of glass. If you are working on a wooden window, check for any signs of rot and renew any decayed parts. Similarly, if it is metal deal with rust. Prime any bare wood, and also the rebates to prevent the wood absorbing the oil from the new putty.

The type of glass used for windows depends partly on the size of the pane and partly on the degree of insulation you want for both reducing noise and retaining heat. 3 mm and 4 mm glass are usual for ordinary sized panes, but for picture windows 6 mm plate glass is normally used because it is strong and also free from distortion.

Measure the exact height and width of the window frame and then subtract 3 mm from the distance between the corresponding rebates; check the diagonals, this will tell you whether the frame is square or not. If it isn't you must allow for it in your measurements.

If you want to cut the glass yourself, rather than having a glass merchant do it, it is a good idea to practice on some waste glass first. It is safer to wear a pair of gloves when handling the glass, rather than bare hands.

To cut glass yourself: put the pane on a work bench or well padded table top and place a rule along the line to be cut. Damp the surface of the glass with a little white spirit (flammable – use with care) which will lubricate the wheel of the glass cutter and make the cutting easier.

Hold the cutter between your index and middle fingers and draw a continuous score line along the edge of the rule. Put a couple of matchsticks under the glass along the scored line and press firmly

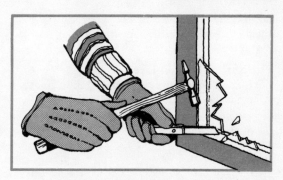
Remove all the old glass carefully

Lay a bed of fresh putty in the rebates

Bed the glass in and fix with sprigs

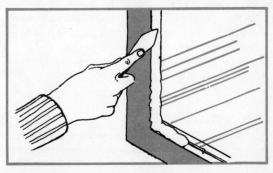
Finish off with more putty, smoothing with a knife

107

downwards on either side of the score. The glass should then snap cleanly along the line.

Fitting the glass in place

For glazing both wood and metal window frames it is best to use universal putty which doesn't need any mixing and can be used straight from the pack.

Lay a bed of putty along all the rebates, then place the pane of glass in position and press evenly round the edges (not in the centre otherwise the glass will break), squeezing out as much putty as possible.

Fix the glass at each side with small sprigs (small headless brads) on a wooden frame, or with metal clips if you are glazing a metal frame window. If necessary add some more putty to give you the thickness you need for smoothing off with your putty knife – a knife with a non-stick finish on the blade is best.

Use the straight side of the point of the knife and draw it across the edge of the frame to press the putty against the glass. Moisten the knife with water occasionally to give a smooth finish. Leave at an angle so that rain water will run off.

Remove any surplus putty, and leave to dry for a week before painting.

Reglazing leaded lights is generally a job for a professional.

Picture framing and hanging

Picture framing falls into three main categories: with glass, without glass and with the picture mounted on blockboard or some similar material so that it is flush with the edges. The disadvantage of the last method is that once you have done it, the picture is framed for all time, so it is really only suitable for posters and inexpensive reproduction prints rather than works of any value.

It is essential to put delicate pastels and water colours under glass in order to safeguard them from dirt and dust, but tougher prints and oil paintings can quite well be framed without glazing.

Go to a professional for framing pictures of value.

THE RIGHT MOUNT

The mount is the 'breathing space' between the edge of the picture and the frame. Not all pictures need this, for instance oils are nearly always framed to the edge and block mounting needs neither mount nor frame. Mounts are made of thin board and can be covered either with paper or with fabric such as canvas, velvet or silk. Do not try to use a synthetic fabric because they seldom lie properly.

A mount can be a complete layer behind the picture or a 'window' in front of it. A window mount also serves the purpose of keeping the glass from touching the surface of the picture.

Small pictures can look more important with the use of a double mount. This is a canvas window with a narrow wooden strip between that and the actual picture. You can buy these strips from artists' materials shops.

Wet mounting

Whether you are going to use a window mount or not, it is usually a good idea to stick a picture to card before you frame it, because it helps to keep it flat in the frame. This is known as wet-mounting.

First apply a thin coat of wallpaper adhesive or

starch-based paste mixed to a thin custard consistency to the back of the picture. Then lay the pasted picture on stiff cardboard and smooth out any wrinkles. Cover the picture with tissue paper and then with hardboard, weight it down and leave for 24 hours to dry.

If you are not going to frame the print under glass, it can then be protected with several thin coats of picture varnish sprayed on from an aerosol can. Picture varnish is available from artists' materials shops.

ASSEMBLY

Cut a cardboard backing board to fit your frame and lay the picture in place, allowing suitable margins. It is an interesting optical illusion that if all the margins of a mount are equal, the bottom one will appear to be narrower than the rest. Making it slightly wider will give a better balance to the eye.

Attach the picture to the backing board with gummed paper tape. Then put on the window mount and the glass front, if you are using one. When cutting a window, you will need a set square and a metal straight edge to be sure that the sides of the picture, the mount and the frame are all parallel and the corners are all right angles.

Be careful to measure the rebate in the wood at the back of the frame exactly before cutting the glass, or ordering it from a glazier. Picture glass is available, which is more expensive than ordinary window glass but thinner and without flaws. A non-reflective quality is also available and is a little more expensive than ordinary picture glass. Clean it carefully with methylated spirit to get rid of any trace of grease.

Now make your assembly front-to-back by laying the glass in the frame rebate, followed by the window mount, the picture, face downwards, and the backing. Seal the gap between the backing card and the frame with wide gummed paper tape.

MAKING A FRAME

Attractive frames can often be found fairly cheaply in second-hand shops, or you can buy picture frame mouldings in sections, complete with rebates for holding the glass and picture, from art supply shops and some timber merchants. You can also buy frames in kit form, usually sold in pairs (two sections of moulding), you just select the lengths you need to make up the frame size for the picture.

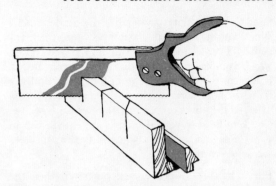

A mitre block will enable you to cut accurate 45° angles for the corners of the frame

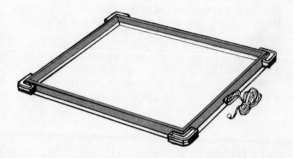

A frame clamp, pulled tight with a cord, holds the frame rigid while the glue dries

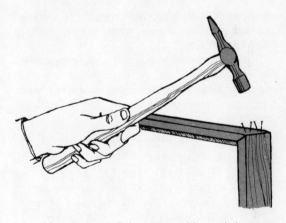

After glueing, nail the corners with panel pins

If you buy moulding by the length, then the important thing is to mitre the corners exactly, and for this you should use a mitre box or block. These have slots cut so that when your tenon saw is fitted into the slots diagonally, the angle is 45°. When you have cut all the mitres, glue them together. Then clamp them firmly in a frame cramp, which comprises four plastic corner pieces with a tough cord which can be pulled tight around the frame to hold it rigidly in position while the glue dries, so the joints cannot be hammered out of line. Check to be sure your diagonals are equal. Tap in panel pins in a dovetail shape, fill in the pin holes and sand down.

For a heavier picture, you can strengthen the join by sawing two small slots across the outer side of the mitre and letting in slips of plywood. Cut the slots with a fine tenon saw so they are the same thickness as the plywood slips. Apply the glue and tap the plywood into place with a mallet. Trim off the projecting plywood when the glue has dried and smooth off with glasspaper.

Finishing the frame
You can either wax the wood for a natural finish, stain it if the grain is attractive enough to stand being highlighted, or prime the wood and paint it.

HANGING
Generally speaking, prints, engravings and small pictures are most effective when they are framed and mounted alike and grouped together on one wall. If two or more larger pictures are to be hung on the same wall, hang them roughly at eye level and with the base of the frames, not the tops, in line with each other.

Light pictures can be hung on picture hooks with hardened nails that are driven into the wall at an angle. For larger pictures you will need screw hooks which are screwed into plugs let into the wall (see page 95).

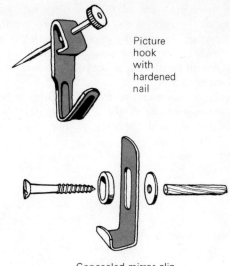

Picture hook with hardened nail

Concealed mirror clip

At the back of the picture frame insert screw eyes and tie a cord between them. The eyes should be inserted just above the half-way mark, because the golden rule of picture hanging is to keep the cord behind the picture, not showing above it. For light pictures use nylon cord; this is available in various grades. Heavy pictures should be supported by special picture wire or hanging plates fixed to the two top corners.

If the combination of cord and screw hooks cause a picture to slope at the bottom towards the wall, you can straighten it by glueing small spacer blocks to the back of the frame. You may find, however, that a picture framed under glass is less affected by reflections if it does not hang completely flush.

HANGING MIRRORS
Framed mirrors can be hung on picture hooks or plugged screws just like a picture. **Corner clips** are specially designed for frameless mirrors. One type has screw holes that leave the screw heads visible. The other is a concealed fitting in which the clips slide into place (and lift up again) after the glass has been positioned.

> ### A HINT ON FIXING MIRRORS TO TILED BATHROOM WALLS
> Fix a small piece of sticking plaster over the drilling position and mark the exact place for the hole on the plaster. Push the drill bit firmly against the mark, and you will find it goes in without slipping or skidding.

Electrical safety

This information refers to Great Britain only. Elsewhere contact your local electricity authority for information. In some countries it is illegal to carry out any electrical work unless you are a qualified electrician.

MAINS WIRING
Good wiring is the first essential of electrical safety. A well wired house should have the right – and the right number of – electrical circuits to take all the equipment that will be used. These may include special circuits for a cooker and an immersion water heater as well as one or more ring circuits. Each ring circuit is a single loop of cable designed to take any number of plug-in appliances up to a total load of 7,200 watts; this is the maximum amount of electricity it can supply at any one time. Lighting has a separate circuit (not a ring circuit) of its own.

Colour coding
Ring circuit cables are usually covered with a grey or off-white insulating material; inside this the supply wires are colour coded
Live : red
Neutral : black
Earth : usually a bare wire.

Rewiring
Electrical wiring can become faulty with age. So you should have the wiring of your house inspected every five or ten years (depending how old it is). After 25 years it is likely that it will need renewing.

Basic wiring, or rewiring, should always be carried out by an approved electrical contractor on the list of the National Inspection Council for Electrical Contracting. Your nearest Electricity Board shop will be able to give you a local name from their list.

PLUGS AND FLEXES
Plugs, too, need to be properly wired but it is simple to deal with these yourself (see page 115). Always bear in mind the colour coding for flexes, which is different from that for main supply wiring:

Live : brown
Neutral : blue
Earth : green/yellow

Never use a two-pin plug to connect with a three-wire flex, and do not use the earth terminal when connecting a double insulated appliance which has a two-wire flex – such as a vacuum cleaner or a food mixer – to a three-pin plug. Double insulated appliances are marked with a ▣ symbol on the nameplate.

Flexes should always be kept in good condition; have any damaged or frayed flex replaced rather than trying to repair it with insulating tape (see page 116). Make sure the flex is the right length, neither too short nor trailing. Never allow a flex to get wet, or to pass over a hot area. Do not run flex under a carpet; walking on it can wreck a wire inside the insulation.

Cartridge fuses
Most modern plugs carry their own cartridge fuses which will 'blow' in the case of trouble without affecting the other outlets. It is important, however, to use the correct size fuse for the appliance to which the plug is connected. Use a 3-amp fuse (coloured red) for anything up to 720 watts, such as lamps and electric blankets and a 13-amp fuse (coloured brown) for appliances with a loading of over 720 watts up to 3000 watts – eg kettle, iron, radiant heater or washing machine. Using too small a fuse will cause it to blow. Refrigerators, freezers and vacuum cleaners usually have a 13-amp fuse, even though the loading is below 720 watts because their motors need a high starting current. A colour television needs a 13-amp fuse.

SIMPLE SAFETY PRECAUTIONS
Unplug
Always unplug appliances that are not in use, particularly TV and radio sets. This is important because if there is any fault in the wiring or components in the set, electricity will continue to flow into the appliance and cause overheating and possibly a fire. Switch off the appliance **before** you pull the plug from the socket, as it might spark and cause damage or give you a shock.

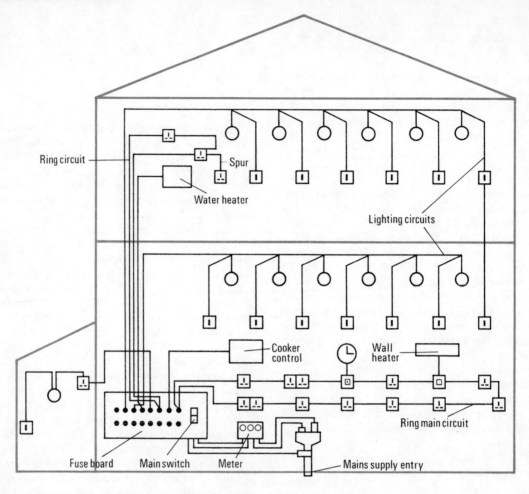

Ring circuit

Spur

Water heater

Lighting circuits

Cooker
control

Wall
heater

Ring main circuit

Fuse board   Main switch   Meter   Mains supply entry

A typical domestic wiring installation, showing ring circuits for plug-in appliances, separate lighting circuits and heavy duty circuits for major appliances such as cooker and water heater

Do not overload

It is often tempting to use a multi-plug adaptor, but if you do, be careful not to overload the socket. It is safer to have another socket put in.

Follow the instructions

When shopping for new electrical equipment, always look for a BEAB (British Electrotechnical Approvals Board) label on anything you buy. It means that an identical sample of the model has been successfully tested by the Board and that it meets the relevant British Standard Specification.

The tests are designed to check that the appliance can be handled normally without giving an electric

shock or causing a fire. But take note of the word 'normally'. Misuse is not only dropping things, but also using them carelessly or in the wrong way. Always check the manufacturer's instructions **before** you switch on a new appliance.

Electric heaters If you have children or old people in the house, electric fires should be placed behind a fire guard. Do not leave fires near curtains or upholstery. Never use a portable electric fire in a bathroom, or any other appliance with the exception of a shaver in a special socket and a radiant heater fixed to the wall out of reach of wet hands (switches for this and for lighting fittings must be of the pull-cord type or fitted outside the bathroom door). Do not drape damp clothing or washing over heaters to dry unless, like towel rails, they are designed for the purpose.

Kettle Always see that the element in the kettle is covered by water before you switch on. Switch off and withdraw the connection from the kettle before filling or pouring out. Never leave the flex un-plugged from the kettle but still plugged into a switched-on socket. Do not let the flex get wet.

Washing machine Be sure the machine is connected to the supply with a properly installed three-pin plug connection.

Refrigerator Do not cover ventilation areas of refrigerators and freezers. This may cause over-heating.

Cooker Do not try and clean the cooker (or any other electrical gadget) without first switching off. Never, never leave a deep-fat fryer unattended. Do not hang tea towels over the cooker to dry.

Toaster Do not try and prise wedged toast from a toaster; switch off, turn it upside down and tap gently to dislodge it.

Steam iron Switch off and unplug the steam iron before filling or re-filling it with water.

Electric blanket Always read the instructions carefully. Do not crease or fold the blanket or leave heavy things on it while it is switched on. Do not wash the blanket unless the label is clearly marked 'washable'. Send it back to the manufacturer for servicing every other year.

Lamps If you want to wash a lampshade, take it off the fitting first. Most lampshades are sold with an indication of the wattage bulb that can be used with them. Too powerful a bulb in certain types of lampshade can cause a fire.

CHILDREN AND ELECTRICITY
Never let children tamper with anything electrical. Since toddlers love to poke their fingers into holes, if you have 5- or 15-amp old-type sockets it is wisest to buy some of the special plastic plugs available, which can be used to close the sockets when they are not in use. (Modern socket outlets have shutters which close automatically when the plug is removed.)

If your washing machine has a power wringer, be especially careful to keep small children well away.

Electrician's tools

To cope with electrical maintenance and repairs in the average house requires only a small tool kit. The main point is to keep the tools where they can be quickly and easily to hand especially if a fuse has blown and you are left in complete darkness. Do not mix the tools up with others in your toolbox, keep them separately in a special box or drawer or better still hanging up near the fuse box and mains switch.

The tool kit should contain a medium **screwdriver** with a 6 mm blade and a smaller one with a

3 mm blade; preferably both of these should have plastic handles and insulation that projects about halfway down the shaft.

A pair of **pliers** with insulated handles and cutting edges will deal with twisting up the wire strands of flexes and cables and cutting through them.

Removing the insulation from flex is best carried out with a **wire stripping tool** and there are several different types to choose from in a reasonable price range.

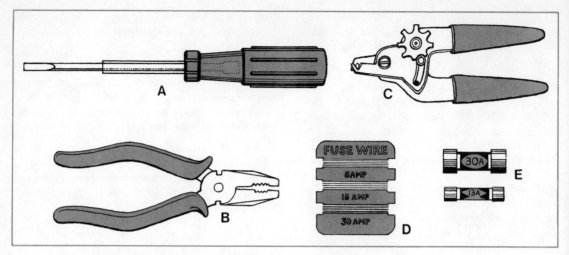

A. Insulated screwdriver B. Insulated pliers C. Wire stripper D. Fuse wires E. Cartridge fuses

A **sharp knife** is needed for cutting and trimming away the outer insulation from the flex and the braiding. When using a knife take care not to damage the insulation on core wires.

A **torch** completes the kit – wherever you decide to keep the tools make sure the torch is lodged near the fuse box. Check it now and again to make sure it works and the batteries have not run down.

Finally have a selection of **cartridge fuses** of all the sizes used in your fuse box or a card of **fuse wires** of different gauges for the rewirable types of fuse carrier.

Basic electrical repairs

REPAIRING A FUSE
Ring circuit wiring A modern ring circuit has two types of fuse as a protection against overloading – a small cartridge fuse in each plug and a main fuse in the consumer unit or fuse board. In houses with modern wiring, if an appliance stops working, switch off at once, both at the appliance itself and at the socket outlet. Remove the plug, unscrew the top, take out the cartridge fuse and click in a new one. Be sure you use a fuse with the correct rating (3- or 13-amp) for the job. Do not rely on the blown fuse as a guide, it may have been wrong in the first place. On most appliances you will find the wattage rating plate either on the base or on the back. For the correct fuse to use, see page 111.

If when you have put in a new fuse you find the

114

appliance still does not work, it is worth checking to see if the new fuse itself is working. You can do this quite simply by taking the base of a metal torch and placing one end of the fuse on the battery and the other end on the torch casing. Switch on the torch and if the bulb does not light, then your new fuse is a dud. Alternatively, try the fuse in another plug on a piece of equipment you know is working.

If the fuse is working, and the main fuse is intact, then have the appliance itself checked by a qualified electrician.

Radial circuit wiring If you live in old property or if you still have the old type of radial circuit wiring your plugs will be the round-pin, unfused type and you will probably have an old-type fuse board and switch. In this case if trouble occurs, eg if an appliance stops working, you will have to trace the fault back to the fuse box. Switch off the appliance and remove the plug from the socket. Find the main switch controlling the circuit and switch this off. Trace the blown fuse in the fuse box by removing one fuse at a time. The blown one will be immediately noticeable by the melted fuse wire and blackened fuse holder. Replace it with fuse wire of the correct size following the procedure described below under **Main fuses**.

Main fuses

Make the job of finding a blown fuse easier by labelling each fuse in the box beforehand so that it is easy to tell which fuse belongs to which circuit and which rooms or appliances it serves. Always have in your tool kit at least one spare cartridge fuse of all sizes or a card with the different sizes of fuse wire used in your fuse board.

If a main fuse blows, first **turn off the main switch**. This may be on the consumer unit or on a separate switch box nearby.

There are three types of main fuse you may find in your fuse box. A modern fuse unit will have cartridge fuses.

A cartridge fuse is an insulated cylinder with a cap at each end like a plug cartridge, but with a different wattage and bigger diameter. The fuse carriers are colour coded:

5-amp: white (for lighting)
15-amp: blue (for immersion heaters and other 3 kw circuits)

20-amp: yellow (for some types of water heater)
30-amp: red (for ring circuits)
45-amp: green (for cookers).

These you replace in the same way as plug fuses (above).

An older-type fuse unit may have protected fuses or bridge fuses.

In a protected fuse, the wire is threaded through a protected porcelain cover. You will need to remove this cover by loosening the screw at the end to see if the wire is burnt. If so, thread through a new piece of wire of the correct current rating. Do not strain the wire too much when tightening the terminals.

In a bridge fuse, the wire is held at either end of a small hump, or bridge. If the fuse has blown you will be able to see that the wire has broken or melted. Replace it as for a protected fuse.

Circuit breakers

Some of the newer systems have miniature circuit breakers. Looking like ordinary switches or push buttons, they automatically flick themselves off if any circuit is overloaded, or if a fault in an appliance fails to blow the plug or socket fuse. Instead of the troublesome business of rewiring a fuse carrier, the circuit can be brought back into use simply by pressing the switch down or pushing the button in.

'Company fuse'

If you suspect the 'company fuse', in the Electricity Board's own sealed unit, has blown call the Electricity Board's emergency service.

WIRING A PLUG

The standard 13-amp plug has three square pins which fit into the mains outlet socket. The three wires in the flex are colour coded:
Live: brown
Neutral: blue
Earth: green/yellow.
These connect to the terminals in the plug marked L, N and E. (Some older appliances may carry the now obsolete colour coding. This was: Live: red; Neutral: black; Earth: green.)

Wiring a plug is quite straightforward, but if you are in any doubt whatsoever, stop at once and get expert advice.

1 Using an electrician's screwdriver with an insulated plastic handle, undo the main centre screw

and loosen the cord grip screws. Take off the plug cover.

2 Push the cord grip to one side and loosen the three terminal screws. Remove the cartridge fuse from its clips and put it aside.

3 With a sharp knife or wire strippers carefully remove about 5 cm of outer sleeving from the flex of the appliance to which you are fitting the plug. Trim the three cores back about 1 cm and make neat the bare wires by twisting them into a loop.

4 Slip the flex under the cord grip and fix the bare wires into each terminal hole or under washers held down by screws, making sure they are connected to the correct terminal. Tighten the cord grip screws. Replace the cartridge fuse and screw the plug cover back. The procedure for replacing a round pin plug is similar, except that there will be no cartridge fuse.

Never connect three-core flex to a two-pin plug.

REPLACING A FLEX

While fitting a plug is simple enough, there may be times when you want to replace a flex, either because the existing one is worn, or you want to alter its length, and this can be more difficult.

On some appliances the terminals are hard to get at, so it is a good idea to take a look before you spend money on a new flex. Unplug the appliance and undo the screws on the cover so that you can see where the flex is connected inside. If the appliance is assembled in such a way that you would have to take it to pieces to connect another flex, do not attempt it. Get in touch with the manufacturer and if possible get him to do it. If that is not possible, take it to a qualified electrician. If the terminals are easy to get at, you will be able to do the job yourself.

When buying a new flex, make absolutely certain that you buy the right grade for the appliance. Take the old flex with you to be sure. Flexes measured in millimetres and the commonly used grades are: $0.5 \, mm^2$ (3-amp) for up to 700 watts

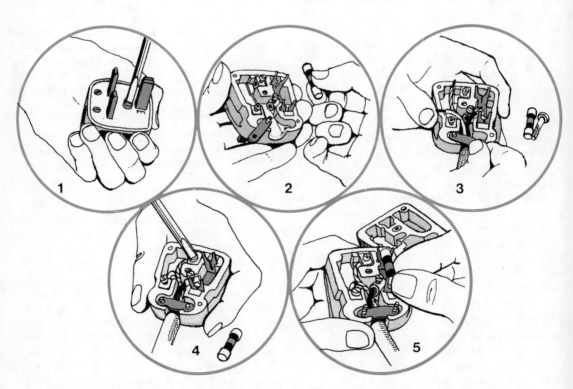

Wiring a plug. 1. Loosen the centre screw and cord grip screws 2. Remove the plug cover, push the cord grip aside and take out the fuse 3. Strip and trim the wires so that they reach the terminals comfortably. Check colour coding (*see page 115*) 4. Fasten the flex under the cord grip and screw the wires firmly into the terminals. Check colour coding again 5. Replace the cartridge fuse and screw the plug cover on

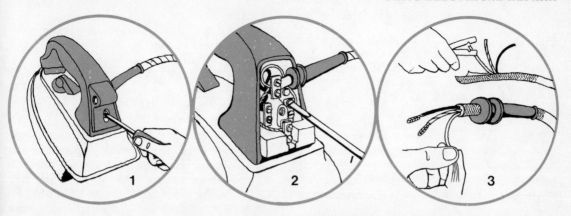

Replacing a flex. 1. Undo the screws on the appliance cover **2.** Unscrew the terminals and remove the flex. If the terminals are not marked, note carefully which is which **3.** Strip back the outer casing of the new flex with a knife and pare the insulation from the core wires with a wire stripper. Twist the ends of the bare wires neatly before inserting into the terminals. Check the colour coding

(for lamps, radios and blankets); 0·75 mm^2 (6-amp) for up to 1400 watts (for irons, refrigerators and small fires); 1·5 mm^2 (13-amp) for up to 3000 watts (for two bar fires and kettles). If you use flex that you have been storing, be sure not to use the old, twisted, unsheathed type for appliances.

If your appliance is double insulated it will be marked ▣ on the label. There will be two cores inside the flex, live and neutral, and no earth wire. If you have a three-core flex, the third, green/yellow core is connected to the earth terminal in addition to the brown to live and blue to neutral.

Always disconnect the appliance before you begin. Then follow this step-by-step guide (the example given is for an iron):

1 Undo the screws on the cover of the appliance to reveal where the cord and cores enter through the rubber grommet to the terminal connectors.

2 Unscrew each of the terminal screws and see which core goes into which terminal. Remove the cores in turn. Remember blue: neutral; yellow/green: earth; brown: live.

3 On your new flex, strip back about 5 cm of outer casing with a knife and carefully pare about 1 cm of the insulating material off each core using a wire stripper. Twist each of the bare wires neatly and secure them into the correct terminals. Replace the cover and screw tight.

EXTENDING A FLEX
Never extend a flex by joining wires with insulating tape. If you are extending a three-core flex, use a flex connector with an earth terminal.

First remove the plug. Remove the plastic cover from the connector, taking care loose terminals do not drop out. If necessary, carefully trim back the outer cover of the flex to expose the inner wires. Push the flex through the rubber sleeve in the connector and pull it through far enough to connect it to the terminals. Trim the insulation of the core away if necessary.

Twist the strands of wires together, connect them to the correct terminals in the flex connector. Make sure that you connect the green/yellow wire to the earth terminal. Next, connect the new length of flex to the terminals. If existing flex has the old colour code, connect new flex colours: brown to red; blue to black; green/yellow to green.

For power tools and other portable appliances it is better to use an extension lead. Before using, make sure the lead is fully unwound from the reel, or it will heat up.

Repairing small appliances

When any electrical appliance fails to work, first check the power supply at the socket, then check the plug, the fuse and the flex. Only when you have proved that all these are in good working order can you be sure that the fault lies in the appliance itself.

The socket Check the socket and power supply by plugging in another appliance, eg a table lamp – and one you know is working – at the same point. If this does not work either it is likely that a fuse-box fuse has blown. Switch off the current at the main switch and replace the blown fuse as described on page 115.

The fuse The appliance may have a cartridge fused plug. Try replacing the cartridge, again with one you know is working.

The plug To check the plug, make sure that the wires are firmly attached to the terminals. Remove the plug cover and lift each wire carefully with the end of a screwdriver to check that it is not loose or broken.

The flex Examine the flex for signs of damage or wear. If when you bend the flex you find a point where it bends more easily, this may indicate a broken wire inside the insulation. Replacing a flex is described on page 116.
Always unplug an appliance before attempting any repairs. Should this be impossible, seek professional advice.

ELECTRIC KETTLES:
replacing the element
The element in an electric kettle is held in place by a threaded shroud. To remove, disconnect the kettle from the electricity supply, hold the element inside the kettle with one hand and unscrew the shroud with the other. Still holding the element, prise off the outside fibre washer with a screwdriver and then twist out the element.

Remove the scale and grease or dirt from round the plug hole with detergent and a rag. If this does not remove the scale, use fine steel wool, but take care not to damage the finish on the body of the kettle. Insert the new element, remembering to put on the rubber washer first and see that it is properly seated against the flange. Slip the fibre washer on the flange and screw the shroud tight. Use a cloth to tighten up, fill the kettle with water and check for leaks, then plug in and test.

ELECTRIC FIRES: replacing the element

Wire coil element fires
Disconnect the fire from the electricity supply. Squeeze the bars of the guard gently inwards to prise it from the fire casing and remove. In some models there are four securing screws which will have to be removed first. Unscrew the terminals at both ends and remove the element from its brackets.

Buy a new element of the same type and size. Replace the new element using the reverse procedure, first wiping over the reflector with a soft cloth moistened in washing-up liquid solution. Buff up with a soft duster.

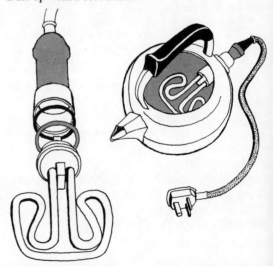

To insert a new element, seat the rubber washer first, put the element in the kettle then add the fibre washer and screw on the shroud

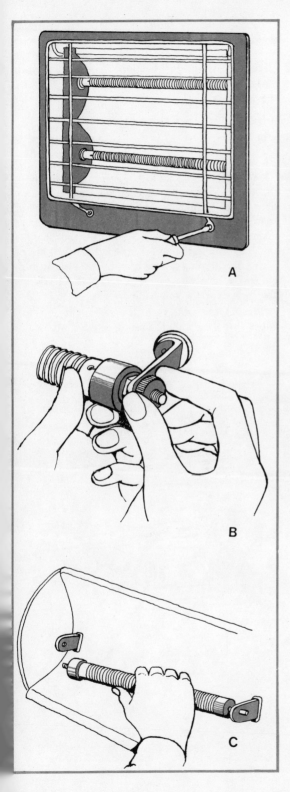

A. Remove the fire guard to get at the elements.
B. Unscrew the terminal nut to remove the faulty element. **C.** Replace with a new element of the same type

Glass rod element fires

Glass rod enclosed element fires are often found wall mounted in bathrooms and kitchens. The element is protected by a cover plate at each end. Disconnect the electricity supply. Press top and bottom of cover plate to remove, then slide it outwards to uncover the terminal brackets. You may find that some of these plates are fixed to the frame by screws at the top and bottom. Unscrew both terminal nuts and carefully lift out the glass-covered element.

Re-fit the new one using the reverse procedure, taking care not to handle the glass section of the element.

FAN HEATERS AND CONVECTORS

Apart from checking the connections at the plug and replacing a fuse, these should always be repaired by a qualified electrician.

VACUUM CLEANERS:

replacing the belt on an upright cleaner

New belts are usually available from Electricity Board shops and department stores – make sure you buy the right one for your particular model of cleaner. Details are often given on the nameplate.

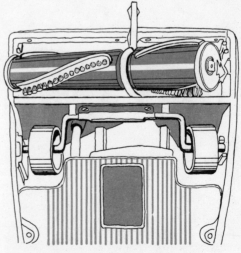

Unclip the roller to remove the old belt

119

Fit the new belt round the centre slot and twist clockwise round the drive shaft

Disconnect the cleaner from the electricity supply, then unclip the cover plate from the front of the cleaner. Remove the belt from the drive shaft and turn the cleaner on its side. Unscrew the metal shield over the brush roller. Unclip the roller and slip off the old belt.

Fit the new belt round the slot in the centre of the roller brush and then place the roller in position in the cleaner. Replace the metal shield. Put the cleaner in an upright position, then twist the belt clockwise round the drive shaft. Finally, replace the cover plate.

LIGHTING

Fluorescent tubes

Fluorescent tubes should last about 5000 hours. If the tube glows white at each end, but does not light when switched on, the starter (automatic switch) is faulty and must be replaced. In most cases you will find the starter on top of the casing or under a cover in the body of the light; it looks like a little tubular plug. Remove it by twisting it anti-clockwise, and buy a new one – be sure you get the right type for your tube, ie 40w or 80w.

Fluorescent tubes that glow red at the ends and tubes that flicker should be replaced. Tubes come

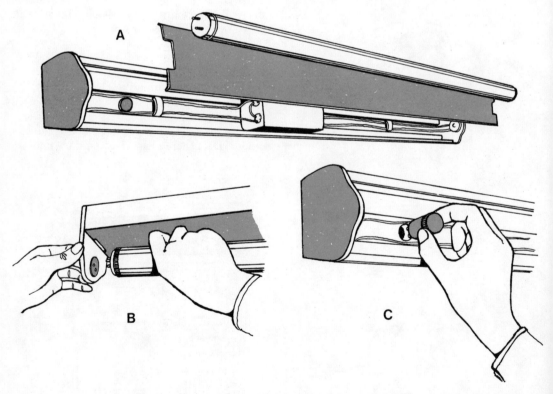

A. All wiring is enclosed in the body of the light, which screws directly to wall or ceiling B. To remove the tube grasp it carefully and put pressure along its length to release spring-loaded lamp holders C. If the tube glows white at each end but will not light replace the starter

with either a bayonet fitting (two little lugs that fit into corresponding slots on the holder) or a two-pin lamp cap, often referred to as a bi-pin.

To remove a faulty bayonet fitting tube first turn the light switch to 'off'; slide back the metal or plastic covers at each end of the tube to expose the lamp holder. Lift out the tube by pressing it against the spring-loaded holders at each end and twisting it anti-clockwise. Replace with a new tube.

Bi-pin tubes have spring-loaded lampholders each end. To remove the tube, first turn the light switch to 'off', then hold the tube with one hand and put pressure along its length while you ease it out of the end brackets; alternatively give the tube half a turn and the pins will slot out at the bottom of the holder. Lift it out carefully so you do not damage the bi-pins, which are fairly delicate. Replace with a new tube.

Christmas tree lights
Older-type Christmas tree lights are wired in series, and if one bulb has failed or come loose the whole lot go out. Tracking down the faulty bulb is a fiddly business, so before you start make sure that the trouble is not in the plug (see page 118).

If the plug is in working order, first try tightening one bulb after the other to see if the lights come on again. If this does not do the trick, take a spare bulb (one that you know is working) and exchange it for each bulb in turn until the set lights up again. Remember to switch off while taking out and putting in the bulb.

Lighting

If you want to modernise and improve the lighting of a house you are almost bound to need extra points. Having these professionally installed can be expensive, so where possible, consider plugging extra lights into the outlet sockets on your main ring circuit. If you have to have new lighting points installed, employ a professional and budget for some re-decoration.

For any major electrical work you should employ a contractor who is enrolled with the National Inspection Council for Electrical Installation Contractors. Your local Electricity Board shop will have a list.

FILAMENT AND FLUORESCENT LIGHTING
There are two main types of electric lamp – the tungsten filament type, usually in the form of light bulbs but also available as tubes, and fluorescent tubes.

Filament type electric light bulbs are either clear, pearl or silica-coated. Pearl bulbs are the most popular because they are just as efficient as clear bulbs but give a softer, less glaring, light. Silica-coated bulbs give a softer light still and are the best choice for any fittings where the bulb can be seen.

Bulbs come with ratings from 5 watts to 200 watts, and the greater the wattage the greater the light given out. The heat given off is also greater – which is why if a lampshade is labelled '60w max' you should not put a higher rated bulb in it as the shade could be singed or even catch fire.

Fluorescent tubes give more than double the amount of light – measured as lumens per watt – for the same amount of current as filament lights. Some give as much as three or four times the amount of light, but these are not satisfactory for use in all areas in the home as they give a cold, hard light. The tubes called Softone 27 and Deluxe Warm White are the closest to filament lighting and so blend well when you have both sorts of lighting together or in adjoining rooms.

HOW MUCH LIGHT
As a general guide a room lit by filament lighting is said to need 20 watts per square metre, and one lit by fluorescent lighting 10 watts per square metre, but this is an over-simplification. The important thing is to get the right amount of light in the right places so you can see to do what you want to do in safety and comfort.

It is important to bear in mind, too, that people's

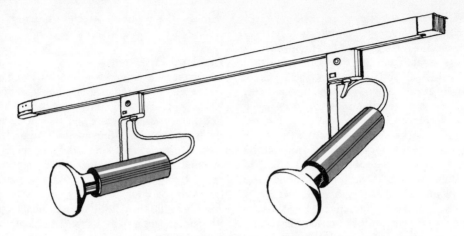

A lighting track with moveable spotlights gives flexible lighting in any room

eyesight deteriorates as they grow older, and in order to read comfortably someone of 60 will need twice as much light as someone of 40.

Fittings and shades
Lighting shops and departments are crammed with a selection of light fittings, lamps and shades; the choice is up to you. It is worth a thought, though, that if you do not want to waste the light you are paying for, shades with large openings at the top and bottom will obviously give you more useful light than those with smaller ones. You also get more light from shades that are white inside. Hesitate before buying shades that give out a coloured light, they can be unflattering as well as uneconomic. And, of course, different rooms call for different kinds of lighting.

Living room Here it is pleasant to be able to ring the changes between lighting that makes the room bright and welcoming when you are giving a party and cosy and intimate for a quiet family evening at home. A quick way of achieving this is to replace an ordinary light switch with a dimmer switch which can raise or lower the light to the intensity you require.

Hidden strip lighting does more than anything to give a room a restful glow – fix it above pelmets or recessed into shelves. Any prized object picked out with a spotlight will take on new importance, and by careful angling you can make sure the shadows fall on corners to which you do not want to draw attention.

If you are stuck with a central ceiling fitting,

consider lengthening the flex and looping it across to a corner where you can fix a more flattering fitting or a spotlight. Alternatively you could have a lighting track connected to the existing point which allows a number of fittings to be placed anywhere along its length. But consult an electrician – too many fittings could result in a blown fuse.

Remember that you get quite a different view of a room when you are sitting down, so check that none of your shades or fittings lets the bulb shine in your eyes or trouble you with glare. See opposite for the recommended positioning of standard and table lamps.

Dining room Whether your dining room is a separate room or a dining area in your main living room, you will need a light over the table so that you can see what you are eating. The simplest solution is probably a 100w pendant lamp hung low so most of its light falls on the table below eye level – or one on a rise-and-fall suspension that allows the height to be adjusted to suit the occasion.

For a formal dining room a chandelier, possibly with a dimmer switch so the candles can be dimmed later in the meal, can look impressive. Or if you prefer to keep the space above the table clear the answer could be one or two downlights recessed into the ceiling.

You will also need a soft background light, perhaps provided by wall fittings, or a table lamp on the sideboard which will help you see to carve.

Hallway and stairs This is sometimes a difficult area to light because of the many corners and

122

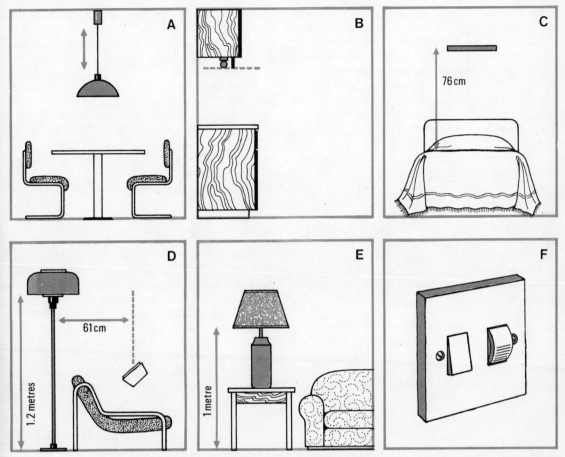

A. A rise and fall unit allows you to adjust the height of a lamp over the dining table B. Screen kitchen worktop lighting behind a pelmet to prevent dazzle C. Position bed lights to give a good reading position D. Position a standard lamp to give maximum light on book or work E. A table lamp should also be high enough to cast a downward light on close work F. A dimmer switch gives a convenient choice of lighting intensity

angles, which cause shadows. It is often possible to overcome the problem with a multi-rose ceiling light with two or three lights that can be pointed in different directions. This way the lighting can be warm and welcoming yet not so dim your guests bump into the umbrella stand.

Stairs should be really well lit to ensure that accidents do not happen. Lighting should show up both where the stair is and how high it is. The best way to do this is to have a good 100w light at the top of the flight to show up the edges of the treads and some general illumination from the bottom to take the deceptive shadows off the risers.

Upstairs landings should be clearly lit with 60w or 40w bulbs, depending on the number of fittings. It is sensible to have two-way switches in the hall and on the landing so you can control the light from wherever you happen to be.

Bedroom Two-way switches are useful here, too, so you can control the main light once you are in bed.

Bed lights must give you enough light to let you read comfortably, so if they are fixed to the wall they should not be positioned too low (see above). A double bed or twin beds should have two fittings, switched independently.

Fix a good light by the dressing-table mirror and make sure it is you not the mirror that is being lit. It is best to have a light both sides, shielded to prevent glare. For a full-length mirror long vertical strips, again on both sides, make a good solution.

If you are using fluorescent tubes, Deluxe Natural can be a good colour choice as it is the kindest one to the complexion but Deluxe Warm White gives the closest effect to ordinary tungsten lighting and is therefore good for making up for the evening.

An interior cupboard light which switches on when the door is opened costs very little to run and is a great convenience in wardrobes and fitted cupboards (good, too, for the glory hole under the stairs).

In a small child's bedroom, a light on a dimmer switch is safer than a nightlight.

Bathroom Safety is the vital factor here, and all electric fittings (with the exception of specially designed shaver sockets) must have pull-cord switches or have the switch outside the bathroom door. For the main ceiling light you can buy a special damp-proof globe with rust-proof metal parts. Many bathroom wall cabinets incorporate their own built-in lighting.

Kitchen Here is another place to consider maximum safety, not only because of electrical hazards but because you may slip or cut yourself if you cannot see properly. Where cupboards project over worktops, fit small fluorescent tubes or tubular tungsten lamps under the front edge and screen them with a small pelmet. This way you will not stand in your own light while you are preparing food.

Some cookers have their own hob lights, but otherwise use a spotlight to illuminate the hob if necessary.

If you are using fluorescent tubes in the kitchen, Deluxe Warm White is the best colour. Avoid the tube that is called Daylight, and also White; these emphasize yellow and green and mute red in a way that makes food look its least attractive.

If you eat in the kitchen you will need a light over the table. Or if your kitchen is small you could fix a spotlight to shine on the table while leaving the working parts of the kitchen dim.

Outside lighting Any lights outside the house must be weather-proofed and are best controlled by switches inside the house.

Try and position a porch light so it illuminates the name or number of your house to guide first-time guests, as well as helping you see to put your key in the lock. An illuminated bell push, correctly positioned, also helps you to locate the keyhole.

Ideally, have lights on all the outside walls of the house because burglars tend to avoid lit-up houses.

Plumbing tools

Simple plumbing is not a problem for the handyman but you should be aware of the water authority regulations. These are fairly strict and you should check them before you attempt anything which is more complicated than re-washering a tap or lavatory cistern.

On the whole plumbing tools are fairly expensive items and often do not warrant buying for 'one off' jobs, in which case it is best to consider hiring them. The tools listed below are probably the minimum needed for most jobs in the house and would double up if need be for use on the car and in the garden, eg repairs to the lawnmower or fixing heavy gates and doors, hinges etc.

An adjustable spanner is probably one of the most useful tools for general purpose and plumbing use. A medium size one is the 20 cm version with jaws that open up to about 2·5 cm. This will be useful for copper pipe compression fittings and other nuts and bolts.

Open ended spanners are for fine work where an adjustable spanner would probably cause damage to the nut or bolt head. A set of these – six spanners in sizes from ¼in to 1 in BSW will deal with most nuts you are likely to find inside and outside the house. Anything in between can be loosened carefully using the adjustable spanner.

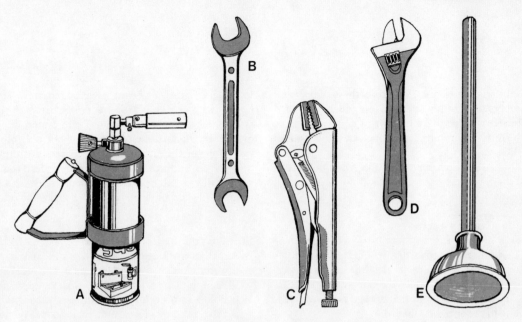

A. Butane blowtorch B. Open ended spanner C. Adjustable grip D. Adjustable spanner E. Cup-plunger

A pair of pliers There is no need to duplicate these if you already have a good pair in your toolkit for electrical work. These are needed for cutting wire, pulling out splitpins and other similar jobs. Try not to use them for undoing nuts, they will slip and damage the nut and the thread of the bolt.

A pair of adjustable grips has jaws that can be locked on to a bolt, or piece of tube or bar to clamp it in position so you have a free hand to manipulate another spanner. This is a very useful tool for removing rusted nuts and bolts, or loosening up corroded parts, because when it is clamped on to the part, it grips well and a lot of leverage can be applied without it slipping off.

A blowtorch with butane gas cartridges is another utility tool. It has many uses for the handyman, but in plumbing is ideal for 'sweating' on the solder type copper water pipe fittings and for heating up corroded fittings to loosen them. It is a very easy tool to handle but take care not to use it near flammable materials or leave it alight but unattended. Take particular care not to use it near gas pipes or a car petrol tank. Other types of blowtorch are equally useful but not so convenient.

Finally a **medium size cup-plunger** is necessary for dealing with lavatory and sink blockages; take care when using it in the lavatory otherwise you will damage the glazed finish on the pan.

Simple plumbing

Plumbing repairs are expensive these days, and plumbers are not always available when you need them. So it helps to know how to cope with some of the minor plumbing faults that can occur around the house.

Before you reach for your tools, though, it is as well to have some idea as to how a plumbing system works.

The hot water system

A domestic hot water system works on the principle that water expands when it is heated and so becomes lighter and rises to the top of the boiler. From the top of the boiler the hot water makes its way up the flow pipe to the storage tank, which is usually in the airing cupboard.

As the hot water rises up the flow pipe, cold water from the hot water storage tank travels down another pipe, known as the return pipe, into the bottom of the boiler to take its place. This circulation continues until all the water in the tank is hot. If none of this hot water is drawn off through the taps, you might expect that the water in the tank would eventually boil. But to prevent this there is another pipe, called the expansion and vent pipe, which is fitted to the top of the hot water storage tank to take the unused hot water and run it back into the cold water storage cistern, which is normally in the roof. The draw-off pipe which supplies hot water to the taps is connected to the top of the storage cylinder, where the water is hottest.

This is known as a direct hot water system, in which the water is heated in the boiler, then stored in the hot water tank and used as required. In a house with water-heated radiators, an indirect system is used. Here, because the water which heats the radiators is circulated but not drawn off, the water for the taps is heated separately with the help of an additional hot water cylinder, sometimes called a calorifier but normally known as an indirect heater, situated inside the main hot water cylinder.

Storage and lavatory cisterns

Every modern house has two types of cistern. A cold water storage cistern (the one in the roof) and wc flushing cisterns, the type used in lavatories. Water flow into both types of cistern is controlled by a valve fixed to a lever and a ball float. The float rises as the cistern fills, the other end slides along an arm until it presses on a piston which closes the water inlet. To prevent a flood if the valve sticks or breaks, an overflow pipe is fitted inside the tank near the top, leading to the outside of the house.

AN OVERFLOWING CISTERN

An overflowing cistern may be only a minor domestic disaster, nevertheless it is one that calls for a speedy repair.

One cause can be that the float arm is set too high. Turn off the water supply to the cistern before you start to make adjustments. (The supply may be direct from the mains or from the storage cistern.) Then loosen the nut holding the ball in place and move the ball down 1 cm. If the ball is not attached in such a way that it can be moved

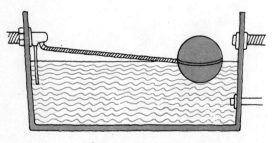

Storage water cistern

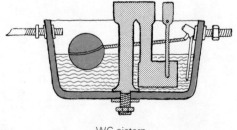

WC cistern

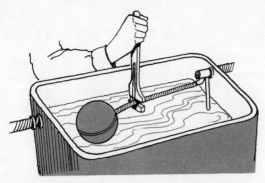

Bend the arm to adjust the ball valve

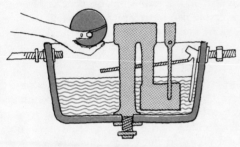

If the ball float is faulty, screw on a new one

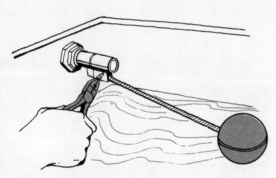

Remove the split pin to take off the float arm

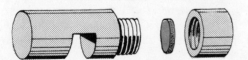

Replace the valve washer if worn or perished

(*Right*) Mains pressure may be enough to force the airlock out of the system

then, using a spanner or pliers, carefully bend the arm down near the ball end by about 1 cm. This will cause the water to be cut off at a lower level in the tank.

If this does not cure the fault, check the ball itself. It may be corroded or split and letting in the water. If so unscrew the ball and replace it with a new one, preferably plastic. These are available from ironmongers and DIY stores. If the repair is going to take more than a few moments, extinguish all forms of water heating or central heating boiler.

A third possible reason for an over-flowing cistern – or a flush which sticks or fails altogether – can be that the washer in the inlet valve is worn or dirty. Turn off the water supplying the cistern, close and remove the split pin and take out the piston. Clean off with fine steel wool.

Unscrew the end cap of the valve and remove the rubber washer. If it is worn or perished, re-place it with a new one. Replace the piston, and refit the split pin to the arm and valve assembly. Turn on the water supply and check to see if the fault is cured.

If you have a modern valve it is a simple job to unscrew the end cap with a pair of grips, and fit a new diaphragm. Assemble again and tighten the screw cap.

AIRLOCKS

If, when you turn on a tap, the water comes out in a trickle or spurts out in a jet and finally stops, and if this is combined with knocking noises in the

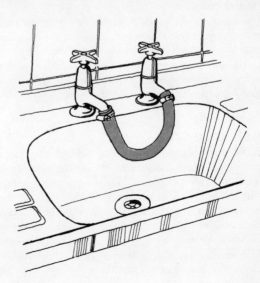

pipes, then you have almost certainly got an airlock in the system. You can correct this yourself only if you have separate hot and cold taps in the kitchen; if you have a mixer tap you will have to call a plumber.

To attempt a remedy you will need a short length of hosepipe, two adjustable hose clips and a screwdriver. Use the clips to fit the hose in a U-shape between the hot and cold (mains) taps in the kitchen; tighten up with the screwdriver. Then turn on first the hot and then the cold water taps and let them run for a few minutes. The theory is that the mains pressure through the cold tap will force water and air back through the pipes up into the hot water storage tank or cylinder and so clear the airlock. If it does not work the first time, try again, but if after 20 minutes or so you are making no progress, call a plumber.

Airlocks in radiators

If a radiator is not heating properly or is making gurgling noises, this too is likely to be because of an airlock caused after the system has been off for the summer.

'Bleed off' the excess air by opening the vent valve at one of the top corners of the radiator, holding a jar or cup ready underneath to catch any water that flows out. As soon as the trapped air has stopped hissing and the water is flowing freely, tighten the valve again. Most radiators open and close with a square-ended hollow key which you can buy at ironmongers.

'Water hammer'

Ironmongers also stock a useful plumbing aid that puts a stop to water hammer. This consists of a flat plastic disc which you fit to the end of the ball valve in the storage cistern to stabilise the action of the valve and prevent the arm jumping up and down causing a hammering noise in the pipes.

BURST MAINS

Burst mains outside the house beyond the water authority's stop cock are a job for the authority. The authority's stop cock is under the ground outside the boundary of your property and cuts off the whole of the household water supply, but this can only be done by the water authority. The same stop cock may control the water supply to several neighbouring houses. You will find your own stop tap either inside or just outside the house close to the

point at which the supply enters. If a rising main bursts, turn this off while you wait for the Water Board to come.

Before turning off the water supply you should always switch off gas or oil fired boilers or an electric immersion heater. If your water is heated by solid fuel, shovel this out of the boiler if you can safely do so to help it cool down faster.

LEAKING PIPES

If a pipe supplied from a cistern goes, look for a stop tap close to the cistern itself. If none exists then turn off the main stop tap, as described above. Also extinguish water heaters. Open all the taps in the house to help the system drain quickly and turn off the stop cock on the outlet tap of the cold water storage cistern.

Copper pipes usually fail at a compression joint where two pipes are linked together. Tightening the two large nuts on each side of the joint may well stop the leak. For a more serious leak you will need a plumber, but for a temporary repair while you are waiting for him to come, wipe the surface of the pipe dry and give it a quick coat of paint. Then bind it, first with rags and finally with strips of polythene cut from bin liners or plastic carrier bags.

A leak in a lead pipe may well mean that the pipe itself has split and binding is unlikely to be effective. Try to close the split by tapping it with a hammer; keep the water supply shut off till the plumber comes.

REPLACING A TAP WASHER

Dripping taps are annoying and wasteful. One drip a second wastes over 1350 litres of water a year. The reason a tap drips is because the washer inside, or the washer seating, is worn and is no longer providing a waterproof seal against the water in the pipe. The remedy is usually to replace the washer; if it is the seating then you will probably have to have new taps.

First you will need to turn off the water supply to the tap. If you are going to be some time doing the job switch off the electric water heater or gas or oil central heating boilers which might burn out without water. Let a solid fuel boiler fire go out.

In most houses you will find the stop cock for the mains supply somewhere near the kitchen sink;

if it is not there look in the front garden adjacent to the pavement where there should be a stop cock, though to turn this off you may need a special fork-ended key with a long handle. Taps to turn off the supply from the cistern will be somewhere close to the cistern itself.

Clear the water out of the pipes by turning on the taps until they run dry; you will only need to do this if you are re-washering a tap fed from the cistern in the loft.

Unless you are dealing with a double-action tap (which is described later) never attempt to dismantle a tap until the mains supply has been cut off and the water has run out.

Step-by-step re-washering

1 Modern taps with plastic tops can be removed by levering out the top disc and undoing the small retaining screw. If the top will not pull off, you may have to lever at either side with a knife blade.

2 To unscrew the chrome head (called the shroud) of a traditional tap, use a piece of cloth under your spanner to protect the chrome from damage and to give a good grip. Apply the pressure slowly.

3 To remove the head section from the body of the tap you will need an adjustable spanner to unscrew the large hexagonal nut. Open the tap fully so that the chrome head moves upwards to allow the spanner to fit on to the nut. Lift out the head section and remove any loose bits of old washer from the inside of the tap.

4 Remove the jumper, the part that holds the washer, if you can and unscrew the retaining nut

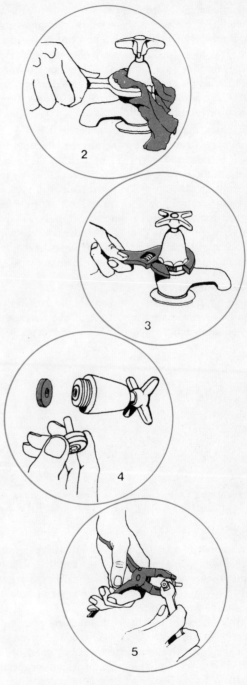

2. The shroud on a traditionally styled tap unscrews; use a cloth to protect the chrome 3. Use an adjustable spanner to release the large nut holding the head section 4. Lift off the head and take out the jumper 5. Remove retaining nut from jumper and replace the washer

Replacing a tap washer. 1. To remove the cover from a modern tap undo the retaining screw and lever off

with pliers and a spanner. If the jumper will not come off, just unscrew the retaining nut and carry on. Replace the washer with a new one of the same size. Usually it is 12 mm for sink and basin taps and 19 mm for bath taps. (Black synthetic washers are suitable for both hot and cold taps, leather ones for cold taps only; leather washers are not often used now.) Refit the retaining nut.

5 Tighten the nut with a spanner, taking care not to damage the washer. Fit the jumper back into the head section and screw it back into the body. Tighten the hexagonal nut and reassemble the tap carefully; a little grease on the threads will make it easier to take apart another time. Turn on the water at the mains to make sure the tap is flowing properly, but in the case of the hot water system, do not start the boiler until all the pipes have filled up and the water is running freely at all hot taps.

Double-action taps

While in the normal way you should never dismantle a tap without first cutting off the water supply, double-action taps provide the exception to this rule. Even with these it is prudent to establish the whereabouts of the relevant stop valve before you start.

Most double-action taps have their handle and nozzle in one piece, pointing downwards. The water is turned on in the ordinary way, but when the capstan head is given a few more turns, the water pressure forces up a special spring-loaded washer against the underside of its seating and the flow of water is cut off.

To change the washer, first loosen the locking nut above the nozzle, using a spanner. Hold the nut and unscrew the whole nozzle anti-clockwise. Any water coming out will stop as soon as you remove the nozzle. Turn the nozzle upside down and tap it gently on a flat surface.

The washer and its mounting should then fall out, attached to the anti-splash device. Prise out the washer mounting and re-fit a similar one. Reassemble the tap again. Remember you need a special washer for these taps, so if you do not know the make, take the old washer with you, so the assistant can match it.

Frozen/burst pipes

If a sudden cold snap catches you unawares, it can play havoc with your plumbing and the drains. Here, then, are some suggestions on preparations you can make before winter sets in, and how to cope if the worst happens.

As a first step, overhaul your general plumbing system. Repair any leaky taps (see page 128) and see that the ball valves for cisterns are in good order and that overflow pipes are working properly. Insulate the roof space and the cold water pipes as described on pages 151–4. Check where the stop cocks are, so that in an emergency you can turn off the water quickly.

As the temperature drops towards freezing, keep the plugs in position in baths, basins and sinks to prevent the outlets being blocked by ice. If you did not get round to fixing any dripping taps, putting salt in the waste traps also helps to prevent freezing.

If the main stop cock is in the house, turn it off at night so if a burst happens you do not wake up to a flooded home. If the stop cock is outside, keep it, and the way to it, free from snow and ice so you can reach it easily.

If you are going away for a short period, overnight or for a weekend, it should not be necessary to drain the system, especially if you can leave the central heating on. But if you are going away for a longer period, turn off the stop cock, turn on all the taps and drain the system completely. (Be sure

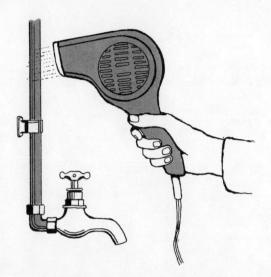

Hot air from a hair dryer may thaw a frozen pipe

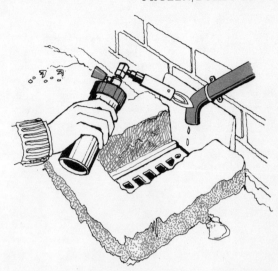

Outdoors, on a metal pipe, use a blowtorch

you have remembered to turn off the water heating appliances.) If you have a central heating system with water-filled radiators check with a plumber that you know how to drain your system correctly, because you could be in trouble if you leave it only partially drained.

FROZEN PIPES

To thaw a frozen pipe that is part of the hot water system first turn off the heater or boiler. Then turn on the tap and apply heat to the exposed pipework using hot cloths or a hot water bottle with a blanket over it. Another method is to play hot air from a hair dryer on the pipe, working along it from the tap to the tank end. If you cannot thaw out the pipe fairly quickly, call a plumber.

If copper piping freezes up, inspect the joints carefully as freezing often pushes the pipe out of the compression fitting. Loosen the nut on the compression fitting, push the pipe back into the joint, then carefully tighten the nut and check again for any leaks.

Outdoor drains that have frozen can often be cleared by throwing a handful of kitchen salt down them, followed by a kettleful of boiling water. If an outlet or waste pipe freezes, try pouring hot water over it until the ice inside melts. If this does not work – and provided the pipe is not a plastic one – apply heat with a blowtorch, but work with care.

If an s-bend in a lavatory pan becomes frozen, thaw it by wrapping the bend in hot wet cloths. Use the same method to clear the u-trap under a sink. Remember to lay newspapers and old towels underneath to protect the floor from drips. Do not be tempted to pour hot water directly into a lavatory or fireclay sink; the sudden change in temperature could crack it.

The ball valve in a storage cistern, however, can safely be thawed by pouring boiling water over it. Move the pivot arm up and down carefully until it comes free, but do not try and force it.

COPING WITH BURSTS

When water freezes, its volume increases by nearly 10 per cent. The resulting pressure in the pipes may then cause the metal to 'burst' and so cause a flood when the thaw begins.

When pipes burst you should immediately turn

Make a temporary pipe repair with epoxy resin adhesive and a cloth bandage

131

on the cold water taps and turn *off* the main stop cock and wrap rags or towels round the burst section. If pipes feeding the hot water system are involved, be sure and turn off the heater or boiler. As soon as the flow stops, a temporary repair may be possible. A lead pipe can often be lightly hammered together; use epoxy resin adhesive (or a coat of paint) and a bandage for copper or one of the repair kits for making first aid repairs to pipes.

In the case of a burst pipe leading from a storage water cistern in the loft, turn off the valve in the pipe. If there isn't one, damage can still often be reduced by plugging the open end of the pipe in the cistern with a suitably shaped piece of wood, such as a broom handle.

Then call a plumber.

Blockages

The best way to prevent your drains and sink getting blocked up is to take care you do not let anything go down the waste pipe that cannot be easily flushed away. Things which are most likely to cause trouble are large quantities of tea leaves or coffee grounds, vegetable peelings and grease. To prevent a build up of grease pour boiling water down the drain about once a week. Cement and mortar, which set solid, are especially likely to cause a stoppage if you let them get into the drainage system.

TO UN-BLOCK AN OUTSIDE DRAIN

1 Remove the grille over the drain and, if necessary, scrub it well with hot water and washing soda. Wear rubber gloves to protect your hands. Then swill out the drain gully with a bucket of clean water or with the garden hose, and scrape off the sludge which has collected on the inner walls of the drain.

2 Tie an old spoon to a length of cane and use it to break up the blockage and lift the silt from the gully bottom. Flush out with clean water and disinfectant and replace the grille.

TO CLEAR A SINK OR WASH BASIN

A blocked sink can often be cleared with a proprietary drain cleaner (follow the manufacturer's instructions carefully) or with a handful of washing soda dissolved in $\frac{1}{2}$ litre hot water. If this does not work, try a sink cup-plunger.

Block off the overflow and work the plunger up and down. With a wash basin do not be too forceful or you may loosen the wall brackets. If this treatment also fails, get to work on the U-bend.

1 Put a bucket under the U-bend, to protect the floor, and carefully remove the screw plug at the bottom of the bend.

A cup plunger will often free a blocked sink or basin; use with care on porcelain

A blockage in the U-bend can be cleared from underneath; remove the screw plug for access

Use a piece of flexible wire or a bottle brush to clean out the pipe

2 Push a piece of flexible wire – a length of curtain wire is ideal – down the sink outlet. Using a twisting action, work the wire up and down and try and loosen the blockage.

3 If this section of the pipe is clear, push the wire along the section of the pipe which leads away from the bend to the outside, and continue with the twisting movement. Then flush through with water. Replace the screw plug. Run the tap for a few minutes to check that the blockage has been cleared.

TO UN-BLOCK A LAVATORY PAN

If possible use a larger plunger than that for a sink. Work the plunger up and down in short bursts and take care not to damage the pan. When the blockage starts to move flush with water from a bucket to help it on its way. Call a plumber if this treatment does not work.

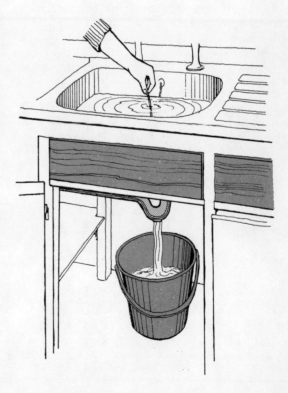

Run water through the pipe to flush it out

133

Plumbing in a washing machine or dishwasher

When your new automatic washing machine or dishwasher is delivered, your pleasure could be spoiled if you have over-looked the cost of having it plumbed in. If your pipes are of lead or iron, there is no way of avoiding this. But if you have standard copper piping of 15 mm diameter you will be able to plumb in the machine yourself, without too much difficulty, and much more cheaply than employing a professional. Water regulations are fairly strict and the by-laws vary in different parts of the country; therefore you should consult your local water authority (you will find the address on your water rates bill). They will be able to advise you about their regulations and tell you how to comply with them.

Using a kit

Electricity Board shops and many department stores sell kits that make the job particularly easy. Several types of kit are available (with some you do not have to drill a hole in the pipe until the end connection is fitted and tightened up), and most come in two versions, one to connect to the hot water system and one to the cold. You will need both versions if your washing machine is a model without its own built-in heater, but usually only the cold version for dishwashers.

Without a kit

If you are a competent handyman it is possible to plumb in a washing machine using standard plumbing fittings. The type with compression joints are easiest because they do not require solder or sealants and only need the minimum of tools. You will need a tee, stop cock, a male coupling with ¾in male iron thread on one end, some copper tube and spacer saddles to fix the pipework to the wall.

1 Turn off the water at the mains. If you are connecting up to the hot water supply as well you may have to drain the system so do not forget to turn off any water heating appliances (immersion heater, boiler).

2 Measure up carefully and determine the most suitable place to cut the pipe so that the taps are in a convenient place for the machine.

3 Mark the pipe and cut through with a hacksaw.

4 Hold the tee against the pipe and mark the amount to be cut off so the tee will fit in.

5 Cut off this section with a hacksaw and smooth off all rough edges and the internal circumference with a fine file.

6 Remove the two compression nuts and rings from the tee piece. Slide a nut and ring on to each end of the cut pipe. Fit the tee to the pipe and slide the nuts down so that they engage with the thread on the tee piece. Tighten up by hand then give a final turn with a spanner.

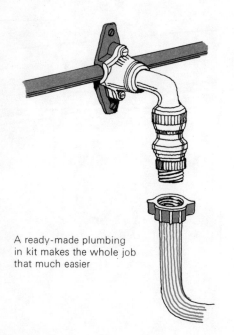

A ready-made plumbing in kit makes the whole job that much easier

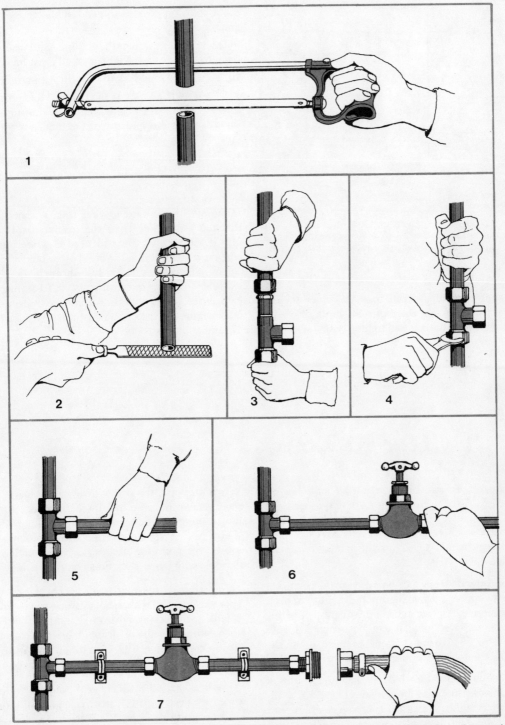

Plumbing in a washing machine. **1.** Cut the pipe with a hacksaw **2.** File off all rough edges **3.** Fit in the tee piece
4. Tighten the nuts with a spanner **5.** Insert the new pipe into the tee piece and tighten the nut **6.** Fit a stop cock
and a further length of pipe with a male coupling **7.** Fasten all pipework firmly to the wall and connect the hose

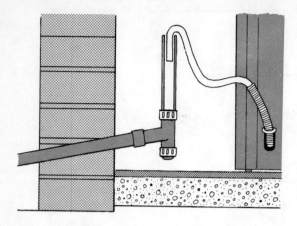

The waste pipe from the machine connects to
the outside drain through a stand pipe

7 Remove the nut and ring from the remaining end
of the tee and insert the required length of copper
pipe. Screw up the nut and tighten with a spanner.

8 Fit the stop cock to the end of the copper pipe
and secure.

9 Insert the next length of pipe with the male
coupling on the end. Tighten up all the nuts again.

10 Secure the pipework to the wall with saddles.

11 Turn on the water at the mains. Hold a bucket
under the end of the pipe and open the stop cock
slowly so that dirt and any bits of metal are flushed
out.

12 Connect the hose from the washing machine to
the male coupling and test.

The waste pipe
If the machine is next to your sink, you may find
that the waste pipe from the machine will reach
into it. Otherwise you will need a waste pipe to
take the water out into the drain or gully.

You will have to cut a hole through the brickwork, in a convenient position, with a hammer and
cold chisel. Check with the machine manufacturer's
instructions regarding waste outlet size (usually
32 mm) and construction.

Building tools

Building tools are fairly specialised and, like all
tools, expensive to buy if they are not going to be
used frequently. Most hire shops have large equipment like a concrete mixer, wheelbarrow or roller,
the things which speed up the job and make it
much easier.

A spotboard A piece of board or plywood makes
a good support for making up and holding mortar
and concrete. A piece about 1 m square will be big
enough for most jobs; it can be supported on a
couple of 50 × 50 mm battens to raise it off the
ground, or four old housebricks can be used.

A hawk is essential for holding small quantities of
mortar when pointing brickwork. These are available from builders' merchants or you can make one
with a piece of plywood about 25 cm square with a
20 cm length of broom stick as a handle, nailed or
screwed to the top.

A bricklayer's trowel with a 25 cm blade is a
good general purpose tool for bricklaying, cutting
and cleaning off bricks and placing small quantities
of concrete. A smaller version with a 12 cm blade
is used for pointing brickwork. Some models are
available with a non-stick finish on the blade.

You will need a **spirit level** for checking levels.
A 1-metre version with metal or wood frame will be
suitable for checking horizontal and vertical levels
when building walls of brick or blocks. It can be
used in conjunction with a length of straight board
to check the levels of a concrete path or paved area.

For breaking up small areas of concrete or brickwork, you need a **club hammer** and **cold chisel**.
Do wear **goggles** to protect your eyes when doing
this.

Larger areas can be dealt with far more quickly

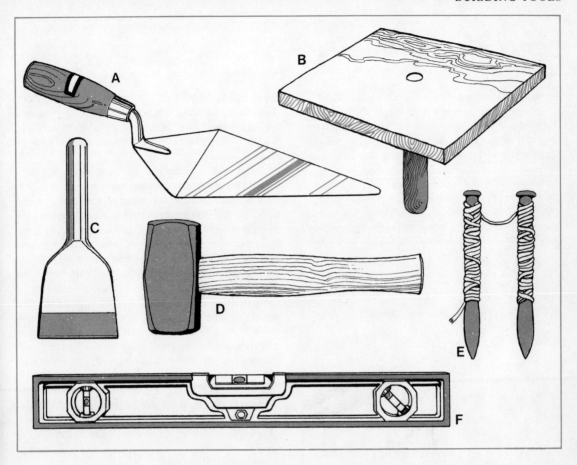

A. Trowel B. Hawk C. Bolster chisel D. Club hammer E. String line F. Large spirit level

using a **sledge hammer**. Whether you buy or hire this check each time you use it that the head is not loose.

For cutting and trimming bricks and stone slabs use a **bolster chisel**. One with a 10 cm blade is adequate for most jobs.

When laying foundations and building brick walls you need a **string line** for marking out. You can buy one of these which has metal spikes that can be driven into the mortar course or earth to hold the string taut. A home-made line will usually suffice although you must watch out for the string stretching if you use cotton string. Attach the string to a couple of 150 mm nails or hardwood battens to use as spikes.

A garden spade will be alright for mixing sand and cement and moving ballast, but if you are doing a lot of work it is a good idea to hire a shovel with the rest of the large equipment.

Remember always keep tools used for building clean. If cement or concrete is allowed to harden on them it is very difficult to remove and only slows the job up.

Building a wall

Building a wall is not difficult, but it does take a bit of practice, and the correct tools for the job. This is why it is a good idea to try your hand at putting up a test section, and knocking it down before it dries, before you start the wall itself.

BUILDING WITH BRICKS

There are over 2000 varieties of brick manufactured in Britain in many different facings, textures and colours, and at a wide variety of prices. Your wisest course when choosing is to consult a builders' merchant who will be able to tell you which type of brick is best suited to the job you want to do.

Apart from bricks you will also need mortar – and if the job is only a small one, you may prefer to save yourself trouble by using a ready-mix mortar (a 6·5 kg bag will lay about 30 bricks). Otherwise it is quite simple to mix your own.

Mortar for bonding bricks is made from a mixture of one part cement to one part lime and six parts sand by volume. Use a level box or tin for each volume measurement. Blend the dry ingredients with a shovel, bank up the edges and pour water into the well, a little at a time. Keep turning it over until the mixture reaches a consistency of whipped double cream. Then transfer two bucketsful to a wetted spot-board – a piece of plywood or board about 1 m square, supported on four bricks; this serves as a place to deposit working amounts of mortar mix so it is easy to pick up and transfer it to the job. Cover the rest of the mix with a sheet of polythene to keep it moist till you need it.

Laying foundations

For an outdoor wall, the foundation should be of concrete (plus some coarse aggregate) 7·5–10 cm deep and at least 10 cm wider than the wall itself. (If the wall is to be a retainer, the foundation will need to be at least 15 cm deep.) For how to mix concrete – see page 142. Dig a trench 45 cm deep and 45 cm wide and fill it with broken bricks and rubble, rammed down firm and to a finished level of 30 cm below the ground level. Then fill in with the concrete to the required depth and level off.

When the concrete has set, fix a peg at each end of the trench adjacent to the concrete base and stretch a string between the two pegs to give you

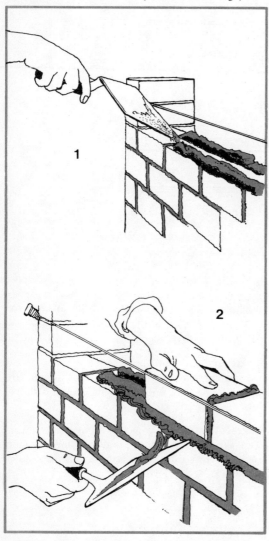

1. Lay the mortar bed in short stretches 2. Spread the head of each brick with mortar and lay it frog down into the bed of mortar. A string line helps to keep each row level

the front edge of your first course of bricks. Next, place a bed of mortar at each end of the concrete base and bed a brick at each of the two corners. Check for level in each direction and then move your string up to the top edge of the placed corner bricks. Lay the mortar bed in short stretches at a time so that it does not dry before you are ready. Start laying your bricks from left to right until the whole course is filled. Remember that for a non-load bearing wall the bricks should be laid frog down, that is, the dented side to the bed of mortar.

Once the first brick is laid, the method of continuing the course is to pick up the second brick in your left hand (or right, if you are left-handed) with your thumb on one side and fingers on the other. With your trowel, saw off a small sliver of the mortar and draw it towards you, squashing it into a neat sort of sausage shape. Now lift the mortar sausage by sliding the trowel into it from the back. Press the mortar on the bottom edge of the header (the short edge of the brick). Then with your trowel, smooth it upwards to cover the whole of the header surface in one sweeping movement, as if you were buttering a piece of bread. Place the brick into the mortar bed alongside the first brick, with the mortar-spread header between them. With your trowel, tap the brick flush with the string line and cut off any excess mortar that has squeezed out.

Continue to the end of the row (or 'course' as the professionals call it) then use your spirit level placed on a batten to check that the horizontal is true. Now build up successive courses of the wall by adding more bricks, alternating these so that each vertical joint comes half way along the stretcher (the long side of the brick) below it. Use half-bricks at the ends of alternate rows, checking often that the rows are both level and upright.

Before the mortar hardens completely, you can improve the look of your wall by 'pointing' it. Rub down the vertical joints with a rounded length of metal to give a slight hollow, then rub the horizontal joints and brush off the excess powdery mortar (see also page 140).

BUILDING WITH CONCRETE BLOCKS

Attractive as the finished result may be, there is no denying that brick-laying can be fairly tough work. Concrete blocks are on average larger than bricks so – especially if you use the special lightweight kind – you will find your wall is finished faster. It can also work out cheaper.

The main point to remember, as with brick-laying, is the importance of frequent checking for level. Concrete block walls also call for piers or other supports at intervals. Piers are built with special blocks, which should normally be twice the thickness of the wall, and bonded into it. (In the case of supports made of ordinary bricks these can be held in with metal bars or reinforcing to hold them to the blocks.) Concrete block walls also need a 'weaker' mortar mix than you would use for bricks. (This is to ensure that any cracks that might develop, either due to settling or movement caused by temperature changes, will follow the mortar joints rather than going through the blocks themselves.) The correct mix for concrete blockwork is one part of masonry cement to five parts of 'builder's' – not 'concreting' – sand.

Most concrete blocks should be laid with staggered vertical joints in the same way as brickwork. There are exceptions, however, such as the decorative pierblocks which are often used for screen walls. These blocks are often square and so must be 'stack-bonded'. That is, laid one on top of the other with matching vertical and horizontal mortar joints to preserve the decorative pattern. Stack-bonding is not as strong as staggered, so you will need to be sure your piers are reasonably close together.

Pointing brickwork

Pointing is the finish given to mortar joints in a brick wall. Neither pointing nor re-pointing are difficult; but if you are working on an area more than 2·5 m above the ground, you should borrow, hire or at worst buy a mini-scaffold. A ladder will not do, because you must always be directly in front of the section you are working on, rather than to one side. Heights up to 2·5 m can be tackled quite safely as long as you have a sturdy pair of steps.

DIFFERENT JOINTS

There are three different types of joint you are likely to come across, a joint being the way mortar is finished off between bricks when they are laid. If you are repointing you will need to match up your existing type or the new pointing will stick out like a sore thumb.

Recessed joints have some of the mortar scraped off from the front of the joint, which is then smoothed off with a rod that has a rounded end, so the face of the mortar recesses between the bricks in a gentle curve.

Flush joints just have the excess mortar wiped away from the face of the bricks and the joints.

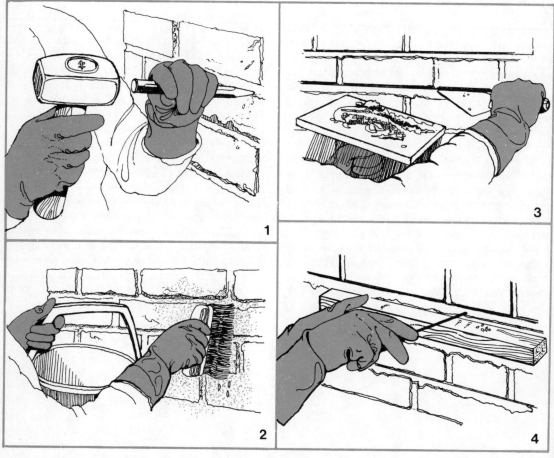

1. Remove all crumbling mortar, but do not chip too deeply 2. Wet the joints well before applying new mortar
3. Using a hawk and trowel, fill the joints firmly with new mortar 4. Use a straight batten to help make weathered joints

Weathered joints have the mortar sloped from the top of the joint outwards, so the rain runs off and is not absorbed by the bricks.

A more unusual joint is the **square recessed or raked joint,** used mostly for decorative effect.

Mortar

The mortar for pointing is usually made from a mix of one part cement to four parts soft sand. It is cheaper to buy the sand and cement separately and mix it yourself, but if you have only a small area to do, or are in a hurry, you could use a dry ready-prepared mix. Then all you need to do is add the right amount of water.

Whichever method you choose, be careful as you add the water. The mortar must have a stiff consistency, without being too dry. If it is sloppy, you will not be able to pick it up on the pointing trowel and you will waste a lot of it, but if it is too dry it will be crumbly. Mix the mortar on a board, and do not mix too much of it at any one time.

Before you start pointing, lay a couple of old sheets along the base of the wall. This will protect any concrete surfaces and also make it much easier to retrieve any dropped mortar.

Work on about a square metre at a time; wear goggles to protect your eyes from grit.

REPOINTING

1 Use a hammer and cold chisel to remove all the crumbling mortar, but do not chip any deeper than 1 cm or you may loosen the bricks.

2 With the aid of an old paintbrush, get rid of the dust and then wet the joints with the brush and water. This stops the brickwork absorbing the moisture from the new mortar, and so preventing it from sticking.

3 Put some of the new mortar on a hawk and pick up a small amount on the back of your trowel. Press it firmly between the bricks and spread it along the length of the joint. Work on the vertical joints before the horizontal ones.

4 If you are making weathered joints along the horizontal lines, form the slope as you are going along. With other joints, fill them flush and then shape them. Neaten all joints, removing excess mortar with the point of the trowel. Finish off weathered joints using a straight piece of wood laid against the bottom edge of the horizontal joints and running the trowel along it to remove excess mortar and leave a neat edge. The neatening process will be easier if you make yourself a simple tool known as a 'frenchman'. Take an old knife, heat the tip of the blade and bend over about 1·5 cm of the tip.

Laying concrete

If you are tired of coming back with muddy shoes every time you go out into the garden to hang out washing or to cut a cabbage, then the time has come to lay a garden path. Concrete provides a practical answer, either in the form of paving slabs or laid *in situ*, because once down it gives you a strong, hard-wearing surface that needs hardly any attention.

Getting a level

Whatever kind of path you plan to lay, once you have marked out the course you want it to follow the next step is to get a level. The professional way to do this is with the help of sighting rods, known in the trade as boning rods. These are made from two pieces of wood screwed together to form a T, with the top arms of the T at right angles to the upright.

Drive in pegs at each end of the path until their tops are the height you want the finished surface of the path to be. Get two helpers to hold boning rods on these pegs while you drive in a halfway peg

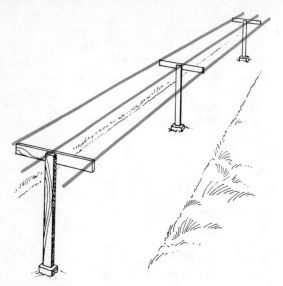

Use boning rods as a guide for levelling the site before concreting

Enclose the site with a wooden frame; check the level with a spirit level on a long board

to a depth where when you stand a boning rod on it this makes a perfect line with the other two rods.

Then level the ground for the base of the path, allowing for the required thickness of concrete, using the pegs as a guide.

Fill in any soft areas in the ground with hardcore or broken stones and roll or tamp it down to give a good firm base. Then check again for level. If the path is not too long you can set a level with a spirit level on a long length of board.

LAYING A PATH *IN SITU*
Enclose the path site with strong pieces of wood along both sides, supporting them with pegs from

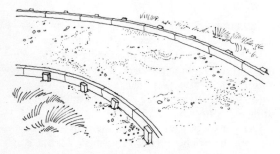

For a curved path put saw-cuts in planks so they bend; then support with pegs

the back. These are going to act as the frame in which your concrete is cast, so their top edges should be in line with your planned finished surface. Remember to allow for a crossfall of, say, 5 mm for every 30 cm of path width so rainwater can drain away.

Divide up the path into sections about 2 m long, using strips of 12 mm timber as wide as the concrete is going to be deep. (An average path is 7·5 cm thick; a driveway needs to be 10–15 cm.) These timber strips in the concrete will allow it to expand in hot weather without cracking.

Mixing concrete
Mix your concrete in the proportion one part cement to five parts washed ballast (a combined aggregate of sand and gravel prepared for the purpose), adding water until you have a mix that is workable but not too sloppy; too much water in concrete makes it 'weak'.

Shovel the concrete generously between your frame boards, working it around to get rid of any air bubbles. Then rake it level until it is about 1 cm higher than the edges of the frame. Compact the concrete with a length of 100×50 mm or 150×50 mm timber, slightly wider than the path. Work from both sides moving the board up and down in a chopping action. When the concrete is thoroughly compacted, go back over the surface working the timber tamper back and forth with a steady sawing

Level and compact the concrete with a length of heavy timber

motion to remove any excess concrete. For a brushed texture, brush with a stiff bass broom.

As soon as the concrete is firm enough, cover it over with polythene or damp sacks for at least three days to protect it from sun, wind and rain. Then remove the support boards, but do not walk on the path for at least a week.

CONCRETE SLABS

You can get ready made concrete paving slabs in a wide range of sizes, textures and colours. But if you have more energy than money it is not difficult to make slabs yourself, though hand-made slabs will never be as strong as commercially manufactured ones.

First you will need to make up a rectangular frame 76 × 50 cm from strips of timber 50 mm wide.

To make the slabs you will need a mix of one part cement to three parts sand. Make it up in the usual way, first combining the dry ingredients, then adding water slowly until the mix is workable but not runny. Keep the mix moist while you are working by covering it with damp sacks or poly-thene.

Shovel the mixture into the mould, making sure all corners are well filled, and level it off about 1 cm above the top of the framework. Tamp the mix thoroughly with a length of timber on edge, exactly as for an *in situ* path (see above), and finish off in the same way. For a slightly rough finish, rub over the surface with a wooden float in a 'fish scale' pattern when the concrete has stiffened slightly; for a smooth surface use a wooden float first and a steel plasterer's trowel after about an hour.

After a couple of hours remove the frame, and because slabs this large would be heavy to work with, divide the slab into smaller ones with an old, stiff knife. Cover the slabs with polythene sheet or damp sacking. Two days later, lift them up and stand them on edge for a further week to harden.

Laying paving slabs: the dry method

If you feel you have done enough mixing in making the paving slabs, you can lay them 'dry' on a bed of sand or ash as long as the ground is level and well compacted.

Dig foundations at least 10 cm deep and spread a 4 cm layer of coarse sand or ash and tread it down well or roll it with a garden roller. The foundations should be at least 5 cm below the finished surface level – do not forget to allow for a crossfall, and that paths near lawns should be 2·5 cm below the grass verges to make mowing easier.

Lower the paving stones carefully on top of the foundations, leaving 1 cm between them, all round, for the filling. Tap the slab with a wooden mallet to make sure it is lying snugly and does not rock. Use a spirit level to check that each slab is lying correctly before going on to the next one.

If you need to break a slab to fit into your pat-tern, lay it on sand or soft earth, then mark a line and carefully score along it using a bolster chisel and hammer. Go right round the slab, and when you have a deep score line tap with the hammer until the slab breaks along the line.

Fill the gaps between the slabs with sand, damp-ing it down with water and then adding more sand and water alternately until all the gaps are com-pletely full. Leave for 24 hours before attempting to walk on the path.

If you wish, grass or small hardy plants can be planted between the slabs. To do this you must leave large gaps or leave out an occasional paving stone; this breaks up a large expanse of slabbed area.

The mortar method

To 'wet lay' slabs using mortar, make up a mixture of one part cement to three of sand. Bed each slab on five small pats of mortar about 5 cm high, one pat at each corner and one in the middle. Tap each slab with a wooden mallet.

Using small pats of mortar rather than an over-all mortar bed makes levelling easier, and if a slab should settle out of true you can simply prise it up with a spade and bed it down again.

CRAZY PAVING

A crazy-paving path gives a pleasantly old-fashioned country look to a garden and, in fact, works best if the gaps between the slabs are allowed to vary a bit in width so the effect is not too geometrical and even.

Local councils sometimes sell off broken paving stones cheaply and these are perfect for crazy paving. Failing this, you can buy purpose cut stones in all kinds of textures and colours. Alternatively, make your own rectangular slabs, as large as possible, and break them up with a sledge hammer when they have hardened.

Crazy paving can be laid either 'dry' or on pats of mortar, but often the pieces are too small to bed down safely and are better set in an overall mortar bed. Crazy paving also needs very firm founda-

tions to make sure the pieces do not sink or crack.

Dig down 10–15 cm and put in 7·5–10 cm of broken stones or well-rammed rubble. Cover this with a dry mixture of one part cement to seven parts sand to a depth of about 4 cm.

Begin by arranging the larger stones round the edge of the path and filling in with the smaller ones until you have an effect that pleases you. Then, starting at the edges again, lift up each stone, spread a bed of mortar and press the stone firmly into place. Tap down with a wooden mallet, correcting any stones that are out of alignment. Fill between the stones, where necessary, with the mortar, trying not to get the stones stained with the concrete mix. Smooth off the joints after an hour or so when the mortar is just beginning to dry. Do not walk on the paving for at least a week.

Guttering repairs

Gutters play an important part in keeping a house free from damp, so even if your gutters are not in any apparent need of repair it is worth going up aloft to look them over from time to time. Signs of a blockage building up will be easy to spot but look, too, for defective joints, loose screws and brackets fixing the gutter to the wall and any signs of cracking or splitting in the bottom of the gutters.

When you are putting up your ladder, do not rest it against the gutter itself, because apart from being unsafe this can cause a plastic gutter to distort and the joints to loosen. It is best to use a ladder stay which fixes to the top of the ladder and raises it away from the guttering and the wall. For safety, tie one of the upper rungs of the ladder to an eye screw let into the fascia board; this will prevent the ladder moving in a high wind and perhaps slipping sideways.

If you find the gutter is in need of repainting or other repairs that might make a mess, protect the ground below with old sheets. Do not use poly-

thene, because a ladder standing on this is liable to slip. If you have considerable work of this type it is worth hiring a work tower or scaffold (see page 57).

CLEARING BLOCKAGES

Although gutters are made of different materials which call for different maintenance and repairs (see later in this section), a problem they share is that they all tend to get silted up from time to time with dead leaves, bird droppings and so on.

Before cleaning out a gutter, plug the downpipe opening to stop any loosened debris getting into the pipe and so into the drains. Take up a bucket with you and hook this on to the ladder as a container to hold the rubbish. Metal and asbestos gutters can be cleaned quite effectively with an ordinary trowel, but for plastic gutters you will need to use an old paintbrush with a scraper made of either wood or hardboard, to avoid scratching.

Once you have cleared the gutter, exchange your

bucket of debris for one of clean water and flush this down the gutter from the highest point and check that it runs down smoothly to the downpipe. If instead of running away it collects in a puddle at any point, this is a sign that a section of the guttering has sagged and you will need to tighten or renew the brackets.

Clogged downpipes
Clogged downpipes can often be cleared with a piece of wire or a flexible cane. If the downpipe discharges into a gulley, put a bowl or some other container there to stop the debris getting into the drains, and flush down the pipe with a jug of water.

To prevent the pipe becoming blocked again, cover the mouth with garden net or buy a small wire cage to put over the opening.

CAST IRON GUTTERS
The most usual problem with cast iron gutters is rust. Remove as much rust as you can with a scraper and a stiff brush. A wire brush attachment on a power tool will cut down the work if your extension lead is long enough; **wear goggles to protect your eyes and gloves to protect your hands.**

Treat the metal with a rust inhibitor (**these contain acid, so handle with care**), then paint the inside of the gutter with two coats of black bituminous paint. The outside of cast iron gutters should be treated with zinc chromate primer, followed by a top coat of gloss paint.

Loose joints
Cast iron gutter sections are joined together with bolts and the joints sealed with putty or mastic. To repair a loose or leaking gutter joint, remove the bolt that holds the sections together and gently prise the two sections of the gutter apart. A screwdriver is a good tool for this purpose. Rake out any hard or broken jointing compound, remove as much grit and rust as possible and brush out thoroughly with a soft brush.

When the joint is quite clean and dry, treat it with a rust inhibitor and repack it with one of the branded mastics. Replace the bolt, using a new one if the old bolt is damaged or rusty. Check the screws and brackets fixing the guttering to the fascia board and renew them if they seem weak, then paint both sides of the joint with primer and good quality paint.

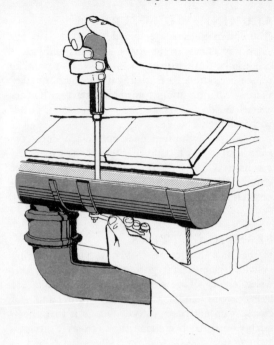

Tighten the connecting bolts to reseal a joint in a cast iron gutter

Cracks and splits
It is quite common to find a long crack or split on the bottom of a section of guttering. This has usually been caused by frost. The simplest way to repair a crack is with the help of a branded impregnated waterproof tape.

First clean the gutter well, remove any rust and prime with a metal primer. Take the end of the tape and press it along the surface of the crack. Make sure all the air is excluded by smoothing first down the centre of the tape and then working outwards along the length. See that the edges are firmly stuck down.

Cheaper, but rather more trouble, is to make your own tape by getting a piece of linen 5 cm wide and 15 cm longer than the crack. Apply a coat of bituminous paint to the gutter, then bed down the linen with a broad paint brush, making sure that the linen overlaps the crack at each end. Cover the linen with another two coats of bituminous paint.

An alternative to taping is to 'patch' the crack with epoxy resin applied following the manufacturer's instructions. For small cracks you can buy special kits consisting of membrane patches and a bituminous compound.

145

ALUMINIUM GUTTERS

Aluminium gutters are joined and sealed in the same way as cast iron gutters, so joints and cracks can also be dealt with in the same way. A point to remember, though, is that galvanic action takes place when aluminium comes in contact with other metals. So do not try and fix an aluminium gutter with iron fittings.

Although aluminium does not rust it does corrode, forming a white powder which will eventually eat its way through the metal. A coat of zinc chromate primer before painting gives a degree of protection against this.

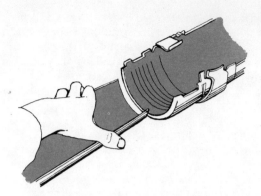

Plastic gutter sections are sealed with a rubber seal and union clips

PLASTIC GUTTERS

If the time has come to renew your guttering system, then plastic gutters are probably your wisest choice. This is because plastic gutters are light, easy to handle, never need painting and – of course – do not rust. A disadvantage is that cheap quality ones may become brittle in frosty weather.

Leaking connections

When a plastic gutter leaks, the source of the trouble is most likely to be a perished rubber seal in one of the union clips – the pieces which hold the sections of the gutter together. To replace the seal, disconnect the union clip by squeezing the front edge inwards and pulling the lip at the back of the clip up over the edge of the gutter. Fit a new seal (obtainable from builders' merchants) and fit the union clip back between the gutter sections.

As well as being secured by union clips, some plastic gutters also have the joints cemented to give them extra water resistance. If, in spite of this, the joint begins to leak you will need to let in a new length of gutter. Cut through the gutter with a fine toothed saw about 23 cm on either side of the joint, unclip the brackets and the unions, remove the length of gutter and use this cut section as your pattern for the new length.

Take two new union clips and if they are the type needing adhesive, apply solvent cement to one side of each and fix them to the ends of the new length of gutter. Cement the other side of the first clip and

put it together with one cut end of the existing guttering, then do the same to the second clip and push the other piece of guttering into the clip.

ASBESTOS GUTTERS

Asbestos gutters are more prone to blockages than other forms of guttering because of their tendency to attract scum and mossy growths.

Because of the dangers from dust when working on asbestos, especially old material, it is essential to observe certain safety rules. Damp the guttering before brushing down; and keep the work wet all the while you are brushing it off. This will prevent the dust becoming airborne where you might inhale it.

Once the surface of the gutter has been brushed clean, paint it over with a solution of household bleach, diluted one part bleach for one of water, to get rid of any lingering infection from mould growths and leave to dry for a couple of days before painting. Use bituminous paint on the inside of the gutter and exterior quality emulsion outside; do not use oil-based paint because the alkalinity of the asbestos will cause this to flake off.

Small cracks and leaks in an asbestos gutter can often be made good with a coat of bituminous waterproofer. If the damage is serious, however, it will probably be more satisfactory to have the old gutters removed and replaced with plastic ones.

Roofing repairs

It may take you some time before you realise there is a leak in the roof – perhaps not till brown patches appear on a ceiling. You may then be able to spot the cause of the trouble by carrying out an inspection of the loft or standing back in the garden and examining the roof for missing slates or tiles.

Most roofing work, however, calls for expert knowledge, special ladders and tools as well as a good head for heights, so in most cases it will be better to consult a roofing specialist. Prices vary considerably, so get at least two estimates as to the amount of time and work involved.

There are some jobs, though, which you should safely be able to tackle yourself – provided they do not involve climbing to any great height. For example, a flat roof over a bay window or a room extension which can be reached from a short ladder or a pair of steps is something you could mend yourself. Remember, though, that the roof itself may not be strong enough to take your weight, so you will need to lay boards across it and work on these.

Repairing a roof joint
One of the main faults that occurs with flat roofs is water getting in at the point where the roof meets the wall. This joint is sealed and waterproofed with either a mortar mix or a strip of metal, usually zinc or lead, known as the flashing. (Flashings are also used to make waterproof joints between chimney stacks, valleys between sloping roofs and anywhere else where a horizontal waterproof joint is needed.)

Both mortar and flashings tend to deteriorate with age and so let water penetrate the joint, which causes dampness to appear in the adjoining walls. Putting in a new metal flashing is a bit too tricky to tackle yourself, but you can, however, quite easily replace it with a special bitumen or mastic impregnated strip made for the job. Remove the damaged metal flashing with a hammer and cold chisel, brushing away any loose bits and brick dust, and make sure that the surface is clean and dry. If necessary prime the wall surface then lay the strip in position and press it firmly against the wall and the roof.

A mortar joint can be replaced with a bitumen or mastic strip, or with new mortar. If you are using mortar, make a mix of one part cement to four parts sand and apply the mortar with a small trowel to the well-wetted surface and leave the finished job levelled off at an angle so the rainwater runs off it.

RE-SURFACING
If rainwater is penetrating parts of a flat roof other than at the joints, you will probably need to re-surface the whole area. This can be done by using roofing felt, fixing it in position with a special adhesive usually applied round the edges and at the seams. Alternatively, you can use a bitumen compound product. Two thick coats of this applied with a large paintbrush or a broom will effectively seal the roof against water penetration. If the roof was originally covered with gravel or mineral chippings, this should be replaced to protect the felt from the sun.

Eliminating damp

Neglected damp will not only ruin your decorations but will also provide a nursery for the germination of mould or fungal spores, cause decay in the structure of the house and – most dangerous of all – rot in timbers.

Rot

There are two kinds of rot, dry rot and wet rot; both are forms of fungal decay, and dry rot is far the worse of the two.

Dry rot germinates from minute airborne spores which thrive on damp wood, usually in out-of-sight places, and throw out long strands of white fungal growth which can spread right through the house. The first warning sign of dry rot may be a faint but unpleasant musty smell. Test the woodwork in the area where the smell seems to be coming from by probing and tapping it – infected timber gives a dull sound, quite unlike that given by healthy wood. The surface may also appear cracked or buckled and a fine reddish brown dust (the fungus spores) may appear when you tap.

If you have any suspicion you may have dry rot in the house, send for a wood preservation specialist immediately (look in the Yellow Pages). Effective treatment must be both drastic and thorough. All traces of fungus must be exposed and removed and timber showing any signs of infection taken out, after which the sound wood must be cut away for at least 45 cm beyond the last visible signs of decay. The infected wood must then be burned to prevent any risk of damage spreading.

Walls and brickwork which have been in contact with the infected timber should be wire brushed and sterilised by soaking with two or three applications of a fungicidal timber fluid. The surrounding sound timber and any replacement timber should be well soaked in this dry rot fluid or better still, use new timber which has had a special preservative treatment.

Even when the fungus has been destroyed and the diseased wood replaced, the damp that caused the trouble may still remain, and unless you deal with this the dry rot may occur again.

Wet rot is often found in window sills or at the base of exterior door frames. The wood looks charred and black, and when wet seems spongy.

Wet rot does not spread in the same way as dry rot, so once you have traced and dealt with the cause of the damp, you may be able to cure the rot yourself. Cut away any infected parts and replace with new wood which has been treated with preservative.

CONDENSATION

Condensation is one of the commonest causes of damp, and one of the simpler to deal with – even if it cannot always be remedied completely.

As air warms, it expands and absorbs moisture. But when the moisture-laden air comes in contact with a cold surface, it contracts again and deposits its moisture in the form of condensation droplets. So anything that warms up cold areas will help, such as filling in cavity walls and double-glazing.

If you have walls without cavities, you can make the surface of these warmer by lining them with expanded polystyrene, which you hang like wallpaper. Treat any damp or mouldy patches on the wall with a fungicide before you hang the covering; once it is up you can either wallpaper over it or give it a coat of emulsion paint. Do not use gloss paint, though, because the solvent in the paint dissolves expanded polystyrene and it could also be a fire hazard.

In steamy kitchens and bathrooms, fitting an extractor fan helps overcome the problem of condensation.

RISING DAMP

Rising damp is often a problem in houses where the damp proof course is defective or, as in many older properties, non-existent.

A damp proof course is a horizontal membrane at the bottom of a wall to stop moisture being drawn up from the subsoil into the wall itself. The course may be of asphalt, bituminous felt or slate and should have been introduced into the wall of

Some possible causes of damp: A. Brickwork needs repointing B. Putty, woodwork or mortar may be damaged C. Tile missing or cracked D. Faulty flashing E. Guttering blocked or damaged F. Cement on chimney stack cracked G. Damp course absent/damaged/bridged H. Sill cracked I. Drain blocked or cracked J. Downpipe blocked or damaged K. Ventilation brick blocked L. Wall cracked

the house at least 15 cm above ground level and below any timber construction (to prevent the possibility of dry rot).

In older houses the damp course is sometimes set dangerously low, so that it may get covered up by earth from a flowerbed or piles of dead leaves. Check regularly to see that your course is clear, and if it is but still shows signs of being defective, call a builder.

Damp courses: new techniques
If your house has no damp course at all, it is possible for a professional to put a damp course of heavy duty plastic into an existing structure. New techniques, however, have made it possible to stop damp rising in a wall by methods which are considerably quicker and cause less disturbance.

One method suitable for mature brickwork consists of injecting a silicone waterproofing fluid into holes drilled at intervals in the bricks. The fluid forms a water and water vapour proof barrier, and the holes are then filled in to match the bricks.

Another technique works on what is known as the electro-osmotic principle. This means it removes the difference in the electrical charge between the damp wall and the earth beneath. It is done by looping a copper strip into holes drilled into the wall at the height the damp course would normally be. These are then connected to copper covered rods driven into the ground. This process can be used for walls of any thickness and for basements and it can be used on brick or stone.

Waterproofing from inside
If your budget will not stretch to the techniques described above – and, being jobs for specialist firms, neither method is cheap – there are still a number of steps you can take to prevent damp

from the outside getting in. The effectiveness of the treatments depends, of course, on the severity of the problem, and in some cases may only give a temporary remedy.

One solution is to waterproof the inside of the wall with a special laminated covering. This is bought as a kit and includes primer, laminate and adhesive. Remove all the existing wallpaper and as much paint as you can scrape off. Remove any loose or crumbly plaster and rub down to get the wall as smooth as possible. Prime the wall, then leave it to dry for at least an hour while you apply clean water to the brown side of the laminate strips and leave them to rest.

When the wall is dry, brush on the adhesive and apply the laminate, overlapping the strips by approximately 1 cm. Smooth out any trapped air bubbles as you go. The laminate should be left for at least 24 hours, longer in winter, after which it can be either wallpapered or painted over.

Another way of waterproofing an inside wall is to apply metal foil to the cleaned plaster surface and hold it in place with a waterproof adhesive. If you want to paint, rather than paper, line the foil surface first with a lightweight lining paper.

If the damp coming in is only very slight, an easy – though only temporary – remedy is to brush over the walls with a branded waterproofing solution. This will need to be renewed every year or so.

Damp through floors

If rising damp caused by a defective damp course is making its way in through a concrete floor, cheaper and easier than inserting a traditional damp-proof membrane is to paint the floor with a special water-proof coating. Once it has set it is resistant to water and water vapour.

POROUS BRICKS

Even when your damp course is sound, water can still seep in through an outside wall for several reasons. It may be that the bricks themselves have become porous through age. In this case paint them over on the outside with two coats of a silicone solution. This is colourless, so as well as strengthening the solution the second coat helps make sure that you have not missed out anywhere – easy to do when you are working with transparent materials. The treatment lasts about ten years, after which you will need to repeat it. Specialist damp proofing firms have other compounds that may give longer protection.

The seal will not work, however, if the rendering is cracked or the pointing between the bricks has gone. Deal with these first. If the mortar between the bricks has deteriorated too much for a patch-up job, you will need to repoint (see page 140).

GUTTERS AND PIPES

An over-flowing gutter or a leaky downpipe can soon result in damp patches. Gutters need trowelling out from time to time to stop them silting up with dead leaves and bird droppings, and you should also make sure that the grilles at the bottom of the down pipes have not become blocked up, causing the water to overflow instead of running down the drain.

Check, too, that overflow pipes from internal cisterns are set at an angle to prevent water running back along the pipe to the wall. At the same time scrape out any cobwebs and paint that may be gumming up the pipe outlets.

DAMP ROUND WINDOWS

Dampness often occurs round a window, and this is most likely to be due to faulty pointing or porous bricks in the adjacent wall. In this case, patch up the pointing and apply two coats of silicone solution to the affected bricks. If the pointing, the mortar fillets, between the window frame and the surrounding masonry, have cracked, rake them out and refill with a branded mastic compound which 'gives' with structural movement.

If the damp patch is under the window, the fault may be that there is insufficient slope to the sill to allow rainwater to run away, or it could be that the rain is running under the sill into the wall.

See that the channel on the underside of the sill is kept clear; in a wooden sill this often gets filled with paint which will need scraping out until it is completely clear.

A wooden sill can be taken out and replaced at a steeper angle. A stone or concrete sill is difficult to remove, but you can roughen the surface with a cold chisel and hammer, then trowel on a ready mix filler or use one part cement to three parts sand. Insert a narrow strip of bituminous roofing felt at the back to keep the window frame dry.

ROOF PROBLEMS

Damp may come in from round a chimney, where there are worn-out or faulty flashings or valley

HOW TO MAKE STYLISH CURTAINS SIMPLY ... WITH SPANTAPE

SEWING INSTRUCTIONS

1. Join widths of fabric and sew side hems.
2. Pull out 2″-3″ of cords from the end of the tape, tie cords together securely and trim surplus tape. This end should always be the edge of the curtain to the centre of the windows and in the case of Spantape 111 (triple one) should start between pleat groups).
3. Fold under the knotted end, place the tape along the curtain about ¼″ from the top and pin into place making sure that the pockets are correctly positioned for the way your curtains will hang (ic, in front or below your track).

NOTE: *Sew along lines indicated*

4. At the other end of the tape follow the instructions in paragraph 2 but leave the cords free for drawing up the heading.
5. Sew the tape to the curtain following the sewing lines indicated in the diagrams on the left for the style you are using. Always sew each line in the same direction.
6. Secure both ends with a row of stitching, making sure that you avoid sewing the cords at the unknotted end.
7. The curtain is now complete except for the bottom hem which should, where possible, be sewn by hand, preferably after the curtains have been hung for 24 hours.

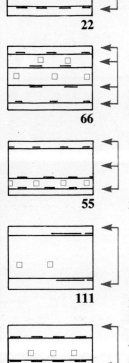

22

66

55

111

11

33

FORMING THE HEADING

1. Hold the cords firmly at the free end push the tape along the cords until the pattern begins to form and you have sufficient free cords to tie securely together.
2. Hook cords over a firm object (a door handle is ideal) and using both hands continue to draw the fabric towards you down cords, forming the pattern as you go.
(With Spantape 111 (TRIPLE ONE) form first set of pleats and advance to second set. (Spaces must be kept flat and unpuckered) Repeat process until curtain is fully pleated).

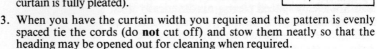

3. When you have the curtain width you require and the pattern is evenly spaced tie the cords (do **not** cut off) and stow them neatly so that the heading may be opened out for cleaning when required.

GENERAL HINTS

1. When calculating the fabric required always allow for pattern match and possible shrinkage.
2. Always use a suitable thread and ensure correct tension for the fabric.
3. After hanging curtains draw back into even folds and allow to hang for 24 hours to "train" the fabric.
4. A cording set will prolong the life of curtains by reducing handling.
5. When using a lining (other than loose) attach only under the bottom row of stitching on the heading.
6. When washing net curtains made with Spantape it is not necessary to release the heading.
7. If desired the pleats on Spantape 111 (Triple One) may be pinched together with a small stitch at the base of each group. The addition of a self covered button at this point may also enhance the effect.
8. Always space hooks evenly (e.g. Spantape 66 every third pocket) to form a neat effect when curtains are opened.

A Stilsound Holdings Product, Spantape Services Ltd, Mersey Industrial Estate, Heaton Mersey, Stockport SK4 3EQ
Telephone 061-432 5303

SPANTAPE
Curtain Headings

Simply . . . for effect

gutters and round skylights, as well as through gaps between slates and tiles. (See page 147.)

If you have a slate roof in a poor condition, an overall waterproofing system may well provide the best answer. This consists of a liquid bituminous proofing which is used in conjunction with a rein-forcing fabric membrane and makes sure that all the gaps between the slates are completely bridged and sealed, while the membrane ensures that loose slates are held firmly in position. Other systems are recommended for different types of roofs. This is a job for a roofing contractor.

Insulation

Whenever the temperature inside the house is higher than that outside, heat is lost. A well insu-lated house can reduce the amount of heat you need to generate to maintain your present level by up to 60 per cent. This is because the 'tea cosy' effect of insulation slows down the rate of heat dis-persal. At a rough estimate, 20 per cent of the heat wasted in an uninsulated house goes through the walls, 20 per cent through the roof, another 25 per cent through the windows, doors and draughty cracks, and 10 per cent through the floor. Good in-sulation also helps to cut down noise and reduces the possibility of condensation caused by warm air meeting cold surfaces.

Heat loss is indicated by U-values. U-value is a rate of thermal transmittance expressed rather in the same way as miles per hour. It represents the rate that heat is lost or will flow through a material, eg glass, brickwork or air. The lower the U-value (rate of loss) the better the insulation. For exam-ple, if you are building a new house or an extension, current regulations stipulate a maximum U-value of 0·6 for a roof (it would be hard to keep down to that figure without good insulation) and a 1·8 U-value for a whole wall area, including a window.

The idea behind any insulation, whether it is for walls, windows or a roof is to sandwich millions of tiny pockets of still air between two surfaces. The best materials for this are airy solids like expanded polystyrene, mineral wool, glass fibre and vermicu-lite (light weight mineral granules).

There are some forms of insulation, notably filling cavity walls, that call for the knowledge and skill of a professional, but many others are reasonably easy to do yourself.

ROOFS
Even if your house is built to the Building Regula-tion Standards which came into force in 1960, you will probably need to increase the existing insula-tion to bring the roof to today's acceptable rate of heat loss of 0·6.

An insulating blanket
For a pitched roof, the most-used material for the job is a blanket, either of glass fibre or mineral wool, which is sold by the roll. These materials are rot and mouse-proof, do not hold moisture and are non-combustible. For the average house you need a thickness of 10 cm.

To lay the blanket, first sweep well between the joists. (Lay down some boards so you do not put your foot through the ceiling.) Then, starting at the eaves, unroll the blanket between the joists, trimming it off with scissors or a sharp knife. Tuck the covering well in and make sure the ends are fixed down so draughts cannot get underneath. Do not seal up the eaves completely, though, or you may get condensation building up. Do not put any insulation under the cold water storage cistern; heat coming up through the ceiling at this point will help to prevent the tank freezing.

Loose-filling insulation
An alternative method of insulation is to loose-fill

Lay an insulating blanket up to 10 cm thick
in the loft

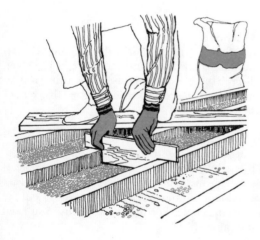

Make yourself a wooden rake to level loose-fill
insulating granules

with granulated vermiculite or pelleted mineral
wool scattered between the joists. These materials
come in bags and they, too, are claimed to be rot
and mouse-proof and non-combustible. They are
slightly more expensive than the blanket type of
insulation but particularly useful where the space
between the joists is irregular or where there are
awkward corners to fill.

To lay a loose filling, just pour the granules out of

the bags and smooth them off with a rake or something similar to the required 10-cm level.

An unfelted roof
If your roof is draughty, the granules may blow
about and finally end up all huddled together in
one corner. Modern houses have a layer of waterproof felt between the rafters and the tiles, but
older houses do not and any irregularity in the tiles
may be enough to let the wind whistle through.
The solution is to line the underside of the rafters
with hardboard panels. Start at the top – the ridge
board – and work sideways round the roof, using
screws rather than nails, because hammering could
displace the tiles.

Even better than hardboard are aluminium-
backed fibre insulation boards which have an insulating core of rigid urethane foam cast between
a gypsum facing and a backing of tough waterproof
foil. These are rather expensive, but they seal and
insulate the roof in one, which could prove useful
if you ever decide you want to convert the loft into
an extra room.

Ceiling insulation
If you have no way of getting into the loft to lay a
blanket or loose-filling, insulation can be fitted to
the ceilings of the rooms below. Polystyrene tiles
can reduce the loss of heat through a roof and for
safety buy the self-extinguishing grade. Because
some grades of expanded polystyrene burn easily
(and then give off poisonous gases) these tiles must
never be used near cookers or boilers, or painted
with gloss paint because gloss paint acts as a solvent
and dissolves the expanded polystyrene. If the tiles
do need painting you should use a fire resistant
grade of emulsion paint.

Hardboard sheets or tiles can reduce heat loss
but are not so efficient, and these need to comply
with the Building Regulations surface spread of
flame requirements. Pre-decorated boards are
available and you can use them for insulating solid
walls (unsuitable for cavity filling) as well as for
ceilings.

Flat roofs
Do not try to insulate a flat roof yourself. Call a
builder and ask his advice because it is usually
difficult to get at.

One method he may recommend is to fix aluminium foil or glass fibre to the ceiling, held in place

with battens and then covered with polythene sheeting and plasterboard. Another way is to insulate the outside of the roof using expanded polystyrene slabs covered with bituminous felt.

TANKS

Once you have insulated the loft floor, the roof space itself will, of course, be much colder. This means that the cold water storage tank is in that much greater danger of freezing.

Mineral wool or glass fibre blanket or insulating board make a cheap way to insulate, especially if you can use up left-over blanket from the loft. Put a first layer of blanket round the lower edge of the tank and tie it with thick string. Carefully cut the blanket with scissors where the pipes go into the tank and tuck it round the pipes. Fix the second piece of blanket, allowing it to come slightly above the top edge of the tank and with a generous overlap on the first piece, and tie it in position. Finish with a layer of blanket over the lid, letting it overlap at the sides.

You can also insulate a cold water tank with slabs of expanded polystyrene. These come in various sizes and you tape the slabs around the tank making U-shaped cuts with a padsaw where the pipes come. Another slab of expanded polystyrene makes the

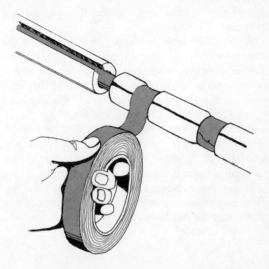

Preformed plastic sections are taped on to insulate pipes neatly

lid, which should be wedged to prevent it blowing off.

Even if you can get at it, do not cover the base of the tank, because you want to allow the warmth of the house to rise up at this point.

Hot water cylinders

An un-lagged hot water cylinder can double the cost of your hot water. Buy a ready made padded jacket at your Electricity Board shop or builders' merchant. You will recoup the cost in a short time.

Even if your hot water tank already has a jacket, check that it is thick enough. With today's heating bills, it is worth having one 7·5 cm thick. If yours is less than this, put a second jacket over it.

PIPES

These, too, need to be properly lagged – cold water pipes to keep cold out, hot water pipes to keep the heat in.

The cheapest insulation is with strips of felt, mineral wool or glass fibre bandaged round and tied or taped at intervals. Wrap the pipe with strips of material overlapping by about half the width of each strip. If you have to make a join, be sure you have a good overlap so as not to leave a gap.

Pay special attention where there are taps or valves. It is a good idea to wrap the stem of the tap separately and bandage this over and on to the

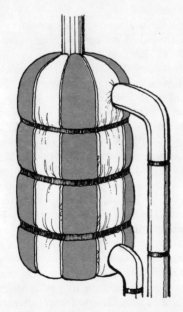

Specially made jackets are the easiest way of insulating hot water cylinders

pipe. Leave the tap head uncovered so you can get to it easily if you need to.

A neater looking and easier, but slightly more costly, method of lagging pipes is to use pre-formed plastic pipe sections, which you can buy in 90 cm lengths. Be sure you buy the right diameter to fit your pipes. Slip the plastic over the pipe and fix along the edge with adhesive tape.

Whichever system you use, pay particular attention to the pipes in the coldest spots near the eaves, even though they may be awkward to get at. Even a tiny gap is enough to cause a frozen pipe.

If you have used granules to insulate the loft floor, you could leaves the pipes unlagged, but box them in with hardboard and insulate them with left-over granules.

WALLS

Remember that uninsulated walls mean that about 20 per cent of your total house heat is being lost.

Solid walls

Provided that your inside walls are damp-free to start with, an inexpensive method of insulation is provided by expanded polystyrene sheet. Stick it to a clean wall with heavy-duty anti-fungal wall-paper adhesive, then cover it with wallpaper, or lining paper if you want to paint it. Again, remember that expanded polystyrene can be a fire risk, so do not use it on walls near the cooker or fire.

A good way to insulate solid walls is to nail small (20 × 10 mm) battens about 60 cm apart across the wall and to tack on a glass fibre blanket. Top this with sheets of plasterboard.

Cork wall tiles help keep warmth in as well as being decorative, and hessian wallcovering also has insulating properties.

Best of all would be aluminium backed insulation boards. These are bought in panels about 2·4 × 1·2 m, and are rather expensive. But it could be worth it for an especially cold north-facing wall.

Cavity walls

Cavity wall insulation is not a DIY job. You must call a firm of professionals. Until recently, you also needed the permission of your local council but now, provided your chosen installer has an appropriate Agrément Certificate and notifies the council, no formal permission or investigation is necessary in most areas for conventional bungalows or two storey houses.

Most houses built since 1935, and many before, have cavity walls but not all the walls in the house are necessarily cavity walls (only the main exterior ones). A cavity wall is one which consists of two walls, or 'leaves', with a gap of about 5 cm between them. The outer wall may be of brick or concrete blocks, the inner is usually of brick or building blocks, and the two walls are connected at intervals by metal or plastic wall ties.

The purpose of the cavity is to prevent driving rain getting through to the inner wall. The air in the cavity provides little insulation since it is normally moving through. Insulation can be greatly increased by filling the cavity completely with either a ureaformaldehyde plastic foam or treated mineral wool. But whatever the material, it is essential that the primary purpose of the cavity is not impaired.

The foam filling is pumped through holes drilled by the installer in the outer walls. The foam sets inside the cavity, trapping millions of tiny air pockets which prevent heat escaping. The holes are then sealed with mortar coloured to match your bricks.

The alternative treatment consists of mineral wool fibres blown through fewer but slightly larger holes. This generally costs rather more than foam. However, it cannot shrink or crack and is suitable for walls that are exposed to even the most extreme weather conditions.

Cavity wall insulation can reduce the U-value of a wall by around 65 per cent and the reduction can be as high as 75 per cent depending on the structure.

Most houses with cavity walls are suitable, and the responsibility for advising on this lies with your installer. Before you agree to employ a firm, check on their credentials. A government-sponsored organisation that can help is the Agrément Board. It operates a certificate of approval system whereby it stipulates the suitability of a firm's methods and materials. The address at the time of going to press is: Agrément Board, Lord Alexander House, Waterhouse Street, Hemel Hempstead, Herts. Your local authority building control officer can also help you.

Even with an approved installer, it is wise to obtain competitive estimates before the work starts. Compare the Agrément Certificates and guarantees carefully, and ask the firm to put in writing that your walls are a suitable case for treatment. Should their work fail in any way, you are then in a strong position to make sure they put it right.

Draught proofing

While fresh air in a room is essential, draughts cause considerable discomfort as well as wasteful heat loss. A well planned heating system and effective wall and roof insulation do a lot to improve matters, but nevertheless you may find local remedies are necessary from time to time. First you need to trace the source of the draught, and a good way to do this is to go round the room with a lighted candle.

DOOR DRAUGHTS

A door is a likely culprit. The easiest and cheapest draught sealer for an internal door is a self-adhesive foam strip. Clean all the dirt and grease from the frame first, or the strip will not stick properly, then cut the length you need with scissors, peel off the backing paper and press home the seal. This foam, however, does tend to come adrift after a few months and you will need to do it again.

More permanent is rubber or felt draught tubing, though since this needs to be nailed into place it takes up quite a bit of space and is rather obvious to look at. Nevertheless it provides a good solution where the draught is coming in through an uneven crack, for instance where the space is wider at the bottom than at the top.

For an outside door, bronze or plastic strip should be nailed all round the cleaned door frame, taking care that it is securely fixed in the corners. Be careful, too, not to kink the strip.

Under-door draughts

For under-door draughts you must either bring the door down to meet the floor, or the floor up to meet the door.

Rising type excluders come in standard lengths which may need cutting to fit exactly. Measure the length you need, then screw it to the base of the door, following the manufacturer's instructions.

Floor-fitted excluders are either wood, metal, plastic or rubber humps which build up from the step. A threshold excluder is the best kind for exposed outside doors with a large gap at the bottom. If you have a stone step, drill it with a masonry drill and plug it before fixing the screws (see page 94).

WINDOW DRAUGHTS

If you live in an exposed position, double windows probably offer the best solution to chilly window draughts, although it is expensive to use them for this purpose. Double glazing is intended to prevent heat loss rather than stop draughts (see page 157).

A cheaper answer – at least at night time – is to combine roller blinds with full-length lined curtains in thick wool or velvet. Thinner curtains can have their warmth increased by lining them with a special insulating fabric or quilted interlining.

Any gaps between the window frames and the brickwork should be closed with a patent sealing compound, and you can also buy water-resistant sealing strips for use on exterior frames.

GAPS BETWEEN FLOORBOARDS

In bad cases it may be necessary to lift the boards and then re-lay them closer together, fitting in one or two new boards to fill up the remaining space. While the boards are up, take the opportunity to put down glass fibre blanket between the joists (see page 151). But be sure your underfloor space still has some ventilation to the outside, or you could get damp, leading to dry rot which is a great deal worse than draughts.

If the gaps between the floorboards are only small, pieces of wood can often be slipped in (apply some wood glue to hold them in place), then planed down and stained to match the rest of the floor. Alternatively, you might use a filler.

Gaps between the floor and the skirting board can be covered with quadrant beading which you can buy from timber merchants or DIY shops. Nail it in place with panel pins. Another method is to fit a plastic coving, which is usually glued in position.

An excellent draught protector for all floors, and the only non-structural solution to the problem of cold with concrete ones, is wall-to-wall carpet over an underlay of thick felt and grey felt paper next to the solid floor. If your budget will not allow wall-to-wall, any area of carpet helps, as do cork and thermoplastic tiles and even lino. If you are converting a house or having a new one built, special insulation can be built on top of solid floors to stop the cold.

Self-adhesive foam strip is the cheapest draught excluder for doors and windows

Floor fitted excluders are best for outside doors with large gaps at the bottom

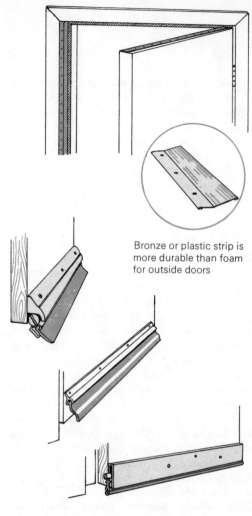

Bronze or plastic strip is more durable than foam for outside doors

Various designs of rising type excluder can be fitted to the bottoms of draughty inside doors

FIREPLACE DRAUGHTS

In every room where an open fire is burning there is a natural air current towards the grate. You get draughts when you have a faulty fireplace design that pulls in too much air. A throat restricter fitted in the chimney will probably help.

The next step is to control the source of ventilation needed by the fire, because if its air supply is cut off altogether the fire will smoke, or even refuse to burn at all. In this case the air supply should be taken direct to the fire by means of an underfloor duct, supplied by two vents in the outer walls of the room, set below floor level and terminating in two grilles either side of the fireplace. If, however, the floor of the room is laid directly on the ground, or is of solid concrete with no intervening cavity, you will need a special structural job with pipes to duct the air to the fire grate.

GOOD DRAUGHTS

While sensible draught prevention brings benefits

in terms of comfort and fuel saving, do bear in mind that some draughts are good draughts. The average living room should have all the stale air replaced by fresh about four times an hour to stop it getting stuffy.

All bathrooms and kitchens need a free circulation of air to prevent condensation and mould growth. The air changes recommended for a kitchen are about 10–15 an hour, for a bathroom about 15–20 an hour. These figures are a guide and will depend on several factors, such as how often the rooms are in use and the size of the rooms.

Moreover, it is essential not to block up vital ventilation to gas cookers, fires and flued heaters. Check with your local British Gas Region if you are in any doubt at all.

Double glazing

Double glazing can save about 12 per cent of your fuel bill. It also brings other benefits such as increased comfort and usable floor space (you can sit near windows in winter), reduced condensation and less noise from outside.

Insulation and heat loss
The principle on which all kinds of thermal insulation works is to sandwich a pocket of still air between two surfaces. Windows, even properly fitting ones, are a notoriously cold area – you can tell by feeling how cold the glass is, even in a centrally heated room. And not only is the cold coming in, your expensive heat is escaping out at a faster rate than anywhere else in the house. Double glazing can cut this rate of heat loss considerably.

Reducing condensation
The warmer air is, the more moisture it can hold. But when warm air comes in contact with a cold surface – such as window glass – the change in temperature causes the air to give up some of its moisture content, depositing this in the form of droplets of condensation.

With double glazing, the room face of the inside glass is not as cold as that of an ordinary single pane and, in normal circumstances, less contrast of temperature means less condensation. Sometimes, heavy curtains drawn over double glazed windows prevent the room warmth reaching the glass, creating the conditions for condensation. Adequate space between curtain and glass, with gaps at top and bottom, will allow the warm air to circulate and prevent condensation.

Cutting down noise
Double glazing helps to cut down on noise partly because you have two panes of glass and a pocket of air between you and the outside world, and also because in the fitting of the assembly any gaps and cracks round the window are sealed.

Different kinds of double glazing cut down noise by differing degrees, and if noise from heavy traffic or aircraft is your problem as much or more than heat loss, you will need a type that is specially designed and fitted. In some cases a grant may be available – check on this with your local authority.

FITTING
Not all types of double glazing need to be fitted professionally, some you can fit yourself, perhaps making use of a special kit. And of course you do not need to double glaze the whole house at once – for example, you could start with a north-facing wall or living rooms only. If the work is being done professionally, though, it will obviously cost more done in two or three goes than in one complete session.

The Glass and Glazing Federation is a reliable source of information. This organisation will supply names of member firms who make and install double glazing to its required standards. One way to find out about double glazing is to ask

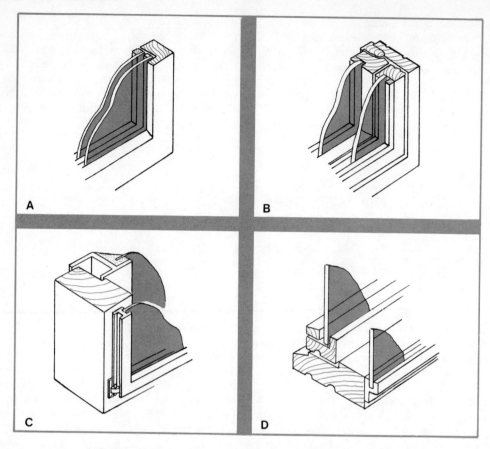

A. Sealed unit B. Coupled frames C. Secondary sash type D. DIY kit

friends about their systems so you can get the names of firms who have proved to be reliable. Even so, it is worth asking for quotations from two or three different firms; some require a minimum order of so many windows or so much money before they are prepared to undertake the work. Consider very carefully before buying from a salesman or from a pamphlet if there is no complete system on show.

Do-it-yourself double glazing materials are widely available from builders' merchants and glass merchants and you can buy in small quantities. Remember the glass will cost extra, so allow for this.

TYPES AVAILABLE

Sealed units consist of two separate sheets which are hermetically sealed together in the factory with an air space in between. They look just like a single piece of glass and are used to replace the glass in your existing window frames so that the appearance is not altered and cleaning is the same – just two surfaces. It may be necessary, though, to fit new window frames if the present ones are very large or an odd shape.

Sealed units normally require professional fixing, though very expert handymen should be able to cope provided it is a standard window frame they are being fixed into.

Coupled frames are two frames, each with glass, joined together with hinges at one side so they can be separated for cleaning – when you will have four surfaces to cope with. On the whole, coupled frames are suitable mainly for new houses or conversions where the window frames are being replaced anyway.

Professional fitting is necessary for these.

Secondary sashes are inner frames that fit over existing windows. The frames may be of aluminium or plastic and come hinged, sliding or fixed depending on the type of windows in your house. Remember that fixed secondary sashes cannot be opened easily once they are in position, so you will need to take them down in summer and find a place to store them.

Do-it-yourself kits are the secondary sash type and may be made from flexible plastic channelling, rigid plastic frames or aluminium. Some kits come complete with glass and are made-to-measure to fit your windows so you need only to install them; others come in bits which you cut to size and make up yourself. In this case you will need to find a glass merchant to cut the glass to size for you.

With DIY installation on metal windows, it is often best to put an inner wooden frame rather than drilling and fixing the unit directly into metal.

Points to consider
Before going ahead with double glazing, check the condition of your existing window frames – the experts will do this when quoting for a professional installation. Although double glazing will stop draughts from broken or ill-fitting window frames to some extent, it will work much more efficiently and pay for itself more quickly if these faults are remedied first.

No one type of double glazing is really better than another, though a certain kind may be best for your house. Your wisest course is probably to find friends who have already double glazed a similar type of house, and if they are happy with the result, to follow their example.

Burglar proofing

Just imagine for a moment that you have locked yourself out of your home. If you would have to send for the police to get you in, congratulations.

It is only too likely, though, that you will be able to manage on your own. Maybe up a drainpipe and in through the bathroom window, or perhaps using a ladder you have left in a rickety-doored shed. You may even have left a spare key 'hidden' under a handy brick. To a burglar, your house is offering an open invitation.

Experience shows that if someone really wants to break in, he will find a way. But delay is the key to preventing a lot of might-be burglaries. Unless you own some special article that a burglar has found out about and deliberately set out to get his hands on, he will probably give up if entry proves to be a problem because your security precautions mean he has to take time and make a noise. Statistics tell that the average domestic burglary takes only 90 seconds from get-in to get-out.

Below are some precautions you can take to discourage the thief before he has a chance to get started. For further information on other burglar deterrents consult the Crime Prevention Officer at your local police station. Your insurance company will also give you free advice.

MAKING MAIN DOORS SECURE
A lock that is commonly found on front doors is a 'nightlatch'. You need a key to open it from outside and it has a knob to turn it on the inside. If the door is well fitted into a rebate, this is the ideal type of lock. However, when a nightlatch (sometimes called a springlatch) is fitted to a badly fitting door or to a door sited in a non-rebated frame it is possible to push back the bolt with a bankers' card or something similar.

A nightlatch fitted to a door with a glass panel adjacent is an open invitation to the thief – he

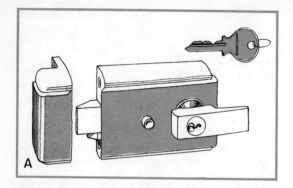

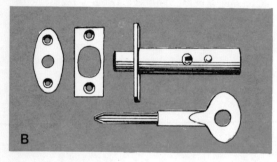

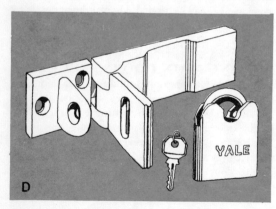

A. Security night latch B. Mortise bolt and key
C. Sash lock D. Padlock and locking bar

simply breaks the glass, inserts his hand and turns the knob. The same is true of a door with a wood panel insert; a small hole drilled in the panel, a greased padsaw blade and the thief can cut out a hole, making less noise than he would breaking glass.

In any of these situations, what you need is a security nightlatch, with a double-locking action. When the key is turned to the final locking position, the tongue is held rigid in the jamb fixing and cannot be moved by pressure on the end of the bolt. These locks are also known as deadlocking nightlatches. The best ones can be locked from the inside, so you feel safe at night, and also from the outside so that a burglar who breaks a glass door panel or a nearby window cannot open the door by putting his hand inside.

It is not difficult to change an existing rather flimsy two-lever lock to a more secure type because you should find that the keyhole and spindle line up, unless your present lock is very old or a foreign one.

To make the front door even more secure, it is a good idea to add a mortise lock as well as a dead-locking nightlatch. This will involve cutting a recess in the door to fix it. Bolts at top and bottom give even further protection.

Locks and bolts, however, can only be as strong as the door they hold. If your door is flimsy or hollow replace it with a stouter one before you put on the new safety fittings.

Chains and spyholes

Burglary is not always a matter of breaking in; sometimes you open the door to the thief yourself. So it is a good idea to have a chain on the front door which you need not open until you have proof of a caller's identity.

Alternatively, or additionally, you can fix a small spyhole with a magnifying glass to show you who is on the doorstep before you decide whether or not to open the door.

Side and back doors

In nearly 70 per cent of burglaries the thieves get in through the side of the house or the back. Most often this is at a time when you are unlikely to be feeling security conscious, between two and four o'clock in the afternoon.

So make sure your back door has a mortise lock and in addition secure all outside doors, including back door and french windows, with bolts which

Spy hole with magnifying glass

mortise into the door at top and bottom. These are hidden in the door and are invisible from outside. You open them with a fluted key – the same one for all the bolts – so keep it well hidden when you are out of the house.

Sliding doors
An ordinary deadlock will not hold sliding doors in position. For these you need a mortise deadlock with a hookbolt which can be opened with a key from outside. Mortise bolts can also be fitted at top and bottom of each door, but these are no good when you want to come in from outside because the key works from the inside only.

For glass sliding doors a disc tumbler window lock works well, though this, like the mortise bolts, is fixed inside and cannot be opened from the outside with a key.

INTERNAL DOORS
In the interests of safety, the police and fire service recommend that internal doors should never be kept locked and bolted. The exception is when you have a flimsy external door – say into a sun lounge – then the inside door to the rest of the house should be treated as an outside one. But be sure you know where the key is kept so you could open it quickly in an emergency.

GARAGES AND OUTHOUSES
Garage and outhouse doors can be secured in the same way as main doors, or with a good padlock with a padbar of equal strength. There is no point in fitting a high security padlock if the bar and hasp are weak. Special hardened steel sets are available.

WINDOWS
More thieves break in through windows than through doors. This is probably because most normal window fastenings can be opened with a knife, or by breaking enough glass to reach the catch by hand. To get in through a properly locked window, however, a thief has to make a lot of noise and take time breaking an area large enough to climb through.

Be particularly careful to protect upstairs windows and skylights if they are near drainpipes or a strong creeper, or if they might be reached by way of the garage or a porch roof. A number of special window locks are available.

Sash locks, which fit into the window sashes are inexpensive and easy to fit.

Stay locks are designed for casement windows. Purpose made locking stays are also available if your existing ones are too flimsy to fit a lock on to. Some makes have the additional advantage that they can be locked in a half open position, not as an anti-thief precaution but to prevent young children falling out. They are designed for installing under the casement stays on either wooden or metal windows.

Handle locks are available for metal casements.

It is worth noting that double glazing acts as a security measure, especially if the inner frames are fixed, ie not hinged.

LOOKING AFTER LOCKS
Like all mechanical things, locks need care. Keep them clean by wiping over the exposed parts with a soft cloth. Do not be tempted to use metal polish, paste or glasspaper because apart from spoiling the look of the lock they can get into the keyhole and jam the works.

Never use oil in keyholes as this will attract dirt and clog the internal pin tumblers or levers. Graphite will help a lock run more smoothly and although you can buy this as a special compound from shops where locks are obtainable, the easiest way to apply it is to run a pencil over the key before turning it in the lock.

LOCKING UP
No lock in the world will be any protection if you do not remember to use it. This means impressing

161

everyone in the household to lock up every time the house is left empty, even if it is just for a moment or two. *Somebody's* house gets burgled every few minutes. Make sure it is not yours.

Locks are useless, too, if you do not take care of your keys. Carry them with you. Never leave a spare key under the mat, inside the letterbox or any other 'secret' place. Thieves know them all. If you feel you must have a spare key, leave it with a friendly neighbour.

If you move house, change the locks on your new home. It may seem unnecessarily pessimistic, but there is always a chance that the previous owner may have left a key with someone, or in some forgotten hiding place in the garden. Change the lock, too, if at any time you lose a key. Never keep keys on a ring with your name and address marked on it.

Other steps to take

Burglars normally avoid well lit houses. Ideally, you should have exterior lights on all the outside walls of the house. If you go out, leave a room light on rather than the hall one.

If you are going away for a few days, stop the newspapers, milk and other deliveries, either by telephone or by letter. Do not leave notes outside for passers-by to read. Take jewellery, silver or other prized possessions to the bank for safe-

keeping. If you are going away for more than a day or two, tell the police.

A burglar alarm can prove itself a worthwhile investment. Before installing one, though, have a word with your insurance company to be sure you are using a firm that meets their standards. The same applies before you put in a home safe.

Burglars do not like dogs. But do not buy one as a protection unless you do!

Know your possessions

If the worst happens and thieves break in, you will have a better chance of getting your possessions back if you can give the police a detailed list of the missing items.

Cameras, typewriters, hi-fi and stereo equipment all have serial numbers, as do many domestic appliances such as foodmixers and irons. List these down along with any distinguishing features on other items, such as hallmarks on silver. Jewellery, pictures and *objets d'art* are much easier to trace if you can give the police a photograph. They do not need to be professionally taken, snapshots will do.

Finally, remember that the crime rate, especially among young offenders, is growing. While it may be impossible to prevent a determined professional from breaking into your home, the more trouble you make it to do so, the more likely it is that the thief will go somewhere else.

Fencing and gates

A good-looking fence makes an attractive frame for your home. It can also, depending on the type you choose, serve a useful purpose keeping your own children and animals *in* and the neighbours' *out*.

In a boundary fence, the posts or other supports must be entirely on the owner's land. It is usual to nail the pales on the outside of the cross members, so the point of the nail is inwards towards the property. If your fence adjoins a public highway you can be held responsible for damages if anyone

is injured because you have let it lapse into a dangerous condition.

WOODEN FENCES

Wood is the traditional material for fencing; oak is best because it is hard wearing but various others such as red cedar can also be used. Chestnut paling is cheap and easily erected. It is always best to use pretreated timber as it will have a longer life. That treated by vacuum process can last up to 20 years.

Untreated timber used for fencing (with the exception of chestnut paling) should be protected with several coats of creosote or a wood preservative over a period of a few weeks before you start building. This treatment should be repeated every couple of years. Another point to remember is that all the nails and staples used in the fence should be of galvanised iron to prevent – or at least delay – rusting. Tops of posts should be sawn off at an angle or capped with wood or metal to shed rain more easily and guard against rot. Post and rail or ranch style fencing are primarily boundary markers, though they can look attractive. If your fence needs to form a physical barrier between your property and someone else's, choose close-boarded or panel fencing.

Close-boarded fences are a good choice for rear and side boundaries which you want to screen to avoid being over-looked. However, some local by-laws restrict the height to which a fence (or wall or hedge) may rise to a maximum of 2 m so it is wise to check with the local authority before you begin to build.

Close-boarded fences consist essentially of substantial wooden pillars placed 2 to 3·5 m apart, supporting cross members known as arris rails, to which are fixed upright feather-edged boards. Concrete pillars are sometimes used instead of wooden posts. It is a sensible precaution to have a continuous board, known as a gravel board, running along the foot of the fence at ground level to provide a base on which the upright boards can rest. This is because it is much simpler and cheaper to replace a gravel board if it rots than to replace all the uprights individually because the base of each has rotted.

Ready-made fencing is available in kits, and usually comes in the form of posts and pre-formed panels. These can be either of boards or woven wood – thin pliable strips of wood interlaced to form a continuous surface.

It is usually more expensive to buy ready-made fencing than to buy the timber and cut it to size yourself – but it does save time.

Erecting a fence
Before starting to build your fence, treat all except pretreated timber with creosote or other wood preservative, especially the base of the posts.

Lay a string line parallel to the line for the fence and about 20 cm out from it. Dig holes about 30 cm

Firmly bedded and upright posts are essential to support any fence

square and 55 cm deep to take the posts, at 2 m or so intervals – or depending on the length of the panels if you are using ready-made fencing.

Using a plumb line or a spirit level to make sure the post is upright, take the first post and support it in its hole with three 12 × 100 mm temporary wooden stays. Fill in the first hole with rubble to within 10 cm of the top and make sure it is well rammed down round the post.

Then line up the board or panel with the marks on the post and nail it into position, using 62 mm nails at 7·5 cm intervals. Do not forget to leave space at the bottom for the gravel board. If you are making up the fence yourself, fix the arris rails into the pre-cut slots in the posts, or use metal brackets specially made for this job. Fix the gravel board to the base of the posts. Featherboard and weatherboard are available in pre-cut lengths from 1 to 2 m and the boards should overlap by 2·5 cm.

Once your fencing and posts are up, mix some dry sand and cement and shovel a 5–7·5 cm layer on top of the rubble round the posts and pour in a bucket of water. Check the level of the fence by running a line along the top and make any necessary adjustments to the uprights with temporary stays, which should be left in place at least overnight.

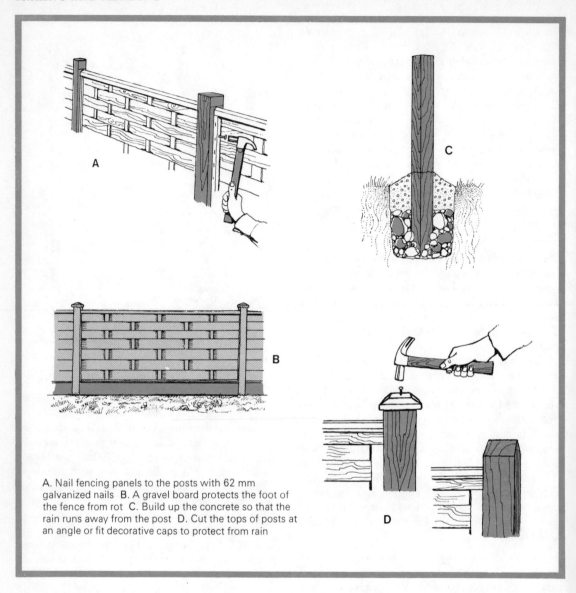

A. Nail fencing panels to the posts with 62 mm galvanized nails B. A gravel board protects the foot of the fence from rot C. Build up the concrete so that the rain runs away from the post D. Cut the tops of posts at an angle or fit decorative caps to protect from rain

Prepare a mix of one part cement, two parts gravel, and four parts sand, and fill up the holes round the posts with it, building the mix up round the posts with sloping sides so the water will run off when it rains. Once the posts are firm, put a decorative capping on the tops, to shed rain.

Repairing fences
Any damage to a fence should be repaired at once. First because you may be liable for damages if anyone gets hurt, and also because the damage could spread and make the repair much more expensive.

If it is just an odd board that needs re-fixing, remember to use galvanised nails and try to nail through an undamaged part of the wood – reversing the board if necessary. If you are fitting in a new board, do not forget to treat it with creosote or wood preservative first.

When a post needs renewing, the old one can be used as a pattern to cut mortise slots. Before inserting it, remember to creosote the ends of the arris rails and the mortise slots. Secure the ends of each arris rail by drilling 12 mm diameter holes through the post and the arris tenon and fixing with dowels, or use purpose-made metal brackets.

If it is only the base of a post that has decayed, it may be possible to insert a concrete spur. You can buy these at builders' merchants. The bottom of the post is cut off above the decayed part and the broken stump and part of the concrete bed removed, so that the spur can be inserted in a position that will bring it up closely alongside the upper part of the post, to which it is then bolted. Settle the spur in a bed of new concrete.

A broken arris rail may need to be completely replaced if the wood is decayed, but if it is a clean break and no other damage has been done, you may be able to repair it with metal repair brackets, fixing the top and the bottom with woodscrews. If the damage has gone beyond the tenons, you may still be able to refix these using special arris rail brackets – but if not or if the wood has decayed, you will need to buy a new section of a rail from a timber yard. Remember to allow for a 6·5 cm tenon to fit into the post at each end, and to creosote the new rail before fixing it.

VINYL FENCING
Vinyl fencing is virtually maintenance free. It never rots, needs no painting and to clean it you simply hose it down or wipe it over with ordinary household detergent and water.

Once the posts have been concreted into the ground, the rails are slotted into the apertures provided and a locking device on the ends of the rails make sure they stay in place. If a plank has to be cut so that the locking nib is removed, you can make a new one by cutting the end of the plank with a saw and using a pair of pliers to prise up a new nib.

GATES
A wide choice of ready-made gates is available in many materials from wrought iron to vinyl.

To hang a gate, first measure the size of the opening needed – especially important if it is a vehicle entrance. Then dig holes for the gateposts the correct distance apart, making the holes about 60 cm deep and large enough to pack with a reasonable amount of rubble or concrete as well.

Stand the posts in the holes and check the distance between them, allowing about 5 cm extra between the edge of the gate and the upright (on each side for a double gate) to make room for the hinge support. Check that the posts are upright and of equal height. Then wedge them in place with a few lumps of rubble.

Now pull the posts slightly outwards to compensate for the inward pull they will get from the gate. Fill up the holes with well-rammed rubble or a concrete mix of one part cement to three parts sand.

Re-check the position of the posts before the concrete sets and leave for as long as possible before hanging the gate.

Fixing the gate
Support the gate on blocks while you are working, so that it rests about 2·5 cm above the ground and 5 cm from the upright, according to the type of hinge. Mark the position of the hinges on the gate and on the post and check the ground over which the gate will swing is level.

All the necessary fittings should be supplied with the gate. As well as the catch to keep the gate closed, it is useful to have one to hold the gate back when it is open: a double gate will also need a central gate-stop set into the ground, or a dropdown bolt fixed to the gate which slides into a hole in the ground.

Repairs to gates
The most common troubles are caused by hinges or the gate fastening coming loose. Check the screws and if necessary replace them with longer, thicker ones or plug the holes and replace them with screws of the same size.

If the edge of a wooden gate scrapes on the ground, lift it off its hinges and place two or three 12 mm iron washers over both top and bottom hinge pivots. These will lift the gate.

To fix a loose gate post, cut a piece of batten so that it makes a tight fit between the gate posts at ground level. Take the gate off its hinges. Now use the batten as a strut between the posts at the top to keep them upright as you work. Drive a stout piece of wood into the ground at each of the four sides of the loose post, making a cavity about 2·5 cm wide by 25 cm deep. Fill this cavity with concrete and press in several turns of strong wire as reinforcing. Make them horizontal, and as near as possible to the outer edge of the concrete filling. Alternatively, fix concrete spurs as described for fence posts. Allow time for setting in either case, and when really firm, re-hang the gate.

2. Care and cleaning

Stain removal

Most stains are not difficult to remove if they are treated immediately after they happen. The idea is to mop up the excess and to dilute the stain as much as possible to prevent it having the chance to become absorbed into the fabric.

Once spills and deposits have had the opportunity to penetrate into the fabric and become absorbed by the fibres, stronger preparations and more vigorous methods will have to be used at greater risk to the fabric, and without necessarily guaranteeing a satisfactory result. In addition, old dried-in stains are often difficult to identify and treating them wrongly could cause an irreversible chemical change.

Stains can be divided into three groups:

'Absorbed' stains These are spilt liquids such as tea, coffee, milk or beer which have been absorbed into the surface.

'Built-up' stains Thicker preparations which leave a surface deposit, but with little actual penetration. For example, thick grease, nail varnish and paint.

'Compound' stains A combination of the two above which leaves some surface residue as well as penetrating into the fabric.

INSTANT ACTION

Provided you can get to them immediately after they occur, it is usually possible to rinse out absorbed stains from washable fabrics in lukewarm suds. Squeeze the stained section gently and rub the fabric together, face to face. Take care that the water is not too hot, because this can actually set

PROFESSIONAL CLEANING

It may be better to consider professional cleaning when expensive garments or furnishings are stained, particularly if you are not sure what the stain is, or if there is a special finish to the fabric. In this case, do not try home treatment. Mark round the stain with tacking thread and take it to the cleaners as soon as possible, telling them what the stain is if you can.

certain stains. If necessary, you can safely leave some articles soaking until you have time to wash them, but never soak wool, silk or any fabric with a flame-retardant finish.

Even on fabrics which are normally dry cleaned, with the exception of those which would watermark, the immediate use of water is usually the safest way of dealing with absorbed stains rather than resorting to the use of bleaches or other commercial stain removers. Use clear lukewarm water, sponging gently from the outside of the mark in towards the centre to avoid spreading it. Then dab with a towel to leave as dry as possible.

Built-up and compound stains, which leave a surface deposit, should be scraped with a knife or a spoon and the surface blotted with paper tissues or sheets of kitchen roll to mop up as much of the substance as possible, then treated by the method recommended for the stain in question.

First aid

Rinse non-greasy stains with cold water.

Sprinkle talc on greasemarks to prevent them from spreading.

Throw salt on tablecloths to stop wine, fruit or beetroot stains spreading, but do not use salt on carpets, where it may discolour them.

Drinks and other liquids spilt on carpets can often be flushed out with a quick squirt from a soda water siphon.

STAIN REMOVERS

Because time can be vital, it is helpful to keep a selection of stain removing agents handy so stains can be dealt with as soon as possible.

A stain removal kit should also contain a selection of applicators and absorbent pads. Use only white cotton cloths or cotton wool, never coloureds. Orange sticks, round which you can wrap pieces of cotton wool, are useful for small areas. Dispose of old applicators safely, where they will not be a danger to children or pets.

Remember, too, that practically all stain removers are poisonous. Keep them well out of children's reach, preferably in a locked cupboard, and clearly labelled. **Do not decant solvents into misleading containers, such as squash bottles.**

Another point to bear in mind is that grease solvents and stain removers may give off intoxicating vapours and some are flammable. So use them sparingly, work in an airy place, wear rubber gloves and do not smoke.

WHEN USING STAIN REMOVERS REFER TO THESE NOTES

Acetic acid Do not use on acetate fabrics or Tricel. Rinse other fabrics thoroughly after treatment. Use diluted: two parts to five parts of water. Can cause some dyes to bleed so test carefully. Keep off the skin.

Acetone is highly flammable. Work with the window open and do not smoke. Do not use on acetate fabrics or Tricel. Can affect some dyes so use carefully.

Ammonia Household ammonia removes certain stains, neutralises acid ones. Use it diluted, one part to at least three parts water, and always in a well ventilated room. Ammonia can cause bleeding of some dyes, so do a test patch first. Do *not* add to hydrogen peroxide for use on wool. Avoid contact with the skin.

Amyl acetate Usually used neat. Safe on most fabrics but causes some dyes to bleed, so test carefully. Flammable.

Borax Laundry borax is safe on most fabrics and is specially useful when stains have 'dyed' into the fabric as it has a mild bleaching action. Use 1 tablespoon to 500 ml warm water for sponging or soaking washable fabrics (10–15 minutes). For white fabrics sprinkle borax on dampened stain, stretch the item over a basin and pour hot water through it.

Cellulose thinners is highly flammable. Work with the window open and do not smoke. Can damage some synthetics so test first.

Enzyme (biological) washing powder This is good on protein stains like blood, egg and perspiration, also tea, coffee and wine. Follow the manufacturer's instructions. When soaking colourfast fabrics, immerse the whole article in case there is a slight colour change. Do not use for soaking wool, silk, non-fast coloureds, flame-retardant or rubberised fabrics or articles with metal fastenings. Enzyme soaking might possibly fade polyester/cotton mixtures; sponging may be preferable here.

Glycerine lubricates and softens stains on any fabric and colour. Use it diluted one part to two parts water. Spread over stain, leave up to 1 hour. Rinse with water. Insoluble in white spirit and dry cleaning solvents.

Grease solvents These remove grease and oil marks and in certain cases are effective on other stains. They may be either liquids, aerosols or in the form of a paste/jelly. It is important to handle them with care and to follow the manufacturer's instructions exactly.

Hydrogen peroxide Like borax, hydrogen peroxide is a mild, slow-acting oxidising bleach. Use 20 volume strength, diluting it one part peroxide to six of cold water. Suitable fabrics can be soaked for up to 30 minutes. You can speed things up by adding ½ teaspoon ammonia to every 1 litre of the solution, but do not try this if the item is made of wool. Hydrogen peroxide is safe for most fabrics (including wool and silk) with the exception of nylon, some viscose (rayon) fabrics and those with flame-retardant finishes.

Lighter fuel is highly flammable. Work with the window open and do not smoke.

Methylated spirits Used neat (unless in doubt) methylated spirits acts as a solvent, but is unsuitable for acetate fabrics and Tricel. It is both flammable and poisonous, so work with care. Surgical spirit is an alternative but contains some oil so should usually be followed by a grease solvent.

Nail varnish remover Use a non-oily brand or, better still, use acetone. On acetate fabrics or Tricel and other fabrics where a test area with acetone proves unsatisfactory use amyl acetate (flammable).

Proprietary grease solvents These remove grease and oil marks and in certain cases are effective on other stains. They may be either liquids, aerosols or in the form of a paste/jelly. It is important to handle them with care and to follow the manufacturer's instructions exactly.

Proprietary spotting kits for use on carpets and upholstery can be used on numerous stains and a variety of fabrics. These should also be used exactly in accordance with manufacturer's directions.

Turpentine substitute (white spirit) is highly flammable. Work with the window open and do not smoke. Safe for use on most fabrics.

Vinegar (white) Can be useful on certain stains; remember to rinse well afterwards. Do not use on acetate fabrics or Tricel.

White spirit See Turpentine substitute.

Using stain removers

1 Always tackle the stain as soon as possible. Stains left in synthetics, particularly drip-dry fabrics, can be absorbed into the fibres and iron mould (rust) can weaken cotton, acetate fabrics and Tricel and may eventually cause holes.

2 When selecting your method, try and be sure you know both the nature of the stain and the fabric, and if dyes or a special finish are involved.

3 Milder methods repeated are far more effective than a stronger solvent applied after the stain has dried.

4 When it is necessary to apply solvents to absorbed stains which have not responded to sponging or laundering, work from the right side of the stain, supporting the wrong side with a dry absorbent pad if possible. Built-up or compound stains should be treated from the wrong side, if you can, with a dry pad held over the mark. Keep changing the position of the pad to present a clean surface. In this way the deposit is driven out of the fabric, not through it.

5 Always start from the outside of the stain and work towards the centre to avoid spreading it. Dab rather than rub; rubbing pushes the stain into the fabric and can leave a roughened surface.

6 Always carry out a test area on an unseen section of the article first and examine the fabric and the colour before proceeding.

STAINS–HOW TO DEAL WITH THEM

Adhesives

Scrape off excess, then follow instructions for type. Large areas on carpet will need professional cleaning.

Clear adhesives on fabrics and upholstery Hold absorbent pad on stained side; dab from wrong side, if possible, with acetone* or non-oily nail polish remover*. On acetate and Tricel, it is best to use amyl acetate*.

On carpets dab lightly with acetone* or non-oily nail polish remover*. On unidentifiable pile, use amyl acetate*.

Contact adhesive on fabrics and upholstery Hold absorbent pad on stained side, dab from wrong side, if possible, with acetone* or non-oily nail polish remover*. On acetates and Tricel use lighter fuel* or amyl acetate*.

On carpets As for contact adhesives on fabrics. If tests prove unsuccessful, try lighter fuel* or amyl acetate*. Some makers of contact adhesives also manufacture their own proprietary remover.

Epoxy resin on fabrics and upholstery Hold absorbent pad on stained side, dab from the wrong side, if possible, with cellulose thinners*. On synthetic fibres use lighter fuel*.

See notes pages 170–171

171

On carpets Dab with cellulose thinners*. On synthetic fibre pile or synthetic mixture use lighter fuel*. If stain has dried, trim pile with scissors.

Sticky label leftovers on china, glass and enamel If soaking or rubbing with a damp cloth does not work, try white spirit*, methylated spirits*, nail varnish remover* or cellulose thinners*. Then wipe with a damp cloth.

Latex adhesive on fabrics and upholstery This comes off with a damp cloth when wet. When dry, loosen with a liquid grease solvent*, rub off as much as possible; sponge or launder. Some manufacturers make their own solvent.

On carpets Scrape off with the back of a knife. Remove rest with the maker's solvent.

Model-making cement on fabric, upholstery, carpets Wipe off what is possible; dab remainder with a moist pad of liquid grease solvent*. This cement is very hard to remove when dry; some makers have their own solvent, but even with this a test area is essential and some discoloration may remain.

Alcoholic drinks
Beer on washables Rinse or soak fresh stains in lukewarm water, then launder. Dried stains: launder then bleach remaining stains on white cottons or linens in hydrogen peroxide* solution. Sponge coloured fabrics with a solution of 2 tablespoons of white vinegar* to 500 ml warm water. Sponge acetate and Tricel fabrics with borax* solution. Launder.

On non-washables Blot well and wipe with a cloth wrung out in lukewarm water. Sponge dried stains with an acetic acid* solution (two parts acetic acid to five parts water) then sponge with clear water. Blot well. This treatment is not suitable for acetates and Tricel. Instead sponge with clear water, let dry, then use a proprietary aerosol spot remover*. Treat upholstery with a spotting kit*.

On carpets Flush out fresh stains with a soda siphon or sponge with warm water. Blot well. Treat dried marks with carpet shampoo or a spotting kit*.

Spirits on washables Rinse with clear warm water, then launder.

On non-washables Sponge with warm water, blot dry. Rub a lather from washing-up liquid or upholstery shampoo into any remaining marks. Wipe

with a cloth wrung out in warm water, blot dry. Alternatively, use a spotting kit* Clothes that might watermark should be professionally cleaned.

On carpets Blot up excess fluid and flush area with a soda siphon or sponge with a cloth wrung out in warm water. Blot well. Remaining stains should be treated with carpet shampoo lather or a spotting kit*.

Wine on table linen Pour white wine (if you have it handy) over a fresh red wine stain to neutralize it and make it easier to remove. Pour boiling water through a fresh wine stain, or rinse in warm water and soak in a borax* or enzyme detergent* solution before laundering. Similarly soak or sponge dried stains; on white fabrics sprinkle borax straight on to the mark and pour hot water through before soaking. Use a proprietary colour and stain remover on stubborn stains on white fabrics. Domestic bleach in solution can be used on white cottons and linens without easy care or drip dry finishes.

On washables Rinse in warm water and if necessary soak or sponge in borax* or enzyme detergent* solution before laundering. Dried marks: treat similarly or use a hydrogen peroxide* solution on white wool or silk. Rinse and launder. On white fabrics use colour stripper or bleach as for table linen.

On non-washables Blot well and sponge with warm water. Sprinkle french chalk or talc on remaining marks on the damp fabric and brush off after a few minutes. Repeat if necessary. Dried stains: lubricate with a glycerine solution*, sponge with warm detergent solution, then with clear water. Alternatively, use a spotting kit*.

On carpets Flush with soda siphon or sponge with warm water; blot. Apply lather of made-up shampoo plus 1 teaspoon vinegar in each 500 ml. Rub gently and repeat as necessary. Alternatively, use a spotting kit*.

Artists paints
Acrylic on fabrics If wet, blot off excess; sponge with cold water. Soak and launder if possible. If dried in, place absorbent pad on non-stained side and use a proprietary paint solvent (do not smoke). All the colour may not come out.

Oils on fabrics Hold absorbent pad to non-stained side, dab with turpentine* or white spirit*.

Where hardened, use proprietary paint solvent (do not smoke).

Poster/powder paint, water colours on fabrics Sponge with cold water, leave to soak if necessary. Laundering should remove all traces.

Beetroot juice
On table linen Rinse immediately in cold water. Soak in borax* solution then launder. Soaking in an enzyme detergent* solution also works. Treat dried stains on white fabrics with a proprietary colour and stain remover, following the instructions.

Bird droppings
Laundering removes most dropping stains, though you may need to use hydrogen peroxide bleach* on white and colourfast fabrics if the bird has eaten berries. Use a diluted solution of a proprietary bleach on white cottons and linens, but not on crease-resistant, drip-dry, embossed or piqué fabrics.

On non-washables wipe or brush to clear deposit and use repeated applications of an aerosol grease solvent*.

On carpets Wipe or brush to clear the surface deposit; sponge with warm water or a tepid borax* solution if necessary. Rinse and blot dry with paper or a cloth.

Blood
On sheets and washables Sponge fresh marks with cold salt water then soak in enzyme detergent* solution; launder in cool suds. Stubborn dried-in stains may respond to soaking in hydrogen peroxide* solution with added ammonia*; rinse well.

On non-washables Wipe or brush lightly to remove surface deposit; sponge with cold water containing a few drops of ammonia*. Rinse with clean water, blot well. Alternatively, use a proprietary spotting kit*.

On mattresses Tip mattress on its side and, with a towel pressed to the stained area to avoid spreading, sponge with cold salt water then with cold clear water. Upholstery cleaner may also prove effective.

On carpets Soda siphon fresh stains or sponge well with cold water; blot. Repeat until clean, or use a spotting kit*.

Candle wax
On washables Carefully lift off surface deposit with your fingernail. Sandwich stained area in clean blotting paper, melt out remainder of deposit by pressing the paper with a warm iron. Keep moving the paper so the clear sections absorb the wax. Use a grease solvent* to remove final traces; launder to clear any dye.

On close-woven upholstery Melt out wax with a moderately hot iron over clean blotting paper; remove remaining colour by dabbing with methylated spirits*.

On loose-woven fabrics Do not pull off the deposit – you may pull threads too. Melt out with blotting paper and iron.

On pile fabrics Rub off as much deposit as possible, then hold blotting paper to pile side and apply warm iron to the other, taking care not to depress the pile. Clear traces with aerosol grease solvent*.

On carpets Scrape off with the bowl of a spoon; melt out remainder with the toe of a warm iron applied through blotting or brown paper. Keep the iron from touching the pile and move the paper around for maximum absorption. Clear traces with proprietary grease solvent*. Remove any remaining colour by dabbing with methylated spirits*.

On wallpaper Do not lift or scrape the deposit because this might tear the paper. Use a warm iron over blotting paper to absorb the wax. Finally treat with aerosol grease solvent*.

On vinyl wall covering Allow wax splashes to harden, then lift off carefully with the back of a knife blade. Dab gently with methylated spirits* or liquid grease solvent* to remove colour, then clean area with a household cleaner.

On polished wood Hold plastic bag of ice cubes over the mark to harden the wax then chip it off carefully with a fingernail or plastic spatula. Rub with duster to remove any film, then repolish. If there is heat-marking, rub hard along the grain with a cloth dipped in liquid metal polish.

Chewing gum
On upholstery A proprietary aerosol gum remover is available that freezes the deposit so you can crack it and pick it off. Try a test area first; work with care because the low temperature can 'burn' the skin.

---

* *See notes pages 170–171*

On carpets Use aerosol remover (see above); brush deposit up by hand – the bits could gum up a vacuum cleaner.

On clothing Put the garment in the fridge or hold a plastic bag of ice cubes on the gum to harden it; crack and pick off. Use liquid grease solvent* (not on proofed articles) to remove the rest. Launder if possible, or sponge with warm water.

Chocolate

On washables Scrape off excess with back of knife blade; launder at temperature recommended for the fabric, using enzyme detergent* solution. If staining remains, sprinkle wet mark with borax*, pour hot water through and rinse to clear.

On non-washables Scrape off excess, treat with grease solvent* or use a spotting kit*, sponge with warm water. For fabrics that will not take proprietary cleaners, sponge with warm water then rub dry borax* into the mark. Leave for half an hour, then sponge off.

On carpets Scrape off excess with blunt knife. Use carpet shampoo. When dry apply proprietary grease solvent* to any remaining stain.

Cocoa

On washables Rinse thoroughly; soak and launder in hand-hot suds using enzyme detergent* solution. Alternatively, soak in borax* solution, then launder in plain hand-hot suds. When dry, use a proprietary grease solvent* to remove any traces. For stubborn marks on white cottons and linens, try a proprietary colour and stain remover.

On non-washables Sponge with warm borax* solution then clear water. Rub dry gently; use proprietary grease solvent* to clear any traces. Alternatively, use a spotting kit*.

On carpets Spoon and blot up then flush with soda siphon or sponge with warm water; blot well. Use carpet shampoo or spotting kit*. When dry, remove traces with grease solvent*. Sponge dried stains with borax* solution then blot. Rub glycerine* solution into remaining stain, leave for a few minutes, then rinse and blot. Repeat this last treatment if necessary.

Coffee

On washables and non-washables Treat as for cocoa. On acrylic upholstery velvet woven into a backing of cotton or cotton and man-made fibre, coffee can often be removed with an aerosol upholstery cleaner. Lubricate old, dried-in stains with a glycerine* solution; leave for half an hour then rinse with a cloth wrung out in warm water.

On carpets Treat as for cocoa. Soda siphon flushing and blotting may clear black coffee. Even dried stains may respond to repeated soda siphon flushing; allow time to dry in between.

Crayon

On wallpaper No treatment, alas. Stick on a fresh piece of paper, torn roughly to shape for a less obvious join.

On vinyl wallcovering and bedheads Wipe with a damp cloth, and if necessary use a liquid household cleaner.

Creosote

On washables Hold an absorbent pad on stained side, apply lighter fuel*, or eucalyptus oil to other side; launder. Old stains may be softened sufficiently with glycerine* solution to let you wash them out.

On non-washables Professional cleaning is best for creosote.

Curry

On washables Rinse well with lukewarm water; rub in glycerine* solution and rinse again. Soak in enzyme detergent* solution and launder with same detergent. Stubborn stains: use a hydrogen peroxide* solution.

On non-washables Sponge with lukewarm water; if unsuccessful it is best to have the article professionally cleaned.

Dyes

On washables Soak whites and fast-coloureds in enzyme detergent* solution. If the stain is not cleared on whites use a proprietary dye stripper. Sponge coloured fabrics with methylated spirits* containing a few drops of ammonia*. Rinse well; launder.

On non-washables Try the method above, or have the article professionally cleaned.

Egg

Whole egg on washables Sponge with cold salt water then launder, using enzyme detergent* solution.

See notes pages 170–171

For dried stains, give an enzyme* soak followed by laundering.

Egg yolk on washables Launder, using enzyme detergent* solution; when dry apply a grease solvent* to clear traces.

On non-washables Scrape off surface, work in a lather of washing-up liquid solution or upholstery shampoo, wipe with damp cloth; when dry, use grease solvent*. Alternatively try a spotting kit*.

Embroidery transfer
Touch lightly with methylated spirits*, applied on a cotton wool bud. Test carefully, especially with synthetic fabrics. Launder if possible. Where methylated spirits cannot be used, try laundering.

Flowers and grass
Laundering usually removes light stains on washables such as sportswear. Otherwise rub marks with methylated spirits*. Rinse with warm clear water.

On cricket flannels If these are washable, treat as above. Otherwise, have them dry cleaned. Small stains may respond to a proprietary aerosol spot remover*. Repeat applications, if necessary until clear.

Fly specks
On fabric lampshades Try aerosol spot remover*, carefully. Alternatively, make up a warm solution of heavy-duty detergent and brush stains from both sides of the shade with a soft brush. Rinse the area in the same way with clear water. Blot and let dry away from direct heat to prevent ring-marking and splitting. Do not wet the trim.

Fruit juice
On table linen Stretch the stained area over a basin, pour boiling water through. Lubricate remaining marks with glycerine* and launder. Soak dried stains in a borax* or enzyme detergent* solution. Alternatively, use a proprietary colour and stain remover on whites.

On washables Rinse under running cold water. If this fails, stains on white silks, nylon and wool may respond to a dye stripper: other fabrics soak and launder using an enzyme detergent* solution. It's advisable to lubricate dried stains with glycerine* solution before treating this way. Stubborn dried stains may respond to hydrogen peroxide*; stains on white cotton to soaking in a product designed for cleansing nappies.

On non-washables Sponge with cold water and blot. Use a spotting kit* to remove any remaining traces.

Gravy
On washables Soak in cool water, launder in warm detergent suds. When dry treat grease marks with grease solvent*. Soak dried stains in enzyme detergent* solution before laundering.

On non-washables Use grease solvent*; sponge with warm water if necessary.

Grease, fats, oils
On table linen Blot off excess. Cotton and linen can be washed at temperatures high enough to clear.

On other washables Scrape off the excess. Fabrics that can withstand high temperatures should be laundered in detergent suds; for others, use a grease solvent* before laundering. Heavy deposits, including car and cycle oil, can be removed by gentle rubbing with a proprietary hand cleanser available through motor accessory shops. Delicate fabrics and wool can be dabbed with eucalyptus oil. Finally launder or sponge.

On upholstery and non-washables Spread french chalk, talc or powdered starch over small marks. Brush off and add more as it soaks up the oil; leave several hours then brush clear. Alternatively, use a grease solvent*. Take care with foam backings. Marks on flat woven or velvet pile acrylic fabrics are best treated with a liquid grease solvent*. For larger areas (not acrylic velvet or pile fabric) press with a warm iron over clean blotting paper and then use grease solvent.

On shoes Shoe polish manufacturers make special products for removing oils and tar from suede and leather shoes. Follow the instructions. It's usually best to treat the whole shoe to avoid a patchy look.

On suede coats If rubbing with the manufacturer's cleaning pad or brush fails rub with a special suede cleaning cloth. Do not use liquid cleaner as chemicals may affect the dye. Large stains need professional cleaning.

On wallpaper Use a warm iron over blotting paper; treat any remaining marks with a paste grease solvent*.

---

* *See notes pages 170–171*

On hessian Use an aerosol grease solvent* sparingly and do a test area first – hessian dyes are fairly weak.

On carpets Blot or scrape off excess with a spatula. Apply a grease solvent* very sparingly where there is a foam or plastic backing. For heavy deposits use a warm iron and blotting paper, as for candle wax. Then rub in a lather from a made-up carpet shampoo, or use an aerosol foam carpet cleaner. Repeat as necessary.

On beachwear Use eucalyptus oil or a proprietary tar remover.

Hair oil

On an upholstered headboard Treat small areas with grease solvent*. Acrylic velvets respond best to a liquid or aerosol grease solvent; apply sparingly over foam padding. For large areas, make up a paste of french chalk plus a little liquid grease solvent, spread over the mark and brush off when dry.

On a wooden headboard Rub with a cloth moistened with white spirit*. Buff up with a soft cloth.

Ice cream

On washables Wipe off excess, soak in an enzyme detergent* solution; launder in the hottest water the fabric can safely take. When fabric cannot be soaked, or if the stain has dried, sponge with warm borax* solution before washing. When dry, treat any remaining marks with grease solvent then bleach with hydrogen peroxide* if fabric can withstand this.

On non-washables Sponge with warm water. When dry treat any traces of left-over grease or colouring as above; alternatively, use a spotting kit*.

Ink

Washable ink on fabrics Act quickly before the stain dries. Sponge or rub under cold water until no more ink comes out. Launder to remove traces, or apply a paste grease solvent* when dry, repeating if necessary. For dried stains rinse as above, then apply cotton wool pads soaked in a hot soapflake (not detergent) solution, changing the pad every 15 minutes. Rinse. If this does not work, seek the manufacturer's advice. Delicate fabrics should be cleaned professionally.

On carpets Sponge fresh stains with cold water then apply lather from a hand-hot soapflake solution. Rub in lightly, rinse; repeat as necessary. Dried stains may respond to the same treatment or repeated use of a spotting kit*; larger areas should be cleaned professionally.

Permanent ink on fabrics Remove as much as possible with cold water. Try spotting kit on small marks, or contact the ink manufacturers for their recommended treatment. Alternative: professional dry cleaning.

On carpets Sponge with cold water. The manufacturers of permanent inks can usually advise on their removal; professional cleaning is likely to be necessary for large dried stains.

Ballpoint ink on upholstery and fabrics Dab lightly with cotton wool dipped in methylated spirits*. Or use a liquid grease solvent* or an aerosol for light stains. Sponge with warm water or launder. If this does not work, write to the manufacturer for advice. Delicate fabrics or bad marks should be cleaned professionally.

On vinyls, vinyl wall coverings and dolls Tackle mark immediately with nail brush and warm water plus soap or detergent. If ink has soaked in there is nothing you can do.

Felt tip ink on fabrics and upholstery Dab small marks with methylated spirits*, or use an aerosol or paste grease solvent*, launder where possible. Contact pen manufacturers for advice on heavy staining. Have delicate fabrics, bad marking cleaned professionally.

On vinyls, wall coverings and dolls Try a liquid household cleaner or methylated spirits* on cotton-wool. If these fail, use neat washing-up liquid on fabric wrapped over one finger, then a proprietary vinyl cleaner.

Iron mould

On linens, handkerchiefs Rub rust marking with lemon juice then rinse. Alternatively use a proprietary rust remover following the maker's instructions. Rinse well, holding the fabric horizontally under running cold water.

Jam

On linens and washables Fresh stains usually wash out. Soak old stains in borax solution* for half an hour or in an enzyme detergent solution*; then launder.

---

* See notes pages 170–171

On non-washables Wipe off deposit, sponge with a cloth moistened in a warm solution of washing-up liquid. If stain remains, rub on a little dry borax* and leave for a few minutes before rinsing. Or let the fabric dry and use a spotting kit*.

Make-up
Foundation cream on washables Wipe fresh stains; if possible soak for 5 minutes in a weak solution of 1 teaspoon ammonia* to 500 ml warm water; rinse well. Launder in detergent suds at the highest temperature the fabric can take. Brush dried stains, then soften with glycerine solution* before laundering.

On non-washables Wipe up deposit, or brush a dried one. Apply grease solvent* using an aerosol for markable fabrics. Or, on light coloured fabrics you can rub in talc or french chalk. After two hours, shake and brush lightly. Or use a spotting kit*.

Lipstick on washables Most stains wash out. Tough marks: damp and rub first with glycerine* or eucalyptus oil. Use hydrogen peroxide* solution to bleach out remaining colour on whites.

On non-washables Dab lightly with eucalyptus oil or use an aerosol grease solvent*.

Trodden into carpet Scrape carefully then treat with grease solvent* or a spotting kit*. Clear remaining colour with a careful application of methylated spirits*.

Mascara on towels, clothing, upholstery Apply grease solvent*. Dab any remaining stain with ammonia* diluted one part ammonia to three parts water. Rinse the area well.

Mayonnaise
On washables Sponge with warm water – if it is too hot the egg content will set. Soak in enzyme detergent* solution where possible; launder.

On non-washables Remove residue with a damp cloth but do not spread the mark. Treat the dry fabric with an aerosol grease solvent*. Have expensive articles cleaned professionally.

Metal polish
On carpets Spoon and blot up the residue then dab the area with white spirit*. When dry, brush off powdery deposit; shampoo if necessary. Brush dry stains before treating.

Mildew
On leather Difficult to eradicate as fungus grows into the pores. Specialist cleaning is recommended.

On plastic shower curtains Sponge light marking with a weak solution of household bleach or antiseptic. Swab heavily marked areas with a mild detergent solution, then rinse with a proprietary fungicide solution.

On wall surfaces Wash down with a mild detergent solution, and rinse with a proprietary fungicide solution.

On washables While growth is fresh, laundering usually removes it. Bleach out marks left on whites with hydrogen peroxide solution*. Use a household bleach solution on white cottons and linens, but not on crease-resistant, drip dry, embossed or piqué fabrics. On coloured fabrics, rub damped areas with hard soap and dry in the sun. Regular washing reduces mildew marks.

On non-washables Professional cleaning is recommended. If the article is an heirloom a museum may be able to give you advice.

Milk
On washables Rinse item well in lukewarm water then launder in warm detergent suds. When dry, treat remaining marks with a grease solvent*. Treat hot milk stains immediately with liquid grease solvent then wash in warm detergent suds. Soak dried stains in enzyme detergent* solution, then launder.

On non-washables Sponge with lukewarm water, treat remaining marks with grease solvent* when dry. On acrylic flat-woven and velvet pile fabrics, use a liquid or aerosol grease solvent or a spotting kit*.

On carpets Treat quickly – when milk penetrates and dries you cannot get rid of the smell without professional cleaning. Flush with soda siphon or rinse with lukewarm water then use carpet shampoo or a spotting kit. For marks left when the carpet dries, use a liquid grease solvent*, but do not let it soak through to a foam or plastic carpet backing.

Nail varnish
On fabrics, upholstery Wipe immediately with tissues or cotton wool. With an absorbent pad under the stain dab with acetone* or nail varnish remover*. On acetate fabrics or Tricel use amyl

* See notes pages 170–171

acetate*; also use amyl acetate on other fabrics where a test with acetone proves unsatisfactory. If you use nail polish remover, you may need to remove oil marking with an aerosol grease solvent* or by laundering. Dab any remaining colour with methylated spirits*. With a bad spill on acetate fabrics and Tricel, go for professional cleaning.

Paints

Speed is essential. Scrape and wipe up then follow the appropriate method below. With newer paints which can be washed out in a mild detergent, immediate laundering or sponging should clear the stain.

Oil-based paint Dab fresh stains with white spirit* then sponge with cold water; repeat if necessary. Launder where possible; shampoo carpets and upholstery. Alternatively, use a spotting kit*. Treat dried stains with a paint brush cleaner or as a last resort, a chemical paint remover. Test first. Bad marks and delicate fabrics need professional cleaning.

Emulsion paint Sponge fresh stains with cold water, then launder. Treat dried stains with methylated spirits* or a chemical paint remover. Test first. Sponge and launder. Again, delicate fabrics need professional cleaning.

Paraffin

On carpets Do not smoke. Tackle immediately as oil which penetrates the backing can cause dye seepage and deterioration of foam or latex backing. Mop up as much as possible and apply aerosol grease solvent*. Vacuum to remove deposit; repeat treatment if necessary. For large stains, have professional cleaning.

Perfume

Rinse washables immediately. Lubricate dried stains with a glycerine solution* before laundering. On non-washables first lubricate with glycerine* then wipe lightly with a cloth wrung out in warm water; blot. Expensive clothes, especially silks, should be cleaned professionally.

Perspiration

On washables Sponge fresh stains with a weak solution of ammonia* then rinse out. Where colour is affected, sponging with vinegar* solution (1 tablespoon vinegar to 250 ml warm water) may

help, followed by rinsing. Bleach white cotton or linen with a solution of hydrogen peroxide* or soak in enzyme detergent* solution. A little vinegar in the rinse water helps clear odour.

On non-washables Dab with white vinegar solution (see above) to help clear stain and deodorize area. Where dye is affected, rub lightly with methylated spirits*. Suits should be cleaned professionally if lined with synthetic fabrics.

Pet stains

Urine/vomit on upholstery Remove deposit with absorbent paper, taking care not to spread the stain; blot. Remove covers if possible; gather fabric and tie string round to isolate affected area. Rinse under running cold water: or use a pet stain remover after testing for colour fastness. Launder or sponge.

Mess on carpets Remove deposit with absorbent paper or spoon. Flush area with soda syphon or sponge with warm water and blot. To clear mark and deodorize area use a proprietary pet stain remover. If instructions advise using remover before sponging, do so, then shampoo if necessary. If deposit has dried, soften with the proprietary remover before scraping off.

Plasticine

Scrape off as much as possible. Hold an absorbent pad under the stain and dab with liquid grease solvent* to dissolve the deposit. For small areas use lighter fuel* but take care on synthetics. Avoid wetting carpet backing. Finally, launder washables or sponge with warm water and blot dry.

Rain and salt water

On calf leather Wipe lightly before the spots dry with a cloth well wrung out in lukewarm water to dampen the entire surface. Let dry naturally then use a proprietary hide food, or saddle soap (not on aniline calf).

On suede Allow rainspots to dry naturally, then use a suede cleaning pad or brush.

On suede shoes Use a proprietary stain remover made by a shoe polish manufacturer, but treat both shoes as the colour may lighten.

Rust, see Iron mould

Scorch marks

On washables Rub light marks immediately under

cold running water, then soak in a warm borax solution*. Rinse well, launder if possible. On whites, careful bleaching with hydrogen peroxide* is a last resort. Bad scorching: no remedy.

On non-washables Lubricate light marks with glycerine* solution then sponge with warm water. Heavier marking: rub lightly with a cloth wrung out in borax solution*, rinse and repeat if necessary.

On carpets Brush with stiff bristles to remove loose fibres, then use glasspaper or a wire brush in gentle circles to hide the mark. Some carpet stores undertake to retuft damaged areas.

Shoe polish
On carpets Scrape deposit without spreading the mark. Dab with white spirit* or use grease solvent to lift spot. Dab with methylated spirits* to clear any remaining colour; finally use carpet shampoo. Alternatively, use a spotting kit.

On vinyl floors Rub lightly with a cloth moistened in white spirit* then wipe with a damp cloth.

On washables Use grease solvent*, or launder with a few drops of ammonia* in the water. Treat heavy stains with white spirit* or a liquid grease solvent; rinse and launder.

On non-washables Scrape up the deposit without spreading the mark. Dab with white spirit* or use an aerosol grease solvent*; repeat if necessary. Clear colour by dabbing with methylated spirits*; rinse with clear water if possible.

Smoke and soot
On brick and stone Use a proprietary brick or stone cleaner.

On carpets, rugs Vacuum or shake, do not brush. Treat small marks with a grease solvent*. Large areas are best cleaned professionally, but may respond to light brushing with lather from made-up carpet shampoo. To avoid wetting light coloured carpets, use repeated applications of french chalk, Fuller's Earth or talc, rubbed in lightly and vacuumed off when the soot is absorbed.

Tar
On carpets Scrape off deposit, apply grease solvent* or use a spotting kit*. Soften dried tar first with glycerine* solution.

On beachwear Scrape off surface deposit. With a pad held over stain, work from underneath with eucalyptus oil on cotton wool. Alternatively, use a proprietary tar remover.

On leather and suede Use a proprietary grease and tar remover, working it slowly and carefully across the mark.

Tea
On table linen Pour boiling water through fresh stains. Soak and launder in enzyme detergent* solution to clear traces. Dried marks: damp, stretch over basin, sprinkle with borax* and pour hot water through. Alternatively treat whites with a colour and stain remover, or use a bleach solution on white cotton or linen without a crease resistant or drip dry finish. Rinse and launder.

On washables Rinse in lukewarm water. Sponge with or soak in warm borax* solution or soak in enzyme detergent* solution. Launder in warm detergent suds. Soften dried stains by rubbing in glycerine* solution an hour before washing.

On non-washables Treat as for **Cocoa**

On carpets Blot well. Flush fresh stains with soda siphon or sponge with warm water. If milky, follow up with carpet shampoo. When dry apply grease solvent* if necessary. Alternatively, use a spotting kit*. Sponge dried marks with warm borax* solution. If stubborn, follow by rubbing in a glycerine solution*; leave for a few minutes before rinsing and blotting with a towel.

On blankets Rinse quickly in warm water. Some dried stains can be bleached carefully with hydrogen peroxide* solution, then laundered.

Urine
On washables Cold rinse then launder. Soak dried marks in enzyme detergent* solution. Try careful hydrogen peroxide* bleaching for stubborn marks.

On non-washables Sponge fresh stains with warm salt water, rinse, blot well. Get dried stains professionally cleaned.

On mattress Tip the mattress on its side. Holding a towel under the stained area, sponge with warm solution of mild synthetic detergent or upholstery shampoo. Wipe with cold water plus a few drops of antiseptic. Or use spotting kit*. A permanent ring may be left on the mattress but treatment is essential to clear the urine and the smell.

On carpets Blot well, flush with soda siphon.

---

* See notes pages 170–171

Sponge the area with made-up carpet shampoo, adding an eggcupful of white vinegar to each 500 ml. Rinse and blot again. Dried stains may have affected dye but cold water sponging with added ammonia* 1 tablespoon to 500 ml water may help restore appearance.

Vomit

On washables Remove surface deposit, rinse well under running cold water. Soak and launder using enzyme detergent* solution.

On non-washables Remove deposit and sponge with warm water that has had a few drops of ammonia*

added. Blot. Alternatively, use spotting kit*.

On mattress Scrape and wipe up solid matter, try not to spread the stain. Tip mattress on its side and sponge with a warm solution of a mild synthetic detergent or upholstery shampoo. Wipe with cold water plus a few drops of antiseptic.

On carpets Remove deposit and flush with soda siphon or sponge with warm borax* solution. Gently rub in lather from made-up carpet shampoo with 1 teaspoon vinegar* added to each 500 ml. Repeat as necessary, rinse. Or use spotting kit*.

---

* See notes pages 170–171

Laundry work

Washing powder

Powders, liquids and flakes are all scientifically prepared to make a good job of your laundry, but some do it better in soft water than in hard, and some are best for delicate fabrics, others for cottons, etc. And you not only need to use the right type of product, but also the right amount of it to get the best results.

Heavy duty powders These are formulated for both soaking and washing the bulk of the white and colourfast wash, which includes some fairly grubby things like overalls and shirts. Some powders are soap-based and some are synthetic detergents, and all the well known brands contain fluorescers (the light-reflecting ingredient that makes whites and colours brighter) and a mild oxidising bleach to assist stain removal. The bleach works only at temperatures above 60°C so it is safe to use these products for colour-fast cottons, any nylons and such things as easy-care shirts which need lower temperatures and a strong washing powder. Modern washing powders and the right temperature wash virtually cut out the need for separate bleach products.

Synthetic detergents work equally well in hard

and soft water and do not form scum. Soap powders work most efficiently in soft water areas, although most do include a water softener. Never use a soap powder on a fabric with a flame-resistant finish as soap can mask the properties of the finish.

To make sure that you are using the right amount of powder, especially if you switch from one kind to another, check with the maker's instructions on the packet.

Biological washing powders These are heavy duty powders which contain enzymes which help remove protein stains by breaking them down. (Protein stains are ones such as blood, egg and perspiration which may not come out in ordinary powders.) Enzymes are most effective at temperatures above 50°C and below 60°C. Some biological powders also include a solvent to cope with oil and grease marks including grease transferred from the skin and hair.

Low-foaming powders It is essential to use a low-foaming powder in a front-loading automatic and those top-loading machines with reverse tumble action. Ordinary powders make too much lather so the clothes cannot tumble properly and will not come really clean. Often, too, the machine overflows if you try and use an ordinary powder and you end up with suds all over the floor.

Some washing machine manufacturers advise using a low-foaming powder with top-loading machines with other (ie not reverse tumble) actions; so check the instructions.

Light duty powders, liquids and flakes These are milder washing products formulated to deal gently with delicate fabrics. They usually contain a fluorescer but none of the light duty products contain bleach. A powder or liquid synthetic product can be used in hard or soft water, but soap flakes perform best in soft or softened water. Dissolve the soap flakes in a little hot water before adding to the cool wash water.

Some products are made specially for washing wool in luke-warm or even cold water. They contain a detergent, a conditioner and special brighteners and are also suitable for washing delicate nylon, silk and blended fabrics.

Fabric conditioners
A fabric conditioner is a liquid added to the final rinse to give things like towels, nappies and woollens a soft, fluffy feel. It also helps to cut down static in synthetic fabrics so that they do not cling during wear.

Always dilute a fabric conditioner before it comes in contact with clothes, and do not add it to rinsing water that still has washing powder in it or a scum will form. If you add fabric conditioner to an automatic washing machine, pour it into the appropriate section of the detergent dispenser. For rinsing in a spin dryer, add the fabric conditioner to a bowl of water, pour over the clothes and allow to stand for a minute or two before spinning off the water.

Starches
Starching gives a crisp finish and adds body to a fabric. It is used to greatest effect on cottons and linens.

Powder starch is the traditional one and needs to be 'turned' with boiling water. For a small quantity of fabric it is more economical to make up the starch in a bowl and dip things in it; for larger loads, or if you are machine washing, it is easier to add the prepared starch to the final rinse.

Instant starch is also a powder but does not need 'turning'. Just mix it with cold or luke-warm water.

Spray starch comes in an aerosol and is most useful when you are ironing for stiffening small items such as collars. It is expensive to use on large items and difficult to obtain an even spray over a large area.

Other stiffeners There are also non-starch products which add body and a good feel to the fabric. They are applied by aerosol before ironing and can be used on most fabrics.

SORTING THE WASH
With so many new fabrics and finishes, it is becoming increasingly difficult to sort clothes and household linens into 'loads' for washing. The best way around the problem is to follow the instructions on the care labels which usually give all the information you need. Do exercise care with deep dyed articles such as towels. The manufacturer may recommend washing them separately for the first two or three washes, but some may need separate treatment throughout their lives.

The international textile care labelling code
Although care labelling is not compulsory the system described below is now used by the majority of manufacturers. The international code is based on four symbols, each of which is variable; they are:

The washing symbol indicates the article is washable, both by machine and hand. The figure above the 'waterline' ties up with the programmes indicated on automatic washing machines, so you can set the machine to the appropriate cycle. The figure below the 'waterline' gives the water temperature for machine washing. A hand symbol in the tub means the article must not be washed by machine; the wash tub crossed out means the item is not washable.

Chlorine bleaching A triangle containing the letters Cl indicates that the article may be treated with household bleach. If the triangle is crossed out, this means that household bleach must not be used. The symbol refers to chlorine bleach only, and does not apply to other types of bleach.

181

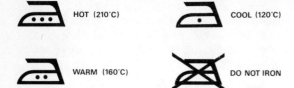

HOT (210°C)   COOL (120°C)

WARM (160°C)   DO NOT IRON

Ironing There are four variations on the ironing symbol. The temperatures shown in brackets are the maximum sole plate temperatures indicated by the dots in the symbol. Where the symbol is crossed through, the article should not be ironed.

Dry cleaning Letters placed in a circle indicate that the article may be dry cleaned and which type solvent may be used. Point them out when you take the article to be cleaned, and if you use a coin-op machine, ask the attendant which dry cleaning solvent is being used.

(A) cleanable in all solvents.

(P) cleanable in perchloroethylene, white spirit, Solvent 113 and Solvent 11.

(F) cleanable in white spirit or Solvent 113.

(X) do not dry clean.

Drying Care labels may also include one or other of the following symbols recommending a particular drying method:

⊡ tumble drying beneficial but not essential

▽ line dry

||| drip dry; for best results hang when wet

— dry flat; do not hang to dry.

Reading the label
An example of an international care code label is

shown below. You will see that in this case in addition to the wash symbol the label also gives a description of the wash process – and this is helpful where you have a machine without numbered programmes. Maximum wash indicates the longest period of washing action recommended for any particular machine. For a medium wash, allow about half this time, and for a short wash the machine should be set to give approximately a quarter of the washing period.

2 / 60°	MACHINE	HAND WASH
	Hot	Hand-hot
	maximum wash	
	Spin or wring	

On some labels handwashing, rinsing and drying instructions may also be included.

In the absence of care instructions, you can get some washing guidance by checking the fibre content label on the article and following the treatment recommended in the international textile care labelling code for the fibre/fibres in question. In the case of a mixture, always wash at the lower temperature. However, such treatment could damage a special finish such as 'easy care' or articles which, because of their trimmings, require dry cleaning, so try to check with the retailer or, failing this, the manufacturer concerned.

WASHING TEMPERATURES

100°C	Boil	Self-explanatory
95°C	Very hot	Water heated to near boiling temperature
60°C	Hot	Hotter than the hand can bear. The temperature of water coming from many domestic hot taps.
50°C	Hand-hot	As hot as the hands can bear
40°C	Warm	Pleasantly warm to the hand
30°C	Cool	Feels cool to the touch

SUMMARY OF WASHING SYMBOLS AND PROGRAMMES

Symbol	Washing Temperature Machine	Hand	Agitation	Rinse	Spinning/wringing	Fabric
1/95	Very hot 95°C to boil	Hand hot 50°C or boil	Maximum	Normal	Normal	White cotton and linen articles without special finishes
2/60	Hot 60°C	Hand hot 50°C	Maximum	Normal	Normal	Cotton, linen or viscose (rayon) articles without special finishes where colours are fast at 60°C
3/60	Hot 60°C	Hand hot 50°C	Medium	Cold, to minimise creasing	Short spin or drip dry	White nylon; white polyester/cotton mixtures. Do not wash these fabrics with those from other groups.
4/50	Hand hot 50°C	Hand hot 50°C	Medium	Cold, to minimise creasing	Short spin or drip dry	Coloured nylon; polyester; cotton and viscose (rayon) articles with special finishes; acrylic/cotton mixtures; coloured polyester/cotton mixtures.
5/40	Warm 40°C	Warm 40°C	Medium	Normal	Normal	Cotton, linen or viscose (rayon) articles where colours are fast in warm (40°C) but not hot (60°C) water
6/40	Warm 40°C	Warm 40°C	Minimum	Cold, to minimise creasing	Short spin. Do not hand wring. Dry chunky knitteds flat	Acrylic; acetate and triacetate, including mixtures with wool; polyester/wool blends
7/40	Warm 40°C	Warm 40°C	Minimum, do not rub	Normal	Normal spin do not hand wring. Dry knitteds flat	Wool, including blankets, and wool mixtures with cotton or viscose (rayon); silk
8/30	Cool 30°C	Cool 30°C	Minimum	Cold, to minimise creasing	Short spin do not hand wring	Silk and printed acetate fabrics with colours not fast at 40°C
9/95	Very hot 95°C to boil	Hand hot 50°C or boil	Maximum	Cold, to minimise creasing	Drip dry	Cotton articles with special finishes capable of being boiled but requiring drip drying
	Do not machine wash. (The appropriate hand washing instructions are usually given alongside this symbol.)					

Soft furnishings

Keeping soft furnishings free from dust means that they will not only look brighter, but will also last longer – because dust that becomes ingrained in the weave will, in time, cause fabrics to deteriorate as well as making colours dull. Rid curtains and upholstery of dust by going over them with the dusting attachment of your vacuum cleaner or a soft brush at fairly frequent intervals. Pay particular attention to the crevices down the sides and backs of seats of upholstered chairs and settees and in the folds of curtains, particularly in the headings, because these are the places where the most dust gathers, providing a cosy spot for moths to lay their eggs.

Removing stains See pages 169–180.

Vacuum cleaning curtains regularly will help keep them looking good for longer

WASHING AND CLEANING

Even with regular dusting and spot cleaning, it is important to wash or dry clean soft furnishing fabrics every so often to get rid of the embedded soiling that comes from handling and use. For detailed instructions on the care of different fabrics, see pages 11–14.

Even if a fabric is washable, before washing the whole item for the first time check an out-of-sight patch of the fabric for colour fastness. Do this either by damping a piece of the fabric and pressing it under a piece of white cloth with a moderate iron or, if this is not possible, by rubbing the fabric with a damp white cloth.

Many furnishing fabrics should be dry cleaned. Very large curtains of any material and interlined curtains are also best dry cleaned. It is always best to tell dry cleaners what the fabric is and about any cleaning instructions supplied by the manufacturer. In particular, inform them when an item contains acrylic fibres, otherwise it may be put through too hot a process. To be safe, the cleaning/pressing process given to acrylics should never exceed 50°C.

Washing curtains and loose covers

Even when you have made certain that your fabric is washable, remember that loose covers and large curtains can be very heavy when wet. Ask yourself if you will be able to cope and whether you have appropriate drying facilities. It could be that professional laundering or cleaning, or coin-op cleaning would be easier. If you are proposing to machine wash the article at home, check that it will fit into your machine/spin dryer before you wet it. Too large a load can unbalance the drum.

If you decide to go ahead, remove all curtain hooks and other metal or hard attachments and loosen curtain heading tapes. Close zips and other fastenings. Shake the article outside if possible to get rid of any loose dust, then follow the hints below:

1 You will be able to get rid of a fair amount of soiling by soaking the cover or curtains in cold water before washing.

2 Wash in warm water, never more than hand hot,

and make sure the washing powder is thoroughly dissolved before you put the fabric in. Use the powder at the strength recommended on the packet for the most delicate fibre involved.

3 Do not use bleach.

4 If you are washing by hand, keep any rubbing and wringing to a minimum. If you are using a machine, follow the recommended wash programme for the most delicate fibre involved.

5 Rinse thoroughly immediately after washing.

6 To dry, squeeze gently, spin dry or wring carefully and hang up at once to minimise creasing. Parallel drying lines will help to spread the weight evenly and avoid strain on the fibres, some of which are weaker when wet.

7 Iron (where necessary) while still evenly damp. Curtains are best ironed lengthwise (along the warp thread) on the wrong side of the fabric, stretching gently as you go – this helps to improve their appearance and avoid puckering along the seams. Have the iron at the correct temperature setting for the fabric concerned.

8 If the fabric has become too dry – or has dried unevenly – before ironing, it is better to damp a synthetic fibre fabric down completely rather than sprinkling it, as this is liable to make spot marks on some fabrics, viscose in particular. Cotton and linen can be sprayed if necessary.

9 It is easiest to put loose covers back on the chairs while they are still warm and slightly damp, and complete the ironing with the covers in position. This counteracts possible shrinkage and ensures a good fit. Remember to use a cool iron on a cover over foam upholstery – and in all cases continue to iron until the cover is completely dry.

Net screening curtains
Net curtains hang closest to windows and so tend to get particularly grubby; also static electricity in some synthetic fabrics attracts dust which can discolour the fabric if neglected.

A half-hour soak before washing will help to remove surface soiling, after which the curtains should be washed as recommended for the fabric concerned (see page 183). Do not exceed the recommended washing and drying temperatures, otherwise permanent creasing will result. Special dye treatments are available to help keep white screening curtains white but they are not really effective on badly discoloured nets.

Most net curtains do not need ironing.

Use an upholstery shampoo solution in a special applicator to make the job easier and prevent over-wetting

CLEANING *IN SITU*
If you cannot remove covers from upholstered furniture to wash or dry clean, you will have to care for them *in situ*.

Always check the maker's instructions before attempting to shampoo the fabric, and even then try a test area on an unseen section first. If in doubt, take professional advice (look in the Yellow Pages under 'Carpet and Upholstery Cleaners').

One should vacuum or lightly brush the furniture before and after shampooing – initially to remove the dust, and afterwards to clean off all traces of the dried shampoo plus the dirt it has absorbed.

Special upholstery shampoo kits are available, using an upholstery shampoo and water solution or you can get a foam aerosol with a special applicator head which only slightly damps the surface. Follow the manufacturer's directions carefully whichever you choose.

FINISHES NEEDING SPECIAL TREATMENT

Glazed cotton
In the absence of specific instructions, glazed cotton can be washed by hand or for a short period in a machine in hand hot water (50°C). Special care must be taken to keep rubbing to a minimum. Do not wring. Remove moisture by gentle squeezing or the shortest possible period in a spin dryer. Line dry over a taut line with plenty of

support. Iron on the shiny side with the iron on cotton setting. Do not use starch.

Acrylic velvet
Acrylic velvet can be shampooed with an upholstery shampoo as described under **'Cleaning in situ'** but it is advisable to carry out a test on an out-of-sight patch first. Be careful to use the foam of the shampoo only, to avoid over-wetting which could cause the cotton backing to shrink. Remember all acrylics can be damaged by heat so make up the shampoo with cool to lukewarm water. When dry, vacuum or lightly brush in the direction of the pile. Do not use an aerosol shampoo.

For greasy marks on acrylic velvet proprietary liquid grease solvent can be used – but sparingly, to avoid damage to the backing of the fabric.

Leather
All leather (but not suede) benefits from an occasional treatment with a hide food. This gives it some protection against stains, and also helps keep the leather supple and stops it cracking.

Good quality furnishing leather is usually cowhide with a final dressing of oil-based lacquer which gives colour fastness and also a degree of waterproofing, so you can sponge it. Other leathers are not spongeable, however, so it is particularly important to keep and follow any manufacturer's instructions.

To remove surface soiling from spongeable leather, wipe it over with a soft cloth well wrung out in a warm solution of glycerine toilet soap. You can buy the tablets of glycerine soap from most chemists. You can make do with ordinary toilet soap or soap flakes, but never use household soap which is too alkaline. Do not use detergents either, as these weaken the protective finish.

Take care not to over-wet the leather or you could damage the stitching, or cause a stain through water soaking into the padding. Finish with a clean damp cloth, but do not rinse off the soap, it helps the leather stay supple. Then let the leather dry naturally.

Treat any greasy marks on non-washable leather with gentle dabs of white spirit. For oily stains such as spilt food, use the rubber solution from a cycle puncture repair kit – but only on darker coloured leathers as the solution has a slight colouring in it which could stain the hide. Squeeze a layer over the mark and let it dry for 24 hours. Roll it off and hope that it has absorbed most, if not all, of the oil. If the stain has penetrated the padding of the leather upholstery there is nothing you can do.

Simulated hides
Imitation leathers should be cleaned with a soft cloth moistened in lukewarm soapy water; never use detergents. Rinse with clean water and dry with a clean cloth before buffing up with a soft duster. Take care when working round wooden frames or you may transfer more dirt on to the upholstered section. Wipe off spills with a damp cloth as quickly as possible. If the upholstery becomes badly stained, seek advice from the retailer or manufacturer.

Vinyl and plastic
Generally these can be treated in the same way as simulated hide. Vinyls with a grain finish are difficult to clean when soiled and you will need a special branded product. Some of these come with a brush type applicator which is helpful for loosening the dirt. Never use a polish on these materials unless the makers recommend it.

Vinyls and plastics do not stain easily but may get marked by felt tip pens or ballpoints. This can sometimes be removed if you treat the mark immediately with a damp cloth and soapy water. Otherwise, dab with methylated spirit, rinse and buff. Do not let the spirit stay on the surface for a prolonged period or it will mark it.

186

Blinds

Keep and follow any care instructions that come with a new blind.

Venetian blinds

Dust the slats and tapes as necessary with the dusting attachment of your vacuum cleaner, or a specially designed two or three pronged brush, or cleaning tongs with foam-covered blades. From time to time the slats can be cleaned with the tongs dipped in, or a cloth wrung out in, a weak solution of synthetic detergent followed by buffing with a soft, dry cloth. Wear protective gloves – the slats are sharp and could cut your hands.

At the same time, wipe over the tapes with a damp cloth and a warm solution of synthetic detergent. Finish with a cloth wrung out in clear, cold water. Let the blinds hang full length with the slats open till the tapes are dry to prevent them shrinking.

If a kitchen Venetian blind has attracted a lot of dust and grease, the best way to give it a thorough cleaning is by washing it in warm soapy water or a

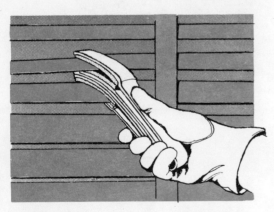

Special foam covered tongs are made for cleaning Venetian blinds

detergent solution in the bath. Keep the roller mechanism out of the water, and put a cloth or a towel in the bottom of the bath to guard against scratching. Rinse well and hang the blind up to dry.

Roller blinds

These need fairly frequent dusting, taking care to keep the roller springs free from fluff. If the blind is beginning to look a bit shabby, take it down and lay it out flat and brush or vacuum both sides, using the dusting attachment. Provided the material is spongeable, you can then wipe it over with a weak solution of soap or detergent in warm water – avoid over-wetting – followed by a wipe over with a cloth or sponge wrung out in clean cold water. Leave to dry flat before re-hanging.

If the material is not spongeable, you may be able to freshen it up by going over it with a soft rubber or a piece of dry bread.

Pleated paper

Again, dust regularly. When necessary, wipe over with a well wrung out damp cloth, using a little synthetic detergent to remove bad marks. Avoid overwetting and never immerse in water.

Canvas sunblinds and awnings

These can be scrubbed with washing soap and warm water, or a synthetic detergent solution, followed by a cold water rinse. The best place to tackle the job is outside on a patio, having covered the paving stones with a large sheet of polythene. Allow the canvas to dry thoroughly, over parallel lines if possible, before it is folded up and put away.

If the water-resistance of the canvas has become impaired, it can be re-treated by painting it over with a water-proofing solution – the type used for tents and available from camping equipment shops is suitable for this.

Beds and bedding

BEDS

Do not leave the protective polythene wrapping on a new mattress or divan base. When you sleep on it, the warmth from your body traps condensation inside the bag and leads to mildew.

Do not make a habit of sitting on the edge of a bed. Concentrating your weight on the same area weakens the edge of the mattress and the base as well (but you can get special firm-edged divan bases for bedsitting rooms – these have reinforced sides to guard against this sort of damage). Try, too, to discourage small children from bouncing on a bed. Apart from the fact they could fall off and hurt themselves, it is not good for the bed or the mattress.

The body gives off moisture during the night so when you get up in the morning, throw back the bed clothes and leave the bed open for at least 20 minutes, with the window open, to dry out and air before re-making.

Most foam mattresses have a layered construction and do not need turning. There are however some made of single density foam, usually found on bunk beds. These should be turned over once a month. Spring interior mattresses should be turned and swung round on the bed to reverse the head and foot ends every three months or so. Never bend a mattress, and get help with turning a double mattress if you can; it will save strain on the handles, not to mention your back.

Every few months, the mattress and upholstered base should be carefully cleaned with a soft brush to remove dust and fluff. The upholstery tool on a vacuum cleaner can be used for removing dust from the surface of a foam mattress, but do not use this on a spring mattress because the suction could dislodge the filling under the cover.

On a metal bedstead with an exposed spring base, clean out the springs with the vacuum attachment or a brush and rub them over with an oily cloth to protect them from rust and prevent them from squeaking.

About every three months, check the bed head and legs. They stand considerable strain and may have worked loose. Make sure that castors are running freely, and do protect the carpet or floor surface with castor cups.

Spills and stains

It is worth buying a washable, bag-style cover or fitted mattress overlay in unbleached cotton or other suitable fabric. It keeps the mattress clean and can be removed for washing. For young children and incontinent people it is sensible to use a protective rubber sheet. If something is spilt, act quickly to stop water or a stain getting to the mattress filling where it could cause real problems. Strip off the bedclothes and stand the mattress on its side – seepage is slower on a vertical surface. Blot off as much liquid as possible with an absorbent cloth, old towel or paper towels.

Immediate sponging with cold water clears many liquid stains. Do not worry about leaving a small watermark; it will not show when the bed is made. It is more important to get rid of any smell.

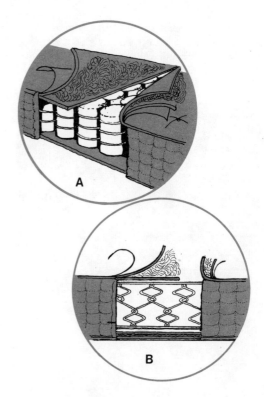

Spring interior mattresses. A. Pocketed springs where each spring works independently
B. Continuous wire construction

Avoid over-wetting by blotting as you work. If further treatment is necessary, follow the instructions under **Stain removal**, pages 179–180.

PILLOWS
Pillows with natural fillings These should be aired regularly – outside in summer.

It is possible to hand wash down or feather filled pillows, though unless you have a large spin dryer, drying them takes so long you may think it worth while to have them done by a professional laundry. The addresses of laundries that operate special pillow cleaning services in your area are obtainable from the Association of British Launderers and Cleaners Ltd, Lancaster Gate House, 319 Pinner Road, Harrow, Middlesex HA1 4HX.

Down or feather filled pillows should never be dry cleaned, either in the ordinary way or in a coin-op machine, as toxic fumes may linger in them.

Machine washing is not recommended in a domestic machine, due to the bulk of a pillow, but a short wash in a launderette machine should be fine. Wash one pillow at a time, with enough towels to balance the load. Follow the drying method recommended for hand laundering, below. Before starting to wash a down or feather pillow, check carefully to see that the cover is in good condition, or the filling may leak.

To wash by hand, use a large container – the wash tub of a top-loading machine is a good choice, otherwise the bath. Wash in warm water using soap flakes or a mild detergent. Squeeze the pillow gently in the suds so the lather penetrates the filling. Rinse in two or three clear, warm rinse waters. Squeeze out the excess moisture, or if you have a large spin dryer wrap the pillow round to fit in the drum and spin for not more than two minutes – longer might draw the filling through the cover. It is not advisable to put a pillow in a tumble dryer; it could cause overheating in a domestic model and the actual tumbling process may weaken the seams and cause the pillow to leak.

Finish by hanging the pillow out of doors firmly pegged by two corners along the line. Re-peg it and shake it up from time to time and be prepared to take it in at night and put it out again in the morning until the pillow is completely dry. Air well in a warm airing cupboard.

Synthetic fibre pillows are normally hand or machine washable, although again more suited to a launderette than a domestic machine. Drip-drying is usually advised, although spin drying followed by tumble drying may be possible in a launderette machine. To get the best results, it is important to follow the manufacturer's instructions. Synthetic fibre pillows should not be dry cleaned.

Foam pillows Vacuum clean foam pillows with the upholstery attachment to remove dust. Washing foam pillows is not recommended. However, accidents happen, and if something is spilt or a child is sick, try to sponge off the stain while it is still on the pillow cover and before it penetrates into the foam below. The cover can be unstitched and taken off for washing. You will need to handle the coverless foam carefully, because it will tear with rough treatment, and is also sensitive to light. Put it in another pillowslip while its own cover is being washed; do not use it, of course.

If, though, when you take the cover off, you see that the stain has already penetrated into the foam, try sponging the surface very gently with warm soapy water, wetting the foam as little as possible. Follow with clean water sponging and blot with a towel. If this is not sufficient, as a last resort, put the cover back on again and wash the pillow complete with cover in warm soapsuds. Squeeze very gently (without twisting or wringing) then rinse till the water runs clear. Press out as much moisture as you can, then wrap the pillow in a towel and press again. Leave the pillow in its close cover in the top of a warm airing cupboard until it is perfectly dry – but never expose a foam pillow to sunlight or direct heat.

SHEETS
Washing
Sheets, particularly synthetics, should never be allowed to become too grubby before washing or it will be harder to remove the dirt. Wash the sheets according to their care label or, failing this, the instructions for treating the fabrics involved – see page 183. Deep-dyed coloured sheets should be washed on their own the first few times as the colour may run slightly. Most synthetic fibre sheets, or those made from a synthetic and natural fibre mixture, will need little or no ironing. Cotton sheets will need ironing; linen ones need careful ironing from damp.

Mending
Darn or patch a sheet the minute you see any

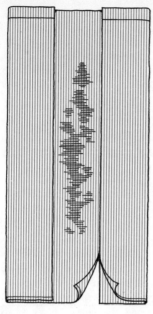

Fold the sides towards the centre and cut the worn part of the sheet away

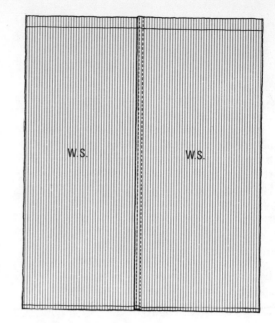

Double stitch the selvedges in a flat seam down the centre and hem the cut edges

damage – otherwise someone will get a toe caught in a small hole during the night and turn it into a big hole by the morning. (For darning and patching, see pages 32–34).

Sheets that have worn in the middle can be turned 'sides to middle' to give them a new lease of life.

1 Lay the worn sheet out flat and fold the sides towards the centre, but leaving the worn area showing in the middle. Keep the folds level with the edges and cut the centre worn part away.

2 Place the right sides of the selvedges together, sew a plain seam about 5 mm from the edge. Fold the edge of the seam to one side and press. Sew along the seam, stitching it to the sheet.

3 Turn in a narrow hem along the cut edges. This will give you a sheet that is once more firm and unworn in the middle.

Storing
Although sheets should always be aired following laundering and before use, do not store them for long periods in a heated airing cupboard or they may become marked along the folds from rising dust in the warm air currents or yellowed by the constant heat. If a white cotton or linen sheet has discoloured in store, wash it and dry it outside in the sun.

BLANKETS
Both natural and synthetic fibre blankets should be shaken out of doors from time to time to keep them fluffy and fresh. Most blankets can be washed either in a machine or by hand; the label or swing ticket will say which. Follow the instructions carefully but before you start, make sure the dry blanket is not too big to go in your machine, and into the spin dryer in the case of a twin tub model. A good machine in a reliable launderette may be a better proposition as the weight of a blanket could unbalance a domestic machine and most launderette machines have a larger capacity.

Woollen blankets that do not carry a 'Superwash' label, or other machine or hand washing instructions, should be dry cleaned. If you use a coin-operated dry cleaning machine, air the blanket very thoroughly before putting it back on the bed as the toxic fumes may linger.

Some laundries and dry cleaners operate special blanket washing and cleaning services; you can get a list of local addresses from the association mentioned on page 189. Certain blanket manufacturers operate their own reconditioning service, so it is worth checking if this is possible in the case of good quality blankets.

Washing a blanket by hand If you have decided to wash a blanket by hand, choose a good drying day so you will be able to hang it out of doors.

Fill the bath, or the tub of a top loading washing machine, with warm water (40°C) and work up a rich lather using a mild synthetic detergent, which is easier to rinse out than a soap-based product. Let the blanket soak for a few minutes, then work it up and down in the suds until the dirt is released. Rinse thoroughly in plenty of warm water, keeping the temperature constant to avoid shrinkage. Squeeze out as much water as you can (but do not wring or twist) or spin dry. Do not tumble dry, however, unless the label specifically states that a tumble dryer can be used, because mechanical movement could cause a blanket to shrink or felt. Wool or wool mixture blankets particularly should not be tumble dried unless labelled accordingly or (more likely) labelled 'Superwash'.

Hang the blanket in a breezy part of the garden, evenly suspended if possible by two parallel lines; striped blankets should be hung with the stripes running vertically to prevent the possibility of the colours running. Shake the blanket occasionally during drying to bring up the pile.

When the blanket is thoroughly dry, brush up the pile lightly with a clean brush. Ribbon bindings may need a light press with a warm iron.

Blankets should be thoroughly aired before storing in polythene bags in a cool cupboard where they will not be crushed. A moth repellant sachet should be included with wool or wool mixture blankets.

ELECTRIC BLANKETS
Many electric blankets can be washed once you have detached the switch and lead assembly. Follow the maker's instructions carefully and even if the blanket is clean and working perfectly, it should be returned to the manufacturer every other year for a thorough overhaul. Unless recommended by the manufacturer, never send an electric blanket to be dry cleaned, because solvents used in the cleaning process could damage the insulation.

To store an electric blanket, fold it as little as possible and keep it in a box in a cool place. Do not use a moth repellant, because this might harm the wiring.

BEDSPREADS
It is essential to follow any washing or cleaning instructions that come with a bedspread – and if none are given, dry cleaning is probably the wiser choice. Certainly never attempt to wash an un-labelled bedspread until you have tried out a test on an inconspicuous corner, plus any trimmings, and checked colour fastness by pressing the damp section between white cotton fabric with an iron. If the tests appear satisfactory, you could risk hand washing.

As with a blanket, make sure the dry bedspread will fit your laundry equipment before you begin. Even if you are hand washing, you will probably need to use the spin dryer and possibly a tumble drier if you have one.

Handwashing is best carried out in the tub of a large top loading washing machine or the bath. Make a good lather of mild detergent and treat the fabric according to type (see page 183). Rinse very thoroughly. If you have to line dry, hang equal amounts of the fabric over two lines to take the strain. Finish as for the material concerned.

CONTINENTAL QUILTS/DUVETS
A duvet should always be protected by a coverslip which as well as taking the place of a top sheet, protects the cambric cover of the quilt from dirt and spillage. Coverslips made of a mixture of man-made and natural fibres are easy to look after and more comfortable to use than an all synthetic fabric. Wash them as for the fabric involved but remember that deep-dyed colours may tend to run in the first few washes, so deal with these separately.

Should anything become spilt on the duvet, mop up immediately to stop it penetrating, then push back the filling so that you can isolate and sponge that section of the cover.

Even if the manufacturer gives washing instructions there is no method of cleaning a duvet without degrading the filling and the lining, therefore only wash when absolutely essential, when it is probably advisable to use a large capacity launder-ette machine because duvets are really too big and bulky to wash at home. Alternatively have it professionally laundered by a firm which offers this service.

Never have any duvet dry cleaned, or cleaned in a coin-op machine, because of the danger of toxic fumes from the solvents remaining in the filling.

A blow in the fresh air from time to time will freshen up a duvet and for the rest, all the routine care it needs is a daily shake to keep the filling evenly distributed.

Carpets and rugs

New carpets sometimes shed an alarming amount of fluff when first laid. This is quite normal, though, and all you should do is brush the surface lightly or use a carpet sweeper until the pile has settled down and the loose fluff has stopped coming away. After this regular vacuuming becomes important, not only to remove surface dirt but to get rid of any embedded grit which can cut into the fibres and so shorten the life of the carpet.

Two or three times a year, any carpets that are not fitted should be lifted and, unless foam-backed, thoroughly vacuumed on the back as well. When you re-lay the carpet, turn it to even out the wear.

Man-made fibre carpets may need a little more attention than wool as dust tends to cling to the fibres due to build-up of static electricity resulting from friction from footwear and a dry atmosphere. If you are buying a new man-made fibre carpet, it might be as well to look for one with an anti-static finish. If static electricity is a problem some carpet cleaners will apply the finish to a carpet that is already laid, failing this, a humidifier helps.

Because the pile of a man-made fibre carpet is not as resilient as wool, as well as vacuuming it may also need a brush-up with a hand brush from time to time in places where the pile has been crushed down.

Avoiding excessive wear
Carpets will stay cleaner if you put mats in front of any doors and french windows giving on to the outside of the house.

On fitted carpets it will even the wear if you move the furniture from time to time. Heavy furniture should be fitted with castors, and when you want to move furniture without castors, lift it; pushing furniture with sharp-edged legs across the carpet damages the fibres. Metal tipped heels and crêpe soled shoes are also bad for carpets because they twist and pull the pile. Try and persuade the family to change from shoes like these in the house.

Wear on stair carpet is particularly hard and concentrated and this should always be laid with the lay of the pile pointing down the stairs and with enough extra length to allow you to move it up or down to spread the wear.

Moth-proofing
Most good British wool pile carpets are moth-proofed when they are manufactured and the information is normally printed on the manufacturer's label. If your carpet has not been moth-proofed you can treat it yourself with a special

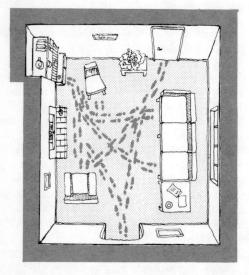

A typical pattern of wear on a living room carpet. Moving the furniture would help to even it out

spray. If possible, spray the back as well as the front of the carpet, and both sides of the underfelt as well. Do not use the spray on a latex or foam carpet backing.

Stains

Carpets can be professionally treated with silicones to protect them from normal household stains. The treatment does not alter the colour, texture or feel of the carpet, but means that spills can be wiped away with a clean damp cloth.

Any spills on carpets, even treated ones, should be dealt with as quickly as possible after they happen. Not only will they be easier to remove but you will also know what caused the mark and be able to treat it accordingly. For details see pages 169 to 180.

SHAMPOOING

No matter how efficient your vacuum cleaner, it cannot remove all the heavy soiling and grease which in time will cling to the fibres and dull the carpet's colour. All carpets need shampooing from time to time, how often depends on the type of fibre, where the carpet is laid, where you live and how many children and pets you have. Indian and long-pile carpets should always be cleaned professionally.

Professional cleaners with portable machines will undertake cleaning on the spot, and the whole process, including stain removal, usually only takes a matter of hours. Alternatively you can send carpets away to a professional firm. Be sure to find out, though, whether the price includes the cost of lifting and re-laying a fitted carpet. It is possible to re-lay a fitted carpet yourself (see page 82) but if invisible fixings have been used you will need to hire special tools for both the lifting and re-laying.

Always warn the cleaners if the carpet you are sending is a fitted one, because there is sometimes a slight shrinkage in the cleaning process and they may need to take special precautions.

Professional cleaning is expensive, however, and nowadays there are a number of different types of carpet shampoo available that make it not too difficult to tackle the job yourself.

Dry foam shampoos are probably the best to choose. These are concentrates that you dilute with water and apply with either a brush, an electric or a non-electric applicator. They produce a foam

The underside of a shampoo applicator, showing the foam rollers and brushes (see page 194)

which dries reasonably quickly. No rinsing is needed; when dry, the foam leaves a crystallized residue which has absorbed the dirt and which you simply vacuum up.

Aerosol foam shampoos need no mixing or diluting. You spray the foam directly on to the carpet and then work it into the pile with a sponge or brush floor mop. Aerosol foam does not damp the carpet as much as other shampoos, so it dries more quickly, and you just vacuum up the loosened soiling. Aerosols are, however, relatively expensive and tend to run out suddenly, so you may be left with an uncleaned area if there turns out to have been less in the can than you expected.

Liquid shampoos are the original and cheapest type. You dilute them with water, following the manufacturer's instructions, then apply them with a soft brush or a shampoo applicator. Their disadvantage is that they wet the carpet more than other kinds of shampoo, which prolongs the drying time. Also they have to be wiped or rinsed off with a cloth in addition to vacuuming, which adds an extra process to the operation.

Applying shampoo

Whichever shampoo you choose, do be sure to read the manufacturer's instructions before you start. Then test the shampoo on an out-of-the way area to make sure the colour of the carpet does not run.

Vacuum the carpet to remove loose dust, and deal with any stains. Unless you are using an aerosol, you will find a shampoo applicator of help, because these cut out backache and also regulate the amount of liquid so the carpet should never get saturated. Applicators can often be hired from carpet, hardware or do-it-yourself shops, also from some dry cleaners and launderettes. It is usually possible to buy the shampoo from these sources. Applicators vary from those which are hand-operated to electrical machines which clean the pile by way of rotating brushes or by high pressure water jets in combination with extraction.

Try and clean the carpet late in the day so it can be left to dry overnight. If you have to put the furniture back before the carpet is perfectly dry, put pieces of aluminium foil under metal castors and legs to prevent rust stains.

RUGS

Most rugs can be shampooed, using the same method as for a carpet, and some are machine washable; look for the manufacturer's label giving the cleaning instructions.

Do not be tempted to try and clean Persian and Chinese rugs yourself. For these and skin rugs, such as goatskin, professional treatment is always advisable. You can, however, hand wash a sheepskin rug, provided you work with care.

Washing a sheepskin rug

Try and choose a sunny day when the wind is blowing, because a sheepskin rug dries best over a clothes line in the open air.

1 In a large saucepan boil up 175 g of good soap flakes with 50 ml of olive oil and 1 litre water, stirring well to emulsify the oil thoroughly.

2 Add this, together with 50 ml glycerine to a sink full of warm water – enough to wash the skin. The wash water should be 40°C.

3 Wash the skin well, drain off the wash water, then give the skin one deep warm rinse. It is important not to rinse out all the soap.

4 Squeeze surplus water out of the rug, then rub both the wool and the skin back with dry towels. The rug has a far better chance of drying out soft if it is hung up in a partially dry condition, not wringing wet.

5 Mix together 125 g of fine oatmeal and the same amount of flour, and when the skin is almost dry rub this mixture into the skin back; this helps make good the loss of tanning materials, and is well worth doing to make the skin soft.

6 When the rug is perfectly dry, comb or brush the wool.

NON-SLIP

Rugs that slip can be kept in place on hard floors or carpets by treating the back with latex carpet adhesive. Make sure the rug is clean, then place it face down on layers of newspaper and apply a coat of latex adhesive over the back. Strips of adhesive about 2·5 cm wide will be more economical if the rug is a large one. Do not put the rug down again until the adhesive is dry.

Alternatively use a piece of proprietary rubberised netting that you cut to size and put under the rug. It doesn't mark floors, and as you don't fix it to the rug, it can be taken up at any time. Other types of gripper are available for rugs that creep on carpets.

Paintwork and wall coverings

Painting or papering a room is always a major upheaval, not to mention a major expense, so you want to keep your decorations fresh as long as possible. The secret is to clean them before they start to turn shabby. Whatever the finish, there are ways to help it stay looking bright and new.

PAINTED WALLS

Use the same technique and cleaning products whether the paint is emulsion or gloss.

First remove loose dust with a soft brush or cloth. You can reach higher levels with a soft duster tied over a broom head, a ceiling brush or the brush attachment of your vacuum cleaner. After dusting, begin washing carefully, starting from the bottom and working up. This way, any dirty streaks that roll down will reach a clean surface where they can be wiped off easily. Dirt rolling on to dirt tends to get ingrained and is much harder to remove.

If the wall is lightly soiled, wash it over with a warm, well diluted solution of washing-up liquid. Do not use washing powders because these contain fluorescers which could affect the colour of the paint. For heavily soiled walls you will need a general purpose household cleaner diluted according to the manufacturer's instructions or a mild solution of sugar soap. Have two bowls of water, one to wash and one to rinse, with a sponge or absorbent cloth in each. Wash an area about 1 m square, rinse and dry; clean the next patch, overlapping the edge of the first so you do not leave hard lines. Do not stop washing a wall in the middle once you have started or a tidemark will form which is very hard to wash off.

For extra dirty patches like greasy fingermarks use the cleaner straight from the bottle. Rub lightly till the marks disappear, then rinse. Take care when you are using water round light switches and electricity sockets. Turn off the electricity at the mains if you can.

Painted wood

For lightly soiled paintwork use an aerosol polish,

which will also contain a cleaning agent. Wipe dirtier areas with a cloth wrung out in a warm washing-up liquid solution, followed by rinsing. Stubborn marks may need a special paintwork cleaner, used according to the manufacturer's instructions.

Ceilings

Ceilings do not need cleaning as often as walls (no grubby fingermarks), but when they do, you should tackle them first.

For painted ceilings (or paper painted-over) remove the loose dust with a ceiling brush or the brush attachment of your vacuum cleaner. Then clean up any particularly dirty parts first, such as those that appear over radiators and chimney breasts, using a soft scrubbing brush and a warm solution of washing-up liquid. Next go over the rest of the ceiling using a soft cloth wrung out in the solution.

Do not make the solution too strong. Apart from wasting money, far from being more effective it

Wash walls from the bottom up to avoid runs

Use platform steps for safety

systematically, or the wall could end up looking streaky.

Greasy marks may come off with a spray from an aerosol grease solvent such as you would use on clothes (but remember to test a small area first). These cleaners dry rapidly without penetrating the paper. When dry, they form a deposit of powder which should be lightly brushed off. Alternatively, for flat wallpapers, you can draw out the grease with a warm iron held on a sheet of clean blotting paper over the stain.

Ordinary wallpapers should not be washed as the colours may run or the paper become loosened from the wall. If you are not sure whether a paper is washable or not, squeeze a sponge out in clean, warm water and rub it very lightly over a small, out of the way area of the wall. If the pattern does not blur, then it is probably safe to go ahead.

Washable papers can be sponged over lightly with a warm, well diluted washing-up liquid solution, rinsed well with a sponge squeezed out with clean water and patted dry with a clean, soft cloth.

Vinyl wall-coverings
Vinyl wall-coverings are usually washable. Brush or vacuum them first, then wipe over with a cloth wrung out in warm washing-up liquid solution, followed by clean water. Take great care not to over-wet as water collecting on the top of the skirting board can loosen the wallcovering. For heavy soiling, especially on light-coloured or greasy kitchen walls, use a solution of general purpose household cleaner with a soft brush. Rinse well.

Vinyl is resistant to most household stains, which can usually be wiped off with a damp cloth. Stubborn marks such as paint splashes or ball-point ink can often be removed with white spirit or methylated spirits (both flammable: work with care).

Hessian-covered walls
Brush, or better still vacuum, over the surface of hessian-covered walls to remove the dust which seems to collect more on them than on other wall coverings. Remove any grease marks with an aero-sol grease solvent (but only after checking a test area first).

CORK TILES
Cork tiles can be wiped clean with a damp cloth;

could actually harm the surface. Do not use too much water, either, it could cause the paint to flake.

Finally, wring out the cloth in clean warm water and, holding it flat rather than bunched (you cover the area faster this way), wipe over the ceiling. Change the water often to make sure all traces of detergent have been rinsed away.

If you can, use a pair of platform steps with a top rail for holding on to when cleaning a ceiling or other high surface.

PAPERED WALLS
Papered walls should be cleaned very carefully or you may damage the paper beyond repair. Always test what you plan to do on a patch of wall that is normally out of sight.

First clean the surface with a soft brush or the brush head attachment of your vacuum cleaner. Take special care on embossed papers, because too much pressure on the face will spoil the pattern.

Light stains on wallpaper can often be removed by rubbing them gently with slightly stale bread. Or you can use a commercial cleaner that looks a bit like a lump of dough and can be bought in hardware stores. Overlap your strokes and work

196

be careful not to over-wet them. For soiled and marked areas use an aerosol cleaner/polisher. Untreated open texture cork tiles should be dusted lightly and soiling or marks removed as recommended by the manufacturer.

CERAMIC TILES
Ceramic tiles are easily cleaned with an absorbent cloth wrung out in a hot washing-up liquid solution. Rinse with clean water and buff up when dry. See also page 210.

Furniture

All wood looks the better for regular dusting and occasional buffing with a soft cloth. But wood comes in many different finishes, and these call for different treatments when you need to do more than remove the dust.

Waxed wood
Wax is the traditional finish for good wooden furniture and to keep it looking good, the important thing to remember is not to polish the wood too often. It is a fallacy that furniture will benefit from generous dollops of polish to 'feed the wood'. Wherever possible, follow the manufacturer's instructions, but normally a regular dusting and an occasional light rub up with polish is all the routine care needed to keep polished wood furniture in good condition.

Any finger marks or smears on polished wood can usually be removed by light buffing, a further application of polish or by wiping over the surface with a damp cloth well wrung out in a 1:8 solution of vinegar and warm water. When using the last method be careful not to over-wet the wood (especially veneer) and always dry off thoroughly before repolishing as damp trapped under a layer of polish will cause white patches to appear.

In the case of stubborn stains, rub gently in the direction of the grain with a soft cloth moistened with a little white spirit. This is flammable so ensure adequate ventilation and avoid smoking during the process. Re-apply polish.

Avoid putting hot plates and dishes directly on to a polished surface – always use heat resisting table mats.

When using any type of polish, avoid using too much at a time and follow the maker's directions. It is advisable not to mix different kinds of polish, or you may set up a reaction. If you want to try a new polish, use turpentine substitute (or white spirit) on a cloth to remove all traces of the old one first. Take care; this is flammable.

On antique furniture it is advisable to avoid using aerosols as these are designed to clean as well as polish and will therefore tend to remove some of the patina of wax which has built up over the years. The best polish to use is a paste wax which does not contain silicones.

French polish
Remove any sticky marks on a french polished surface by wiping over with a cloth well wrung out in a little warm soapy water and dry thoroughly. Polish occasionally with a little furniture cream.

When french polish wears off, a new coating can be applied by a professional – or you can do it yourself, using a special kit.

Oiled woods
Some teak and afrormosia furniture, as well as other woods, is sold with a sealed finish, in which case you can safely use an aerosol or any other good polish. More often, though, these woods are finished by oiling, and oiled woods should never be treated with traditional furniture polish.

Instead, use a proprietary teak oil or cream, applied very sparingly and only two or three times a year or an aerosol teak polish at more frequent intervals. Rub up with a soft cloth.

197

If the wood has been marked by heat or water, the marks can often be removed by rubbing with a cloth moistened in pure turpentine or by dipping very fine steel wool into the teak oil/cream and rubbing gently, following the grain. Do not try this, though, unless you are sure the wood has been oiled and not sealed, or if it has a veneer. If in any doubt write to the manufacturer.

FIRST AID FOR FURNITURE

However good your routine care, wooden furniture is always at risk to being marked, stained, scratched, burned or even attacked by woodworm – although in the latter case regular care, not forgetting the backs of furniture, will help prevent this. An anti-woodworm polish, for instance, is a good deterrent.

If the furniture is a prized antique, repairs are best left to an expert. Otherwise there is a good chance you may be able to deal with any blemishes yourself. (For repairs to veneer, see pages 103–104.)

Heat and water marks on all types of finish with the exception of oiled woods.
These often show up as a white mark on a polished surface. Try treating them with a few drops of liquid metal polish on a cloth, rubbing the surface gently but briskly, following the direction of the grain. Dry off. Finish by polishing as usual or, if necessary, tint the wood with a similar colour shoe polish, rubbing in then buffing up the surface.

Water-marking which has roughened the surface of solid wood (not veneer or french polish) should be rubbed over with fine steel wool dipped in a wax polish; handle very gently.

Marks on oiled woods should be treated as above under **Oiled woods.**

Ink stains on all finishes except french polished and sealed surfaces.
Ink stains are often difficult to remove if they are old stains. The simplest remedy is to use household bleach, applying it to the mark with a matchstick and agitating it slightly. Dab off with a wet cloth, but take care not to spread the bleach over the rest of the surface.

If this does not work, the stain has probably penetrated deeply into the surface and a branded woodworker bleach will be necessary. These are usually acidic and can be dangerous to use, so follow the maker's instructions closely.

Other stains except on french polished and veneered surfaces.
Stains which have not penetrated into the surface can generally be removed by rubbing gently with fine steel wool dipped in paste wax or liquid wax. Deep stains may need harsher treatment, starting with steel wool then a coarse grade glasspaper, working down to a fine grade. Always work in the direction of the grain – never across – and sand the whole surface evenly, otherwise you will get an indentation. If in any doubt seek professional advice.

Scratches
Scratches can usually be concealed by applying a proprietary scratch covering preparation or a similar colour shoe polish. Apply the polish with a matchstick, leave it for a short time, and then finish off by rubbing up with furniture polish.

Bruises and dents
Slight dents or bruises in solid wood (not veneer: for this see page 103) can usually be raised by covering the bruise over with damp blotting paper and pressing with a warm iron. Remove the existing polish first, using white spirit on a cloth, and afterwards apply a suitable colour shoe polish to blend the damaged area in with the surrounding wood. Buff well.

Cracks and holes
Small cracks and holes can be filled by applying wood stopping, plastic wood or filler in a colour to match the wood; allow to dry, then rub down. Larger holes, where handles have been removed, for example, can be filled with a piece of dowel of suitable diameter.

Burns
Light burns may respond to rubbing with metal polish. For oiled woods, use pure turpentine. For deeper marks, sand the whole surface, restain and polish. Serious damage will require professional treatment.

Woodworm
Danger signs of woodworm at work are a lot of very small holes and a fine deposit of sawdust. Treat with a generous application of proprietary woodworm fluid, following the manufacturer's instructions. In the case of a valuable antique, seek professional help.

CANE, WICKER AND BAMBOO FURNITURE

To clean cane, wicker and bamboo furniture, dust regularly with a brush or the dusting attachment of your vacuum cleaner. When it becomes notice-ably dirty it can be scrubbed gently with a soft scrubbing brush and warm soapy water (soap flakes, not a laundry detergent containing fluores-cers) with a teaspoon of laundry borax added to each 500 ml water; alternatively use a weak solu-tion of washing-up liquid. Avoid over-wetting.

Rinse carefully, with a final rinse for natural cane and wicker furniture of warm, salted water (2 teaspoons of cooking salt to 1 litre water) to stiffen and bleach it. Mop up surplus moisture with an old towel and leave out of doors or by an open window to dry, never near a direct source of heat which could cause warping. Polish with a sparing application of furniture cream.

Painted cane furniture is kept in good condition and made easier to clean if it is treated occasionally with a little furniture polish. Any scuff marks can be removed with a mild abrasive on a damp cloth.

GARDEN FURNITURE

Garden furniture has to be tough in order to with-stand the variable British summer. Even so, it will benefit from some attention to keep it in peak con-dition and improve its life expectancy.

Tubular metal furniture

Come the spring, folding chairs and loungers should be carefully eased open, so as not to strain the hinges, and given a drop of household oil. If the hinges have seized up, treat them with a proprietary aerosol lubricant. Aluminium framed furniture should need only a wipe with a damp cloth and washing-up liquid solution. Rub the frames with a little wax polish to brighten them up.

Furniture made from tubular steel usually has a rust-resistant finish, but this may deteriorate after long exposure. Combat rust with a smear of oil or grease – but remember to wipe it off before anyone sits down.

The coverings of tubular chairs are usually rot-proof canvas or plastic and can be wiped over with a damp cloth to remove soiling. Mend any small tears before they get worse and patch or replace damaged covers before an accident happens (see below).

Large pieces of tubular furniture, for example swing-type canopy seats, which cannot be moved and have cloth covers and awnings, should be pro-tected on wet days by stout canvas covers with tapes to hold them in position; hinges will need oiling from time to time to keep them free from rust and squeaks.

Cast iron and steel furniture

With an enamel painted finish in good condition, these materials need only a wipe or hose down to keep them clean. Oil any hinged parts and treat any rusted or chipped paint with a chemical rust re-mover. Then prime with a metal primer and re-paint with a good exterior quality gloss paint.

Wooden-frame furniture

The wood frames of deckchairs and folding chairs are best treated with a lacquer seal or exterior quality varnish.

Lightly smooth the wood with steel wool or fine glasspaper, dust off, and apply the lacquer with a paintbrush in a thin, even coat. Repeat this treat-ment each year to keep the chairs in good con-dition, but always make sure that the wood is dry before you start.

Hardwood furniture

Teak, cedar, iroko and other hardwoods will with-stand all kinds of weather for many years but may eventually become discoloured after long damp spells.

Remove any markings with steel wool rubbed in the direction of the grain – wear gardening gloves as it is hard on the hands. If the wood is still dis-coloured, use a proprietary wood bleach. Finally, treat with an exterior grade wood preservative. Remember that creosote should never be used on garden seats as it will stain clothes.

For any wood furniture that you leave outside permanently it is wise to put a wood block under each foot during the winter months so the furniture itself is not in constant contact with damp ground.

Cane furniture

Cane furniture is attractive in the garden, but you should always store it inside in the winter as cane suffers badly from long exposure and may warp. (But keeping it in too warm a place – against a radiator, for instance – will dry out cane and make it splintery.)

There is little you can do to restore untreated cane that has become warped and discoloured.

Treated cane should be cleaned by brushing to remove loose dust, then using a small scrubbing brush and warm soapy water to remove soiling from the weave. Re-treat with a liquid preservative or an aerosol spray, which is the easiest form of application to an uneven surface of this type and gives a more complete surface covering to the weave.

RE-COVERING A GARDEN CHAIR

If the damage to a canvas-covered chair is only a simple split you can often use an adhesive to stick a patch of hessian or canvas on the cover of the chair. Equally, if the old canvas is in good condition and has merely torn away from the frame, you can machine a wide strip of firm carpet binding across the end of the canvas and re-fix in position.

If the damage is due to rotting, however, it is better to replace the canvas completely. Most shops specialising in garden furniture will sell pre-cut seat and back covers which you can put on yourself. Or you can buy canvas by the metre.

First remove the old material, then turn in the edges of the new material and machine them. If the chair has a wood frame, wrap the new canvas firmly round the rail and fix it with staples, using a staple gun, or attach it with domed tacks or nails. For a tubular framed chair you may need to sew on the new cover with a darning needle and nylon thread or heavy twine. Some tubular chairs are designed to take apart completely so that all seams can be machine sewn; if yours is this type, use the old cover as a guide for measurements and make casings at top, bottom and the back of the seat for the removable rods to go through. Put the chair back together with the new cover in place.

If the woven plastic back or seat of a tubular chair needs repairing you will need to remove the damaged section and re-weave new plastic – sold by the metre – on to the frame.

Floors

Neglected floors spoil the look of a room irrespective of the rest of the furnishing, while a clean, shining floor can make the whole room look fresh and bright. Here, then, first of all are four general rules that will help make floor cleaning an easier job:

1 Have good door mats to reduce the amount of dirt brought into the house.

2 Vacuum or sweep up loose dust and dirt before applying any kind of polish. Some surfaces will also need to be washed to ensure that they are clean before polishing—see under instructions for different types of flooring.

3 Apply the minimum amount of polish to achieve the best result and to avoid a build-up.

4 If necessary strip off old polish from time to time to avoid a build-up of polish and dirt.

Most flooring manufacturers give instructions for care and also make their own cleaners and polish—use these when available. In any case, it is important to bear in mind the difference between the two types of polish—solvent wax and the self-shining floor polish that is also called emulsion polish.

Solvent wax polishes come in pastes or liquids and are a mixture of natural and synthetic waxes with spirit cleaning solvents. You have to buff them to get a shine. They should never be used on vinyl or rubber floors as they tend to soften the surface and fade the colour over a period. An electric polisher is useful to cut down the effort required in polishing floors treated with a solvent wax polish and some have an applicator for putting on the polish.

Emulsion polishes generally contain a blend of

natural and synthetic waxes and resins. Some need no buffing and dry to a shine as you apply them, others can be buffed up when thoroughly dry and between applications to restore the shine. There are also emulsion polishes which incorporate a cleaner. These are suitable for lightly soiled floors and save time. They are not always efficient for heavily soiled floors, however, for which it is better to clean off all the dirt with a proprietary floor cleaner before applying more polish.

Never put one type of polish on top of another, eg emulsion on top of solvent wax; they are designed for different surfaces and are not compatible. Mixing brands is also inadvisable as they are rarely chemically the same; clean off one before you start with another. **Never polish under rugs or runners. It is dangerous.**

WOOD BLOCK AND STRIP FLOORS
A wooden floor with a waxed surface should be swept or dry mopped regularly to remove dust and grit. Water should never be used to clean this type of flooring, though a damp cloth may be used to wipe up sticky marks or spills. But be careful not to over-wet; water seeping between blocks or boards can loosen them. Allow to dry thoroughly before repolishing.

If wax has been allowed to build up on a wooden floor surface, remove this with a cloth moistened in white spirit (turpentine substitute). **Take care, this is flammable. Turn off gas pilot lights and ensure adequate ventilation.** Alternatively, use steel wool dipped in liquid or paste wax and allow the wax you have just applied to harden and then polish up. Wear protective gloves for this type of work. Stubborn marks can also be removed by the steel wool treatment. Do not apply an emulsion polish to an unsealed wood floor.

Sealing wood floors
Wood floors look better and last longer when they are sealed. Before this is done sanding may be necessary to ensure a clean, flat surface (see page 77). On wood strip floors always work the sander with the grain. On wood block floors the floor should be sanded twice, in two directions at right angles to each other. After sanding make sure all the wood dust is vacuumed up from the surface and fill in any nail holes with a wood filler. (If a large area of uneven floor is involved, commercial-type sanding machines can be hired by the day.)

An electric polisher cuts the hard work out of polishing floors

New and untreated wood can be sealed with one or two coats of floor sealer, following the maker's instructions. It is usually necessary to sand old or previously treated floors prior to resealing to obtain a good finish, but for small areas it may be sufficient to use dry steel wool.

Once a wood floor has been sealed with a varnish or polyurethane finish it can be kept clean by damp mopping, or an occasional application of wax or an emulsion (self-shining) polish, whichever you prefer.

VINYL SHEET OR TILES
Regular sweeping goes a long way towards keeping vinyl floors clean. When necessary damp mop vinyl floors which have a 'built-in' shine, or have been treated with emulsion polish. Use a weak solution of general purpose cleaner if the floor is really dirty. From time to time it may be necessary to remove a build-up of old polish. Follow the manu-

201

facturer's recommended formula for removing the polish or use a proprietary floor polish remover. Work on small areas at a time and mop up the softened polish as you go. Rinse, and when the floor is thoroughly dry, give it a fresh coat of emulsion polish.

Scuff marks can be removed by rubbing lightly with a moistened cloth dipped in the polish or cleaner, but use this carefully or you could damage the surface.

Never use solvent-based wax polish on vinyl floors

LINOLEUM
Lino is easily cleaned by damp mopping with a weak solution of a general purpose household cleaner. Do not over wet. When dry, re-wax with a liquid or paste wax polish. For the kitchen and bathroom, where water splashing is likely, use an emulsion polish which will not water mark like a wax polished surface would. Treat scuff marks as for vinyl.

QUARRY TILES
Glazed quarry tiles need only mopping over with water with a little liquid household cleaner added. Unglazed tiles may need scrubbing with the same solution to remove ingrained dirt and, when dry, should be polished with a liquid or paste wax polish with slip-retardant properties, or an emulsion polish, to protect the slightly porous surface.

If a quarry tiled floor has lost its colour, remove the old wax with steel wool and white spirit, wash and rinse. When dry, put on a light application of pigmented wax to restore the colour. Buff with a soft cloth to prevent loose wax collecting on shoes.

When quarry tiles are first laid, white patches may appear on the surface. This is likely to be the result of the presence of lime in the concrete used for laying the floor underneath them. The patches will fade naturally in time, but meanwhile do not polish. You can speed up the process by washing them over with a solution of four tablespoons vinegar to five litres water. Wipe over the surface and leave to dry without rinsing. Repeat after a few days if the patches reappear, and do not polish until they have completely gone.

CERAMIC TILES
Clean with an absorbent cloth wrung out in a hot washing-up liquid solution. Rinse with clear water and buff up when dry. If the grouting between the tiles is dirty, clean with a soft bristled brush, used gently so it does not loosen it.

Never polish ceramic tiles. It would make them much too slippery.

CORK
Cork tiles should have a sealed or waxed finish or a clear vinyl coating as the surface is slightly porous and some form of treatment is necessary to prevent dirt and grit becoming embedded in it. Tiles are available with these finishes; alternatively it is possible to wax or seal the surface yourself.

To seal cork tiles, apply the seal evenly on to a clean, dry floor surface. Some seals are slightly coloured and will make the cork darker in appearance. Old cork floors can be sealed, but it is essential to remove all the wax first with a special de-waxing cleaner, otherwise the new seal will not take properly. If the floor is badly worn it will be necessary to sand the surface first to remove the damaged areas. Sealed cork floors can be kept in condition by damp mopping and a light coat of emulsion polish.

Wax-finished cork tiles should be maintained by occasional applications of a paste or liquid wax polish. However, this finish does tend to get water-marked; remove by rubbing lightly with a cloth dipped in liquid wax polish.

Cork tiles with a clear vinyl surface need damp mopping only, although an occasional application of emulsion polish will brighten up their appearance.

RUBBER
Rubber floors can be spoiled by the wrong treatment, so it is particularly important to follow the manufacturer's recommendations. Generally you should never use a solvent-based wax polish or a synthetic detergent, both of which can soften the surface.

Mop off soiling with a solution of soap flakes and warm water, then rinse off thoroughly and allow to dry. Then apply a light layer of emulsion polish.

Remove stubborn marks as recommended by the manufacturer, or with an abrasive powder floor cleaner that does not contain bleach, used on a damp cloth.

Kitchen appliances

THE SINK

Never pour any solids down the sink that could collect in and block the waste pipe. If possible, use an outside drain for greasy liquids which might otherwise solidify in the pipe and cause a blockage. From time to time, dissolve a handful of washing soda crystals in 500 ml of boiling water and pour this down the sink outlet to clear any solidified grease. (Blocked sinks – see page 132.)

Stainless steel

After use, rinse thoroughly with hot water and leave as dry as possible. This is particularly important in a hard water area as any water spots that dry on the surface can leave a deposit. Pools of tea or coffee can also cause discoloration. Rub with a damp cloth and neat washing-up liquid to remove surface soiling. When necessary, clean with a preparation specially formulated for stainless steel according to the manufacturer's instructions.

Do not use harsh abrasive cleaners or cleaning pads on a stainless steel sink, and **do not** use undiluted or strong disinfectants or leave clothes soaking in the sink in a strong bleaching solution.

Never clean silver by the immersion dip process on a stainless steel surface; these cleaners can cause permanent staining.

Rubber or plastic mats in the sink or on the draining board are not necessary with a steel sink because the surface does not chip and is unlikely to cause breakages. If you like to use a mat, remember to remove it after use because any gritty particles trapped underneath can cause scratching.

Vitreous enamel

Use a product marked with the recommendation seal of the Vitreous Enamel Development Council for 'general' or 'bath' cleaning, which will contain no abrasives or chemicals fierce enough to damage the finish.

A plastic washing-up bowl protects an enamel surface from chipping, but be careful not to give gritty particles a chance to collect underneath it or they may scratch the surface.

Fireclay

Clean this as for enamel. If the sink has discoloured because the glaze has worn, use a mild solution of household bleach, following the manufacturer's instructions.

COOKERS

Wipe up splashes and spills on cooker tops and in the oven as soon as possible, preferably while the cooker is still warm, so the deposit does not have time to harden. Use a diluted washing-up liquid to shift heavy spills.

Follow the manufacturer's instructions when the cooker needs more thorough cleaning. Or in the absence of these, follow the procedure below:

Gas cookers

Turn off the pilot light or lights.

Burners and pan supports Wash removable parts in hot washing-up water using a nylon cleaning pad. If necessary, soak in hot sudsy water and clean with a soap impregnated steel wool pad, using a paste or ammonia-based liquid cleaner for stubborn marks.

Cooker hobs, back-splash and spillage trays Clean with a soapy cloth and wipe dry. If further cleaning is necessary, treat according to surface finish.

For vitreous enamel use a liquid or paste cleaner approved by the Vitreous Enamel Development Council for 'cooker' or 'general' use, applying it with a cloth or a nylon cleaning pad to remove heavy deposits.

For stainless steel use a special stainless steel cleaner; never use abrasives.

Grill The high temperature reached during grilling burns off any grease. When necessary use a soft dry brush to get rid of any residual soiling.

A removable grill cover should be cleaned at the sink in a hot washing-up detergent solution.

Oven The cleaning depends on the internal finish.

Continuous cleaning linings vaporize grease splashes during cooking, so they do not form the usual deposits. The hotter the oven, the more effective the cleaning – so if you have been using the oven at

Fitting rollers to a cooker may make access easier for cleaning

A small lever, easily operated with one hand, locks the rollers when not in use

relatively low temperatures for some time, you will need to cook a dish at a high temperature to give the surface a really thorough clean. You can wipe the oven over with a damp cloth, if you think this necessary, but do not use any form of oven cleaner, vitreous enamel cleaner or abrasive.

Continuous cleaning linings cannot cope with heavy spillage, so the oven base may have a non-stick surface which should only need a wipe over with a damp cloth. If the oven base is vitreous enamel, use a liquid cleaner or paste approved for vitreous enamel, or for heavy deposits use an impregnated oven cleaning pad, a paste or gel oven

cleaner, again one approved by the VEDC. Follow the instructions carefully and do not let it get into contact with the treated lining or into the holes of the burners. Oven cleaners are strong so it is advisable to wear rubber gloves during the process. Clean the oven shelves with a nylon cleaning pad and hot washing-up water.

Vitreous enamel linings should be cleaned in the same way as a vitreous enamel baseplate. An aerosol oven cleaner may be used, but have adequate ventilation and leave the room for a few minutes after application because the fumes are very strong.

Finally, wipe over the outside surfaces of the cooker with a cloth wrung out in a hot detergent solution. Relight the pilot light/lights.

Electric cookers

Turn off the cooker at the wall switch.

Hotplates Radiant rings and solid hotplates usually burn themselves clean during use. In the case of a ceramic hotplate, it is especially important to wipe up any spills immediately to stop them spreading and solidifying. Be careful though; it is easy to scorch the cloth or burn your hand. Always use the manufacturer's recommended cleaning preparation for ceramic hotplates when thorough cleaning becomes necessary.

Cooker hobs, back-splash and spillage trays Clean these as for gas cookers, above.

Grill The grill burns itself clean in use and should only need an occasional wipe with a damp cloth.

Oven Clean continuous cleaning, non-stick and vitreous enamel oven linings as for gas cookers.

High temperature cleaning ovens should be cleaned as advised by the manufacturer. The oven door locks automatically during the cleaning period when the soiling on shelves and linings is carbonized and reduced to ash which can later be brushed away. The individual spillage trays from beneath the radiant rings and the grill pan and roasting tin accompanying the cooker can often be cleaned in the oven at the same time.

Finish by wiping over the outside surfaces of the cooker with a cloth wrung out in a hot detergent solution. Turn on the cooker at the wall switch and remember to re-set the clock on the control panel.

Glass oven doors

Clean with a nylon cleaning pad or, for stubborn

marks, a paste or liquid household cleaner in conjunction with this. Do not use steel wool – which could scratch – and do not use an aerosol type oven cleaner which could cause the glass to disintegrate.

REFRIGERATORS
Keep food covered and wipe up any spilt food or liquid right away to keep the refrigerator hygienic and prevent staining the lining.

Defrost the refrigerator (unless this is done automatically) as soon as the frost round the frozen food compartment is 5 mm thick. Some models have a rapid defrosting device; those without will need to be switched off at the electric socket outlet.

To defrost, follow the maker's instructions – or in the absence of these, use the procedure below.

Defrosting
Remove any food from the frozen food compartment. Wrap it in newspapers or put it in an insulated bag and leave in a cool place. Take out the ice cube trays, empty them and refill with hot water and put them back. Keep the drip tray in position to catch the melting frost and empty it as necessary. Leave the door open.

Once the refrigerator has defrosted, empty the drip tray, wipe the frozen food compartment dry, wash and refill the ice trays with cold water and replace. Return the food to the frozen food compartment. Close the door and switch on the electricity.

Cleaning
The inside of the refrigerator should be cleaned about every 2–3 weeks following defrosting.

Remove all food, shelves and fitments. Wipe the inside surfaces, except metal sections, with a cloth wrung out in a warm solution of bicarbonate of soda (1 level tablespoon to 1 litre water). Wipe metal sections with a damp cloth and clear water. Dry well. Marks left by milk bottles on plastic shelves can be removed with a general purpose liquid cleaner suitable for use on plastics.

Wash shelves and other fitments at the sink. Rinse, dry and replace. Wash over the outside of the refrigerator with a warm detergent solution when necessary. An occasional rub over with a liquid or aerosol polish will brighten the surface.

Turn off a refrigerator that is not in use, defrost it, empty it and leave with door wedged open so the air can circulate.

Smells
To clear the smell left by food that has been allowed to go bad in a refrigerator, defrost and leave the refrigerator turned off with door open for two or three days, washing repeatedly with the bicarbonate of soda solution (see above), followed by wiping over with an antiseptic solution in the strength recommended for sterilizing babies' bottles.

It is possible to buy a small refrigerator freshener for standing or hanging on one of the shelves, and this will combat any lingering smell.

FREEZERS
Clean the outside by wiping first with a damp cloth and then with a dry one, or use a little aerosol polish. Vacuum or brush to remove dust from the condenser at the back (see page 206).

Freezer interiors may be either enamelled steel, stainless steel, aluminium or plastic. Wipe up any spills at once – particularly acids on an aluminium surface. With plastic linings, take especial care not to puncture with sharp objects.

Defrosting
Unless they are frost-free models, chest freezers usually need defrosting once or twice a year and upright models two or three times, but follow the manufacturer's instructions. Normally it's time to tackle the job when the frost becomes 5 mm thick.

Switch off the electricity and – wearing gloves – remove all the frozen food and pack it tightly into a large box or other suitable container; the more tightly it is packed, the colder it will stay. Cover it with layers of newspaper and a blanket to insulate it and minimize air circulation.

Unless the instructions say otherwise, leave the freezer open. Speed up the melting rate by placing bowls of hot water on the shelves of an upright freezer – and in a chest model too, provided the instructions recommend it.

It helps to cover the lowest shelf in an upright model with aluminium foil with the edges turned up to catch and retain the water. Make a hole in the centre of the foil and put a bowl underneath it to catch the water. Some models have a drain tube which makes this unnecessary.

Start scraping down the sides and shelves as soon as the ice is loosened; never, though, scrape with anything metal as it will damage the surface of the freezer. A wooden or plastic spatula is ideal.

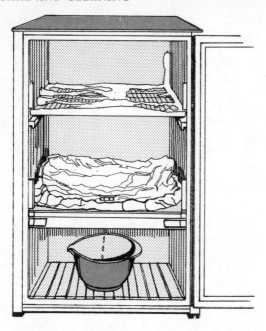

A sheet of foil on the lower shelf will help to funnel melting frost into a bowl (*page 205*)

When the freezer is defrosted, wipe round the inside with a solution of bicarbonate of soda (1 level tablespoon to 1 litre of warm water). Make sure the freezer is thoroughly dry before switching on the electricity again. The whole defrosting process should only take about an hour, though it is best to wait another hour before putting the food back again.

Frost-free freezers
From time to time dust will need to be cleaned away from the fan and blades which are found inside frost-free models. Switch off the freezer at the socket outlet and remove the plug, unscrew the inlet grille and remove the dust with a soft brush or the dusting attachment of a vacuum cleaner. Replace the grille and switch on.

Although a frost-free model does not need defrosting, it should be turned off and cleaned out inside – as for other freezers – approximately once a year and at a time when stocks are low.

Smells
If food has gone bad in a freezer, treat as for re-refrigerator smells, above.

WASHING MACHINES
Washing machines should be clean and dry inside when you put them away. Check carefully that no metal objects such as safety pins or hair grips have been left in the washtub – these could cause rusting. Brighten the outside with an occasional rub over with an aerosol or liquid polish.

Automatic machines are virtually self-cleaning, but should be wiped over with a clean cloth or sponge after use. Remove any fluff from the lint trap.

Twin tubs Rinse out the wash tub with clean water after use. Remove any tidemarks with a little paste cleaner. If the tub has a removablé agitator, lift this out and rinse it in the sink. Wipe dry before replacing it. It is also sensible to rinse the rubber filling hose since washing detergent deposits tend to soften the rubber and make it sticky after a time.

Single tubs Clean as for twin tubs. Rinse wringers well and leave them with the pressure released and a clean tea towel or other cloth between the rollers.

Most washing machines have storage space for the flex – use this as it will help keep the flex in good condition.

DISHWASHERS
Always follow the manufacturer's recommendations on loading, choice of detergent and method of operation.

Wipe the outside surface of the machine with a damp cloth wrung out in a detergent solution when necessary; use a liquid or aerosol polish if the sur-

Vacuum clean the back of a freezer to remove dust from the condenser

face is looking dull. If you have to pull out the machine to clean at the back, replace it carefully or you may kink the hose and prevent the water flowing properly.

The insides of dishwashers are self-cleaning, but you may need to remove stubborn grease marks or other soiling from the racks with a hot washing-up liquid solution, or a paste or liquid cleaner on a soft cloth.

Clean out the filter after every wash; if the machine has a second filter, this will need looking at about once a week. Follow the manufacturer's instructions.

IRONS

Stand and store an iron on its heelrest or on a vertically mounted iron stand where the flex can safely be wound round the protective rim during the cooling down period.

To fill a steam iron, follow the maker's instructions and make sure that the iron is disconnected from the electric socket. After use, empty the tank while the iron is still hot.

Use demineralized or distilled water to prevent trouble. Hard water will gradually cause scale to form in the tank and block the vents in the soleplate of a steam iron. Although special cleaning fluids are available, it is better to buy a bottle containing crystals for demineralizing tap water; otherwise buy distilled water from a chemist. Never use distilled water from a defrosted refrigerator, nor buy it from a garage as it may contain impurities.

Clean starch or brown marks from the soleplate of an iron by rubbing it over a coarse damp cloth stretched over the edge of the ironing board. For stubborn marks, use a proprietary iron soleplate cleaner – and in the case of a steam iron, make sure that nothing gets lodged in the steam vents.

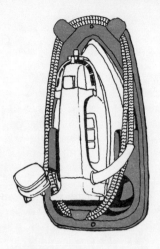

A special stand with flex holder helps protect an iron while stored

KETTLES

Disconnect an electric kettle before filling. Switch off – or in the case of an unswitched socket, unplug – before pouring. Never switch on the kettle unless the element is covered with water. Never allow the flex to trail across the top of a cooker, and replace a worn flex immediately (see page 116).

For general cleaning, wipe the outside of the cold kettle with a damp cloth and buff with a dry one. Water marking can usually be removed with a general purpose liquid cleaner.

In a hard water area scale will build up inside the kettle; remove this periodically with a proprietary kettle descaler. With automatic kettles it is important to check the maker's instructions for the type of descaler to use. Boil up the kettle once or twice and throw the water away before boiling water for use.

Bathroom fittings

BATHS

Most baths are made of vitreous enamelled steel, porcelain enamelled cast iron or acrylic (plastic). When you buy a new bath always keep any care instructions that come with it and follow these closely using the cleaning products the makers recommend.

Provided any type of bath is rinsed immediately after use, whilst still warm, with hot soapy water and wiped dry, day to day care will be reduced to a rub over with a little neat washing up liquid on a damp cloth, followed by rinsing. This treatment will maintain the original surface of the bath and prevent staining.

In the absence of specific cleaning instructions, a vitreous or porcelain enamelled bath can be given a more thorough clean, when necessary, with one of the proprietary bath or general vitreous enamel cleaners carrying the Vitreous Enamel Development Council's recommendation seal (see inset).

VITREOUS ENAMEL DEVELOPMENT COUNCIL

Tested and recommended for use on vitreous enamel

For plastic baths, keep to the manufacturer's recommended cleaner or to a cleaner labelled for use on plastic baths.

Tidemarks These are formed by a scale of soap scum and lime salts and are most likely to occur in hard water areas. Marks on vitreous or porcelain enamelled surfaces usually respond to one of the proprietary bath or general vitreous enamel cleaners mentioned above. On no account use vinegar or any other acid for this purpose as it may damage the glaze.

For a tidemark on a plastic bath rub with a little brass metal polish on a soft cloth. This treatment can also be used to reduce scratches on plastic baths, although deeper scratches may require rubbing gently with fine grade glasspaper and the finest grade 'wet or dry' abrasive paper before the metal polish.

Blue-green marks These can be the result of a dripping tap, especially where the piping is made of copper. First re-washer the tap (see pages 128–130) then treat as for tidemarks.

Rust marks are best treated with a branded sanitary ware cleaner with rust removing properties. These are poisonous and very strong. Follow the manufacturer's instructions implicitly and test a small area first to check that it does not damage the glaze. Rinse thoroughly.

General discoloration In hard water areas an overall discoloration is sometimes caused by a film of hard-water salts on the bath. Treat as for tidemarks. In some cases discoloration on white enamelled baths may be improved by using a chlorine bleach in a very weak dilution and well rinsed away after use; follow the maker's instructions. **Do not use bleach if the glazed surface of the bath is cracked or damaged in any way.**

A really badly stained bath can often be improved with a branded cleaner specially formulated for removing difficult stains from vitreous enamel and vitreous china sanitary ware. These are available through good household departments and stores but should not be used for regular cleaning as they are very fierce. Read the instructions carefully and test a small area in the least noticeable place first. If this does not work professional resurfacing will be necessary. This will not be enamel, but the appearance will be similar.

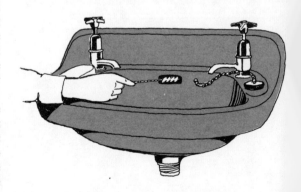

A bottle brush may be the only way to clean the washbasin overflow

BASINS

Washbasins should be cleaned with a damp cloth or sponge and a bathroom cleanser, followed by thorough rinsing. Clean out the overflow from time to time with a bottle brush.

TAPS

Chromium taps on basins and baths should be wiped over with a damp cloth, then polished with a soft duster. Any marks or corrosion which does not respond to washing-up liquid should come off with a liquid metal cleaner or impregnated wadding, but never use an abrasive powder or steel wool as this could damage the plating.

Gold-plated taps and fittings should be dried with a soft cloth after use, because water allowed to dry on the surface leaves a sediment. Gold is much softer than chrome so no polish or cleaner should be used on this type of fitting as the gold plating will wear away.

LAVATORIES

Use a lavatory brush of a non-scratch type, either rubber, nylon or a good bristle. Once the surface of a lavatory pan has been allowed to become scratched, hygienic cleaning becomes much more difficult. Wash the brush often in hot soapy water, rinse in cold water with a few drops of disinfectant in it, then hang out to dry.

Wipe over the lavatory seat and cover, both top and underneath, every day and once a week or so go over the outside of the pedestal with a cloth damped with warm water containing a little disinfectant. A

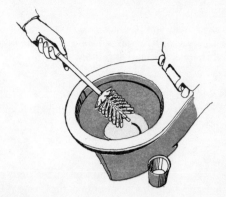

Regular brushing with a non-scratch brush is an essential part of hygiene

flush cleaner or a toilet block permanently in the lavatory provides continuous cleaning and a defence against germs.

Powders and liquids

Powder cleaners usually contain bleaches and/or acid cleaning agents and scourers. They can safely be used on coloured as well as white lavatory pans as the colour is under, and protected by, the glaze. These cleaners kill germs (mainly bacteria, they are not so good on viruses) as well as clean the pan. Powder cleaners containing bleach tend to fix any rust stains; the acidic type help to remove rust.

Liquid bleaches can be used on white and coloured lavatory pans as long as the glaze is in good condition; do not use if the surface is damaged in any way. They are more effective than powders on ordinary soil-staining but not very good on rust. They also kill more germs than powder cleaners and are effective against viruses as well as bacteria, which makes them particularly valuable if there is sickness in the house. You can safely use a liquid cleaner every night if you wish, but do not forget to flush the lavatory before using it in the morning; a splash-back from the liquid could cause skin irritation.

Never use a powder and liquid bleach cleaner together because toxic gases could be released.

WALLS AND CEILINGS

Bathroom walls should be wiped down fairly frequently with an absorbent cloth wrung out in a mild detergent solution, followed by clear water. Wipe dry.

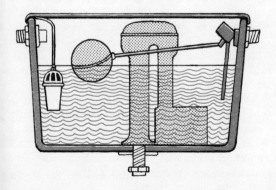

A continuous cleaner in the cistern provides a mild disinfectant action with each flush

Mould

Painted ceilings should be wiped over from time to time. Use an anti-fungal solution on ceilings and walls if there is any sign of mildew growth.

MIRRORS

Clean hairspray off mirrors with methylated spirits and a soft cloth.

TILES

Wipe over ceramic tiles regularly with a detergent solution and buff dry to maintain the shine. Hard water deposits may be difficult to remove so try to avoid any build-up, eg in a tiled shower cubicle. If a film of lime does start to appear use a mild acid such as vinegar, leaving it on the tiles for 10–15 minutes to give it time to dissolve the lime. Alternatively use an acid-based cleaner designed for the purpose, obtainable from specialist tile merchants. Wear rubber gloves if you have sensitive skin.

If the grouting (filler) between the tiles on a ceramic tiled wall gets dirty, clean it with a soft-bristled brush dipped in a domestic bleach solution, but be careful you don't loosen the filler and take care not to get the bleach solution in your eyes.

PLASTIC SHOWER CURTAINS

Shake and wipe down after use to prevent marking with soap and hard water deposits. To remove deposits, soak in warm water with 2 tablespoons water softener added. Rinse and wipe dry.

Ornamental metal and stoneware

SILVER

Whether it is solid sterling silver, Sheffield plate or EPNS, silver needs regular attention. It tarnishes on exposure to certain gases in the atmosphere, particularly in places where there is industrial pollution. Silver cutlery can also be discoloured by the sulphur content in certain foods such as egg yolk, fish, green vegetables and salt – see pages 214–215 on the care of cutlery. Although, unlike rust, tarnishing affects only the surface of the metal, it is unwise to let it develop to the point where you have to use drastic removal methods which could themselves impair the surface. Where bad tarnishing has been allowed to occur, it is best to seek a jeweller's advice.

Silver to be put away for a time should be wrapped in the special acid-free tissue paper or tarnish-proof bags which you can buy from jewellers. Then store the wrapped silver in a dry place, in an airtight box if possible.

Silver polishes come in a wide variety of forms and the one to choose depends largely on the article to be cleaned. Impregnated wadding and foaming polishes are good for getting into the crevices of intricate pieces, the dip process is a quick way of removing tarnish and discoloration from cutlery, while paste or liquid polishes are best suited to large areas and plain surfaces. A silver cloth – a soft cotton cloth impregnated with silver polish – is useful for items that need frequent buffing up. A soft brush may be used to clean intricate articles.

It is also possible to buy tarnish-inhibiting (long-term) polishes, impregnated wadding and cloths containing a chemical agent which forms a film on the surface of the silver which provides protection against atmospheric pollution. These long-term polishes do not remove tarnish as quickly or easily as the other types, though, so it is a good idea to use an ordinary polish or wadding first on heavy tarnish, then a tarnish inhibitor afterwards to extend the time before you need to re-polish.

When you are cleaning silver, avoid hard rubbing over the hall-marked sections. Too much pressure will wear away the mark in time, and so lessen the value of the item.

COPPER AND BRASS

The most frequent threat to copper-based metals, as with silver, is tarnishing caused by atmospheric pollution or damp. More serious corrosion, possibly in the form of a powdery green deposit called verdigris, may result from continued neglect.

Specially formulated polishes and impregnated wadding for brass and copper are available – the long-term type helps cut down on how often you will need to clean.

If you have antique items of brass or copper that have become discoloured or stained, it is best to take specialist advice. Less precious articles that have been slightly neglected should respond to a rub over with a cut lemon dipped in salt or a cloth moistened with vinegar and dipped in salt. Use an old toothbrush to clean the crevices. Then wash with soapy water, rinse and dry.

Badly neglected and corroded items can be treated with spirits of salts rubbed on with a rag tied on to the end of a stick. This is a poisonous and corrosive acid, so take great care – wear rubber gloves and work in a well ventilated place, the garden if possible. Rinse several times in clean water afterwards.

Any green corrosion that does not respond to the acid treatment may be removed by overnight soaking in a strong solution of washing soda and hot water, rubbing it into the surface a couple of times before you go to bed and again when you first get up with an old cloth or brush. Rinse well, then dry and polish.

Lacquer

The shine on brass and copper can be protected for a limited time with a clear lacquer, which should be applied in a dry place to prevent sealing in any moisture. When discoloration eventually occurs under the lacquer, the lacquer can be removed with a cloth dipped in cellulose thinners or nail polish remover (both flammable; take care).

BRONZE

Bronze should be dusted regularly with a soft cloth

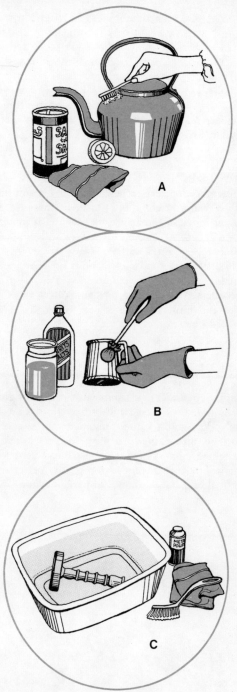

A. Lemon juice and salt will remove normal tarnishing and light deposits of verdigris
B. Use spirits of salts on badly corroded copper and brass; protect your skin and do not inhale
C. If necessary soak in a strong solution of washing soda and water; rinse, dry and polish

or brush. Occasional rubbing with a few drops of oil on a cloth, or a little dark brown shoe polish followed by buffing improves its appearance and will also protect the surface against the green spots which sometimes occur on bronze.

Badly soiled bronze should be washed in very hot soapy water, or cleaned with turpentine or paraffin and, when dry, brushed with a stiff, non-scratchy brush.

PEWTER
Collectors often prefer pewter to have a soft glow rather than a bright shiny finish. In this case it is enough to clean the article by washing it in soapy water and then rubbing up with a soft cloth. To produce a brighter surface use a special pewter polish – or any good metal polish or impregnated wadding.

Neglected pewter develops an oxide scale which films and tarnishes the surface; removing this is best left to an expert.

MARBLE
For general care, marble should be washed with warm soapy water to clean the surface and brighten the colour, then rinsed and buffed dry with a soft cloth. Wax polish without pigment can be applied sparingly on coloured marble to protect it against scratching – but do not use polish on white marble as it will make it go yellow, nor on any surface used for food preparation; it may impart a flavour.

Marble is slightly porous so stains are readily absorbed. Sponge off tea or coffee spills quickly with clear water. Dried stains may respond to sponging with a solution of laundry borax (1 dessertspoon borax to 250 ml warm water). Trickle lemon juice or vinegar on to cigarette burns and the rings made by glasses, but rinse off quickly or it will dull the surface.

Deep marks may need professional treatment.

ALABASTER
Any surface soiling on alabaster can usually be removed by wiping with a damp cloth, but alabaster should never be immersed in water. Discoloration, such as staining on ashtrays, should respond to wiping with a cloth moistened with turpentine, then light rubbing with a mild paste cleaner. Rinse off quickly with a warm weak laundry borax solution (1 teaspoon borax to 250 ml water). Dry thoroughly and buff with a clean cloth.

ONYX
Onyx should be handled as little as possible since it has a porous surface which readily absorbs marks. Dust regularly and wipe off any surface soiling with a clean damp cloth. Light staining may respond to rubbing with a cloth moistened with methylated spirits. Marks caused by spilt drinks or wet glasses should be quickly wiped clean, otherwise expensive professional regrinding and polishing becomes necessary.

Tableware

CHINA
Fine bone china is best washed by hand in a weak solution of washing-up liquid, comfortably warm to the hand. Do not use scouring pads, harsh abrasives, bleach or soda; they may damage the surface or dull the pattern – particularly any gold decoration. The surface of a stainless steel sink is fairly resilient and so unlikely to cause breakages, but it is wise to use a plastic washing-up bowl in a vitreous enamel or a glazed fireclay sink where

dropped china is more readily broken (and could also damage the surface of the sink). After washing, the china should be rinsed in fresh water, drained, and dried and polished with a clean tea towel.

Most decorative glazes are relatively hard, but scratching can be caused by stacking wet pieces of china one on top of the other straight from the sink. Use a plastic-covered rack so all the items can be supported separately.

If acids like vinegar and fruit juice are left in contact with some ranges of decorated china for any length of time they can cause damage to certain colours in the design. So if any of your china shows signs of being at risk make a point of always washing these pieces immediately after use – even if you do not want to cope with the whole of the washing up as soon as you have finished the meal.

Any china with egg on it will be easier to clean if you rinse it with cold water before washing. If the egg has dried on, you can loosen it with a damp cloth dipped in salt. Salt can also be used to remove stains from the inside of a teapot; alternatively rub with laundry borax or use a branded tea/coffee stain remover. A bottle brush will come in handy for the spout.

Washing china by machine

A dishwashing machine is a great time and labour saver when you are dealing with everyday ware, but with better quality china it is wise to check that it is 'Dishwasher proof' (some firms mark this on the individual pieces). If the china is old, or you suspect the pattern may be hand painted, it is always better to wash the pieces by hand.

When you are using a dishwasher, it is clearly important to follow the loading instructions correctly, and make sure you do not overload the machine. It is also a good idea to check that the dishwashing powder you use has been approved by the British Ceramic Research Association. (Powders approved by the BCRA have been tested and found safe for china where the decoration is on top of the glaze.)

If you are not using one of the BCRA approved powders you may find that you have problems after a time with a build-up of dulling film on the crockery. This is due to the fact that drying in a dishwasher is done by heat alone, so that if a scum forms it is not removed in the same way as it would if you were drying up with a tea towel. If you do notice a scum building up – and if a change of powder does not solve the problem – a servicing

agent can usually adjust the dishwasher cycle so that the dishes are rinsed more quickly after the washing process.

Any marks on the surface of china caused by crockery coming in contact with metal objects, such as cutlery, can usually be removed by rubbing the surface lightly with a damp cloth dipped in borax.

Mending china

Mending valuable ornaments is a skilled job best carried out by a professional craftsman, who will often be able to replace chipped parts and make an invisible mend.

With epoxy resin adhesives (see page 71), you can join broken pieces of more everyday ware so effectively that neither heat nor water will affect them and broken china will get a whole new lease of life (although, in some cases, a join line may show).

China must be supported while adhesive sets. You can do this by putting it in a box of fine sand or holding the two pieces together with clothes pegs or clamps. Plasticine makes a firm bed for small pieces, and simple cracks will stay together if you stick strips of masking tape or sticky tape across them at right angles.

How to work

Clean the surfaces to be glued. Soak off any old glue in warm water or scrape it off or dissolve it in a solvent – for example, methylated spirits or acetone.

Mix two-part adhesive according to instructions. Hold the joint with sticky tape until it is set

It is difficult to mend more than one break in the same piece of china at the same time, so if you are dealing with a very fragmented piece it may be necessary to build it up a few bits at a time, letting them set, and assembling the whole thing later.

Apply the adhesive by mixing according to the instructions, then cover both surfaces with a fine film, applied with a cocktail stick. Put the bits in place carefully and in the right order. Keep your fingers clean – gluey fingers can stick to china and pull newly stuck joints apart. Press the two surfaces together until they fit perfectly; you may have to twist them about a bit until they slot into place. Check that they are level by running the tip of a knife over them. Any adhesive that has oozed out should be wiped off with a cloth moistened with methylated spirits.

If you are using a standard epoxy resin adhesive, check after about three hours to see that the edges are joined properly; you will still be able to manoeuvre them into position if necessary (the fast-setting adhesive does not allow this, which is why when repairing awkward articles it is better to use the standard type). Then leave the piece, still supported, until the adhesive has dried hard. Scrape off any surplus and fill in any holes with a filler; sandpaper them smooth after setting and, if necessary, paint to match the rest of the pattern. Special enamels are available for this – or you can buy a complete china repair kit that comprises adhesive, filler, glaze and various enamels.

GLASS

Always wash crystal glasses by hand and separately to make sure they do not bang together and chip. Use a plastic bowl or a sink mat and wash the glasses in a warm, weak solution of washing-up liquid. Rinse in clear warm water and drain on a rubber mat or a plastic-coated drainer before drying and polishing with a non-fluffy tea towel – linen if possible. Take extra care when drying glasses with stems, they are easily twisted off. The facets of cut glass can be cleaned with a very soft brush.

To remove wine stains from inside a decanter, fill it with a warm solution of an enzyme washing powder and leave for several hours. Rinse well afterwards. Alternatively, pour in a mixture of vinegar and salt (1 tablespoon salt to 125 ml vinegar) allow to stand for a while, shaking occasionally. A proprietary stain remover for tableware may

work if these methods fail, but if the glass has become 'etched' there is nothing you can do.

To dry a decanter, reverse it in a heavy, wide-necked jug and allow it to drain naturally.

Glasses should be stored upright as the rim is usually the thinnest part.

When glasses stick together, do not try and prise them apart. Pour cold water into the inner glass and hold the outer one in warm water. To loosen a stopper which has become stuck in the neck of a decanter, pour a drop or two of cooking oil round the mouth of the decanter and let it stand in a warm place for half an hour; then tap the stopper gently, first on one side and then on the other.

Glass and dishwashers

Do not use a dishwasher to clean crystal glass. After a time the detergent used in the machine will spoil the look of them with white marks and etching. If you buy glasses or glass tableware with painted or transfer decorations, be sure and ask if they are dishwasher proof. Cheaper glasses as well as crystal glass can become etched with white marks after continued cleaning in a dishwasher. The borosilicate glass used for cooking utensils and oven-to-tableware is capable of resisting greater extremes of temperature, and with greater chemical resistance can stand hot washing in a dishwasher. Glass ceramics are even more resistant to sudden temperature changes.

Repairing glass

Many repairs to glass can be made by using an epoxy resin adhesive (see page 71). If you chip the rim or break the stem of a particularly precious glass it could be worthwhile having the chip professionally ground out or the stem welded. Look for the name of a local glass repairer in the Yellow Pages.

CUTLERY
Silver and silver-plate

Silver cutlery should be washed as soon as possible after use, dried immediately and polished with a clean tea towel. This guards against tarnishing and discoloration which could otherwise result from prolonged contact with salt, egg or vinegar and other acidic foods. Because silver is a comparatively soft metal, it is important that any cloth you use should be really clean and free from any dust or grit which could scratch the surface – and never use scouring powders or steel wool on silver.

Washing-up liquids, dishwasher detergents and rinse aids (provided they are completely dissolved) are all harmless, and almost all sterling and silver-plated cutlery can be safely washed in a dishwasher. An exception is cutlery with hollow handles or handles made from wood, horn, ivory, mother-of-pearl and certain other natural materials. Cutlery with these should always be washed by hand because it is important to keep the handles as dry as possible; hold the handle in your hand and wash the metal part only in clean, hot, sudsy water. Then rinse and dry the cutlery at once.

When silver and silver plated cutlery has been washed in a dishwasher, it is a good idea to rub it up with a tea towel when it comes out of the machine because the polishing given by the towel helps keep it bright. In addition the cutlery will need polishing from time to time with silver polish.

A quick and easy way to remove tarnish – although it is not a polish – is by the dip process. Here you just dip the silver in a jar of the special fluid, rinse and dry. (But do not use this type of chemical cleaner for stainless steel cutlery, or on a stainless steel draining board – it will stain.)

When silver or stainless steel is put into a dishwasher along with worn silver plate or copper (eg a copper-based pan or anodised lid) the colour from the exposed metal base of the plated pieces or of the copper can transfer to the silver or stainless steel. They are best washed separately. Where colour transference has occurred use a silver polish or stainless steel cleaner as appropriate.

Stainless steel

Under normal conditions, stainless steel cutlery should remain bright without any special care, provided it is washed as soon as possible after use. Prolonged contact with salt and acidic foods can cause discoloration and possibly pitting. Knives, particularly, should not be left in water or undried longer than necessary or some slight corrosion or dried-on waterspotting may occur.

For knives with handles made from natural materials, see above under **Silver and silver-plate.**

When washing stainless steel – or any cutlery – in a dishwasher, make sure it is not allowed to come into contact with dry detergent (which should always be poured into the detergent dispenser, or on the floor of the machine) and that the cutlery

basket is not overloaded. Space individual pieces so that there is enough room between them so the water can wash and rinse effectively. As soon as the washing cycle is over, take out the stainless steel cutlery and wipe it dry with a tea towel.

Stainless steel can take on a blue-grey tinge if it has been allowed to overheat. This can sometimes be removed by the use of a branded stainless steel paste or liquid cleaner (which may also be effective on other stains), but stainless steel cutlery should never be immersed in – or even allowed near – the liquid cleaning 'dips' described under 'Silver', above. This would turn it black.

Bronze

Bronze cutlery is easily finger marked and may need rubbing up with a soft cloth during table setting. It tarnishes and discolours more readily than silver and silver plate so should be washed, rinsed and towel dried as soon as possible following a meal. It requires frequent cleaning with a good silver polish.

WOOD
Salad bowls

Do not immerse a wooden salad bowl in water since this could cause the wood to dry out, warp and crack. Instead wipe it round with a kitchen paper towel or a cloth wrung out in clear, warm water and let it dry naturally in an airy place.

It is a good idea to wipe over the surface of a new salad bowl with a cloth moistened with a little edible oil. Corn oil is a good choice because it never goes rancid. The oil seals the wood to some extent and helps prevent the penetration of staining juices – such as beetroot (although it is really better not to put this in a wooden bowl at all).

If the bowl does become stained, try rubbing the surface with a nylon scourer moistened in clear water; for bad staining you may need to resort to rubbing it over with wet and dry abrasive paper. In either case wipe out the bowl with a dry cloth following the treatment to remove any loosened particles of wood.

Once you have used garlic in a wooden bowl, it will always carry the aroma.

Cheese boards

To clean a wooden cheese board, wipe it over with a cloth wrung out in warm water. Leave it to dry naturally in an airy place – preferably propped up on one edge so the air can circulate around it.

215

Kitchenware

SAUCEPANS

Some pans nowadays will stand up to machine-washing in a dishwasher but, in general, pans with wooden or plastic handles should not go in a machine unless the manufacturer specifically says so. Metal handles are usually safe.

If food has burnt on to the inside surface of a pan, it is safer to try and soak it off rather than risk damaging the pan by the use of harsh abrasives. Fill the pan with hand-hot water and whisk in a little enzyme washing powder. Leave for a few hours, boil up then clean as described below for the material concerned. You may need to repeat the process for heavy burnt-on deposits.

Aluminium

Avoid leaving food or water in an aluminium pan for longer than the cooking period as this can cause the surface to pit. So as soon as possible, wash with hot water and washing-up liquid, rinse thoroughly and dry. If necessary, use a nylon brush to loosen any food that has stuck, and a soap impregnated steel wool pad or fine steel wool to burnish the surface from time to time – except on a non-stick or mirror finish.

When washing aluminium in a dishwasher, take care to load the machine so that the rinse water can reach all the surfaces of the utensils to rinse the detergent solution away completely.

If an aluminium pan becomes discoloured, this will be due to mineral salts in the tap water and is quite harmless. However, it can be removed by boiling up a weak acid solution in the pan (for example, water with apple parings or the squeezed cut half of a lemon); rinse and dry. **Never use soda or bleach for cleaning an aluminium pan.**

It is best to fill an aluminium utensil from the cold water tap, letting the tap run for a moment or two first if the piping is made of copper. This is because water which contains some temporary hardness, dissolved chlorides and traces of copper salts, in contact with aluminium can cause pitting of the surface. Use a wooden, rather than a metal, spoon for stirring food in the pan – metal utensils cause scratches which again encourage pitting, especially if the water is artificially softened.

Never put an empty aluminium pan on a hot-plate or over a gas burner to warm up; it will overheat rapidly. And do not plunge a hot aluminium or any lightweight frying pan into cold water or hold it under a running cold tap. It may buckle and distort.

Where a coloured polyimide finish has been sprayed on to the outside of an aluminium pan, this looks like vitreous enamel but is not as durable. Wash as for aluminium using hand-hot water, washing-up liquid and a nylon brush and avoid the use of any type of abrasive cleaner.

Some aluminium pans have a non-stick interior or an outside coating of vitreous enamel or copper. See below for the maintenance of these finishes.

Stainless steel

Clean stainless steel pans with hot water and washing-up liquid, using a nylon brush. A stainless steel paste or liquid cleaner can be used to remove any stains; separate pads may be supplied with the paste for use on satin or mirror finishes. Liquid bleaches should never be used.

Stainless steel does not conduct heat evenly, so pans usually have a base or core of some other metal. Clean an aluminium base as described above and for pans with a copper base, clean the base when necessary with a special copper cleaning product. (For cleaning stainless steel cutlery, see page 215.)

Vitreous enamel

Wash with hot water and washing-up liquid. Stubborn marks can safely be removed with any household cleaning product that carries the Vitreous Enamel Development Council seal of recommendation for general use. These will not dull or scratch the surface. If the inside of a vitreous enamel pan becomes stained, after boiling beetroot for example, fill it with water and add a teaspoon of household bleach. Leave for a few hours, then wash the pan in the usual way.

In a hard water area it is important to dry pans immediately after washing, otherwise a whitish film may form on the surface.

Where a vitreous enamel pan has a non-stick interior, treat this as for 'Non-Stick ware' below.

Copper lined with tin or nickel

Wash the inside of the pan with hot water and washing-up liquid, using a soft cloth; when necessary, clean the outside of the pan with vinegar and salt or a branded copper cleaner.

Because certain foods react with copper, especially those with a high acid content, copper pans are usually lined with another metal. It is important to have the pans re-lined as soon as the copper begins to show through, to prevent metal taint.

Non-stick ware

Keep and follow any care instructions that come with non-stick pans; some items can be washed in a dishwasher but you need to take the manufacturer's advice. As a general rule, non-stick pans should be washed in hot water and washing-up liquid, but certain ranges of bakeware should be washed in hot water alone as any kind of detergent will impair their non-stick finish.

Never use abrasive powders, steel wool or scourers on non-stick ware as these will damage the coating. However, from time to time it is a good idea to rub over the surface with a nylon or plastic cleaning pad or a stiff sponge (special ones are available for non-stick ware) to remove any grease that may be clinging to the surface. If necessary, a proprietary cleaner is also available that will shift any heavy deposits on non-stick surfaces.

To remove food stains from non-stick ware, make up a solution of 1 cup water, $\frac{1}{2}$ cup liquid bleach and 2 tablespoons of bicarbonate of soda. Boil this in the pan for five minutes, then wash the pan well, rinse and dry.

Metal tools can be used with most non-stick pans nowadays, but certain makes could be damaged – so check when you buy. However, even with a surface which will tolerate metal tools, it is unwise to cut food in the pan with a knife or to use an electric hand-held mixer in it.

The main cause of damage to non-stick ware is overheating – so do not leave empty pans on the cooker while you go round collecting ingredients.

CASSEROLES

For casseroles made from any of the materials dealt with above, the same care and cleaning hints apply but keep and follow any instructions that come with new equipment.

As a general rule, casseroles made from oven glass, ceramic glass, pottery, stoneware, earthen-ware and porcelain can be washed in hot water and washing-up liquid in the normal way. Remove any dried-on food by soaking in hot water and washing-up liquid before washing out; use a nylon brush to loosen any bits that may still be sticking.

Most modern casseroles are dishwasherproof, but check when you buy.

Electric casseroles must never be immersed in water. Switch off and detach the plug, then fill the casserole with hot soapy water and rub the inside with a soft brush, sponge or cloth – never anything abrasive. Rinse with clean water and dry. To keep the exterior looking good, just wipe over with a damp cloth and polish dry. Some electric casseroles have a detachable interior bowl that can be completely immersed.

PLASTICS

Melamine cups should be washed as soon as possible after use since prolonged contact with tea or coffee will result in staining inside the cups. If necessary, however, special de-staining products are available.

Do not use serrated knife blades on melamine plates as these can mark and dull the surface.

Melamine and some other rigid plastics, such as those used for mixing bowls and kitchen tools, can be washed in a dishwasher where the washing action helps to minimize the build-up of stains – though some things may go dingy after a while. Flexible plastics such as the kind used for food storage boxes should be washed by hand since the high temperature of water in a dishwasher will affect them. A blender goblet should not be washed in the dishwasher.

The other plastic material most likely to be found in the kitchen – the plastic laminate used for work-top surfaces – needs only an occasional wipe over with a damp cloth. Remove any stains with washing-up liquid or a thicker liquid household cleaner.

COOK'S KNIVES

Knives made of carbon steel should be washed and dried immediately after you have finished using them. This is because they are easily stained by food acids, and will rust if you leave them damp. If staining has already occurred, try rubbing the blades with a nylon pad. If this is not sufficient rub the blades with the flat end of a wet cork dipped

Clean a badly stained carbon steel knife with the end of a wet cork dipped in abrasive powder

into an abrasive cleaning powder or use very fine emery cloth.

Although cooking knives with plastic handles are usually safe in a dishwasher, do not include wooden or other types of handles unless they have been specially treated to be dishwasher-proof.

Do not keep your knives loose in a drawer where they can get blunted by other cutlery. Many knife sets come complete with a plastic or cardboard holder to store them in, but failing this use a magnetic knife rack. A little vegetable oil rubbed over carbon steel blades will protect them against rust. Correct and regular sharpening is vital for all kitchen knives. As a general rule, saw-edge blades will need professional attention, but knives with a continuous cutting edge or hollow-ground blade are not difficult to sharpen yourself, either with a hand operated sharpener, an electric knife sharpening machine, or using a sharpening steel or carborundum stone, once you've mastered the knack. Scallopped edge blades can be sharpened with a steel or carborundum stone.

Pictures

All pictures need dusting regularly. For a picture framed behind glass, the protecting glass should be cleaned from time to time by wiping over with a soft absorbent cloth moistened with methylated spirits, a chamois leather wrung out in warm water or a branded liquid window cleaner. Whichever you use, take care you do not let trickles seep inside the glass and damage the picture.

Provided the backing is in good condition, a glass-framed picture should need no further attention. Prints and engravings, however, sometimes develop unsightly stains due to mildew. Do not try to clean these off yourself; send the picture away for professional treatment.

OIL PAINTINGS
Oil paintings are often framed without glass and, no matter how often you dust them, sooner or later dirt will build up on the surface. Again valuable paintings should be referred to an art dealer, but for less precious works it is possible to get a branded cleaner from artists' supply shops which removes surface dirt. Nevertheless you should use this with

extreme care – especially if you are dealing with an unvarnished picture – and in all cases it is vital to follow the manufacturer's instructions exactly.

The first step is to remove the picture from its frame. You may be able to do this simply by un-clipping it, but if it is nailed in remove the nails carefully with a pair of pliers. Leave the canvas on its stretcher (the stretcher is the inner wooden frame to which the canvas is fixed; there may also be cross pieces). Insert folded tissue or wads of cotton wool between the back of the canvas and the stretcher to prevent the stretcher marking the canvas.

Apply the branded picture cleaner on cottonwool swabs as instructed, working on a small area at a time. If there is any sign of paint coming off on the swabs, stop work at once. When no more dirt is brought off on the cotton wool, the painting should be wiped over with cotton wool moistened with English distilled turpentine; do this twice, using fresh wool and turpentine each time.

Stand the painting on edge to dry in a warm, dust free atmosphere, well away from direct heat until the surface has re-hardened, which may take a few hours. If you want to revarnish the painting, use the oil painting varnish recommended by the makers of the picture cleaner and follow the instructions implicitly. Keep the picture lying flat until the varnish is dry enough not to run. This may take up to 30 minutes, depending on the varnish used and the temperature in the room. Then to prevent dust dropping on the picture, lean it face inwards against a wall until the varnish has dried completely.

FRAMES

Wooden picture frames should be polished regu-larly with a little furniture cream and then rubbed up well.

When gilt frames become discoloured, rub them over with a cloth dipped in turpentine or turps substitute.

If re-gilding is necessary, first dust the frame well then wipe it over with a damp cloth; or you can sponge it with a warm mild detergent solution and rinse, provided the picture has been taken out of the frame. Next apply a branded wax gilt (from artists' supply shops) over the surface, rubbing it on using a finger or a soft cloth. If the frame is a very intricate one, a liquid gilt which goes on with a brush is also available and is easier to get into the fiddly bits of the mouldings.

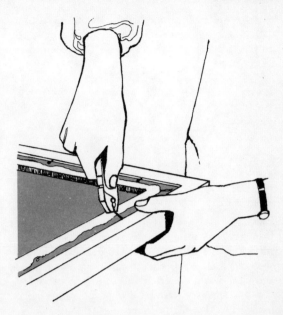

To remove a picture from its frame carefully pull out the nails with pliers

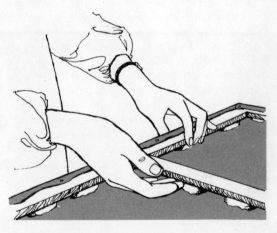

Push pads of cotton wool between canvas and stretcher while you work

An alternative treatment for a shabby gilt frame is to give it a rough white texture, which goes well in a modern room. Mix a little plaster filler into white oil paint (for a specially rough finish, add a little sand or sifted ash) and tint the paint with a little raw umber. Paint the mixture on roughly and thickly, then dab it with a soft cloth or dry brush, so that the underlying gilt shows through here and there, and leave to dry. If the finished effect is too white, mix a little raw umber with turpentine so that it is quite runny and brush this on freely, then dab with a soft cloth till the colour is almost removed, leaving a darker tone in the recessed or carved parts.

Picture cord
Check all picture cords, wire, chains or other fixing from time to time and replace as necessary. (For picture framing and hanging, see page 108.)

Fireplaces

Brick
If the fireplace is only lightly soiled, brush over the surface with a soft brush to remove any dust and soot and then scrub with a hard scrubbing brush and clear warm water. If the soiling does not respond to this, try washing down with neat vinegar followed by thorough rinsing.

Even if the surface is more seriously soot-stained, do not try and clean it with soap or detergents as these get absorbed into the brick and leave a deposit which may well prove impossible to rinse away. Instead, use a proprietary soot cleaner, or make up a solution of six parts water to one part spirits of salts (available from hardware and DIY shops) and apply this to the surface of the bricks, taking care not to let it come into contact with the cement. For heavily soiled areas, strengthen the solution as necessary. Wash down fairly quickly and thoroughly with plenty of warm water. Spirits of salts is corrosive, so **protect your hands and clothes and wear protective goggles.** Spirits of salts also gives off fumes which are extremely strong and poisonous, so **work in a well ventilated room** and do not lean over the surface while applying the liquid.

If there are any burn marks on the bricks, wipe them over with neat vinegar and rinse with clear water.

Stone
Remove light soiling from stone by using clear warm water, a scrubbing brush and a sponge. Using a sponge rather than a cloth makes sure that all the surplus water, dirt and grit are absorbed rather than being left to seep into the stone. To remove heavier soiling, add a few drops of washing-up liquid to the water, then rinse well, but avoid using soap, soap powder or scouring powders

which may affect the colour of the stone. If this does not prove effective, protect surrounding area and scrub with a concentrated solution of domestic bleach. Then rise thoroughly.

The treatment for stubborn marks on a stone fireplace depends on the type of stone, so your wisest course is to get in touch with the manufacturer.

Ceramic tiles
Ceramic tiles should be washed over with soapy water or a washing-up liquid solution; use a very mild abrasive, such as a fine paste cleaner, if necessary, but avoid harsh ones and hard scrubbing brushes which will spoil the glaze. Do not wipe over the fireplace with a damp or wet cloth while it is still hot as this can cause the tiles to crack or craze.

Dry thoroughly, then apply a little furniture polish or cream and rub with a duster.

Polished marble
For detailed treatment, see page 212.

Rustic marble and riven slate
To clean rustic marble or slate, scrub with a stiff-bristled brush and a washing-up liquid solution. Do not use wax polish on either of these materials, and ask the manufacturer's advice on how to remove stains.

Stainless steel
Fireplace trims and hearth plates of stainless steel should be washed with a soft cloth and warm, soapy water. There is no need to use any polish. Tar or soot deposits usually respond to rubbing with methylated spirits.

Sweeping a chimney

Even where a chimney is burning smokeless fuel, it should be swept once a year at least. Where ordinary coal is burned it should be cleaned twice yearly, possibly even more often if you burn a lot of wood. Clean soot out of the lower part of the flue yourself, using a soft brush with a dustpan.

Professional methods
It is well worth the money to have your chimneys swept by a professional chimney sweep. Most sweeps nowadays use the suction method of cleaning, because it involves less mess in the room. By this method, the soot is drawn into a container by suction, after which brushes are used to sweep any clinging dirt from the brickwork lining the chimney.

The traditional method depends on brushes to do the whole job. These are fixed to extending canes and pushed up the chimney till they emerge through the pot.

Whichever method the sweep uses, some soot may escape into the room, so it is wise to cover furniture and remove ornaments and rugs near the fireplace.

SELF HELP
If it proves impossible to find a professional sweep, perhaps because your house is in a very remote area, rather than leaving the chimney unswept it is better to have a go at doing it yourself.

You should be able to buy brushes and rods from a hardware store, or you can probably hire them. Use an old dust sheet to cover the fireplace opening and make a hole in its centre. By taping the sheet to the fireplace with strong adhesive paper, you should get very little soot escaping into the room.

Insert the brush through the hole in the dust sheet and push gently. Screw on an extra length of cane as the end of each cane is reached. Push the brush very gently up the chimney and have an assistant standing by to call out when he sees the brush just emerge at the top. Stop pushing at once at this point, or you could knock off a cowl or do

some other damage. With some types of cowl, you will not be able to see the brush – so take great care and try and judge, by the number of rods, when you are nearing the top.

Remember to remove soot and ash that has dropped down on to the ledge at the back of the fireplace opening.

Chemical soot-removers are also available, but these are not considered very satisfactory. They usually consist of oxidising agents which cause the soot to smoulder. If chimneys are cleaned by this means, lumps of smouldering soot may fall on the hearth, or be blown out of the chimney on to the roof, and the chimney lining, too, may be damaged by the process.

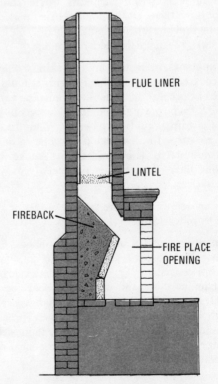

If you have to sweep the chimney yourself, note the likely shape and construction first

Boiler chimneys

Boiler chimneys can often be swept through an outside soot door. It is important to remember to sweep the flue pipe between the boiler and the chimney, especially the sloping part of the chimney, because this can collect a lot of ash.

Identifying and eliminating household pests

Before using any insecticide or rodenticide in the home, read the instructions on the label and follow them exactly when carrying out treatment. Store all pest control chemicals where children cannot reach them, and avoid dispensing pesticides from anything but their original containers. Never, ever, leave any in unlabelled jars, tins, etc.

Any splashes of liquid on the skin should be washed off immediately and hands should be washed before food is eaten. Avoid inhaling vapour or fumes from sprays and do not allow pets to have access to baits, liquids or powders. Many insecticides are carried in flammable solvents, so do not spray near naked flames and do not smoke while applying them. This applies particularly to wood preservatives.

Burn or deeply bury the bodies of rats or mice killed by rodenticides.

When using aerosol insecticides it is best to do this last thing at night, and then close the door of the room concerned. This way the spray can work to maximum effect, and closing the door also has the advantage of keeping pets away, because although licking areas treated with these preparations should not be fatal, it could make them sick.

Never spray near food or cooking or eating utensils.

Ants

It is the foraging worker ants that invade buildings in search of food. These are 5 mm or less in length and are attracted to sweet foodstuffs which they take back to the nest to feed the larvae and the queen.

Flying ants are, in fact, ordinary ants which have been selected to reproduce their kind. Mating takes place in the air during a few days in July and August, and it is for this purpose that the ants grow wings. The female then seeks out a nest site where she stays for the winter, laying eggs the following spring to start up a new colony.

Remedy If you can find the nest entrances – indicated by small piles of earth pellets – pour in a kettle of boiling water and follow this by puffing in an insecticide powder, such as lindane or carbaryl (available from chemists). An aerosol insecticidal lacquer can be applied around door thresholds (yours, not theirs) or wall/floor junctions where the ants run, or spray these areas with an insecticidal aerosol. Otherwise buy tubes of ant killer jelly, that the workers feed on and carry back to the nest, destroying the whole colony. Be careful to cover sweet foods, which ants love.

Bed bugs

The adult bed bug resembles a small brown disc, about the size of a match head. The elongated eggs are cemented in cracks or crevices close to the hosts (which for bed bugs are humans). The bugs generally emerge to feed at night and their bites can cause severe local irritation.

Remedy Insecticidal sprays or even possibly fumigation of the premises, clothing and bedding will be necessary; but this is a job for the experts – either the Local Health Authority or a reputable pest control contractor.

Bluebottles

These are large buzzing flies with shiny, metallic blue bodies 6–12 mm long. One bluebottle can lay up to 600 eggs at a time, which in warm weather will hatch in under 48 hours and produce maggots which can become fully developed in a week.

Remedy Keep dustbins clean with tight lids and away from doors or windows. Keep meat and other food covered. Use an insecticidal dustbin powder. Indoors, use a vaporizing insecticidal strip and keep a fly spray handy.

Carpet beetles

The 'woolly bear' grubs of these small, oval beetles have outstripped the clothes moth as the major British textile pest. The Varied Carpet Beetle is 4 mm or less in length like a small, mottled brown, grey and cream ladybird. The related Fur Beetle is black with one white spot on each wing case, and there is also a rarer Black Carpet Beetle. The larvae of carpet beetles are small, covered with brown hair and tend to roll up when disturbed. As they grow, they moult – and the old cast-off skins may be the first sign of infestation.

Carpet beetle damage consists of fairly well defined round holes along the seams of fabric where the grubs bite through the thread.

Remedy Regularly vacuum all fluff and debris from airing cupboards, shelves, floorboards, carpets and upholstery. Occasionally move furniture to vacuum floor coverings and floors beneath. Spray any affected items with a special carpet beetle killer or moth proofer. As an added precaution dust an insecticide powder between floorboards, under carpets and underfelts and into crevices where fluff may collect and attract the beetles.

Clothes moths

There are several species of clothes moth, of which the commonest is the Brown House Moth with its characteristic golden-bronze wings flecked with black. Adult moths do not do damage in feeding, but their larvae hatch from the sticky eggs and digest wool, hair, fur or feathers – with a preference for blankets, wool carpets, wool garments and upholstery that have been soiled with perspiration or food stains.

Remedy Sensible precautions include the scrupulous cleaning of all woollens and the storing of them in sealed heavy gauge polythene bags; furs should be kept in cotton bags or covered with old sheets and hung in an airy place. Fold in a disc of moth repellent in a cotton bag. Examine these articles at regular intervals.

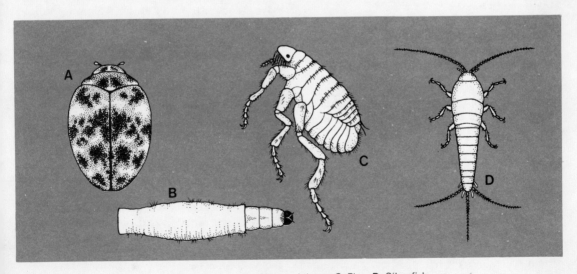

A. Carpet beetle B. Moth grub larva C. Flea D. Silverfish

If you see signs of moth damage, launder washable articles. Otherwise spray any affected garments (not furs), fabrics or carpets with a proprietary aerosol moth proofer, especially along seams and folds; also spray any gaps or shelves where fluff could collect. Furs should be taken outside and carefully but thoroughly brushed, or professionally cleaned in the case of severe infestation. If a carpet can be lifted, vacuum the underside, the underfelt and the floor before putting it back.

Cockroaches

Often confused with black beetles, cockroaches are distinguished by their very long whip-like antennae, flat oval bodies and rapid, jerky running about. The common cockroach is 20–24 mm long.

Cockroaches thrive round the heating ducts and boiler rooms of large centrally heated buildings, such as blocks of flats. They eat any sort of food and emerge after dark to forage and incidentally to contaminate food and food utensils and preparation surfaces. They can be carriers of serious food poisoning.

Remedy Control of cockroaches is seldom easy because of the difficulty of getting the insecticide to the insect. Try a long-lasting one in aerosol form sprayed liberally into and on to all possible harbourages. If the problem persists, call in your Public Health Department or contact a pest control contractor.

Death watch beetle

This is a woodboring beetle whose grubs eat old hardwood structural timbers. When adult the beetles produce a rapid tapping sound by beating their heads against the wood as a mating call.

Remedy Persistent and thorough use of a proprietary woodworm killer will deal with small outbreaks, or call in a wood preservation company. See also woodworm.

Fleas

Fleas are tiny flightless parasites. Their bites cause intense irritation around a central bright red spot.

Remedy Flea powders suitable for treating humans are available at chemists. Treat infested pets and their bedding with a special veterinary powder or shampoo. Remove any old birds' nests you find in the eaves or loft and burn them. For rapid clearing

of an infested building get in touch with a pest control contractor, who may use an insecticidal fog. Fumigation by gas is rarely necessary.

Flies

The Common House Fly is grey in colour with black stripes on the back. The smaller Lesser House Fly is the one that cruises around light fittings, abruptly changing direction in mid-flight when you try and swat it.

Remedy As for Bluebottles.

Lice

The Head Louse is a blood-sucking parasite about 3 mm long, greyish, but adapting to the hair colour of its host. The tiny pearly eggs or 'nits' are cemented to the hair close to the scalp and hatch in about eight days. The complete life cycle takes about 18 days.

The bites cause inflammation and itching, which leads to affected children scratching the scalp and introducing secondary infections such as impetigo or eczema.

Remedy There are effective insecticidal shampoos but preferably these should be prescribed by a doctor.

Mice

The presence of mice is usually first detected from their dark-coloured droppings, or perhaps by damage to food packets stored in the larder. Mice have a compulsive need to gnaw in order to keep their incisor teeth worn down to a constant length. Electric cables, water and gas pipes may all be seriously damaged by mice. They contaminate far more food than they consume and are capable of carrying many diseases, particularly food poisoning.

Remedy Keep a cat. As far as possible, mouse-proof all means of entry by blocking holes with wire wool embedded in quick-setting cement or by fitting metal strips to damaged wooden doors to cover gaps. You will then need to put down some kind of rodenticide. But the trouble is that in many places mice have become resistant to warfarin, the main ingredient of most of the previously successful types. Buy a brand based on alphachloralose or calciferol. Seek the advice of your local Public Health Department or a pest control contractor if the problem persists.

A trap may catch the odd intruder if baited with

nutty chocolate or raisins and placed close to signs of mouse activity. Cheese, oddly enough, is a comparatively poor mouse-baiter, despite what the nursery stories say. Place the trap at right angles to the wall.

Rats
Rats, like mice, need to gnaw to keep their constantly growing incisor teeth worn down and this gnawing can damage woodwork, plastic and lead pipes, and has been known to strip insulation from cables. Rats spread many diseases including food poisoning, murine typhus, Weil's disease, rat bite fever and trichinosis.

Remedy As far as possible eliminate harbourages such as gaps under sheds, loose piles of wood or neglected weed patches. Do not encourage rats by leaving scraps of food out of doors; if you feed garden birds, use a bird table or a feeder basket.

Poison rats with one of the proprietary ready-mixed baits. These can be obtained in sachets to be placed near signs of infestation. Keep replacing the baits until no more are taken.

For serious or persistent rat infestation, call a pest control company or your local Public Health Department.

Silverfish
Silverfish are cigar-shaped silver-grey wingless insects about 12 mm long, found in damp areas of kitchens and bathrooms. Pretty harmless in itself, a silverfish feeds on residues of starchy substances such as some glues, wallpaper paste and carbohydrate food debris; its presence may indicate damp conditions which need attention.

A closely similar species, the Firebrat, is flatter and speckled and favours hot, dry situations.

Remedy Spray harbourages with a household insecticide or insect powder.

Wasps
Large, buzzing insects with yellow and black striped, waisted bodies, wasps have a sweet tooth at one end and a painful sting at the other.

Remedy Close or screen windows with a fly screen if wasps are a major problem. A good spray with an aerosol insecticide should dispose of the odd one or two fairly quickly, and is more likely to prove effective than random swatting (unless your reactions are very much quicker than a wasp's).

If you find a wasp's nest in a wall or bank, wait until dusk, put on gloves and puff wasp killer powder liberally into the entrance. Leave a few days before digging it out. If a nest is in the house, in the roof or under the floor for instance, you will probably need professional help.

Woodworm
First sign of woodworm is the appearance of neat round holes, 2 mm across, in wooden surfaces, often accompanied by tiny piles of wood dust beneath them.

Remedy Woodworm in furniture can be cured by special fluid woodworm killers. Coat all surfaces, polished and unpolished, and inject fluid into a few flight holes with a special injector.

Although it is possible to treat woodworm in structural timbers yourself, it is a complicated job and really better left to experts. Specialist firms will come and inspect and give an estimate free of charge. They usually give a 20 or 30 year guarantee on their work. Pick a reputable company that is not likely to go out of business before the guarantee expires.

Moving house

Moving house calls for a positive plan of campaign if you want things to go smoothly – and who doesn't? So whether you decide to hire a removal company or to cope with the move yourself, below are some of the steps you can take to ease your way to a successful moving day.

EMPLOYING A REMOVAL COMPANY

If you decide to employ a company to move you, get at least three estimates – up to three months ahead of the move. The British Association of Removers (279 Grays Inn Road, London WC1X 8SY) will give you the names of their members in your area if you write to them enclosing stamped addressed envelope.

When the estimator calls, point out to him exactly what has to be moved, not forgetting odds and ends in the garage, the attic and the garden. If you are leaving the carpets behind for the new owner, mention it now so the men will know to bring protective covers for them on moving day.

Insurance

Sometimes your household contents policy can be extended to cover things in transit, but valuable articles may need insuring separately. Most removers offer limited insurance in their estimate, but make sure this covers your needs. If half the load is damaged, for instance, you might only receive compensation on half the sum insured rather than for the value of the individual items damaged. Basic policies for removal firms do not usually cover important documents or jewellery or loss through fire or damage whilst articles are in store. So be sure and read the small print. Almost certainly the contractor will have laid down restrictions as to his responsibilities, so leave the packing (especially of china and glass) to him; he will not be responsible for anything you pack yourself.

Carry jewellery and other precious items with you, or make arrangements to lodge them with your bank over the move. Use your discretion about small pocketable items like transistor radios

and cameras; do not leave these or cash lying around.

Carpets and curtains Alter, make or have these cleaned well in advance. It can be a mistake to move fitted carpets unless they are in really good condition. Some removal firms associated with a furniture or department store may arrange to lift and lay carpets for you, but as a general rule removal men are not skilled carpet fitters so you will need to loosen them beforehand and to arrange for a specialist carpet laying firm to be waiting to re-lay the carpets at the other end.

Freezers Run down the contents in advance till your freezer is empty, defrost it and give it a good clean.

Alternatively, if the move is a fairly short one you may be able to transport the loaded freezer; however, a freezer is not really designed as a travelling container and you would do well to seek the manufacturer's advice. If you decide not to empty it turn the freezer down to the coldest setting 12 hours before the move and have it loaded into the van last so that it comes out first. Unopened, the contents should stay frozen 8–10 hours. (On a longer journey, where a night stop is involved, some removal firms can arrange for the freezer to be plugged in overnight.) Be sure to check in advance that the firm has the necessary lifting gear – a loaded freezer is very heavy.

Other electrical equipment Try to find the instruction manuals for any large equipment. Arrange in advance for a service engineer to disconnect equipment such as an automatic washing machine; it may need transit bolts, special crating and carrying bars. If you are taking any storage radiators with you, remember to turn them off well in advance so they have time to cool down.

Service connections Notify the electricity and gas boards in both districts of your move so that meters can be read, cookers and storage radiators disconnected (and connected at the other end) and power supplies turned off (and on). You should also notify the local water authority at least 48 hours before the move.

Remember that the removal men are not allowed

to interfere with service connections; nor will they dismantle or reassemble electrical fixtures and fittings or take down or put up outside television aerials.

Deliveries Get a form P944B from the post office to arrange for mail to be forwarded, and let the telephone people know you are leaving at least seven days beforehand so that you do not get charged for any calls made after you have gone.

Remember to cancel the newspapers, milk and other regular deliveries and to notify your doctor and your bank that you are moving. Send notice of your change of address to your stockbroker if you have one, and also to any HP companies, Premium Bonds etc. Contact your insurance company to make arrangements on your various policies – not forgetting car insurance.

If the new owners are not moving into the house at once, ask the police to keep an eye on it.

At the new house Clearly the more work you can do at the new house before the move the better – new electric points, decorations, curtain rails, telephone installation and so on. Make sure you have at least some electric light bulbs in their sockets.

Packing

Have the house as tidy as you can but do not (for insurance reasons) start on any actual packing apart from clothing and personal articles. If you do not have enough containers for these, the removal firm can be asked to supply you with some beforehand.

It is not necessary to take things out of drawers but equally do not leave precious and fragile things in them, nor fill them with a lot of heavy things that would make them difficult to handle. The drawers of heavy pieces of furniture should be left unlocked so that they can be carried separately to the van; tie any furniture keys to the piece concerned.

If you wish, you can leave clothes hanging in the wardrobes, though the odds are they will fall off the rails. Some firms supply special wardrobe cartons. Bedding should be taken off beds and folded.

Apart from any other personal belongings, one thing you should pack yourself is a case with things you might need during your first 12 hours or so in the new house. If you have small children, include a favourite toy or two. It is also as well to have matches, candles, a torch and a small tool and first aid kit at the ready, as well as a picnic set and meal, flasks of soup and/or tea and coffee, and a kettle – remember the flex if it is an electric one.

Keep enough cleaning equipment out to give the house a final quick flick round before you leave.

Moving day

As soon as the men arrive, make it clear to the foreman what is to go and what is to stay. Different coloured labels and stickers on furniture indicate what is to go in which room. If you cannot be at the new house when the van arrives, give the foreman a plan showing furniture placing – plus the house keys. (Even if you do plan to be there, it is a good idea to give the foreman an extra key, just in case you are held up.)

Make sure the foreman has the full address of your new house, and give him a clear written description, or better still a simple map, showing how to get to it. Give him a telephone number to call in case of any problems on the way, and have a parking space reserved if possible.

When the old house has been cleared, check that everything is aboard before the van drives off; do not forget to look in the cupboard under the stairs. Remember it is your responsibility to see that everything to be moved is taken out, and also that anything you do not want moved is not put on the van by mistake.

Children and pets both tend to get over-excited on moving day. See if you can entrust them to a kindly neighbour.

Finally, hand over the house keys as arranged.

DO-IT-YOURSELF REMOVALS

Moving furniture is heavy work, so before you decide to pack and move for yourself you would be wise to enlist the help of a couple of good strong friends. You will also almost certainly need to hire a van – look in the Yellow Pages. Some rental companies supply packing cases and ropes as part of the deal, so be sure and ask what is included. For your part, give the company some idea of the size of the load so they can advise you on the size van you will need. (Above a certain size you will need a driver with a Heavy Goods Vehicle licence.)

When you are ready to start packing, put things together in groups – books, linen, crockery, clothes, papers and documents and so on – then pack them in numbered cartons, keeping a list of the type of contents, so you will be able to unpack systematically when you arrive at your new home. Do not make the boxes so heavy that it is a strain to lift them.

Packing glass and china Glassware, crockery and other fragile objects should preferably be packed in boxes with firm sides such as tea chests. If you have to make do with cardboard boxes it is a good idea to reinforce them by lining the inside with extra sheets of cardboard. Line the boxes generously with newspaper, straw or tissue paper.

The heavier the crockery, the closer it goes to the bottom of the box. Put layers of newspaper, corrugated paper or cardboard between each layer, and do not pack too much in any one box. Leave a few centimetres space at the top of the box and fill this with pieces of crumpled newspaper or some other soft filling.

Plates and saucers are best packed on their sides, so that if the case is dropped the shock will not go right across the plate and it will be less likely to break. Put a few layers of newspaper between each plate and make sure the sides are well cushioned. Cups and glasses should be wrapped individually with paper stuffed inside; pots and pans should also be separated by layers of newspaper.

Furniture should be wrapped in old blankets or dust sheets and vulnerable edges are best protected by tying a piece of sponge rubber or old carpet over them. Taking self assembly furniture apart will make it easier to carry.

Where you can, lock all doors and drawers to chests, cupboards and wardrobes to stop them coming open in transit. Tie the keys to the pieces of furniture to which they belong as they are easy things to lose during a move.

Foodstuffs and toiletries should be wrapped separately in polythene bags, as should flasks and bottles, which should also be sealed with sticky tape.

Liquids in plastic containers, oils and paints should be placed in a container such as a bucket. Make sure they are tightly closed by tying a piece of plastic or some other waterproof material over the opening and see that the container is wedged so that it cannot tip over in the van.

Loading the van
Load all the big and heavy items first, tying them to the bars on the sides of the van to stop them sliding about. Put protective padding of some kind between any adjoining surfaces. Watch out that no-one loads cartons containing fragile things one on top of the other, and wedge them well in case you have to brake in a hurry.

Storing furniture and carpets

Putting things in store can be an expensive business, so if you have furniture and carpets that you have no room to store yourself, you might be better getting rid of them by putting a small ad. in the local press, or perhaps giving them to a charity or sending them to an auction.

If you do decide to put things in store, ask round for competitive estimates. Remember that once goods are stored away it can be quite pricey to trace and take out particular items that you want back in advance of the rest – so when you have chosen your contractor, warn him if you think there are any things you are likely to want before the full storage period is up.

It is your responsibility to insure any goods you have in store, though obviously the contractor will take all the precautions that he can. Use some form of moth preventive with curtains and soft furnishings as infestation can spread from other people's possessions. It is also wise to give wooden furniture a generous coating of woodworm preventing polish, not forgetting to polish the sides and back, and the undersides of any drawers as well.

STORING AT HOME
Provided you have the space you can save a good deal of money by storing things that are not in use but that you do not want to part with at home. A dry, airy attic is ideal – although do not use it for storing anything too heavy or it might cause the ceiling to cave in. The floor must be level so that the furniture does not become distorted. If you use a room with a concrete floor it is likely to be dusty, so put thick cardboard down first and stand the furniture on wooden blocks to prevent damp penetrating.

Try and store furniture off the floor (but not too close to the roof where humidity collects) so the air can circulate freely; wooden blocks can be used for this.

Again, it is a good idea to protect wood furniture with polish and soft furnishings with a moth preventive as described above. Wrap each piece in large sheets of brown paper, or thick blankets for delicate things, and tie brown paper round table legs for extra protection. Then cover everything with a loose dust sheet.

Carpets
Carpets should be thoroughly cleaned before you put them away. Vacuum both sides, remove any stains, shampoo and let them get perfectly dry. If they are not permanently moth-proofed, you will need to protect natural fibre carpets against moth and carpet beetle. Use an aerosol insecticide (test first on an out-of-the way area) or enclose napthaline balls (available from chemists) in a double cotton bag. Alternatively, have the carpets professionally cleaned and moth-proofed.

Then roll up the carpet against the way of the pile, and with the pile inwards, and store the roll in 500 gauge plastic sheeting which is particularly suitable for this – cheaper, though not quite so effective, is to wrap the roll with strong brown paper tied loosely round with string.

Store the carpet roll lying down, ideally on some blocks of wood placed a few cm apart to let the air circulate round the carpet. Do not put anything on top of the carpet roll – it could cause permanent creasing. Open the roll from time to time to check that all is well.

Beds
Before you put them away, brush mattresses and bases to remove any dust and air them by an open window for at least a day before storing.

If you can spare the space, it's best to store beds and mattresses flat. If you have to store them on their sides, try and change them over from time to time to prevent distortion. Mattresses should never be stored rolled.

You can use a moth proofer on a mattress before you put it away, and wrap it in an old cotton sheet – do not use polythene because it keeps in any moisture and this could cause mildew.

Refrigerators and freezers
Refrigerators and freezers should never be stored on their sides. They are best stored on wooden blocks if the floor is concrete so the air can circulate. Naturally both inside and outside must be scrupulously clean before you put them away, and a coat of wax polish on the outside will help to prevent any condensation damaging the surface. Doors or lids should be wedged slightly ajar, again for the purpose of air circulation, and the whole thing covered with an old sheet or blanket.

If a refrigerator or a freezer is to be stored for a long period, it would be wise to have it serviced by the local agent for the makers so that it can be suitably prepared to combat any deterioration that might otherwise occur. It is also important to have the appliance serviced after long term storage in case the seal has perished or the motor is in need of replacement parts.

Try to examine stored furniture at regular intervals.

3. Managing with money and the law

Bank accounts and services

Most people open a bank account because it provides a very much safer place to keep their money than in an old teapot or under the mattress. It also makes life easier to be able to draw cash when you need it and pay bills with a cheque. But a bank can also act as your insurance broker, executor and trustee, advise you on your investments and income tax, look after your valuables and offer, at the least, an informed opinion on pretty well any problem you have concerning money.

Below we talk about some of the services offered by the Commercial Banks – often called Joint-Stock Banks – which are the banks with the familiar names you see in every High Street. Trustee Savings Banks provide many of the same facilities.

Current accounts

A current account is the most commonly used type of bank account. Cash, incoming cheques, money orders and postal orders can all be paid into a current account and you draw cash or make payments by writing out a cheque. The bank sends you statements at regular intervals setting out payments made and received, and letting you know the balance in hand.

As well as, or instead of, just being your personal account, a current account can be opened in any number of joint names. You have to let the bank know, in writing, who is empowered to sign the cheques, which can be any, either or all of you. In the case of a joint account held between husband and wife, provided you trust each other, it is probably most useful to arrange for the bank to pay out on either signature, so you can draw out money even if your husband/wife is away or ill.

Banks do not pay interest on current accounts. In fact, if you let your balance slip below a certain minimum you are likely to end up paying them a service charge, the amount of which varies from time to time and from bank to bank. If you do not know what your bank charges are, ask; paying in a few extra pounds could save you money.

Deposit accounts

A deposit account does earn interest. The rate varies according to the economic situation of the country (and again sometimes from bank to bank). You should normally give seven days' notice if you want to withdraw your money from a deposit account, but if you need it urgently most banks will let you have it on demand with a small loss of interest.

Budget accounts

These are designed to even out your household expenses as you foresee them, so that you do not suddenly have to cope with paying a large number of bills all at the same time (just after Christmas, for example).

For a budget account, the bank will ask you to list all your regular bills such as rates, gas, electricity, telephone, car tax, TV licence, insurance, season tickets, etc (and you had probably better add on an agreed figure for inflation). These are then added up and the total divided by 12. You then give the bank a standing order to transfer one-twelfth of the total from your current account to your budget account every month. When the bills come in, you pay them with a budget account cheque, whether there is enough money in the account or not, because this is the one kind of bank account which is intended to go into overdraft sometimes. Over the whole year you should break even, provided you got the original sums right.

Bank Giro

As an alternative to making payments by cheque, transfers of money can be made by the bank's credit transfer system or direct debiting system – known as the Bank Giro. When you have a lot of payments to make at the same time this can be easier (and cheaper, because you save postage stamps) than writing out individual cheques.

Bills for local rates, electricity, gas, telephone and many others now have their own bank giro slip attached to them. All you do is fill these in, sign them and take them to your bank with a single cheque made payable to the bank to cover the whole amount. The bank takes over from there, and makes no charge for the service.

233

Cheque cards

A cheque card reassures shopkeepers and restaurant owners that they can safely accept cheques from you up to a fixed limit, even though they may never have seen you before. You can also cash your own cheques up to a fixed daily limit with a cheque card at any of the major banks throughout the UK and at banks in Europe that show the Eurocheque symbol. The card itself costs you nothing.

Cash cards

Cash cards enable you to help yourself to money (usually £10 but increasingly up to £100) from a sort of slot machine. These cash dispensing machines are installed in the outside walls of some banks, so in an emergency you can get money 24 hours a day, seven days a week.

Travellers' cheques

These are cheques made out to you for fixed sums in either sterling or a foreign currency of your choice. They are exchangeable for currency at banks and other authorized exchange offices. It is safer to carry large sums in travellers' cheques than in currency because they are endorsed with your signature. It is important to order them a few days before you want to travel, and remember to take your passport with you when you collect them. You can use travellers' cheques on holiday in the UK if you want to, but unless you are touring it is probably easier and cheaper to ask your bank to arrange an 'open credit' for you at a local branch in the town you are visiting. Or you can use your cheque card for sums up to the fixed limit.

OTHER BANK SERVICES
Safe-guarding valuables

All banks have strongrooms and/or safes where you can leave important documents such as your will, deeds and share certificates and boxes or parcels of jewellery and other precious items. But although the bank will take 'all reasonable precautions' in looking after your property you should nevertheless cover valuables with insurance; the premiums quoted will be much less than the usual 'all risks' rate you would pay if you were keeping them at home.

Insurance

Several of the big banks have their own subsidiary companies which offer a complete advisory service; life and endowment insurance, householder's comprehensive, employers' and public liability insurance and so on. An advantage of dealing through a bank is that not only should you get impartial advice but, because your bank manager knows you, you will probably also get immediate cover.

Buying and selling shares

Through their own stockbrokers, your bank will buy or sell all kinds of stocks and shares on your behalf. For most investments up to a fixed limit in value, investment through a bank will cost you no more than using a broker direct. However, for investment in gilt-edged stocks on the National Savings Stock Register it is better to buy direct from the Post Office as their charges are very small. All other gilt-edged stock must be bought through a stockbroker.

Income tax

The bank's income tax department will advise you or act on your behalf in any personal tax problems. This includes preparing your tax return, checking your assessments, claiming refunds and dealing with any problems concerning capital gains. For this service they make a charge comparable to an accountant's.

Executor and trustee departments

Many people appoint a bank to act as executor and, if necessary, trustee of their estate when they die. This has a number of advantages over appointing a friend or relative. The bank administrator will be an expert in the subject, and will also have all the other departments of the bank to call on for their expertise in trust law, accounts, taxation, investment, property management and so on. He will also be impartial in the event of a family dispute breaking out.

No fees are payable if you appoint the bank as executor until after you are dead. After this an administration fee is charged on the gross value of the estate, and an annual management fee until the estate is wound up.

OBTAINING A BANK LOAN

Banks are in business to lend people money, although at times the government makes this difficult for them. Below are some of the loans your bank manager can arrange for you; whether he will or not is a matter between him and you.

Overdrafts are flexible loans with interest charged on your day-to-day balance, so as soon as you get in the 'black' again, the interest stops.

Personal loans are for a fixed period, with a rate of interest also fixed at the time the loan is agreed, and repayments by equal monthly instalments.

Home loans are much the same as building society mortgages, and you can claim tax relief on the interest paid up to a certain level of borrowing.

Bridging loans come in useful when you have bought a new home which you need to pay for before you have received the money from the sale of your old house. You can claim tax relief on the interest on bridging loans, but only up to a 12 month period and provided that you have moved into the new house within a year of getting the loan.

On all loans, be sure you are clear as to the rate of interest being charged.

Mortgages

A mortgage is the name given to a document in which the borrower (or mortgager) pledges the home he or she is buying to the lender (or mortgagee) as security for the repayment of a loan, and for payment of the interest on that loan.

A mortgage is usually arranged through a building society or, less often, a local authority and is often linked to a life assurance policy. Other organizations which may provide mortgages are the life insurance companies themselves, although they tend to be interested in big houses and professional people, and banks, who again prefer higher priced property and are usually only prepared to lend for a fairly short period of time.

If you have difficulty getting a mortgage, a mortgage broker may be able to help. He will have firsthand knowledge of the building societies in his area, and how much money they have currently available for lending. Do not be persuaded into paying a fee to a broker until a mortgage has definitely been arranged.

Building society mortgages
Over 80 per cent of home owners borrow from a building society – and you probably stand a better chance of getting a loan if you have been investing your savings with one (see page 237) provided your income is sufficiently high and stable. The societies' lending policies differ quite a bit – some do not like lending to self-employed people, for example, or will only lend on purpose-built and not on converted flats. Most, nowadays, maintain that they treat single women applicants in exactly the same way as men, but some will only lend money to a married woman if her husband joins in the mortgage.

A building society's 'normal advance' is usually about 80 per cent of the property's value or of its purchase price, whichever is less; but higher advances can be obtained. The loan is normally repayable over a maximum of 25 years. Before you are loaned the money you will have to produce a deposit (ten per cent or more) and prove that you are capable of keeping up the instalments and interest on the money you want to borrow.

Happily, the interest on mortgages is allowable for tax relief, and because of the way the scheme operates you tend to pay the interest off first, which means that the mortgage costs you least in the early days, when you may be shortest of money.

Local council mortgages
Local councils can be more amenable than building societies if you want to buy an older (pre-1914) house, a flat or a maisonette. These mortgages are not easy to get, however, as local authorities are only likely to lend on houses in their own areas, and when funds dry up they have to stop lending

235

altogether; they may, however, refer applicants to building societies who have agreed to help.

Local authority mortgages tend to have a higher rate of interest than building societies, but against this they may lend you as much as 100 per cent of the value of the property, and if you are young enough they may allow you as long as 30 or even 35 years to pay.

Option mortgages

This scheme was started to help people to whom income tax relief is no benefit, because they pay little or no tax. An option mortgage may be obtainable either from a building society or a local council and under the scheme, instead of paying mortgage interest at the normal rate and claiming tax relief, borrowers pay interest at a lower rate and forgo the tax relief.

It would probably be wise to talk to an accountant to see if taking up an option mortgage would help you or not, although once you have kept to the scheme for four years you can always switch to an ordinary repayment mortgage (with tax relief) later, if your income goes up.

Endowment mortgages

Although more expensive than ordinary repayment mortgages, for anyone paying tax at the standard rate or above this scheme is certainly worth looking into.

This is how it works: you apply to a building society for a loan for, for example, 20 years. But instead of paying the money back bit by bit as you would with an ordinary repayment mortgage, you leave the loan outstanding throughout the 20 years. At the same time you also take out an endowment assurance (a kind of life policy, see page 239) for an amount equal to the loan and for the same length of time. This policy you assign to the building society. When the policy matures, it is used to pay back the mortgage.

As with a repayment mortgage, you make regular payments which go towards paying the interest on the mortgage and the premiums on the endowment assurance. Both payments qualify for tax relief (although on the assurance premium there is an upper limit of about two-fifths of the premium).

Another advantage of an endowment mortgage is that if a married man is buying a house and he dies, the insurance policy matures immediately and repays the mortgage, so the house belongs to the wife without her needing to make any more payments at all.

Investment

If you have a sudden windfall of a large amount of money, you would be wise to consult your bank manager, or a special investment consultant, as to how to make it work best for you. Here we are looking at ways by which the money you have managed to save can be used (invested) to make more money for you.

SHORT-TERM SAVING

A **deposit account** at a bank, as mentioned earlier, is one of the easiest ways of putting a few pounds away. The interest you will get varies from time to time, depending on the bank's base rate, and you will need to declare any interest received for tax.

Trustee Savings Banks are local banks which offer a complete personal banking service. On an ordinary account they pay a yearly rate of interest, some of which may be tax free. You can pay in and draw out at any TSB branch, and you do not lose any interest you have accrued by taking your money out when you want to.

On a TSB special investment account you earn a

higher rate of interest, but no tax-free allowance, and you need to give a few days' notice before you withdraw your money.

The National Savings Bank also pays interest on an ordinary account, again, some of which is tax free. You can open an account with just a few pence, and draw out a stated amount on demand – once you have saved it, of course – at nearly all branches of the post office. Withdrawing larger amounts usually takes a few days because you have to apply to NSB headquarters, but if you need the money urgently you can use the telegraphic withdrawal service, which will cost you the price of a telegram.

NSB investment accounts are less 'liquid' than ordinary accounts and one month's notice of withdrawal is needed. But, although taxable, the interest rate is considerably higher.

Building Societies These are a particularly good place to put your savings if you think you may need to approach the society for a mortgage at some future date (see page 235). Paying in and drawing out is convenient because you can do this at any branch of the society and you can withdraw quite large sums on demand. Interest rates may vary from time to time, and tax is paid by the society on your behalf at a rate slightly lower than the basic rate of income tax. This means that if you are not eligible for income tax, investing with a building society is not such a good idea, because you cannot prevent the society paying the tax, and once paid, you cannot recover it.

LONGER-TERM INVESTMENTS
Building society subscription share accounts
These pay a higher rate of interest than ordinary building society share accounts. You arrange to pay in a specified sum of money at regular intervals.

As with ordinary share accounts, tax is deducted by the society and is not recoverable.

Building society term shares These offer a comparatively high rate of interest in return for an undertaking to invest your money for a fixed period of say one, two or three years; once you have paid your money in you cannot withdraw it until the agreed period is up.

Life assurance linked building society savings
These are designed as a means of earning higher interest on relatively short term savings. You pay a monthly premium to a life insurance company, which is eligible for tax relief, and they invest your money in a building society where it earns interest. Meanwhile your life is insured for a fixed sum. The return on your investment depends on how long you keep up the premiums, but the best return is after four years.

British savings bonds You buy these in minimum unit quantities at any bank or most post offices. They pay an annual interest which is taxable, plus a tax-free bonus at the end of the fifth year.

Local authority loans It is best to invest in these only when you have already saved a largish sum of money which you want to put to work. Remember, too, that you will not be able to get your money back from a local authority until the time you have undertaken to lend it to them is up.

National saving certificates You do not receive any annual interest on these but at the end of four years you get a tax-free bonus. You can withdraw your money from national savings certificates if you need to, but you lose part of your bonus if you cash them within the four year term.

Index-linked savings
The Department of National Savings also runs two further schemes which are particularly worth considering in a period of inflation because the return you get is linked to the UK General Index of Retail Prices (the RPI).

The RPI is based on the average prices paid for such things as food, clothing, rents, transport and essential services. Once a month the government compares these prices with the prices paid the month before, and if they have risen the RPI will also rise.

Save as your earn Under this scheme you agree to invest a fixed sum monthly for five years. At the end of this time you will be entitled to receive repayment of the total amount of your contributions, revalued to reflect the difference between the RPI for the month you paid the money in and the index figure for the month in which the fifth anniversary of the starting date falls.

If you leave your savings in for another two years, you then become entitled to the return of your contributions at the current revalued rate, plus an additional tax-free bonus equal to two months' contributions.

If you need to take your money out before the first five years are up, after the first year you will receive some interest on your contributions, but otherwise you will only get back the money you paid in, not the revalued sum.

The retirement savings plan These certificates are called the retirement issue, although you do not have to be retired to hold them. You do, however, have to be over 65 if you are a man, 60 if you are a woman. There is a limit to the number of certificates you can hold.

Your investment is again index-linked, but you have to hold the certificates for one year before you can cash them with the benefit of indexation – after this you will receive back your original investment plus an extra amount directly related to any rise in the RPI since you bought them. (The RPI figure applying to purchases and repayments each month is available from post offices.)

If you hold on to the certificates until they mature (five years) you also get a bonus equal to a fixed percentage of their face value. All repayments are free from both income tax and capital gains tax.

INVESTING IN STOCKS AND SHARES

Most newspapers carry a section of city news and plenty of books are available on investment for beginners. The vital thing to remember is that shares have a nasty habit of going down as well as up. For this reason money invested in shares through the Stock Exchange is known as 'risk capital', and you should always be sure that you have enough other money coming in to keep you out of trouble if things go wrong, before you decide to invest.

Unit trusts provide a way of spreading the risk. These are companies that use the money investors pay in to buy a wide variety of securities, generally company shares. By buying units in the trust you can get an indirect share in all these companies. And hopefully if some go down, the others will do well enough to offset the loss.

Life assurance

Many people confuse Assurance and Insurance. Put simply, Insurance is cover against things that might happen, such as an accident or a fire, while Assurance is cover against what is bound to happen to you sooner or later, such as reaching a certain age or death.

Life assurance is a good way of saving for the future, as well as providing protection for your family. As well as getting a fair return for your money, anyone who pays income tax is entitled to relief. This is normally just over one-sixth of the premiums paid, depending on your personal circumstances.

Insurance companies offer lots of different types of assurance policies, and the important thing is to choose the one that is right for you. This is why it may be better to talk things over with an insurance broker rather than an insurance salesman, who represents a particular life office and will understandably do his best to persuade you to take up one of the policies his life office has to sell. In any case it is always worthwhile trying to get several quotations before you make a final choice because premium rates vary a great deal from company to company.

Basically there are four types of assurance cover:

Temporary or Term assurance This type of assurance protects your family against hardship should you die during a certain stated term of years. It can cover the mortgage of your home, or assure an income for the family over a number of years after your death.

Term assurance is much the cheapest form of life assurance, because in the majority of cases the person assured survives the term, so the life office does not need to pay out at all.

Whole life assurance Here, provided you keep up the premiums, the company undertakes to give you assurance cover for your whole life until you die. They will then pay the agreed sum to your dependants. Whole life costs more than term assurance, for the obvious reason that the company is bound to pay out in the end.

Endowment assurance This is a scheme by which you pay premiums that will enable you to save an agreed sum by an agreed date, while ensuring that if you die before the date is reached, the whole sum will be paid to your dependants (see also under **Mortgages,** page 236). Inevitably the premium is higher than for term or whole life assurance, because you are getting both temporary life cover and an agreed sum at the end.

A whole life or endowment policy can be either 'with profits' or 'without profits'. If you have a 'with profits' policy you pay a higher premium, but it entitles you to share in the profits which the life office earns from its invested fund. This way you stand to get a better benefit in the longer term; with bonuses it could be almost twice as much as the 'sum assured' you were expecting. But, of course, it all depends on the fortunes of the life office over the years between.

Endowment policies are essentially for long-term savings. If you cash in the policy early, the insurance company will retain a proportion of your money to pay for the expenses of setting up the policy. You will therefore probably get back less than you have paid in.

Annuities In exchange for a lump sum you can buy an annuity that will give you a guaranteed income for as long as you live. Provided you are young enough, you can also buy an annuity on the instalment plan through regular payments to a life assurance office.

PENSIONS FOR THE SELF-EMPLOYED

If you are self-employed you will not benefit from the two-part pension scheme described on page 247, so you will have to meet the cost of any pension above the basic flat rate yourself. Fortunately any part of your income you use to provide for a pension is exempt from income tax, up to a maximum yearly amount.

Pension assurance is offered by many life assurance companies, part of the cover providing a pension for your dependants and part providing for life assurance cover. At retirement you can usually take a tax-free cash sum in exchange for part of your pension, up to three times the amount of the remaining annual pension.

It is normally possible to vary the amount you set aside from year to year, which is an advantage if your earnings fluctuate.

Risk insurance

Apart from offering life assurance to protect people from financial hardship, insurance companies also provide cover for your possessions in the case of accident, damage or loss. Policies vary widely, however, so it is a good idea to seek the advice of an insurance broker or your bank to help you pick out the most advantageous policy for you – and even so, be sure you read the small print before you sign it.

Property insurance
Your home is really two separate things – the building (and this term includes garage, sheds, fences, the drive and so on) and the contents (the fittings, furniture, your clothes and possessions).

When calculating how much cover you will need on the building, remember that you should insure for the current cost of rebuilding the house, which may be more than its market value. Your insurance company or a surveyor will be able to advise you and you need to revise the sum insured from time to time, to keep pace with inflation.

A householder's policy will normally cover the building for damage by all sorts of calamity – fire, flood, lightning, theft, riot and vandalism, being hit by an aircraft falling out of the sky or a car skidding off the road. In certain accidents, though, you may have to pay something like the first £15 yourself, and liability is limited if your house is empty at the time.

In addition to the above, for no extra charge, some companies will also pay rent for alternative accommodation should you be unable to live in your house whilst it is being repaired/rebuilt; they will cover you against accidental breakage of fixed glass (including double glazing) and sanitary fittings and pay compensation for any legal liability incurred to a third party.

Contents

The protection you get for the contents of your home will probably cover the same disasters as for the building, but additional cover may include a certain amount of loose cash, perhaps the contents in transit while you are moving house and a small lump sum if the insured or his or her spouse is killed by fire.

The important thing about a standard contents insurance policy is that you can claim only the current value of the article damaged or lost. For instance, if your seven-year-old carpet is ruined by fire, your insurance company, when paying the claim, will make a deduction for seven years' wear. Since, due to inflation, the same type of carpet will now be costing much more than when you bought it, the money will not go all that far towards paying for a new one.

New for old policies

It is for this reason that more and more people are switching to 'new-for-old' policies. This means you insure the articles at the current market price, and that is what you claim back. Obviously this costs a bit more, but it buys you a lot of peace of mind. The policy often also throws in cover for accidental damage in the home, such as dropping a hammer on your dining room table.

In any event, your insurance company has the right to insist that you protect your home adequately before they accept your policy. They may require you to change the locks on doors and windows, or even ask you to put in a wall safe.

'All risks' cover

Special valuables are best covered by an 'all risks' policy. This may cover jewellery, furs, camera, tape recorder, even things like contact lenses and false teeth. An 'all risks' policy will insure these both in and out of the home, and including cover for travel in many countries abroad, but not all, so check your policy and ask if in any doubt as these may vary as political situations change. Of course you can then exclude items covered by 'all risks' from your ordinary contents policy.

Freezer insurance

For quite a small sum you can insure the food in your freezer against deterioration due to freezer breakdown. Some companies will not insure freezers more than ten years old.

Credit card insurance

A stolen credit card could cost you a lot of money if you do not notice that it is missing and report the loss at once. You can take out a policy to cover you against fraudulant usage.

Blanket cover

Nowadays, many insurance companies have put all the above policies together under one 'blanket cover' – so that you pay one annual premium for them all.

There are often added attractions to blanket cover, in that if your total premium is more than a certain amount you may earn a discount. It is also worth finding out if you are entitled to special terms for woodworm insurance, or a private health scheme.

CAR INSURANCE

Motorists are compelled by law to take out cover against liability for death or injury of people caused by their cars, including claims arising from the death or injury of passengers.

'Act only' policies provide only this minimum protection demanded by the Traffic Act. Premiums are often higher than for policies giving more extensive cover, because these policies are usually taken out only by people with such bad accident records they find it difficult to get insurance cover at all.

'Third Party' policies give the minimum legal cover, and also cover against liability for accidental damage to other vehicles or property.

'Third Party, Fire and Theft' policies add on cover to vehicles damaged through fire and theft.

'Comprehensive' policies are taken out by the majority of private car owners. As well as providing for insurance against damage to your car through accident, the policy also normally includes accident benefits for husbands and wives, and loss of personal possessions from cars, though this is usually subject to a limit of about £50. Some also include the cost of hiring a car while your own is repaired.

No-claim bonuses can considerably reduce the cost of insuring your car. With these, a percentage of the basic premium is deducted every time you renew after a year of claim-free motoring, usually reaching a maximum after four or five years.

HOLIDAY INSURANCE
For a very small premium (often paid through a tour operator) you can get cover to protect you in a number of different ways:

1 You can be insured against loss of baggage or money, extending to tickets, travellers' cheques, credit cards etc, and against damage to your effects.

2 Accident – where you get a lump sum for disablement or death, or a temporary disablement pension of so much a week. Dangerous sports, such as ski-ing are excluded – though an insurance broker should be able to get you special cover.

3 Cancellation charges up to a certain amount if you have to put off your holiday at the last minute.

4 Medical expenses, up to a stated limit.

5 Substantial indemnity against legal liability to a third party.

Credit cards

Credit cards allow you to buy things or pay for restaurant meals or hotel bills without having to pay cash for them at the time. You sign a chit endorsed with your card – and the issuing company, which may be a bank, group of banks, or a credit card organization, then pays the trader (deducting a discount) and sends in a bill to you at the end of the month.

There are two kinds of credit card. With the first (which includes the cards backed by banks) the card is free, and provided you pay a stated minimum sum when the account first comes in you can then pay off the rest of the sum by instalments. The interest rate on the instalments is usually high.

With the other type of credit card, you pay an annual amount for the card, and you are expected to pay in full as soon as the statement comes in.

If the card is lost or stolen, most companies protect you by limiting your liability to a certain sum *provided you let them know at once*. You can, however, cover your card against fraudulant use with an insurance policy.

Hire purchase and credit sales

When you buy something on hire purchase you obtain possession of the goods as soon as you have paid your deposit and signed the HP agreement; you do not, however, own them. In law, they remain the property of the shop (or finance company) until the last payment is made. This means you have no right to re-sell without the permission of the finance company, who are likely to agree only provided you are prepared to pay off all the remaining instalments there and then.

With a credit sale, although you pay by instalments the goods become yours right away. In this case you can sell the goods if you want to, although you should let the finance company know; again they will probably want you to pay off all the remaining instalments at once.

HIRE PURCHASE LAW

The law on hire purchase is changing substantially as the Consumer Credit Act 1974 is brought into force. At the time of going to press HP agreements where the total credit price is not more than £2000 are governed by the Hire Purchase Act. Most of this Act's provisions also apply to credit sale agreements where the total price is between £30 and £2000, and is to be paid in five or more instalments. See also **Consumer Credit Act 1974**, opposite.

A hire purchase or credit sale customer is protected in the same way as any other customer by the Supply of Goods (Implied Terms) Act 1973, under which:

1 The seller has to guarantee the article is his to sell.

2 The goods must be free from serious defect (though this does not apply to goods marked as 'seconds' or 'defective').

3 The goods must be reasonably fit for the purpose for which you want them, provided you make clear what this is at the time.

Signing the agreement

Before you sign an HP or credit sale agreement, the seller must show you in writing the cash price of the goods you are buying. The actual agreement must give details of the total credit price, the cash price and the instalments so you can see how much extra the credit is going to cost you.

The agreement must also contain a 'Red Box' which warns you, as the customer, that you will be legally bound by the terms. Do not sign a form without this warning – it could well be just a hire agreement (rather than hire *purchase*) under which you will never own the goods however long you go on paying

Never sign a form unless all the spaces have been filled in, in ink, even if the salesman says that to save you time he will do it for you later.

If you are a married woman with no separate income of your own, the finance company will probably ask husband and wife to sign a hire purchase agreement jointly, or they may ask for a guarantor (any person) of suitable financial standing. A woman with an income of her own is treated exactly as would be a man in similar financial circumstances.

The cooling-off period

Once you have signed an HP or credit sale agreement on trade premises, such as a shop, it is too late to cancel it. But if you sign the agreement somewhere else, at home for instance, and provided it is within the financial limits of the act, you have the right to change your mind and cancel, as long as you do it quickly.

When you sign the agreement at home, one copy is left with you and a second copy must be sent to you by post. If you want to cancel, you must do so in writing within three days of the arrival of this second copy (send your letter by recorded delivery). If you have already taken delivery of the goods you ordered it is worth noting that it is up to the finance company to collect them, rather than relying on you to send them back.

Falling behind with instalments

If you fall behind with payments under a credit sale, the finance company can sue you for the money owing, but they cannot repossess the goods.

Under an HP agreement the company has the right to take the goods back, but subject to two conditions; first, they must send you a warning letter giving you at least seven days to pay and second, once one-third of the total price (which includes the deposit you have already given) has been paid, they have to apply for a court order.

Breaking the agreement

You have no right to break off a credit sale agreement, so if you have landed yourself in financial deep water you may have to sell the goods to pay off the debt.

If you find you cannot afford to continue with a hire purchase agreement, you can in practice terminate it at any time. If you have paid less than half the total credit price, however, you will normally have to pay any instalments which are in arrears, plus sufficient to bring the total amount paid up to half the credit price. You will also be liable for any damage if you have not taken reasonable care of the goods.

Goods over £2000

Hire purchase agreements where the total cost of the goods, including credit charges and interest, is over £2000 are not covered by the Hire Purchase Act. Such agreements commonly carry a termination clause calculating the hirer's liability on the basis of the trader's actual loss.

Consumer Credit Act 1974

As this Act comes into force, the credit limit for hire purchase transactions will rise to £5000. In addition agreement forms will have to show the effective rate of interest and the customer will be entitled to a rebate of the charge if he pays off the agreement ahead of time. Many of the provisions which at present protect hire purchase and credit sale customers will be extended to cover other forms of credit and hire or rental transactions.

Income tax

Whenever money is coming in, whether it is to a child appearing in a television commercial, a businessman or woman, an artist or an old age pensioner, it is liable to be subject to income tax. The Board of Inland Revenue issues a range of leaflets covering the taxes due on various sources of income, profits and capital gain, and also describing the personal tax allowances different people in various situations can claim. These are free from any tax office.

PAYE

If you are working for an employer, tax on your earnings will normally be deducted before you are paid, under a system known as PAYE (Pay As You Earn). The amount of tax you pay depends on the code allotted to you by the Inland Revenue and which is worked out on the information available to the tax office about the allowances to which you are entitled (more about these under **Allowances, page 245**).

If you think you are paying too much tax, the first step is to check your code. It could be that a mistake has been made and the code you have been given is lower than it should be. The answer is to get in touch with your tax office or a PAYE Enquiry Office. If, during the previous year, you have not been asked to complete a tax return and want to do so, apply – in person, by letter or by phone – for a return form.

There are a couple of other forms worth mentioning. Shortly after the end of each tax year, which runs from April 6 to April 5, you should receive from your employer a Form P60; this is a record of your total earnings for the year and the amount of tax you paid. Look after this, you will need it if you have any queries. A second important form is the P45, which your old employer should give you when you change your job. It gives the amount you have earned and the tax paid in the year to date and the wages department of your new company will ask you for it.

TAX AND THE SELF-EMPLOYED
Anyone who is self-employed, even in quite a small way, would be well advised to employ an accountant. The self-employed pay tax under Schedule D, which is considerably more complicated than the ordinary PAYE system. It involves preparing a profit and loss account and maybe a balance sheet. In return for these the Tax Inspector will send you an assessment of the tax due, and you have 30 days in which to appeal.

Even an accountant will not be able to help you much, however, unless you keep a careful record both of your outgoings and the money coming in. Keep receipts for any bills paid, because the profits on which you are assessed under Schedule D can be offset by the amounts you are allowed to claim for business expenses, which might include heating, lighting, telephone and so on as well as the more obvious costs such as buying stock and materials.

VALUE ADDED TAX
Although VAT is the concern of the Customs and Excise rather than the Inland Revenue, it is worth remembering that if you are self-employed and with total gross takings above a certain figure you will need to register. VAT is a difficult tax for most people to understand, but you can get a free book entitled '*VAT: General Guide*' from your local VAT office (look in the telephone directory under Customs and Excise).

Separate taxation of wife's earnings
If you are a wife and living with your husband, your income is normally considered as part of his for tax purposes. However, as long as you *both* agree, your earnings can be taxed as if you were single. (This applies only to earned income, any unearned income you may have will still be treated as if it were your husband's.)

The point at which having your earnings taxed separately begins to save you money varies

according to how much you both earn, the amount of any other income, whether you have children and so on. Normally you are unlikely to come out on the winning side until your joint income is over £8000 a year, and if there are allowances and charges (such as interest on mortgage payments) which can be set against income the total may be higher.

Children's income
If you have a child under 16, or over that age but still in full-time education or training, once his or her income passes a certain amount (which varies from time to time, so check) the parent starts losing the child tax allowance. If the child is earning a considerable amount of money (which is why we talked about television commercials earlier) then he or she could themselves become liable for tax. The child tax allowance, which you as a parent claim against your income, varies according to the child's age and the amount of Child Benefit paid by the Department of Health and Social Security.

SOURCES OF INCOME LIABLE FOR TAX
Naturally, everyone wants to pay as little tax as possible. The legal way of arranging your affairs so as to get down to a minimum is known as 'tax avoidance' and is what you hire an accountant for. The illegal method is termed 'tax evasion' and probably means you have filled in your tax return fraudulently. As far as the Inland Revenue is concerned, negligence is no excuse.

Below are some of the taxable sources of income or capital you are legally bound to tell them about:

Earnings As well as your salary or wages, professional fees or business profits, this also includes commission, bonuses and tips.

Expenses Any part of these you do not spend wholly, necessarily and exclusively in carrying out the duties of your employment is taxable.

Fringe benefits You must pay tax if, for instance, you have the free or cheap use of a company car for your private purposes. The value of fringe benefits has to be included as part of the remuneration you receive from your job.

Investment income Any dividends you receive from stocks and shares and interest on bank deposit and other savings accounts is taxable. (But where you have an ordinary account with the Trustee Savings Bank or National Savings Bank a proportion of the interest is tax free.)

Capital gains made on the disposal of a house (except your family home) or any other asset (including investments) which has risen in value since you first acquired it is taxable. Any disposal, even by way of gift, can give rise to a liability for capital gains tax. There are however various exemptions and thresholds before the tax is payable.

Redundancy payments and compensation above a certain level are liable for tax.

State benefits Some state benefits are taxable, so check at your local tax office, particularly in relation to pensions and payments from the DHSS in respect of children.

Rents of property are liable, but some expenses and deductions can be allowed before tax is charged. Check with your tax inspector.

ALLOWANCES
Before arriving at 'net taxable income' – the amount on which tax is chargeable – every tax payer is entitled to a personal allowance, the amount of which can vary from one tax year to the next, and also according to your age and marital status. If you have children you can claim the child tax allowances already mentioned. In addition these are some of the other allowances you may be entitled to claim:

Additional personal allowance for children You can claim this if you are a single parent bringing up a child on your own, or a husband whose wife has been completely incapacitated for the whole tax year.

Housekeeper allowance A widow or widower can claim this for a living-in housekeeper, but you cannot claim this if you are already claiming the additional personal allowance for children, see above.

Dependent relative You can claim this if you have a relative (or relatives) to whom you give financial help where his or her income is under a certain level.

Daughter's services If you have a daughter who lives with you to look after you and you pay for her keep, you may be able to claim an allowance. (It might be better to claim housekeeper allowance. You cannot have both, so check.)

Life assurance Subject to certain conditions you should be able to claim relief from tax on part or all of the premiums on a policy on your own or your own or your husband's/wife's life. Check at your life office.

Age allowance for elderly people This replaces, and can be greater than, the ordinary personal allowance. It is available to people who are 65 or over in the tax year.

Mortgages The payment of interest may entitle you to tax relief. (The rules can be complicated – check.)

Business expenses
If you are self-employed, claiming for all the expenses 'wholly and exclusively' incurred in making your profits is particularly important – hence the advice to get yourself an accountant. With his help you should be successful in claiming for a proportion of your heating, lighting and telephone bills if you work at home, as well as expenses such as travel and stationery (and even the services of the accountant).

National insurance

National Insurance is a scheme to which all working people in Britain contribute some regular amount from their earnings. This then entitles them to a range of social benefits when they are in need.

CONTRIBUTIONS

There are different classes of National Insurance, each with a different rate of contribution entitling you to a different range of benefits.

Class 1 contributions are for employed people. The cost of the contributions is shared between the employee and the employer and the amount is based on a percentage of the employee's earnings. The contributions are collected through the PAYE income tax system (see page 243).

If you are paying Class 1 *contributions* you qualify for the following benefits: unemployment, sickness, invalidity (the name given to the long-term sickness benefit, see later), industrial injuries benefit, maternity grant, maternity allowance, retirement pension, death grant.

Class 2 contributions are for the self-employed, who may also have to pay a contribution (Class 4) based on their profits or gains within certain limits. Contributions are made by stamping a card with National Insurance stamps bought at a post office, or by direct debit through a bank or National Giro. Class 4 contributions are normally collected by the Inland Revenue along with Schedule D income tax (see page 244).

If you are paying Class 2 *contributions* you may qualify for: sickness and invalidity benefits, maternity grant, maternity allowance, retirement pension, death grant.

Class 3 contributions unlike Classes 1 and 2 are voluntary contributions. They are designed for people who are not liable to pay either Class 1 or Class 2 contributions, to help them to qualify for a limited range of benefits, most importantly a retirement pension. They can be paid at post offices or by direct debit through banks or Giro.

If you are paying Class 3 *contributions* you may qualify for: maternity grant, retirement pension, death grant.

Reduced rate contributions Until 11th May 1977, married women and certain widows receiving National Insurance widows' benefits or war or industrial injuries widows' benefits were able to choose to pay a reduced rate contribution (or if self-employed to choose not to pay Class 2 contributions). Reduced contributions give very limited benefit cover. After 6th April 1978 the right to pay reduced rate contributions is abolished. Only women who pay reduced contributions during the 1977/8 tax year will be able to continue doing so; if after this date a woman paying reduced rate contributions becomes not liable for any contribution – basically this will be if she gives up work completely – for two consecutive tax years, she loses the right to pay at a reduced rate in the future.

BENEFITS

You can get free leaflets about all the benefits, and application forms, at your local social security office. Briefly, they work as follows:

Unemployment benefit

You are entitled to claim this for a year after losing your job, provided you are able and willing to take on a new job if you are offered one. After a year the benefit runs out, but if you go on signing on at the Employment Exchange they will continue crediting you with NI contributions (important, because contributions count towards your pension), but you will not receive unemployment benefit any more. Before you can claim this again you will need to go back to work for a minimum of 21 hours a week in each of at least 13 weeks – after which if you lose your job again you should once more be entitled to the benefit.

If after a year you still have no job, but continue to sign on and make yourself available for work, you may become eligible for *supplementary benefit*. Whether you are eligible and how much you might receive will depend on the total resources of yourself and any dependants.

Sickness benefit
You can claim this on the production of a doctor's statement that you are unfit to work, which should be sent to the social security office within six days from the time you fall ill. You can claim sickness benefit for 28 days at a stretch, after that if you are still ill you become eligible for invalidity benefit. The rates for sickness benefit are the same as for unemployment.

Invalidity benefit
The rate for invalidity benefit is higher than for sickness benefit. You also get a larger allowance for dependants, and a man under 60 and a woman under 55 is entitled to an additional weekly invalidity allowance. You do not, however, qualify for an earnings related supplement, see below.

Earnings related supplement
This is paid from the 13th day after you first receive sickness or unemployment benefit; it is also payable to women receiving maternity allowance. The amount you receive depends on the amount of earnings on which you paid Class 1 contributions in the relevant tax year.

Industrial injuries benefit
You can claim injury benefit if you are incapable of work as the result of an injury due to an accident at work, or a prescribed industrial disease due to your job. If the injury or illness persists, you may become entitled to disablement benefit.

Industrial death benefit
This can be paid to dependants if death results from an industrial accident or a prescribed industrial disease.

Maternity allowance
This is usually payable for 18 weeks, starting 11 weeks before the week the baby is expected (an extension can be given if the baby is late). Earnings related supplement is also payable.

Maternity grant is paid to help with the cost of having the baby.

Death grant
This is a lump sum paid on the death of anyone paying National Insurance contributions, or the wife, husband or child of a contributor, provided certain contribution conditions are met. The grant is normally paid to the executors or administrators if the decreased person left a will, otherwise it is paid to the next of kin or to whoever is meeting the funeral expenses.

Retirement pension
To qualify for any retirement pension you must have paid contributions up to a minimum level in at least one of the tax years in your working life. To qualify for a full pension you must in addition have contributions paid or credited to you (see unemployment benefit) in about 90 per cent of these years. If you are a married woman you must have contributions paid or credited to you for half the number of tax years between your marriage and your 60th birthday.

A new state pension scheme comes into force in 1978 under which every employee can look forward to a flat-rate pension of whatever amount then applies and, above this, for the better paid majority, your increased National Insurance contributions, together with your employer's, will go towards providing a second pension of a quarter of what you earn between the basic flat-rate level and an upper limit of about seven times that amount.

A non-working wife or a working wife who has been paying reduced rate contributions will receive a bit more than half her husband's flat-rate sum. If a husband and wife both work and the wife has paid full contributions, then under the new scheme each will get the full flat rate, plus his or her own earnings-related supplement 'inflation-proofed' against rising prices.

The alternative plan
After consulting you and your trade union, if any, your employer may choose to give you your second pension through his own earnings related pension plan, which must at least match the state minimum. In many cases companies' own plans are likely to be more flexible and better-tailored to individual needs, with optional earlier retirement.

Pensions for the self-employed see page 239.

Widows' benefits
Provided that your husband has paid enough National Insurance contributions, you will be entitled to a widow's allowance for the first 26 weeks

after his death. If you are 60 or over when he dies, however, you will not get this if your husband was drawing a National Insurance retirement pension.

If you have a dependant child you may qualify for a widowed mother's allowance when your widow's allowance finishes. If you have no dependant children you will be entitled to a widow's pension when the allowance finishes provided you are 40 or over when your husband dies. You can also draw a widow's pension if you are 40 or over when you cease to be entitled to a widowed mother's allowance (for instance, because the children have grown up).

All widow's benefits stop if you marry again, or live with a man as his wife.

Child's special allowance

If you are divorced and your former husband is supporting a child who lives with you, you can claim this allowance if he dies, provided he has paid enough National Insurance contributions.

The last two benefits described above depend entirely on the husband's contributions; they have nothing to do with any contributions a wife may have made.

Buying a house

Buying a house is probably the most expensive transaction the majority of people are ever involved in, so no-one wants to make mistakes. This is why most house-buyers consider it worth the cost of employing a solicitor – especially important if the house is not registered with the Land Registry (the government department responsible for land registration), or if the property is a flat or a newly built house.

However, if the property is registered, freehold, has no sitting tenants and is being sold by an owner-occupier it could be possible to handle the transaction yourself. In either case it is interesting to know the order in which things happen, and below we give an outline of the procedure involved. There are certain legal and procedural differences in buying a house in Scotland, but in general the information in this section will apply.

MORTGAGES AND MONEY

Once you have found a house you like, either through an estate agent, an advertisement, or by private agreement with someone you know who wants to sell, the next step is seeing about the money. 80 per cent of people buying a house do so

with the help of a building society mortgage (see page 235). If the house is a new one, built by one of the big companies, many of these employ home loan experts who provide a mortgage service free of charge.

Building societies insist that newly built houses taken into mortgage should have been constructed by a house-builder who is a member of the National House-building Council. The only exception is where the construction has been supervised by an architect or qualified surveyor employed solely by the purchaser. Houses built by a registered builder are inspected periodically during the course of construction and are sold with an 'after sales' service and a ten year guarantee against major defects.

If the property is more than 25 years old or a non-purpose built flat you may find the building societies less keen to lend you money – and even when they do, remember that the loan is always based on the lender's valuation of the property, which may be less than the price you are being asked to pay for it.

Unless you are raising the purchase price in cash you must have a firm mortgage offer and mortgage terms agreed before the exchange of contracts.

248

You will also have to find, as your personal stake in the property, an amount equal to the difference between the purchase price and the mortgage loan. A cash deposit, usually ten per cent of the price, will have to be paid at the time of purchase.

Apart from the deposit, you will have to bear initial costs comprising the legal charges for the conveyance and the preparation of the mortgage, government stamp duty if the house costs more than £15,000 and the building society's valuation fee. On top of this you will also have to allow for the cost of an independent survey (not essential, but recommended unless the property is new) and for removal expenses.

'SUBJECT TO CONTRACT'
The first stage in the actual buying of the house is to write to the estate agents, or owner, or builder saying that you want to buy the house 'subject to contract'. These words are essential because they mean your letter cannot be made legally binding if for any reason you want to withdraw later. Some builders of new houses may ask for five or ten per cent of the purchase price at this stage, others will be satisfied with a smallish deposit until the contracts are signed. Remember always to keep copies of any letters that you write.

Surveys
At this point it is wise to have the house surveyed to check that there are no major structural faults, that the roof is in good order, etc. Surveyors' fees vary according to the age and state of the house, its size and how thorough a survey you want. It is a good idea to have a pretty detailed one, and there is nothing to stop you asking the surveyor in advance what his fees are likely to be.

The building society will also want their surveyor to inspect the property, but his report is for valuation purposes only and will be confidential to them, even though you have to pay for it. Some societies allow their surveyor to give you a report direct. You pay a little more, but not as much as your own surveyor would charge; remember, though, that it is unlikely to be a full structural survey.

Draft contract
A week or so later, you or your solicitor should receive a draft contract from the vendor or vendor's solicitor and a list of any restrictive covenants: for

example that you cannot use the house for business purposes, or you must not put up a greenhouse without permission. It is usual for you to receive a copy of these entries as they appear on the register at the Land Registry, giving details to prove that the vendor of the house is indeed the owner.

ENQUIRIES BEFORE CONTRACT
The next stage is 'Enquiries Before Contract', for which you or your solicitor will need a form, Conveyancing 29 Long, and two forms for the Local Search, LLC 1 and Conveyancing 29A (or 29D if the property is in a London borough). These and the other forms necessary in connection with buying a house are obtainable from Oyez Stationery Ltd., 237 Long Lane, London SE1.

The first form contains a list of questions about the house – who owns the boundary fences and whether there are any rights of way and so on. This you send to the vendor's solicitors or the vendor.

The other two forms ask the local authority for details about the house – if the vendor owes them any money for road charges, if any planning schemes, such as a future road-widening scheme, might affect the house (visit the County Council Planning Department to make certain) – and about drainage, mains services and so on. If you have received your surveyor's report you can include any matters he has raised. For example, if he has found traces of woodworm, then you should mention this in the first form; this may make it possible to re-negotiate the price.

EXCHANGE OF CONTRACTS
Only when you have received satisfactory answers to all three forms should you think about exchanging contracts. Draft contracts are drawn up on standard forms and are usually pretty straightforward, but check carefully and make any amendments you think necessary. If the vendor has agreed to include any furniture or fittings in the sale, make sure they are specifically mentioned together with their price.

Once both sides have agreed the contract, then you are ready to exchange contracts. The copy signed by you is sent to the vendor or vendor's solicitor with the rest of the deposit, and the vendor's signed copy is sent to you or your solicitor. Legally this is the point of no return. You are now committed to the purchase or risk losing your deposit, and the vendor must sell to you or risk your suing him.

Insurance
At this point, you become legally responsible for the house – if it burns down before completion you must still go through with the purchase. So make sure you, your solicitor or your building society insures the house from the date that contracts are exchanged; you will have to notify the building society of this date.

Inspecting the register
Once the contracts have been signed you are legally entitled to see the register for the property in full – the vendor's solicitor will send you a copy along with a letter of authority for you to inspect the register at the Land Registry yourself and obtain your own copy. Check the register to see that the details on it tally with those sent to you earlier.

Requisitions on title
If there are discrepancies, and you have been working without a solicitor, now is the time to see one.

If there are no discrepancies, you are ready to prepare your 'Requisitions on Title', a list of further questions about the title of the house, for which you will need Form Conveyancing 28B. You will need to know that the answers you were given last time are still correct, that vacant possession will be given on the date agreed and proof that the vendor's mortgage will be paid off before you take possession of the house. The form goes to the vendor's solicitor.

DRAFT TRANSFER
Now you will need Form 19, 'Transfer of Whole', the most important document of all since this is the one that transfers ownership from the vendor to you. This includes a certificate of value to make sure you pay no more stamp duty than you have to. The rate goes up in steps on the price you pay: up to £15000, £20000, £25000 and £30000. Insert the figure next above your price. Over £30000 you pay the top rate and no certificate is required.

Once you have received satisfactory answers to your 'Requisitions on Title', and the vendor or vendor's solicitor has approved your draft transfer – a copy of which the vendor generally signs ready for completion – there are only two more steps to completion.

Completion statement
You will receive a completion statement from the vendor or vendor's solicitor, telling you how much money is outstanding (the purchase price, less your deposit) plus what you might owe the vendor for rates and water rates that he has paid beyond the completion date. It is as well to arrange a banker's draft at this time, which you will hand over on completion day to cover these costs.

Land Registry search
A final Land Registry search should be made immediately before the date set for completion to check that no changes have been entered on the register since the exchange of contracts; for example, that no new person has been registered as the owner, or some new mortgage made.

To make this search, you fill in Form 94A and send it to the Land Registry with the 'Authority to Inspect the Register' that the vendor's solicitor sent you. They will send you a Search Certificate stating whether there has been any alteration; if there has, consult a solicitor – fast. If not, then you have about three weeks in which to complete your purchase and register yourself as the new owner. During this time the Land Registry guarantees not to register anyone else as the owner, and will not make any entries to the register until your application for transfer of title has been received and the transfer is carried out.

Paying a solicitor
If you have been employing a solicitor, it is at this stage he will present his bill, and you will need to have the cash in hand, because the purchase will not be completed until that bill is met. (The building society's solicitor's bill is deducted from the mortgage money before the money is released.)

COMPLETION OF SALE
On the day of completion, you or your solicitor if you have one, the building society's solicitor, and the vendor's solicitor all meet. Documents are checked and handed over. Any banker's drafts are handed over. Afterwards you are given the keys or the estate agent is authorised to release them to you and the property is yours.

Instead of all the parties getting together at a single meeting, it's possible to effect a completion in stages, or by post. The one meeting, however, is generally agreed to be the most satisfactory way.

250

This isn't quite the end of it though – there are still two more forms to go.

New owner
You will need Form A4 on which you apply to the Land Registry to be registered as the new owner, and Form Stamps L(A)451 (obtainable from head post offices or inland revenue stamp duty offices) which you fill in and take, along with the transfer deed itself, to an inland revenue stamp duty office or a head post office to pay any stamp duty and get the transfer stamped.

If you are buying your house on a mortgage the building society will complete these last two formalities for you, since they take the land certificate after completion and you do not see it again until every last penny of the mortgage is paid off.

Planning and building regulations

Planning permission is needed when you want to make any material change in the use or appearance of your house, and while it may seem like a bit of bureaucratic interference at times, at least it can often serve to protect you from having to stare at some eyesore put up by your neighbour.

If you want to make any alterations to the outside of your property (which, besides the house itself, also includes things like changing a fence to a wall or building a garden shed), and you are not sure whether you need planning permission or not, your best course is to get in touch with your local Planning Officer and ask his advice. It may be, however, that what you want to do comes under what is known as Permitted Development.

Permitted development
This does not call for formal application to the local authority, and as long as there are no restrictive covenants or directions removing your permitted development rights (see page 249) it will probably be all right to go ahead. Full details of when permission is granted automatically are shown in Schedule 1 to the Town and Country Planning General Development Order 1973 (available from HMSO). (But – see **Building regulations**, page **252**.)

Permitted development applies when you want to enlarge or improve your house (but not a flat or maisonette), say by building on a room extension or a garage, as long as it does not increase the size of the original building by more than ten per cent, or 50 cubic metres, whichever is more. It will probably also apply if you want to put up a greenhouse, a dog kennel or some other small outbuilding behind the front of the house, or build a garden wall not more than 2 m high – 1 m if it is alongside a road.

Planning permission
If you want to make a major structural alteration or to change the use of the house, such as by converting it into flats, then formal Planning Permission will be required. To apply for this, ask your local planning office for the necessary form or forms. You will have to certify whether you are the owner of the property and give full details of the work you want to do. The planning officer may also ask for a sketch map showing your house in relation to your neighbours' properties, in addition to a plan (with copies) of the alterations you want to make. The plans do not have to be professionally drawn, but they should be clear enough to illustrate your proposals.

251

Your application will then be considered by the local planning authority and in due course you will receive a decision in writing; this is likely to be a matter of weeks. If your application is turned down, try and find out why from the planning officer and see what compromises would be necessary to get it through. As a last resort you can appeal to the Department of the Environment – or the Welsh or Scottish Office – as long as you do so within six months of the date permission was refused.

Building regulations

Even when the work you want to do comes under Permitted Development, consent under the Building Regulations may still be required. The control under these regulations is additional to and quite distinct from that under planning law. As well as the erection of new buildings, the extension of existing buildings and their structural alteration, both external and internal (such as knocking two rooms into one, changing a bedroom into a second bathroom), the regulations also cover the installation of drainage and heating appliances and may also apply if you wish to alter the use to which the building is put.

Anyone wishing to carry out work to which the Building Regulations apply has to submit plans to the local authority before starting work and when you are clear what you want to do it is a good idea to discuss your proposals with the local authority's Building Control Officer. If you are employing a builder, he can do this for you and also see about getting consent. The Building Inspector may want to inspect the work in progress from time to time.

Compulsory purchase

If your house or flat falls a victim to a compulsory purchase order, then the sooner you can get advice from some professionally qualified person, either a surveyor or a solicitor, the better. (See page 262 on finding a solicitor.) This is because clearly you will want the maximum compensation to which you are entitled and property valuation can be a complicated business. You should be able to claim back any professional fees you pay from the acquiring authority.

Normally the amount of compensation you receive will be decided by negotiation (which is why it is important to have a professional acting for you). As a general rule you will be entitled to the open market price of your property, that is, the amount you would have got if you were selling it privately and if it were not involved in a public authority scheme. If you cannot agree with the authority on an acceptable figure you can refer the case to the Lands Tribunal – but you will have to abide by their decision and if they consider you were being unreasonable you could end up paying the costs for both sides.

As well as compensation for the land and building, you will also be able to claim removal and other expenses, such as the cost of having your curtains altered, telephone reconnection charges and incidental costs, such as conveyancing, involved in buying a new house of the same standard.

If you have lived in the house for five years or more you will also be entitled to a 'home loss' payment which is paid on top of any compensation you may receive.

Partial purchase orders

If the authority want to take over only part of your property, say a chunk of your garden for a road widening scheme, you may be able to make them buy the whole property if, as a result of their activities, your house has become so noisy or in some other way uncomfortable that you do not want to live there any more.

Alternatively, you are entitled to the market value of any land they have taken and compensation for depreciation in value of the remainder. If traffic from a new road produces noise above a certain level you can demand insulation for living rooms and bedrooms in the form of double glazing.

'Blight' notices
If you are an owner-occupier and have tried to sell your house on the open market but failed to find a buyer, except at a reduced price, because an authority with compulsory purchase powers has it on a list to buy at some future date, you may be able to serve a 'blight' notice on the authority. This forces the authority to buy in advance of starting its scheme, and compensation is paid on the same basis as for compulsory purchase. You will not get a 'home loss' payment, though, and probably will not be reimbursed for removal and other expenses. Again, to obtain the most satisfactory compensation, it is best to let your solicitor or surveyor handle matters for you.

Essential services

ELECTRICITY
In England and Wales, the Central Electricity Generating Board is responsible for the national grid and 12 electricity boards share responsibility for retail distribution of electricity to customers. In Scotland the North of Scotland Hydro-Electric and the South of Scotland Electricity Board are responsible both for generation and distribution and Northern Ireland is controlled by the Northern Ireland Electricity Service.

The supply is usually brought into the house underground by a thick cable connecting the house meter to the nearest electricity sub-station. If you live in a country area, your electricity supply may be by overhead cables. If these have to be newly installed the Electricity Board is responsible for having trees and shrubs lopped in order to prevent them impeding the supply lines. Once the lines are there it is your responsibility to keep trees clear of them. If the lines cross your driveway or garage entrance, you must take care if you are bringing in a high van or trailer.

Next to the house meter you will normally find the service cut-out which cuts off the current if there is a fault in the supply to the house. This is installed and sealed by the Electricity Board when the supply is first put in, and both it and the meter remain the Board's property. This means that while the householder will be held responsible for any damage to the cut-out and the meter, it's up to the Board to make sure they function properly.

Wiring inside the house is your responsibility, and while house wiring is supposed to comply with the Institute of Electrical Engineers Wiring Regulations these are not at present mandatory.

If you move to a house where you suspect the wiring may be old, it is wise to ask the Electricity Board to check the system and make a report or give you an inspection certificate. If new wiring is necessary, you should always have this type of work carried out by a recognised contractor who will comply with the recommended regulations.

Reading an electricity meter
Electricity Board officials can demand entry to the house to read your meter and, indeed, cut you off if you do not pay (unless you are living on the national insurance retirement pension, in which case get in touch with the local Social Security office). If the inspector calls when you are out, he may leave a reply-paid card asking you to read the meter yourself.

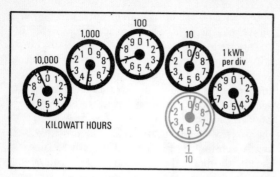

A conventional electricity meter

Most meters have the kind of dials shown above, and the card will have blank dials on it and all you have to do is to mark on it the position of each pointer on the dials of your meter. Some modern meters have digital register (below) which is even easier to read because the number of units of electricity used is shown as a simple row of figures.

A digital register is easier for the consumer

Remember, though, that the reading on a meter is the total number of units used since the meter was installed; to get your consumption between readings, subtract the previous reading (shown on your last electricity bill) from the new total.

To read a traditional electricity meter, ignore the small dials marked 1/10 and 1/100 and read the other dials from left to right. Read off (and write down) the figure each pointer has just passed and not the one it is coming up to.

When the pointer is between two figures, write down the lower of the two (when it's between 9 and 0, write down 9 because 0 is short for 10). If the pointer is exactly on a figure, say 7, write down 7 if the pointer on the next dial to the right is between 0 and 1; but if the pointer on the dial to the right is anywhere else, write down 6. Work along all the dials in this way, writing down each figure as you go. (In the illustration, the correct reading is 9469 units.)

GAS

The Gas Act of 1972 incorporates special safety regulations designed to protect not only you as the householder but also the public at large from any injuries, fire or explosion that could result from the use (or misuse) of gas.

For your part, as the consumer, the Act stipulates that you must:

1 Make sure ventilation from outside is adequate, eg by not restricting or covering up air grilles and ventilators.

2 Never use a gas appliance you know or even suspect may be unsafe.

3 In the event of a suspected gas escape, turn off the gas at the meter control tap and telephone Gas Service immediately – look under 'GAS' in your telephone directory. (Take great care – no naked flames or smoking.) Do not turn on the gas again until the leak has been dealt with.

4 Never try and make repairs yourself. Get a competent installer to do it for you – either British Gas or a CORGI registered installer.

If you break any of these regulations you are liable for a fine of £100. More recent Rights of Entry Regulations also give British Gas the right for their representative to enter any premises where gas is connected to examine fittings and appliances and their flues and ventilation and to disconnect fittings or the supply if in his opinion there is any danger to life or property.

There is no charge when you call about a suspected leak, nor for work British Gas may carry out to the pipe carrying the gas into the house, up to and including the meter. All pipework and appliances in the house are the customer's responsibility and any repair work necessary will be charged for.

No charge will be made if the suspected escape turns out to be a false alarm.

Reading a gas meter
Some gas meters have a direct reading index in which the figures are all in a line. In this case, read only the white figures, not the red ones, to give you the total.

On the traditional type of gas meter, the only dials you are concerned with are the four bottom ones with the black pointers (right). Starting with the dial on the left, copy down the figures in the order they appear. Where the pointer falls between two figures, take the lower of the two. As with an electricity meter, if the pointer is between 9 and 0 you should put down 9. Then take the figures on your previous reading (shown on your

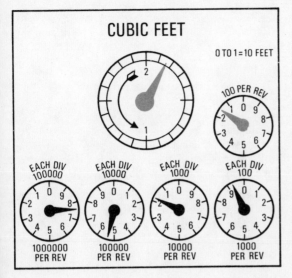

CUBIC FEET

0 TO 1 = 10 FEET

100 PER REV

EACH DIV 100000

EACH DIV 10000

EACH DIV 1000

EACH DIV 100

1000000 PER REV

100000 PER REV

10000 PER REV

1000 PER REV

A typical gas meter

last gas bill) and deduct them from the new reading. You will then know, in hundreds of cubic feet, how much gas you have used since the last reading.

Note though, that while the meter reading is in cubic feet it will be converted into cubic metres by British Gas and you will be charged in metric therms (100 megajoules). If you are curious how the calculation is worked out, ask at your local Gas Showrooms. An explanatory leaflet is available from there.

WATER AND DRAINAGE

If you are on mains water, the water supply to your house will usually be controlled by a main stop cock which is to be found near the perimeter of the property. This cuts off the whole of the household water supply and should only be touched by the water authority, whose property it is.

Your own stop cock is usually inside the house, close to the point at which the supply comes in. There could, however, be a stop cock in the front garden just outside the front door, this would usually be about 75 cm below ground level and may require a fork-ended key for turning it off. You may or may not be responsible for the pipe between the two stop cocks, this depends on the local by-laws. Water regulations are fairly strict and the by-laws vary in different parts of the country;

therefore you should consult your local water authority (you will find the address on your water rates bill). They will be able to advise you about their regulations and tell you how to comply.

Unlike the Gas and Electricity Boards, the water authority have no right of entry to turn off the supply if you do not pay your bills. But then they don't need it, as they can turn you off from the street. As long as reasonable notice is given, the water authority has a right of entry to inspect leaking water fittings.

The water authority is also responsible for sewerage and drains, although in some cases the the local district council act as agents. If you have any trouble with drains that you cannot cope with yourself or with the help of a plumber, get in touch with the district council, or failing help from them, the local office of the regional water authority concerned.

Wells and cesspits

If you have any problems with a well, go to the local office of the regional water authority concerned. With problems over cess pits, go to the local district council or, failing this, the local office of the regional water authority.

WASTE DISPOSAL

Ordinary household waste is normally collected by your local Refuse Collection Authority, ie the district council. In addition to this, your local Waste Disposal Authority, ie the county council in England or district council in Wales or Scotland, has to provide places where you can take the more out of the ordinary rubbish free of charge, but you are usually responsible for transporting it. Also you can often arrange for the local authority to collect large items of rubbish for a charge.

Commercial or industrial waste

If you are concerned with a firm or business which is involved in depositing waste on land, or which uses plant or equipment to dispose of it, you will need a licence. This is issued free by the Waste Disposal Authority in whose area the deposit or disposal takes place, and under the Control of Pollution Act anyone who should have a licence for disposing waste but operates without one is liable to a fine, imprisonment, or both.

255

Renting and leasing

The laws on leasing and renting are complicated, so it is always a good idea to get legal advice before signing a tenancy agreement. Rights and responsibilities on both sides vary, depending on whether the landlord lives on or off the premises, whether the property is owned by the council or a housing association, or whether the agreement is with an owner-occupier letting his home on a temporary basis.

Regulated tenancies

Tenants of furnished or unfurnished houses and flats which are privately owned but not part of their landlord's home, and which are under a certain rateable value, are fully protected by the Rent Acts. These are called 'regulated' or 'protected' tenancies. (The exceptions include places rented for short holiday periods, and those where the rent includes payment to cover the cost of meals or attendance.)

Under a regulated tenancy the tenant has security of tenure even when his lease expires; he cannot be made to move unless a court grants an order for possession against him. This it will only do if the landlord establishes one or more of the grounds laid down in the Acts – that the tenant is not paying the rent, for example, or is causing annoyance to the neighbours, or that he or anyone living with him has damaged the landlord's property or furniture.

Furthermore, a regulated tenancy gives security of tenure not only for the lifetime of the original tenant, but also for the lifetime of his statutory successor; this will be the surviving spouse or, if there is none, some other member of the family who has been living with him for not less than six months. And even after that the tenancy can again be passed on for the lifetime of the successor's successor.

Resident landlords

A tenant living in the same building as his landlord (unless it is a purpose-built block of flats) is not quite so secure. Nevertheless it is illegal for even a resident landlord to try and evict a tenant without an order for possession from the court. He cannot

apply for such an order until the tenancy has been terminated.

The way a tenancy is terminated depends on which sort of tenancy agreement has been used: a fixed-term contract or a periodic tenancy.

A fixed-term contract is for a definite period; for example, it may be for six months, a year or two years from the date at which the tenancy begins. The landlord does not need to give the tenant any notice under this kind of contract – it finishes at the end of the time stated and the tenant should then leave. The contract cannot be terminated before this time, however, unless the tenant agrees, or unless he has been breaking the terms of his contract and the court grants the landlord an order for possession.

A periodic tenancy, on the other hand, goes on until the landlord or the tenant brings it to an end. For the landlord to do this he must give a 'notice to quit' in writing, and if the tenancy is by the week, fortnight or month he must give at least a month's notice. If the tenancy is by the quarter, 3 months' notice must be given, and if the tenancy is for six months or a year he must give six months' notice. The expiry date of the notice must be the end of a rental period, ie a week, month, quarter and so on, depending on the period of the let.

Even after a tenant has been given notice to quit, he can go to the Rent Tribunal and ask them to suspend the notice. This means that the expiry date of the notice, which is also the date on which the landlord can go to court to apply for an eviction order, is put off for the period during which the tribunal suspends the notice – in the first instance this can be for up to six months, longer if the suspension order is renewed. However if the tenant continues to misbehave the landlord can re-apply to the tribunal for the suspension period to be reduced, or can apply straight to the court for an order for possession.

The Rent Officer

Either a landlord or a tenant of a regulated tenancy, or both, can apply to the rent officer to register a fair rent for the dwelling. This then becomes the most the landlord can charge for the accommodation until the rent officer registers a higher rent. This applies even if one tenant moves out and another one moves in. He can, however, increase the rent to cover increased rates and, where the contract allows it and the rent officer has registered a 'variable' rent, increase the rent to cover the increased cost of any services he provides, such as cleaning or provision of a caretaker.

If the rent registered by the rent officer is less than the rent the tenant is currently paying, then the landlord must reduce it at once. If the new rent is higher the landlord can normally only put it up to the higher figure in stages. This is known as 'phasing' and the Housing Rents and Subsidies Act 1975 lays down the way in which the increases must be phased. (The rent officer or your local Citizen's Advice Bureau will have explanatory literature on this).

Once a rent has been registered the landlord or tenant alone cannot apply to have it re-registered again within a period of two years and nine months of the date of the last application for a registration. However, if the circumstances of the tenancy have changed substantially within that period, for example if the landlord has made considerable improvements to the property and wishes to increase the rent, or if it has fallen into disrepair and the tenant considers the rent should be lowered, the rent officer may allow the application.

Repairs
The responsibility for carrying out certain repairs and decorations will normally be set out in the tenancy agreement, but where this is not done and the original tenancy was for less than seven years, then the law imposes certain duties on the landlord. He will have an obligation to carry out any repairs needed to the structure of the property and to installations for the supply of water, gas, electricity and sanitation, and for space heating and water heating.

The Rent Book
Any tenant whose rent is paid weekly is entitled to a rent book. This must give details of the tenant's rights under the Rent Acts, including details of the local authority's rent allowance schemes, a summary of the laws against over-crowding and information about offences against these laws. Suitable books can be purchased at some stationers.

LETTING A FAMILY HOME
Tenants of landlords who do not live in the same house have security of tenure under the Rent Acts (see under regulated tenancies, above). So anyone who lets his family home (perhaps because he is going abroad or working in another part of the country for a spell) could have difficulty if his tenant later proved unwilling to move out. There are certain circumstances, however, in which a county court must grant an order for possession to the landlord. In the case of a temporary let of a family home this right to possession is given by provisions in the 1968 Rent Act (Case 10) but to claim his right the landlord will have to prove three things:

1 That at the beginning of the let (and before the tenant moved in) he gave notice to the tenant in writing that possession might be recovered under Case 10.
2 That every time he had let the property before he had served a similar notice on the tenant.
3 That he wants the house back to live in himself, or for a member of his family who had previously lived there with him, to live in. (Some stationers sell forms for this purpose, but it is advisable to consult a solicitor before entering into any agreement).

Similar rights to re-possession apply to anyone who has bought a home for his retirement (Case 10A) and the letting of short-term holiday accommodation for a longer term out of season (Case 10B).

Before a landlord applies to the courts for an order for possession under any of these cases, it will be necessary for him to terminate the tenancy agreement. If it is for a fixed term he need take no action, the tenant's right to occupy will end with the expiry of the lease. If it is a periodic one he will have to give the tenant at least a month's notice in writing, more if the tenancy is by the quarter or longer. (The same rules apply as detailed under 'Resident landlords' above).

The court may still grant the landlord an order even if he has not given the tenant notice in writing that possession may be recovered under the relevant Case, but only if the court considers it 'just and equitable' to do so.

BUYING A LEASEHOLD
Anyone who leases the whole of a house (but not a flat or maisonette) for which the lease was originally

granted for over 21 years and at an annual rent below a certain figure has the right to buy the free-hold of the house, or to extend the lease for a further 50 years. A proviso is that the tenant must have been occupying the house as his sole or main residence for the whole of the last five years, or for a total of five years during the last ten under the same lease.

If the landlord and tenant cannot agree on a fair price for the freehold, this can be fixed by applying to the Land Tribunal.

If the tenant does not want to buy the freehold, but would like to extend the lease, the landlord is entitled to a new rent from the start of the extension period that will be in line with the current values. If the landlord and tenant cannot agree on a modern ground rent, the Land Tribunal can be asked to determine it. After 25 years of the extension period this rent can be reviewed again.

If the landlord of the property acquired his interest in it not later than 18 February 1966 he has the right to object both to selling it or to extending the lease, provided he does so during the course of the existing term of the lease. He will need to prove that he wants the property either for himself or a member of his family to live in when the lease expires, and that it would cause more hardship for him to be denied possession than having to leave the house would cause the present leaseholder. He will also have to compensate the leaseholder finan-cially for the loss of the 50-year extension.

Public authority and Crown properties

Tenants of public authorities may be refused the right to buy the freehold or extend the leasehold on a property needed for development; the decision is made by the appropriate government minister, and the tenant will receive compensation. Crown authorities are not bound by the Act but behave as if they were; they will refuse to sell a freehold or extend the lease only if the property is needed for development or if there is some special architec-tural, historic or amenity value attached to it.

Scotland

The Leasehold Reform Act applies in England and Wales but not in Scotland.

Shoppers' rights

Most people at some time or other come up against a bad deal or find themselves landed with a rogue piece of equipment for which they want repairs, a replacement or their money refunded. The Sale of Goods Act exists to protect shoppers in this sort of situation, and your first step when you have a com-plaint to make is to be sure you know your rights.

Rights under this Act apply whether you are buying with cash, on credit or with trading stamps, but if you are complaining about a gift the com-plaint must come from the person who bought it. With goods on hire purchase you will probably need to complain to the finance house and not to the shop.

(In areas where consumers' rights are not as yet protected by law, the various Associations in the service industries – such as launderers and dry cleaners, the Electricity Council and the travel trade are increasingly drawing up their own voluntary codes of practice which should give you a degree of protection. The Citizens' Advice Bureau will be able to tell you where to apply for help.)

A SALE IS A CONTRACT

When you buy something from a shop you are making a contract. Under the Sale of Goods Act there are many requirements that must be satisfied if the trader is to keep his side of the bargain, three of these are:

1 The goods must be of 'merchantable quality'. This means that if they are new they must not be broken or damaged and must work properly. This does not apply, however, to any defects that were specifically pointed out to you before you bought the goods, or that you could reasonably have been expected to notice for yourself while you were looking them over.

2 The goods must be 'as described' – whether by the salesperson or on the packet. For instance, a box which says it contains a rose-patterned tea service should not turn out to have in it one patterned with forget-me-nots.

3 The goods should be 'fit for purpose'. The purpose, that is, for which most people would be expected to buy the particular goods. If you want something for a special purpose you must make this plain at the time, and you will still have no right of redress if the circumstances of the sale show that you did not rely on the seller's skill and judgement, ie you asked his advice and did not take it, or if you asked advice from someone who couldn't reasonably be expected to know.

Making a complaint

Although some shops have generous policies about exchanging goods, for your side of the contract you are not legally entitled to claim any money back, or to claim an exchange, credit note or free repair if you have:

1 Simply changed your mind about wanting the goods, or

2 Damaged or marked goods that were of 'merchantable quality' when you bought them.

So when you have a complaint to make, make it as soon as possible. The longer you hold on to the goods the easier it will be for the seller to say you have caused the damage (see **2** above). Do not hesitate because you think it's not the shop's fault but the fault of the manufacturer – even if this is so, it is still the shop that you have made the contract with, and it is up to the shopkeeper to sort it out with the manufacturer direct. (For manufacturers' guarantees, see page 260).

So go back to the shop or firm and ask to speak to the manager. Take the item with you if it is small enough to carry, and also the receipt and any other relevant documents. If your complaint is justified

you are legally entitled to claim either all or some of the purchase price paid, depending on the type of fault and how soon you brought the goods back. For their part, the shop may offer you a credit note instead of cash, but you do not have to accept this. If you and they both agree you may settle on exchanging the item for a similar one, or to have the faulty item repaired.

If you have to spend money as a direct result of the goods being faulty – say a new washing machine broke down and you had to send things to a laundry – you could try claiming the cost of this from the shop. But you must keep such claims to a reasonable minimum.

Claiming your rights

Most firms will accept a genuine claim without the need for threatened legal action, but if you have received no satisfaction or your complaint has been ignored, then the onus is on you to start legal proceedings for the return of your money, or for compensation.

In England and Wales it is possible to do this yourself without the help of a solicitor through the county court (see page 264). In Scotland small claims are dealt with by the Sheriff's Small Debt Court, but in Northern Ireland the procedure is rather different so consult a solicitor or the Citizen's Advice Bureau.

FOOD PRODUCTS

When you buy a food product from a shop it must be 'of the nature, substance and quality demanded, and fit and safe for human consumption'. Again the recommended first step if you get a packaged food product that gives you cause for complaint is to take it back to the shop and ask for a refund or replacement. If for any reason this is not convenient, then this is a case where you are equally likely to get satisfaction by writing to the manufacturer direct.

Return the product and the packaging if possible, with a letter giving as much detail as you can; where you bought the product and when, how it was stored and the full nature of your complaint. If the complaint is justified (or even if there is any reasonable doubt) the least you can expect from the majority of British food manufacturers is a full refund of the cost or a replacement of the product, plus the cost of the postage involved in making your complaint.

LOCAL AUTHORITY PROSECUTIONS

If the complaint is a really serious one, where food or drink has been found to contain a 'foreign body', or someone has been made ill by contaminated food or drink, you should get in touch with the Environmental Health Authority of your local District Council. Public Health Authorities have the power to prosecute in cases like this, and you are allowed to remain anonymous if you wish.

It is important to keep the evidence if you possibly can – it is not much use saying you were sold bad meat if you cannot prove it. (Wrap it up very thoroughly in foil and keep it in the refrigerator till you can hand it over.)

Also part of the local authority are Trading Standard Inspectors. Their field is the correct marking of goods, short measure, false descriptions of goods and services and safety aspects of things like oil heaters, carry cots, electric blankets and so on. The inspectors will deal with both retailers and manufacturers, warning or bringing prosecutions as appropriate.

Both Public Health and Trading Standard Inspectors can be traced through the Town Hall.

You will be doing a public service by having matters officially investigated by them. If on the strength of your complaint they bring a prosecution and get a conviction, the court may award you compensation.

MANUFACTURERS' GUARANTEES

Many manufacturers provide a written guarantee covering faults in their product during the early months or years of its life. This usually has to be signed and returned to the manufacturer by the purchaser. This does not alter your rights against the retailer but it does mean that if a piece of equipment covered by guarantee is found to be faulty, or goes wrong quite soon after you buy it, you have a choice of taking the matter up with the shop or with the manufacturer. Under a manufacturer's guarantee you may well find that he will repair the goods but you will have to pay for labour costs and transportation; a retailer is not obliged to make repairs, but he must give you damages.

Be careful of cards which specifically exclude claims for compensation for damage to property or personal injury; it is better not to send these off.

Mail order shopping

The main advantage of mail order is that it provides a pleasantly relaxed way of shopping in the privacy of your own home. You choose either by seeing something that you want in an advertisement or by studying a catalogue, the goods are delivered to your door so you save on fares and the bother of carrying parcels, and in the case of clothes you can try things on in your own good time and see how they'll match up with the rest of your wardrobe.

Catalogue mail order prices are usually comparable with cash prices in big department stores,

and credit terms (with no interest charged for periods of less than nine months) are available in the case of the large general catalogue companies. Part-time agents receive a commission on sales and a discount on own purchases.

The larger general catalogue mail companies selling through part-time agents or direct to the public are members of the Mail Order Traders' Association of Great Britain, who will help you if you have any complaints against members – you can get the address from the Citizens' Advice

Bureau. Companies within the association do not require payments to be made in advance of delivery. Goods may be held by the recipient for 14 days on approval without any legal obligation and may then be returned at the expense of the company in the case of the agency mail order firms. These large companies are also members of the Retail Trading Standards Association.

When ordering by mail it is always sensible to send the money in the form of money orders, postal orders or a cheque (make a note of the serial numbers) rather than cash. If you are replying to an advertisement, cut out the ad., or keep the leaflet if it was enclosed loose in the publication, and make a note on it where and when it appeared and the date you sent off the order. All useful information just in case of trouble later.

THE MAIL ORDER PROTECTION SCHEME

As a mail order customer your rights are just the same as if you were buying from a shop, but it is a little more difficult to claim them as you never come face to face with the retailer. Sometimes in the past you may have heard or read about mail order firms having gone into liquidation or bankruptcy after accepting customers' money and failing to supply the goods. Now, however, various organizations representing most of the newspapers and magazines have set up special funds for paying any claims their readers might have for failing to receive the goods (or a refund) after answering an advertisement which appeared in their papers or periodicals.

The protection scheme applies to what are known as direct response mail order advertisements, display or postal bargains which often appear in the paper set up under some such headline as Shopping by Post, where cash has to be sent in advance of goods received. The scheme does not apply to classified advertising (where you are likely to be buying from a private individual rather than a company) or direct mail solicitation.

Making a claim

To claim under the scheme, if after one month from the time of posting off your order you have failed to receive the goods or get your money back, or to get an acceptable explanation from the firm concerned, you should write to the Advertisement Manager of the paper or magazine in which the advertisement appeared. Periodicals require that you report your problem within two months, newspapers allow three months. Give the factual details we talked about earlier, ie the date the ad. appeared, the date you ordered and the number of your postal order or cheque – do not, though, enclose the original advertisement.

If for some reason the Advertisement Manager cannot sort things out for you, you should then write to the Newspaper Publishers' Association if the ad. appeared in a national newspaper, or the Newspaper Society if it was in the local press. For an advertisement that appeared in a magazine, write to the Periodical Publishers' Association (all addresses from the Citizens' Advice Bureau, and special associations exist for Scotland).

Provided the publisher is a member of one of these associations, the association will then do its best either to sort out mistakes and inefficiencies or, if need be, to settle your claim from the special funds that have been made available.

SALESMEN AT THE DOOR

A small proportion of salesmen who call at your home can be pests – or worse. Doorstep callers you should fix with a beady eye and ask to leave include 'students' selling magazine and book subscriptions, 'researchers' who do not make it clear they are selling and – though it may seem hard – callers who claim to be selling for charity, perhaps on behalf of the blind or the disabled.

Before you let anyone into the house it is important to ask to see a visiting card or some other means of identification. Most reputable firms selling direct to the home are members of the Direct Sales and Services Association which lays down a code of conduct for its members covering both the quality of the goods they sell and the claims and methods they may use to sell them.

Buying at home

As with direct mail, one of the greatest advantages of buying from a salesman in your own home is that you can afford to take your time (and never do business with a salesman who tries to rush you). Have a good look at the products, see them in action if possible, and read through catalogues or any other promotional literature. On a major purchase when you want a chance to think things over for a day or two before deciding, do not hesitate to ask the salesman to call back. (This will also give you time to shop around a bit and see how prices compare – essential when you are contemplating buying something expensive.) Ask about guarantees and after-sales service.

If you decide to buy, do not sign anything until you have read and understood exactly what you are signing. Watch credit charges and hire purchase terms carefully (see page 242). If you are doubtful over any points, take the form round to your local Citizens' Advice Bureau and ask them to explain it to you. Get a receipt.

If the goods prove faulty, you are entitled to redress under the Sale of Goods Act as with any other purchase (see pages 258–9).

Going to a solicitor

Although it is possible to tackle some legal problems yourself, at some time in your life you will probably have to call on the services of a solicitor. It is most important that you should engage the right solicitor – not just one picked at random from the telephone directory. Different firms specialise in different areas of the law and certain individuals are inevitably better than others at certain types of work.

The best way to find the right man for the job is by personal recommendation; talk to friends or business contacts who may have had a similar problem and try to find a solicitor that way. Failing personal recommendation, the next best thing is to call at the Citizens' Advice Bureau. They will have a list of solicitors in your area and may also be able to draw on experience and recommend one or two particular firms.

Legal costs
By law solicitors' charges have to be 'fair and reasonable'. You can appeal if you think you are being over-charged; if a court case is involved the court will assess a fair charge, if advice only is involved you can appeal to the Law Society. Nevertheless going to law can be an expensive business. For this reason a legal aid scheme exists to make sure that anyone who needs legal advice need not go without because he or she cannot afford to pay for it.

LEGAL AID
The legal aid scheme is sponsored by the government but run by the Law Society through a number of Legal Aid Offices throughout the country. The scope of legal aid in Scotland and Northern Ireland varies a little from that in England and Wales, so seek local advice.

Under the legal aid scheme you can get advice from a solicitor, or be represented in a court case, either free or for a small contribution depending on your means. Legal aid is available for a wide range of civil court proceedings – for example, divorce, personal injury claims, defence of eviction proceedings and so on. It is not available in cases of libel, slander or defamation, nor if you want representation before a tribunal (though it is available for advice before tribunal proceedings); it is unlikely to be available for small consumer claims.

Who is eligible
Whether you are granted legal aid or not depends in the first place on your financial situation. This is assessed both on your savings (disposable capital) and what you earn (disposable income),

less certain allowances for dependants, rent, mortgage repayments and similar unavoidable commitments. For both legal advice and legal aid for court proceedings, a husband's and wife's incomes and savings are lumped together for assessment, unless you are separated or on opposite sides in the same case – divorce, for instance, or a dispute over custody of the children. In a case like this you will be assessed separately.

Before you are finally granted legal aid you will probably have to go to a Supplementary Benefits Commission Office with proof to back up your statement about your finances. In practice it is generally only those on very low incomes, such as a pension or supplementary benefit, and those with large families who qualify for legal aid – but do not let this deter you from applying as the commission can exercise a certain amount of discretion.

What to do
Not all solicitors handle legal aid cases but the Citizens' Advice Bureau will have a list of those in your area who do. If the solicitor you consult advises you that you have reasonable grounds for going ahead with a court case he will complete a legal aid application form for you and send it to the local Legal Aid Office. This office will then consider your application to decide whether they agree you have reasonable grounds for bringing your case, and whether you are eligible for aid on financial grounds.

Legal aid certificates are not retrospective, so any legal costs you incur before the certificate is granted will have to be met out of your own pocket. For this reason the solicitor will do nothing further until he gets a reply to your application from the Legal Aid Office.

If you are turned down for civil legal aid you can appeal, but only if you have been turned down on the grounds that your case is not worth pursuing,

not if the commission decides you are not financially eligible. It is possible, though, to ask the Law Society to ask the Supplementary Benefits Commission to make a reassessment in case the facts have been misconstrued.

Before you are committed to going ahead with legal aid you will be informed of any contributions you may be expected to pay.

EMERGENCY LEGAL AID
Usually there will be up to two months' delay before a legal aid certificate is granted. Where time is important – if you are trying to get an injunction to stop your husband taking your children out of the country, for instance – then you can apply for emergency legal aid. Your solicitor will fill in a special form and submit it immediately to the Legal Aid Office. The certificate may then be granted the same day, in time for your case to be heard the following morning.

Criminal legal aid
If you find yourself facing serious criminal charges in court, then you should apply for criminal legal aid right away. If you are being remanded in custody, you should be given the necessary forms automatically; if you are remanded on bail, then you should go to the court office and fill in the relevant forms there.

If you do not have time to do either before you appear in front of the magistrates, then you should tell them at the earliest opportunity that you want to apply for legal aid. If you do not apply, the court is under no obligation to offer you legal aid, and whether it's granted or not is left entirely to the magistrate's discretion. Legal aid may be granted in less serious criminal cases if the defendant does not have a reasonable grasp of the English language or if he has some mental illness.

Taking out a summons

Pages 258–260 outline consumers' rights under the Sale of Goods Act. Contrary to what many people believe, you do not get these rights automatically. If you have a complaint against a trader which is either ignored or disputed, it will be up to you to take out a summons against him in the county court. (Provided, that is, that the sum involved is less than £2000. Cases that involve larger sums of money must go to the High Court.)

Many disputes and grievances can be heard under a simple small claims procedure in the county court – unpaid debts, damage to property and so on, as well as faulty goods. And this is an area of the law where you are actively encouraged to handle the action yourself without the services of a solicitor. In fact, if the sum involved is less than £100 you cannot usually claim the cost of a solicitor, even if you win. However, the small claims procedure is simple and straight-forward; the hearing is informal, usually held in private before a registrar rather than a judge, and the costs are minimal. Indeed in many cases you may not have to go to court at all. A free booklet *Small Claims in the County Court* is available from all court offices, citizens' advice bureaux and consumer advice centres. It is a step by step guide to the procedure.

Procedure in the county court

Your first step is to submit a 'particulars of claim' and a 'request for summons' to the court. The 'particulars of claim' should include details of the case and any action you have taken so far including dates and references to any correspondence you have had with the person or the company. You do not need a form for this, but if you have any difficulty in setting out the facts the court and CAB have forms for the most common claims, which you are recommended to use.

The 'request for summons' needs a special form (available from the court office), and it is important that you get the name and address of the defendant correct. If you serve a summons on a limited company anywhere but at its registered office, any judgment that you obtain against it will be invalid.

The address of the company's registered office should be on its letterhead but if you have difficulty, then Companies House should be able to supply you with the correct address for a small fee (the Citizens' Advice Bureau will give you details).

If you are suing a partnership, you should sue all the partners in their individual names – check with the Business Names Registry (try your local library) by looking against the name of the firm.

You will have to specify the type of summons you want served – a default or an ordinary summons. A default summons is issued when you are claiming a fixed sum of money, such as an unpaid debt; an ordinary summons is issued when the amount is not fixed, such as a claim for general damages. The court officer will advise you which kind you need. You can also state whether you would like the case to be heard, if defended, by arbitration under the small claims procedure.

The court to which you submit your claim will not necessarily be your local county court – it may be the court for the district where the defendant lives, or where the company's registered office is located but your local court staff will clarify this for you. The court's fee will depend upon how much you are claiming and you can obtain a scale of fees from the court office. However, it is basically ten per cent of the amount you are claiming with a minimum of £1 and a maximum of £15.

If you issue a default summons and the defendant does not notify the court within 14 days of service of the summons whether he intends to defend your claim, then you can ask for judgment in default. You fill in a simple form and state how you would like the money to be paid. There will be no hearing at all.

If on a default summons the defendant does indicate that your claim will be contested or you were claiming damages and so an ordinary summons was issued, then both parties may be called for a pre-trial review before the registrar and matters may be, and usually are, settled here. If this is not possible because there is a real dispute or difficulty between you, the registrar will arrange for the case to go to arbitration, usually before himself, or to trial in court, but if the amount involved is less than £100 the case will nearly always be dealt with by arbitration if you ask for it. In either case the registrar arranges the hearing.

The hearing

If your case is being dealt with by arbitration then it is entirely informal and held in the registrar's private room. He will ask you to tell him your story and he may put questions to you. The defendant will also be asked to tell his story and the registrar may ask him questions too. He will normally expect you to put questions through him for answer by the other party. The registrar will then sum up and give his award.

If you have to go to court then the judge or the registrar will be robed and it will be a little more formal. You will again be able to tell your story but it is the other party who will normally then be allowed to ask you questions. When it is the other party's turn to tell his story then you will be able to ask him questions.

If the case involves more than £100 and you win you can ask the court to award you costs and under the Litigants in Person (Costs and Expenses) Act 1975 this can include an amount for the work you have done in preparing your case and arguing it in court. A leaflet on how to assess your costs is available at the court office.

If your claim was for less than £100 you can normally only have the court fee and your expenses. If you lose in an under £100 case you can only be asked to pay any court fee and any expenses of the other party.

If you win but the firm or person you sued does not pay up the court will, for a fee, enforce the debt for you. The court will tell you how this can be done but it will not advise you as to which is the best method of enforcement to use. Remember it is useless to sue someone who does not have the means to satisfy any judgment you obtain. Also during the hearing, if there is one, make a note of any details you hear about the assets of your opponent. This will help you if you have to enforce your judgment. Often getting judgment is easy but getting your money may well be the difficult part and the more information you can get about your opponent's means the easier it will be.

Jury service

If you are registered to vote you may be called to do jury service in a criminal trial because prospective jurors are selected, at random, from the list of names in the electoral register.

Some people are ineligible: those concerned with the law and with the administration of justice, the clergy and the mentally ill being the three general categories. Other people can be excused if they so choose and these include Members of Parliament, members of the Forces, and the medical and allied professions. However, anyone who has a good reason not to serve can write to the summoning officer and ask to be excused. Family reasons are usually accepted.

You will be summoned to attend the Crown Court on a specified date (you are normally given six to eight weeks' notice). With the Jury Summons, which gives the Court address, date and time, you will also receive an explanatory leaflet on jury service, a sheet with information on how to reach the court house and information about the allowances you will be entitled to receive. These consist of a travelling and a subsistence allowance and if you lose earnings while you are away from work (or unemployment benefit) you will receive a further payment in respect of your financial loss.

When you attend court, your name will go into a ballot once to select a jury in waiting and again when names are drawn in the courtroom to make up the actual jury. If you are not selected you will probably be allowed to go once the case has started, but asked to return in the afternoon or on the following day for another case. If your name is drawn, you are then sworn in, unless the prosecution or the defence objects to you serving on the jury. If someone does make an objection, you would stand down and another juror would take your place. Once sworn in you must attend for the whole case.

Jury service is likely to last ten working days but you could be asked to stay longer.

A word of warning – anyone who, without reasonable cause, fails to attend for jury service, or after attending is not available when called, is liable to a substantial fine.

Marriage and the law

This section deals with the law as it applies in England and Wales. If you live in Scotland or Northern Ireland go to your local Citizens' Advice Bureau who will be able to tell you where to go for help and advice.

If you are over 16, single, one of you male and the other female then you may marry. The law will give you its blessing provided, however, that the person you want to marry is not one of the forbidden group of people already related to you either by marriage or by blood.

If you are a woman you are forbidden to marry your father, son, grandfather, grandson, brother, father-in-law, stepson, stepfather, son-in-law, stepgrandfather, mother-in-law's father, father-in-law's father, step-daughter's son, step-son's son, granddaughter's husband, uncle or nephew. The list applies similarly to a man, with the sexes reversed of course.

If either of the couple although over 16 is still under 18, he or she will need parental consent. This means the consent of both parents, if both are alive, unless they are divorced or separated when it is the one who has custody who has to give the consent.

Bigamy
It may seem obvious of the law to stipulate that you must be single (which includes the widowed and divorced, of course) at the time you get married.

But history is full of cases of people who 'come back from the dead', so if you have any doubts as to whether a former partner really has died it is best to apply to the court for a decree of presumption of death and divorce. Then, should a previous wife or husband later turn up, the new marriage will still be valid.

Intention and consent
Even though a marriage may, if things go wrong, be dissolved by divorce (see later), at the time of entering into it the assumption is that you mean to make it last for life. And, in fact, in the marriage ceremony you have to make a promise that this is so.

As far as consent goes, it does sometimes happen that a marriage takes place under threat of blackmail or some other compulsion, and if you can prove this it can be annulled.

Change of name
It is not legally necessary for a woman to change her name to her husband's when she marries. Any children born to a married woman, however, have to take her husband's name.

Cohabitation
'Cohabitation' means living together and sharing a common domestic life, and is considered part of a normal working marriage. This naturally normally

266

includes sexual intercourse, but a husband has no 'right' in law to demand sexual intercourse from an unwilling wife; equally a healthy wife has no 'right' to refuse it all the time.

Property
As long as your marriage is 'working', any property either of you brought to it or bought later with your own money belongs to you as individuals. This is rather hard on a wife who stays at home to look after the children, because anything her husband buys with the money he earns is looked on as belonging solely to him. At the same time anything she buys from the housekeeping money he gives her (even if she saves up to buy it) belongs to them jointly.

This should not matter much in a happy marriage, and should the marriage break down the divorce court has wide powers to transfer a share of a husband's property to his wife and children.

Maintenance
Both husband and wife have a legal duty to support each other (and any children under 16). Even so, as long as husband and wife are living together the law will not help a wife to get money out of her husband, even to buy food or necessary household goods.

However, a wife may pledge her husband's credit, ie open an account in his name for which he will be liable to pay the bills, for reasonable goods and household services applicable to his income. But if she does not get his consent to this, he can revoke her implied authority and that will end it. This is why you sometimes see notices in the newspapers saying that Mr So-and-so will no longer be responsible for his wife's debts (not that this does much good, because the husband has to prove that the particular tradesman saw the notice or he will still be liable – it is much more effective to go to the shop direct).

DIVORCE
Divorce cases are handled by the Divorce Registry (in London this is part of the Family Court) and by county courts with divorce jurisdiction – the address will be in your local telephone directory, or ask at your police station.

Once you have reached the stage of wanting a divorce, if you have children or joint property a solicitor's help will be essential to sort things out.

(But you may be eligible for Legal Aid, see page 262). In a really straightforward case where children and property are not involved, a 'quickie' or postal divorce which you can handle yourself may be feasible. Your wisest course is to consult the Citizens' Advice Bureau or an officer of the Divorce Registry at the county court, who will be able to advise you as to the steps you would have to take, even though he is not permitted to give you legal advice.

When filing a petition for divorce, the person applying for the divorce is known as the 'petitioner', and the other party as the 'respondent'. If a petition alleges adultery the third party is called the 'co-respondent'.

Grounds for divorce
Under the law of England and Wales, divorces are normally granted only after three years of marriage, and on the ground that the marriage has irretrievably broken down for one of the following reasons – and you will have to be able to prove your claims:

1 Adultery: ie the respondent has committed adultery and the petitioner finds it intolerable to live with him or her.

2 Unreasonable behaviour: ie the respondent has behaved in such a way that the petitioner cannot reasonably be expected to live with him or her.

3 Desertion: ie one partner has deserted the other for at least two years immediately prior to the filing of the petition.

4 Two years' separation with the consent of the respondent: ie that man and wife have lived apart for two years continuously immediately prior to the filing of the petition, and that the respondent consents to the divorce.

5 Five years' separation without consent: ie that man and wife have lived apart for five years continuously immediately prior to the filing of the petition – even if the respondent does not consent to the divorce.

If you are the one filing the petition, separation is the easiest ground for divorce to deal with, and unless there is a dispute about custody of the children or about the family property it is unlikely that it will be necessary for you to attend court. In this case the registrar of the court will issue a certificate on the strength of your evidence contained in a sworn affidavit, upon the acceptance of which the judge will grant a decree nisi. The decree nisi does not finally end the marriage. The decree absolute does that, but it is not granted automatically; you have to apply for it six weeks after the grant of the decree nisi.

If you are petitioning on other grounds, if the case is undefended and there is no dispute about custody or property, the judge will normally interview the petitioner in his private room to discuss the arrangements for the children. If the case is defended, however, and the respondent decides to file an answer disputing the facts in the petition, the proceedings must then be transferred to the High Court, and if you have been managing without the aid of solicitor up to this point you would be strongly advised to consult one now.

Registration of births, marriages and deaths

The registration procedures described below refer to England and Wales; in Scotland and Northern Ireland the requirements are rather different so you would be best advised to take local advice.

NOTIFICATION OF A BIRTH

When a baby is born in a hospital or a large maternity home, you will probably find that you can register him or her there with a visiting registrar. If for any reason the birth is not registered in this way, or if the baby is born at home, one of the parents will need to visit the Register Office within 42 days of the birth – or you become liable for a fine.

If it is quite impossible for one of the parents to visit the Register Office for the district where the birth took place, a declaration may be made before any registrar of births and deaths for transmission to the proper office: there is no charge for this. In certain exceptional cases (for example, in the case of an abandoned baby) the person having charge of the child can register the birth.

The registrar will give you a short birth certificate free of charge. This gives the child's names, sex and place and date of birth. You can buy a 'full' version of the certificate, including the names of the parents, if you wish but the short certificate can be used for most purposes.

At the time of registration you will also receive a card to give the doctor on whose National Health Service list you want your baby entered.

Stillbirths

Even if a baby is stillborn it is necessary to register it. The doctor or midwife who was present at the birth, or who examined the baby, will give a certificate of still-birth and this should be taken to the registrar.

268

MARRIAGE

Civil marriages
A civil marriage must take place in the Register Office of the district in which one of you lives. How much notice you must give depends on whether you are being married by certificate or licence.

For marriage by certificate you will need to have lived in the district for seven days before you go to the superintendent registrar to give notice of your intention to get married. If you and your future husband or wife have both lived in the same registration district for seven days, only one notice need be given; otherwise, you will have to give notice in both districts. You will need to sign an official declaration that the details on the notice are correct, and after 21 clear days, provided there is no impediment, the superintendent registrar can issue his certificate authorizing the marriage.

For marriage by licence, only one notice is necessary – but in this case one of you will need to have lived in the district for 15 days before you can give notice. This qualification met, however, one clear day (other than a Sunday, Good Friday or Christmas day) has to elapse from the date on which the notice was entered in the notice book before the superintendent registrar can issue a licence – again provided there is no impediment.

Both certificates and licences are valid for three months from the date of entry of the notice.

Particulars recorded in the register at the time of the wedding are, in respect of both husband and wife, name and surname, age, marital status, occupation, residence at the time of the marriage; also father's name, surname and occupation. The date and place of the marriage are also registered and the entry is signed by both of you, two witnesses, the superintendent registrar and the registrar. If you want a copy of the entry in the register (your 'marriage lines') – and it is a good idea to have one – this will be available for a fee.

Marriage in the Church of England
The preliminaries to a Church of England marriage may be either:

1 The publication of banns. These must be called on three successive Sundays by the clergyman of the parish in which each of you lives.

2 The issue of a common licence, about which you must consult your vicar.

3 The issue of a superintendent registrar's certificate (see above).

4 The issue of a special licence granted by or on behalf of the Archbishop of Canterbury (but this is only granted in special circumstances or grave emergencies).

At the end of the ceremony the clergyman will register the marriage; the particulars recorded are the same as for a Register Office wedding.

Marriage in a church other than of the Church of England
The marriage may be by superintendent registrar's certificate or superintendent registrar's licence and notice must be given in the same way as for a civil marriage. You must, however, consult the minister or priest and unless he is authorized to register marriages, a registrar will have to attend. The particulars to be registered after the ceremony are the same as for a Register Office wedding.

Marriage by Registrar General's licence
This licence is for a marriage, otherwise than by Church of England ceremony, when one of the persons to be married is seriously ill and not expected to recover and cannot be moved to a building in which marriages are normally solemnized. Notice must be given to the superintendent registrar for the district in which the marriage is to take place but there is no waiting period for the licence and the marriage may be solemnized as soon as the licence is issued. The ceremony may be in hospital or at home.

REGISTRATION OF DEATHS
When someone dies at home, the doctor who has attended will issue a certificate giving the cause of death. He may then send this certificate to the registrar direct or, more likely, give it to a relative of the deceased who is the person liable to register the death.

If it falls on you to register a death, this should be done within five days, although the period can be extended to 14 days as long as the registrar has been informed that the doctor has signed a cause of death certificate. As well as this certificate, you should take the dead person's National Health Service medical card along with you to the registrar's office. Do not worry, though, if you cannot find the card; you can send it on later.

The registrar will give you a certificate of registration of death, which is free and is for claiming national insurance benefits. You will probably need certified copies of the entry of death in the register for probate and for claiming money due under insurance policies etc; you pay for these, but for some purposes a certificate may be issued at a reduced fee. If you tell the registrar what the certificate is needed for, he will advise you of the appropriate type and cost. The fee generally is less if you get certificates at the time of registering the death than if you go back for them later.

The registrar will also give you a certificate (known as a certificate of disposal) to enable the funeral to take place; this is free.

If the body is to be cremated, three forms obtainable from the crematorium or the funeral director will have to be completed; one form by the next of kin, the others by two different doctors. All three forms are then sent to the medical referee, who is also a doctor. If he decides the cremation may take place he issues a certificate which is sent to the crematorium. Fees are payable to the two doctors, but the fee for the medical referee is normally included in the crematorium charge.

Death in hospital

When someone dies in hospital the medical certificate of cause of death is usually completed by the hospital doctor, and if the body is to be cremated the hospital will arrange for the necessary medical forms to be completed. The only difference in procedure for registering a death in hospital from one that took place at home is that the registration must be made at the office of the registrar in whose district the hospital is.

It will be your responsibility to arrange for the body to be taken from the hospital mortuary to a funeral home.

FUNERAL ARRANGEMENTS

If the deceased person has made a will, the executor appointed in it will usually be responsible for making the funeral arrangements, and the cost of the funeral must be the first item paid out of a dead person's estate.

If you are yourself an executor, or for some other reason are making funeral arrangements to help the family, do make sure you know how much it will be reasonable to spend. Ask the funeral director to give you a really detailed estimate and make sure it includes every expense there may be, including cemetary or crematorium fees and the cost of any religious service.

Announcements

Most newspapers will accept a death announcement for their columns over the telephone provided they can ring back and check the text with some responsible person. Unless the funeral is to be private, the notice should give details of the time and place and, if flowers are welcome, an address to which they should be sent.

Making a will

Lots of people do not make wills because they think they have so little to leave. A common excuse with wives is that 'my husband will deal with all that'. But nowadays joint ownership of a house, for instance, could mean that either partner has a good few thousand pounds to dispose of – and

you would be surprised how much money household possessions and personal effects can be worth when executors have them valued for the purpose of Capital Transfer Tax.

There is also the problem that husband and wife may die together in a car or air crash. In this case, if you have not made a will and the law steps in to administer your estate, your money and possessions will be disposed of according to the rules of the Administration of Estates Act, but this could still cause family problems and even hardship. (Different rules apply in Scotland and Northern Ireland, but the principle remains the same.)

Dying intestate (that is, without having made a will) could mean a larger chunk of your money than necessary will go to the government. In fact, if you have no close relatives the whole of your estate will revert to the Crown – which is a pity if you have friends or a favourite charity to whom you would like to leave a legacy.

Even if you do leave an immediate family, the problems of sorting out your estate according to the law of the land, if you die intestate, will cost them a fair amount in legal fees – solicitors make more money out of people who do not make wills than out of those who do.

HOW TO SET ABOUT IT
You can make your will yourself but, unless you have some knowledge of the law, this step is fraught with danger. You may unintentionally invalidate some of the things you wanted done by miswording. You can buy will forms from many large stationers, which come with a set of instructions on how to write, sign and witness them, but far the best and simplest method of making a will is to consult a solicitor (see page 262). This will cost money, but you will be sure the job has been done properly. (If your estate is small enough you may be able to get free help under the Legal Advice scheme – see page 262).

Once you have chosen your solicitor, he will treat your affairs confidentially, advise you on alternative possibilities, help you not to pay more tax than necessary, and draw up your will in accordance with your wishes to make the best possible provision for your family and any friends or charities you want to include.

Choosing an Executor
In your will you will also need to appoint some person or persons to see that your wishes are carried out. These people are known as executors and they have a responsible and sometimes difficult duty to perform. Some people choose friends or relatives to be their executors, but there is always the chance that he or she will not be able to take on the job when the time comes, or may die before you. A way to guard against this happening is to appoint the Executor and Trustee Department of a bank to act as your executor, either alone or jointly with a personal friend (see page 234).

After you have made your will
Make sure that you keep your will in a safe place, such as a solicitor's strongroom or a bank, and that you leave a note as to where the will is lodged among your other papers. It is also a good idea to keep a copy of the will in a sealed envelope among your papers so you can take it out and consider it from time to time in the light of any major family developments. For example, if there are any births or deaths in the family you may want to alter your will. This can often be done by making what is known as a 'codicil' which makes some alteration or addition to a will while leaving the main part standing. Changes in tax laws may also affect it and it is worth taking fresh advice occasionally.

Licences

DRIVING LICENCE

Every driver of a motor vehicle on a public road must hold a current driving licence specifying the groups of vehicles it entitles the holder to drive. The purpose of driver licensing is to ensure that vehicles are driven only by people who are medically fit and entitled to drive the particular type of vehicle and are not disqualified by the courts or by reason of age.

To qualify for a full driving licence you must be at least 17 years old (16 for a licence to drive a moped or agricultural tractor) and have passed a driving test.

A full driving licence is normally valid until you are 70, or for three years at a time if you are over 67 when you apply. If you are over 70 you may need a medical certificate.

A provisional licence is valid for one year, and is issued to allow you to drive, subject to certain conditions, while you are practising to take your driving test.

Sign your licence as soon as you receive it and take it with you any time you are out on the road. If you are stopped when you do not have it with you, you will need to name a police station to which you will take it for inspection within five days.

TELEVISION LICENCE

Television licences are obtainable at any post office or from the Television Licensing Organisation at Bristol. The money goes to the BBC after deduction of collection costs.

You can buy a licence either for a colour television or for black and white. In a family house one licence (which must of course be a colour one if you have colour TV) covers any number of sets, but if you have a lodger with a TV in his room he will need to take out a licence of his own. In a block of flats or a private house divided into flats, occupiers will also need individual licences.

The licence lasts for one year and just before it expires a reminder is automatically prepared by a computer and sent to the licensee. If the licence is not renewed a further reminder is sent, and if you still do nothing an enquiry officer is likely to call.

Dealers in television sets are obliged by law to notify details of their transactions, whether you rent or buy. There are fines for having an unlicensed television set.

AMATEUR RADIO LICENCE

If you want to become a ham radio operator, you must first obtain from the Secretary of State for the Home Department a licence which gives the conditions under which you may establish and use an amateur wireless station.

There are two types of licence: the Amateur Licence A which permits the use of all facilities at present available to radio amateurs in the UK, and you will need to pass the Radio Amateur Examination and the Morse Test to obtain it; and the Amateur Licence B, which has some limitations, but for which you need only pass the Radio Amateur Examination.

The Home Office publishes a comprehensive pamphlet *How to become a radio amateur* and by writing to the Home Office Radio Regulatory Department, Licensing Branch (Amateurs), Waterloo Bridge House, London SE1 8UA, you can obtain a copy free.

DOG LICENCE

A dog licence, which lasts for 12 months from the date of issue, must be taken out for each dog over the age of six months. Exemption is granted for dogs used for guiding the blind and for working sheepdogs. In these cases, apply to the local police station, who will advise you as to how an exemption certificate may be obtained.

In the ordinary way, dog licences are obtainable from the post office. The authorities do not usually issue reminders when the licence is due, or has expired; it is the owner's responsibility to make sure that the licence is up to date.

Anyone who fails to take out a dog licence can be prosecuted and fined.

Passports

Passport application forms are available through main branch post offices. Remember you will need to put in the application and any other documents required to the Passport Office for your area at least four weeks before you need the passport (though special arrangements can be made for anyone called abroad on an urgent business trip or a family emergency). The application can be made by post, which is probably the wiser course, since going yourself may well involve you in queueing, and does not of itself secure priority.

The normal United Kingdom passport contains 30 pages, and one containing 94 pages is also available for a higher fee. Both passports are valid for ten years (five years, renewable for a second such period, for a child under 16).

The notes for guidance supplied with the passport application form give full details of the other documents (birth certificate, marriage certificates, etc) you will need. These must be originals; photocopies are not acceptable. You will also need two identical copies of a recent photograph of yourself, and also two of your husband/wife if you are applying for a family passport. The photographs should be taken full face without a hat and should not be more than 63×50 mm nor less than 50×38 mm. They should be printed on normal, thin, photographic paper and be unmounted; do not submit a black and white photograph with a glazed back, nor any colour photograph unless the supplier advises that the type is 'passport approved'. The person who countersigns your passport application form should also sign on the reverse side of one photograph with the words 'I certify that this is a true likeness of . . .' and add his or her signature.

Special short-term passports known as **British Visitor's Passports** are also available. These are valid for one year and are restricted to short holiday visits to Europe, Canada and Bermuda. These passports are issued over the counter at main branch post offices on the presentation of some official means of identification, such as a birth certificate or medical card, and cost less than standard passports.

4. Miscellaneous

Childhood illnesses

Certain infectious diseases seem to be inevitable however healthy the child. Below is a useful list of the most common infectious fevers, their symptoms, treatment and incubation periods. It may also be helpful to give a few general rules for coping with a child who has one of these illnesses.

Never press the child to eat unless he feels he wants food. The main requirement is that he should have plenty to drink – fruit drinks containing glucose are probably the best choice. Iced lollipops and ice cream are also appreciated. As the mouth can become very dry in many of these illnesses (particularly mumps) it helps if you can persuade the child to rinse his mouth with water, or with a mouthwash, from time to time.

When the temperature is high, keep the child cool by sponging with tepid water. Aspirin helps to bring down the temperature as well as easing the pain if there is any.

There is no absolute virtue in confining a sick child to bed. He may feel much better if he is allowed to lie on a settee where he can watch you at work. Isolating a sick child from the rest of the family is usually impracticable and is, in any case, unlikely to prevent the spread of the disease. In some circumstances, however, this may be necessary (see below). Disinfecting toys, eating utensils and laundry is unnecessary and ineffective.

Strict quarantine regulations are now known to have little effect on the spread of infections so that it is not necessary to keep brothers and sisters home from school if you have an infectious illness in the house. However, as some schools still insist on these measures it might be best to check.

ILLNESS	INCUBATION PERIOD (the time after exposure to the disease during which symptoms may occur)	SYMPTOMS	TREATMENT
Mumps	16–18 days	Swollen, aching face and a rise in temperature. Mumps is confirmed if the swelling fills the finger-sized groove behind the angle of the jaw.	Call the doctor even though medical treatment is seldom needed. Keep the face warm – say with a scarf – and encourage mouth rinses. Isolate from adults who have not had the illness.
Chicken pox	14–16 days	Oval pink spots on trunk; often also on face and scalp. These turn to blisters and then scab over. In more serious cases fever is also present.	Try and prevent scratching by giving tepid baths containing 2–3 handfuls of bicarbonate of soda. Dab the spots with a soothing lotion such as Calamine. Children are infectious until all the spots are crusted over. Keep away from adults who have not had the illness – especially the elderly, who could develop painful shingles.

MISCELLANEOUS

ILLNESS	INCUBATION PERIOD (the time after exposure to the disease during which symptoms may occur)	SYMPTOMS	TREATMENT
Scarlet fever	2–5 days	Headache, chills, malaise and high temperature. The child may complain of abdominal pain and vomit, but although he he has a tonsillitis he will seldom complain of this. The face is flushed with a pale area around the mouth. The skin peels later.	Call the doctor, as antibiotic treatment is needed.
German measles (rubella)	14–21 days	Rash of bright pink spots starting on the face and spreading over the body. Enlarged glands at the back of the neck.	Medical treatment is rarely needed. Isolate from pregnant women as the infection can harm the foetus in the early months.
Whooping cough	7–10 days	Coughing, usually worse at night, developing in a week or two to a spasm of coughing ending with the characteristic whoop. At the end of a spasm the child may go blue in the face and vomit.	Call your doctor – this can be a nasty illness and might lead to complications such as chest and ear infections. The child remains infectious for 4 to 5 weeks after the characteristic cough begins, and during this period should be kept away from babies not yet immunized.
Measles	10–15 days	Cold symptoms and fever, with blood-shot eyes and a sensitivity to light. Small red spots with white centres may be seen inside the mouth before the appearance of the rash, which starts 3–4 days after early symptoms. The rash consists of dark red blotches, starting behind the ears and spreading to face and trunk.	Call the doctor; treatment may be necessary if complications like ear or chest infections set in. There is no need to darken the room unless the child cannot bear the light.
Polio	Up to 3 weeks	This is a mild illness resembling a cold or flu in most children. But in about 10% of cases it can become serious and produce paralysis. The main symptoms are a temperature, sore throat and hoarseness, but the child feels, and is, very ill.	The only treatment is prevention. All children – and indeed all adults – should be immunized against this illness. If diphtheria epidemics are to be prevented from occurring again it is essential that childhood immunizations should continue – so make sure your child is protected.
Diphtheria	2–4 days		

278

Vaccinations

The chart below gives the immunization schedule for children as recommended by the Department of Health and Social Security in 1976. The schedule may have been modified since this book went to press, and in any case it is a good idea to discuss the question of immunization shots and their timing with your own doctor. He or she knows your child and so will be in the best position to give you advice.

Injections can be given either by your own doctor, or at your local Child Health Clinic. If when the immunization is due the child is ill, or seems to be sickening for something, you should postpone it. If you are in any doubt your family doctor or health visitor will be glad to advise you.

After each set of jabs, keep a watch on the child. If he or she develops a temperature or seems to be unwell for more than 24 hours, contact the doctor without delay.

VACCINATIONS FOR TRAVEL ABROAD

Many countries require certified proof of certain vaccinations from travellers who enter them or who have passed through areas where certain diseases – such as smallpox and yellow fever – are endemic. In other cases, there may not be a *legal* requirement under international law to have the vaccinations performed – but travellers are advised to do so for their own protection. These include inoculations against such illnesses as cholera, typhoid and para-typhoid and polio. Read *Notice to Travellers – Health Protection* issued free of charge by the Department of Health and Social Security for general advice on health protection abroad. If you require more specific or up to the minute information – contact the DHSS or the Embassy or Mission in the UK of the country to be visited.

Your own doctor should be able to give all the

DEPARTMENT OF HEALTH AND SOCIAL SECURITY RECOMMENDED IMMUNIZATION SCHEDULE FOR CHILDREN

Age of child	Protection from:	Procedure
1st year	Diphtheria, whooping cough, tetanus, polio	3 injections of combined vaccine, each accompanied by oral polio vaccine, with an interval of 6 to 8 weeks between the 1st and 2nd and 4 to 6 months between the 2nd and 3rd
2nd year	Measles	1 injection of live measles vaccine after an interval of not less than 3 weeks from previous immunization
At or before school entry	Diphtheria and tetanus Polio	1 booster injection of combined vaccine 1 oral booster dose of polio vaccine
10–13	Tuberculosis	Injections of BCG are available to children at risk
11–13	German measles	Injections are available to teenage girls as a precaution against developing the disease in pregnancy
School-leavers	Tetanus, polio	Further booster doses are recommended

vaccinations except the one for yellow fever. Vaccination against yellow fever can be done only at a designated centre. There are centres in most of the larger cities and they are listed in the *Notice to Travellers*.

If you need vaccination against more than one disease, discuss the matter with your doctor well in advance of your journey. Not only might he have to order the necessary vaccine, but he might also have to arrange for the vaccinations to be done in a particular order. For example, it is best to allow at least 3 weeks between yellow fever and smallpox vaccinations. But if time is short, they can be given on the same day. Other points to bear in mind are that international certificates for primary inoculations do not become valid for six to ten days after immunization and you must allow time for your smallpox certificate to be stamped by your local health authority.

Some vaccinations can be carried out free of charge under the National Health Service – it depends on what vaccination is given and where you are going – but a charge may, in any case, be made by the doctor for signing or completing a certificate. The charge will generally be small.

In general, if there is a requirement under the International Health Regulations but vaccination is considered inadvisable on medical grounds, your doctor should provide you with written evidence underlying that opinion. He may do this if you are pregnant, in some cases if you suffer from eczema, or he may do it for young babies. Decision on a claim for exemption from the requirement to be in possession of a valid International Certificate of vaccination is solely a matter for the health authority at the port of arrival. You are, therefore, advised to consult the High Commissioner's Office to enquire about the possibility of being granted exemption from the requirements.

Smallpox	1 vaccination. International certificate valid for 3 years.	**Cholera**	2 inoculations 7 to 10 days apart. Valid for 6 months. Booster dose every 4 to 6 months when in infected areas. With a few exceptions most countries now require only 1 inoculation. This can be given with TAB.
Yellow fever	1 inoculation. International certificate valid for 10 years.		
Typhoid and paratyphoid (TAB)	Complete protection given after a course of 2 injections, allowing 4 to 6 weeks between them. If it is urgent the interval can be reduced to not less than 10 days. Booster injections are needed every 3 years. However, if time is short, even 1 injection will give some measure of protection.	**Polio**	This is advised for travellers of any age going anywhere other than Europe, Canada and the USA, but is not legally required. The complete course or booster is given as necessary.

Pet care

DOGS

A dog that lives indoors should have a basket or box in a quiet corner in which he sleeps. The front should be cut low for easy access and the sides of the bed should be higher than the dog when he is lying down to keep out draughts. If you are using a box, raise it slightly off the floor for the same reason. To lie on, give him either a blanket or better still an old cushion cover filled with wood shavings which can be changed as necessary.

If your dog is going to live outdoors in a kennel, make sure it is large enough for him to stand up and turn round in but small enough for his own body warmth to keep him cosy on chilly nights. It must be waterproof and slightly raised off the ground to avoid damp and cold. Spread the floor with a good thick layer of straw or wood shavings and cover the entrance with a door that can be closed at night, or at least with a curtain of heavy sacking.

Feeding

At eight to ten weeks a puppy will be weaned and old enough to leave his mother. He should be given four small meals a day, mainly of milky cereal, mashed vegetables and puppy biscuits with a little raw or cooked minced meat added. As the puppy grows the four small meals can be cut down to three larger ones and by the time the dog is fully grown he should be given two meals daily. These should be a light meal, mainly biscuits, in the morning, and a larger meal of meat, biscuits and a variety of chopped cooked vegetables (not potatoes) in the evening. Each meal should be given at the same time every day.

If you own a freezer you can save both time and money by buying dog meat in bulk. Several different kinds are available through freezer centres, but try small packs first, in case the dog does not like a particular brand.

Tinned and dried dog foods are a trouble-saving way of feeding, but check the maker's instructions to be sure you are giving the right amount for the weight of the dog. Marrow bones are good for a dog's teeth, but small splintery bones are dangerous and can even be fatal.

Do not leave food down if the dog has left any in the bowl as it will attract flies, but always make sure he has plenty of fresh, clean water.

Exercise and training

There can be no hard and fast rules as to how much exercise a dog needs; it depends on his age, breed and size. As a general rule once a dog has been trained to come when he is called he needs a good run off the lead at least once a day in a park or other open space. (But never let him off the lead on a public road, see Dogs and the Law, below.)

Most dogs are quite easily trained by a mixture of kindness, firmness and patience. If your dog turns out to be highly nervous, however, or for some other reason difficult to train, your local Town Hall or Public Library will have a list of training centres in your area where you and he can go and train together.

Grooming

Again, how much grooming a dog needs depends on the breed. An Old English Sheepdog or Afghan hound presents a very different problem from a smooth haired terrier. But all need a good brushing every day and benefit from a thorough grooming once a week. An adult dog can be bathed occasionally in a good soap or dog shampoo – never a synthetic detergent – but rinse him well and keep him active and warm until he is thoroughly dry.

Health

It is unwise to take a puppy to places where other dogs have been until he has been vaccinated against the major infectious diseases. As soon as the puppy arrives, make arrangements with your local vet to have these carried out. The diseases in question are distemper (including what is often known as hard pad), hepatitis – a liver disease, jaundice and nephritis. The puppy should also be kept in until two weeks after the completion of the course of vaccinations, to allow them time to take.

At present no general vaccination is available against rabies – see under Quarantine, below.

If you have to give a tablet to a dog, place your hand over the back of his head and put your thumb and forefinger between his lips at the back of the

Pour medicine into the lip at the side of the
mouth to funnel it down the dog's throat

mouth where he has no teeth. Put the tablet at the
back of his throat and push it down with your
forefinger. Hold his head well up until he swallows.

To administer a liquid medicine, pull the lip
at the side of the mouth so that it forms a funnel
and pour the correct dose of medicine into this.
Tip the dog's head back a little to allow the
medicine to run down his throat. Stroke the throat
to encourage swallowing. If you cannot administer
the medicine in the manner described after
reasonable perseverance, admit this to the vet who
will be able to recommend an alternative method
of administration.

Boarding kennels
The best way to pick kennels when you have to
leave your dog for a while is on the advice of a
friend or neighbour whose dog has already
boarded there. Even so, go and look them over
well in advance Check that the food is the kind
your dog is used to, and see if the owner will let
you leave your dog's own bed or basket with him.

Dogs and the law
All dogs kept as pets must have a licence from the
age of six months (see page 272), and wear a collar
with a name tag giving your name and address.

Under the Road Traffic Act of 1972 it is a
criminal offence to take a dog on many roads
unless it is held on a lead. If he slips his lead
through negligence and causes an accident or any
other damage you may be held legally liable and
have to foot the bill. It is up to local councils to
rule whether dogs must be kept on leads in parks
and other public places.

If you live in the country, take special care that
your dog does not wander and chase or kill
livestock. Apart from the fact that you will be held
liable, a dog may legally be shot by a farmer on
suspicion alone.

In many places there is a heavy penalty for
allowing a dog to foul a footpath. (Even where
this penalty does not apply all dog-owners should
train their dogs to use the gutter.)

Quarantine
All animals entering Britain from abroad have by
law to spend six months in isolation in a Government authorized quarantine kennel as a precaution
against the introduction of rabies into the country.
Penalties for people caught smuggling animals are
severe and may well include a term of imprisonment.

Before importing any animal (and some birds)
into the country you must apply for a licence to the
Ministry of Agriculture, and make arrangements
for the animal to be collected at the port of entry
by a Carrying Agent on the Ministry's approved
list, to take it to the kennels. During the quarantine
period the animal will be given two injections of
anti-rabies vaccine as an extra safety precaution.

If you are taking your dog out of the country,
check the regulations in force in the country to
which you are going well in advance of your
departure date. You are likely to need a health
certificate from a vet, and some countries may
ask for an anti-rabies vaccination certificate. In
this case, warn the vet so he can put in an order
for the vaccine in good time.

CATS
Pedigree kittens, such as Siamese and Persians,
can be quite expensive, and it's probably wisest to
buy from a registered breeder. Quite often
though, some friend or neighbour will be only too
eager for you to accept an 'ordinary' kitten for
free. The reason for this is that a female cat can
have two, three or even four litters a year – maybe
as many as 100 kittens in a lifetime.

So unless you really want to go into the kitten
distribution business it's better to have a female
kitten neutered by a vet after her first oestrum
(season or heat). While she is young it is a simple
and safe operation.

Neutering a male kitten is even simpler, and
should be done when he is three and a half to six

months old, otherwise he may be wild when he grows up and some males develop dirty habits.

Care and feeding

Some people do not think it necessary to give a cat any special bed of its own, but this is a mistake from the point of view of hygiene as well as for the comfort of the cat. Right from the start a new kitten should be given a small, cosy box lined with something soft and either disposable or washable. When the kitten gets older this can be changed to a larger box or a special cat bed or basket.

A kitten should also be provided with a sanitary tray filled with dry earth, sand or one of the proprietary cat litters – by the time the kitten is ready to leave his mother she will have taught him what the tray is for.

Feeding

Like puppies, kittens should be started on four small meals a day, with two larger ones for an adult cat. It is a widely held belief that cats should be fed mainly on fish but, in fact, too much fish is not at all good for them. Even an adult cat should be given fresh cooked fish only on alternate days. A varied diet is best, including fresh tripe and lights, both well cooked, and other cheaper meats and fish, freshly cooked, in addition to tinned cat foods. Raw beef or marrow bones are good for their teeth.

Some cats are greatly attracted to dried cat foods, and these may be given once or twice a week as long as you make absolutely sure that plenty of fresh water is available, even if you give the cat milk. But don't feed these dried foods if your cat has any history of kidney disorder, because it is suspected they may aggravate this.

Cats and kittens also need to eat grass from time to time because it causes them to vomit and bring up any fur which licking themselves may have caused to accumulate into a hair-ball in the stomach. If you live in a town you can buy special grass seeds to grow on a tray indoors. These are sold at pet shops.

Health

At 12 weeks old all cats should be vaccinated against feline enteritis, which is frequently fatal.

Giving medicine

Cats can be difficult to handle when you want them to do something they do not want to, so

Before dosing a cat protect yourself by wrapping him firmly in a thick towel

before trying to give a cat any kind of medicine it is as well to wrap him in a thick towel, or a duffle bag with the drawstring tightened so that only his head is outside.

Get someone to hold the cat; you will need both hands to give the medicine.

To open a cat's mouth, put your left hand over his head and press gently with your thumb and forefinger on the cheeks at both sides, tilting his head back slightly as you press. His mouth should then open, and if the medicine is a powder or liquid pour it in very gently, and close the mouth quickly and hold it closed until the cat swallows.

A tablet or pill should be given in the same way, but in addition stroke the front of a cat's throat to encourage him to swallow.

Quarantine

As for dogs, above.

HAMSTERS

Hamsters are probably the best choice of pet for young families living in towns. The only cause for sadness will be that their life is short, usually only two to three years.

Hamsters are clean enough to be kept in a cage in the living room, but because they are experts at chewing their way out of places start with a strong hardwood box if you are making the cage yourself, or buy one lined with aluminium sheets from a pet shop. To give the hamster room to exercise and play, his home should be at least 46 cm long, 30 cm high, and with a glass front and a lid made of 13 mm or finer wire netting. Cover the floor with a layer of sawdust and give him a small sleeping box in one corner of the cage, lined with wood shavings or hay. Put a jam jar on its side in another corner for the hamster to use for its droppings.

Hamsters need plenty of light and fresh air but must be protected from damp, draughts and strong sunlight.

Feeding
A hamster thrives on a mash of biscuit meal with tablescraps of meat, cheese, egg and vegetables mixed together with milk. He also needs fresh green vegetables and nuts, raisins and pieces of apple make a special treat. Give him water in a heavy dish so he will not upset it when he is playing.

If you have more than one hamster, they will be better kept apart except at breeding time. Even two of the same sex may fight if you put them in a cage together.

RABBITS AND GUINEA PIGS (Cavies)
Rabbits of the same sex will happily share a cage together, but guinea pigs, like hamsters, are better kept apart.

Both rabbits and guinea pigs can be kept either indoors or out – a garden shed is ideal – and a packing case can be adapted to make a suitable hutch. Part of it should be partitioned off and made draught-proof for sleeping quarters. Cover the floor of the hutch with sawdust and a generous layer of straw. The hutch should be cleaned out daily and scrubbed thoroughly with soap and water once a month.

Feeding
Rabbits and guinea pigs love to nibble, so they should be given plenty of snacks of fresh greenstuff in addition to one main meal a day in the case of a fully grown animal. This should be a bran mash with tablescraps of cooked vegetables and bread crusts added to it, or one of the prepared rabbit foods. Give fresh water every day, more often if needed.

BUDGERIGARS
Budgerigars are cheerful and attractive and need so little looking-after they make an ideal pet for older people living alone.

If you plan to teach your budgerigar to talk, you will need to look for a very young bird, one that is only just ready to leave the nest.

You can tell which sex a budgerigar is by the colouring of the skin covering the base of its beak, known as the 'cere', which is brown in females, blue in males.

The larger his cage, the happier a budgie will be. Perches should be at least 10 mm wide, narrower ones can harm the bird's feet. Never leave the cage by the window in the full glare of the sun, and if you take it outside on warm days – which is good for the bird – be sure you hang it in a shady place well out of the way of cats who can hook their paws through the bars. The bottom tray of the cage should be taken out each day and the soiled sand replaced.

Feeding
In addition to their standard diet of birdseed, budgerigars need greenstuff such as lettuce or cabbage (or groundsel and chickweed, if you can get some). Keep the container in his cage filled with fresh water. A cuttle fish bone or iodine block fixed to the side of the cage gives him something to peck at and helps stop his beak from growing too long.

Measurement

METRIC MEASURES

1 millimetre (mm)		= 0·0394 inch (in)
1 centimetre (cm)	= 10 mm	= 0·3937 in
1 metre (m)	= 100 cm	= 1·0936 yards (yd)
1 kilometre (km)	= 1000 m	= 0·6214 mile
1 square centimetre (cm^2)	= 100 mm^2	= 0·1550 sq in
1 square metre (m^2)	= 10000 cm^2	= 1·1960 sq yd
1 square kilometre (km^2)	= 100 hectares	= 0·3861 sq mile
1 hectare	= 10000 m^2	= 2·4710 acres
1 cubic centimetre (cm^3)		= 0·0610 cu in
1 cubic metre (m^3)	= 10000 cm^3	= 1·3080 cu yd
1 litre (l)	= 1000 cm^3	= 1·7598 pints
		= 35 fluid ounces (fl oz)
1 milligram (mg)		= 0·0154 grain
1 gram (g)	= 1000 mg	= 0·0353 ounce (oz)
1 kilogram (kg)	= 1000 g	= 2·2046 pounds (lb)
1 tonne (t)	= 1000 kg	= 0·9842 ton

BRITISH MEASURES

1 inch (in)		= 2·5400 cm
1 foot (ft)	= 12 in	= 30·4800 cm
1 yard (yd)	= 3 ft	= 0·9144 m
1 mile	= 1760 yd	= 1·6093 km
1 sq in		= 6·4516 cm^2
1 sq ft	= 144 sq in	= 0·0929 m^2
1 sq yd	= 9 sq ft	= 0·8361 m^2
1 acre	= 4840 sq yd	= 4046·9 m^2
1 sq mile	= 640 acres	= 259·0 hectares
1 cu in		= 16·387 cm^3
1 cu ft	= 1728 cu in	= 0·0283 m^3
		= 28·3 litres (l)
1 cu yd	= 27 cu ft	= 0·7646 m^3
1 fluid ounce (fl oz)		= 28·4 ml
1 pint (pt)	= 20 fl oz	= 0·5683 l
1 gallon	= 8 pt	= 4·5460 l
1 ounce (oz)		= 28·3500 g
1 pound (lb)	= 16 oz	= 0·4536 kg
1 stone	= 14 lb	= 6·3503 kg
1 hundredweight (cwt)	= 112 lb	= 50·8020 kg
1 ton	= 20 cwt	= 1·0160 tonnes

SOME USEFUL WORKING EQUIVALENTS

2·5 cm	= approx. 1 in
1 m	= approx. 3 ft 3 in
1 km	= approx. 5/8 mile
28 g	= approx. 1 oz
1 kg	= approx. 2·25 lb
1 tonne	= a little less than 1 ton
1 litre (l)	= approx. 1·75 pints, or 35 fl oz
1 hectare	= a little less than 2½ acres
1 km^2	= approx. 3/8 sq mile

FABRIC LENGTHS

Yards	Approx. cms
⅛ yard	10cm
¼ yard	23cm
⅜ yard	34cm
½ yard	46cm
⅝ yard	57cm
⅞ yard	80cm
1¼ yard	90cm
1⅛ yard	1·0m
2 yard	1·8m
3 yard	2·7m
4 yard	3·7m
5 yard	4·6m
6 yard	5·5m

Note: Fabrics are sold in multiples of 10 cm
Quick reference: 10cm is approximately 4 in

FABRIC WIDTHS

in	cm
36	91
48	122
54	137
72	183

MISCELLANEOUS

	GUIDE TO METRIC COOKING					
	Use these equivalents to make metric recipes that will fit your cake tins and bowls.					
Imperial Measurement	Approx. Metric Equivalent	Imperial Measurement	Approx. Metric Equivalent	Imperial Measurement	Approx. Metric Equivalent	
1 oz	25g	9 oz	250g	1 fl oz	25 ml	
2 oz	50g	10 oz	275g	2 fl oz	50 ml	
3 oz	75g	11 oz	300g	5 fl oz	150 ml	
4 oz	100–125g	12 oz	350g	10 fl oz	300 ml	
5 oz	150g	13 oz	375g	15 fl oz	400 ml	
6 oz	175g	14 oz	400g	20 fl oz	600 ml	
7 oz	200g	15 oz	425g	35 fl oz	1 litre	
8 oz	225g	16 oz	450g			

Bed and linen sizes

Beds
The usual bed sizes are:
Small Single, 90 cm × 190 cm
Small Double, 135 cm × 190 cm
Standard Single, 100 cm × 200 cm
Standard Double 150 cm × 200 cm
Bunk beds vary in size from 69 cm × 175 cm to 90 cm × 190 cm.
  Special sized beds are available to order.

Mattresses
Mattresses come in the same width and length dimensions as beds, but vary in thickness.

Fitted sheets
Fitted sheets are made to fit mattress sizes and are labelled accordingly. They are normally designed for a mattress of average thickness, 18 cm to 20 cm. It is possible to obtain larger size sheets for mattresses exceeding 150 cm × 200 cm.

286

Flat sheets
Flat sheets come in differing sizes which vary according to the amount of shrinkage that can be expected for the type of fabric. Choose the sheet size according to the mattress but large enough to give a good tuck-in allowing for the depth of mattress.

Pillowcases
The standard pillowcase size is 50 cm × 75 cm.

Blankets
The sizes listed in the chart below provide for an adequate tuck-in with the appropriate size mattress of average thickness.

Larger sizes
As well as the dimensions given in the table below, blankets and flat sheets are also available in extra large sizes – blankets up to 300 cm × 250 cm and sheets up to 305 cm × 320 cm.

Bed size	Mattress size		Recommended blanket size		Sheet sizes available				
					Sheets made of: man-made fibres, blends with man-made fibres, cotton with easy-care finish, flannelette with easy-care finish			Sheets made of: untreated cotton, untreated flannelette	
	Width	*Length*	*Width*	*Length*	*Width*	*Length*		*Width*	*Length*
	cm	cm	cm	cm	cm	cm		cm	cm
Small Single	90 ×	190	180 ×	240	175 ×	260		175 ×	255
					180 ×	255		175 ×	275
					180 ×	260		180 ×	275
								200 ×	255
								200 ×	275
Standard Single	100 ×	200	200 ×	250	175 ×	260		175 ×	275
					180 ×	260		180 ×	275
								200 ×	275
Small Double	135 ×	190	230 ×	250	230 ×	255		230 ×	255
					230 ×	260		230 ×	275
Standard Double	150 ×	200	260 ×	250	230 ×	260		230 ×	275

Temperature

To convert degrees Celsius (°C) to degrees Fahrenheit (°F): $°C = \frac{5}{9}(°F) - 32$ $°F = \frac{9}{5}(°C) + 32$

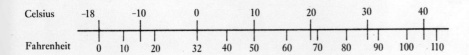

Fire

If a fire breaks out – unless you can put it out quickly and safely – it is *essential* to follow the rules below:

1 Get everyone out of the room where the fire is and close the doors and windows. Even an ordinary door can hold fire back. If the door is left open fire, smoke and fumes can spread through the house to overcome or trap occupants.

2 See that everyone gets out of the house.

3 Call the Fire Brigade by dialling 999 – or your relevant local procedure.

4 When you have called the Fire Brigade you can try and put the fire out – but only if you are not putting yourself at risk to do so.

DON'T open the door of a room you suspect may be on fire. This can cause the fire to grow rapidly.

If you get trapped

1 Go to an unaffected room on the street side of the house. Keep low to avoid smoke.

2 Close the door and block the gap at the bottom with a rug, towel or blanket.

3 Shout for help from the window.

DON'T jump unless you really have to.

Clothes on fire

1 Lie down at once (or force the victim to).

2 Roll across the floor to extinguish the flames.

3 If possible wrap yourself or the victim in a rug, coat, heavy curtain or, best of all, a special fire blanket.

4 For any burn larger than the size of a hand, get medical help as soon as possible.

DON'T delay lying down – time lost could allow flames to reach your face.

FIRE EXTINGUISHERS

Fire extinguishers may work with either foam, dry powder, carbon dioxide (gas) or water. Water extinguishers are not suitable for fires involving live electrical equipment or flammable liquids or 'chip pan' fires. All these types of fire extinguisher need annual servicing, and disposable ones replacing every five years.

Also available are special fire blankets, usually made from glass fibre.

Read the instructions carefully on any extinguisher so you know how to use it in an emergency. Whichever type you buy make sure it is BSI or Fire Officers' Committee approved.

HOW TO DEAL WITH DIFFERENT FIRE OUTBREAKS

Oil heater fires

DO stand at least 2 m away from the heater – then throw buckets of water over it.

DO close the door behind you if you leave the room to get more water.

DON'T try and carry the heater outside until the fire is out. Remember the case will still be hot so wear gloves.

DON'T try and deal with any surrounding fire until the heater fire is extinguished.

Guard against oil heater fires

1 Never buy a heater without the BSI Kite-mark.

2 Never use any liquid in the heater other than paraffin, and never fill it while alight.

3 Always place the heater where it cannot be knocked over, or better still fix it to the wall or floor by the fixing device incorporated.

Oil heater fire: throw water on it

Electrical fire: use a dry powder or carbon dioxide fire extinguisher

Chip pan fire: smother the flames with the pan lid

4 Keep the heater level.

5 Keep it away from draughts.

6 Never carry or move the heater while it is alight.

7 Have the heater serviced regularly.

Electrical fires

NEVER use water on live electrical equipment.

ALWAYS unplug the appliance involved or switch off at the mains. Then you can use water – but a dry powder or carbon dioxide fire extinguisher is better.

Prevent electrical fires

1 Always remember to switch off at the socket and unplug any electrical equipment that is not in use – this is particularly vital with TV sets.

2 Don't overload electrical sockets.

3 Don't leave an electric under blanket on once you are in bed (unless it is a low voltage type marked as safe to be used all night).

4 Have the house wiring checked every five years – it will probably need replacing after 25.

Chip pan fires (or any fires involving cooking fats and oils).

DO turn off the heat, smother the fire with a lid, metal tray, damp cloth or fire blanket to cut off the air supply to the flames.

NEVER pour on water, or put the pan in a sink full of water.

NEVER try to carry a burning pan or to take it outside – the flames may blow back on you.

Prevent chip pan fires

Never leave the pan on the stove unattended.

DIY product fires

If a flammable liquid such as a paint thinner or stripper, methylated spirits, white spirit, adhesive or some kind of cleaning fluid catches fire:

NEVER use water or a water-operated fire extinguisher.

ALWAYS smother the flames with a blanket or dry powder extinguisher.

Guard against flammable liquid fires

1 Always work with the doors and windows open.

2 Never smoke or use naked lights.

3 Keep flammable liquids in cool, airy places – not under the kitchen sink or in a cupboard containing hot water pipes. Do not keep these materials under the stairs. A fire here could cut off your only escape.

4 Don't allow waste to pile up – get rid of old rags, etc as you use them.

Chimney and fireplace fires
Put out a fireplace fire with water. In the case of a chimney fire:

1 Call the Fire Brigade by dialling 999 or the relevant local emergency procedure.

2 Shut down the ventilation to the fireplace and close the doors and windows.

3 Move the furniture and carpets back from the hearth.

4 Check the other rooms through which the chimney passes and if the walls are getting hot, move the furniture back there as well.

Prevent fireplace and chimney fires
1 Use a fireguard conforming to British Standard specification – it is an offence to allow children in a room with an unguarded fire of any sort.

2 Do not use a fireguard for drying or airing clothes.

3 Make sure the fire is out, or very low, and the guard in position before you go to bed.

4 Have your chimneys swept regularly, and do not let soot collect in the lower part of the flue of an open fire – remove it with a soft brush, but let the fire go out before removing soot.

FIRE PREVENTION
1 If you smell gas, extinguish cigarettes and any naked lights such as pilot lights; do not look for the leak yourself. Turn off the main gas tap (next to the meter) and your appliance taps, including the pilot lights.
Then telephone Gas Service.

2 Keep matches away from children – and impress on them the dangers of fire.

3 Remember that, by law, children's nightdresses must be made of material of low flammability and old people can benefit from this precaution too.

4 Last thing at night, make a safety check to see that the cooker is off and all cigarette ends com-

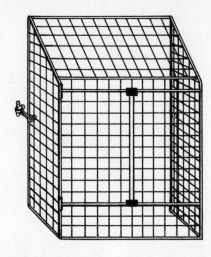

Always use a fireguard in a room where there are children or old people. It should fix to the wall

pletely stubbed out. As you leave downstairs rooms, close the doors behind you – then if fire does break out it may be contained and danger reduced.

5 Never, never smoke in bed.

FAMILY FIRE DRILL
It is a good idea to have a practice fire drill from time to time, so everyone knows what to do in an emergency.

1 Make a list of alternative emergency escape routes, and make sure that everybody knows them. Arrange a place to meet.

2 Make everyone practise keeping low – as if avoiding smoke – and protecting nose and mouth with towels or other material.

3 Check the position of the nearest call box *and* neighbour with telephone. Make sure that everybody knows the procedure for dialling the Fire Brigade, and can give the address of the fire clearly.

4 If escape is impossible, impress on children the importance of getting to the window and shouting for help *at once*. Hiding can be fatal.

First aid

Calling an ambulance
To call an ambulance in most parts of Britain – dial 999. If you are in any doubt or difficulty, dial 100 and ask the telephone operator for help.

ARTIFICIAL RESPIRATION
In any case where the victim is not breathing deal with this first, even before sending for medical help. In most cases the 'kiss of life' or mouth-to-mouth (or nose) method is best.

1 Clear the air passages by pulling the patient's head as far back as it will go and bringing the lower jaw upwards and forwards. Clear the mouth and throat of any obvious blood, vomit, loose teeth or dentures.

2 Pinch the patient's nostrils together so the air you breathe into him cannot escape through his nose.

3 Breathe in deeply and put your mouth over the patient's mouth – for a small child or baby put your mouth over his nose as well.

4 Blow out with just enough force to make his chest rise. If the air is still not going into his lungs, put his head further back and try again until his chest moves as you breathe.

Note: if you find it easier, you can keep the patient's mouth shut with your thumb and put your mouth over his nose instead.

5 Keep up the treatment until the patient begins to breathe for himself.

6 When he is breathing fairly regularly, stop the artificial respiration and turn him on his side in case he vomits (see under 'Unconsciousness' for the recovery position, page 293).

BLEEDING
1 Find where the bleeding is coming from; remove or cut away clothing if necessary. Lay the patient flat.

2 Apply pressure as follows: where the wound is large and no fracture is suspected, or foreign bodies (such as glass) embedded, apply firm pressure directly on the wound. Use a sterile bandage if possible, but your handkerchief, or even your

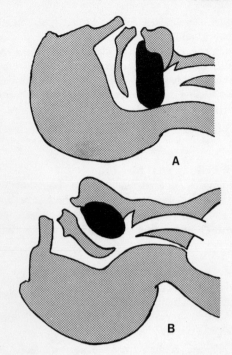

A

B

Unconscious person lying on his back. A. Shows how the tongue may fall to the back of the throat blocking the airway B. Shows that if the neck is extended, the head pressed backwards and the jaw pushed upwards, the tongue moves forward opening the air passages

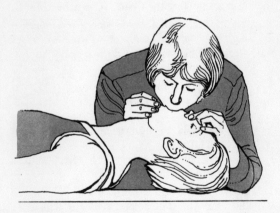

Mouth to mouth method of artificial respiration

fingers will do. If you suspect a fracture or if there are foreign bodies in the wound, apply the pressure around, above and below but not directly on the wound.

3 As soon as pressure appears to be controlling the

291

bleeding, remove any foreign bodies that you can without touching the wound and apply a large dressing of sterile gauze or clean linen. Cover this with a thick pad and bandage firmly. If the wound continues to bleed and soaks through the bandage do not remove it but place another pad on top of the first and bandage again firmly.

4 Treat for SHOCK (see page 293) until the ambulance arrives.

Suspected internal bleeding
In a case of suspected internal bleeding the casualty will look pale and sweaty, the skin will be cold and the pulse rapid and feeble. Keep him lying down and treat for SHOCK until help arrives.

BURNS AND SCALDS
Burns are caused by flame or dry heat such as electricity or chemicals.

1 As far as possible, remove the heat source causing the damage.

2 If clothing is alight, lay the person down and put out the flames by smothering them in a rug or other heavy material.

3 Cool the burn by flooding it in cold water (for at least ten minutes for a chemical or fireworks burn or until the pain has gone). If possible remove any jewellery, watch, socks and shoes near the burnt area before the tissues have time to swell.

4 Cover the area with a sterile – or at least clean – dressing, but do not use cotton wool or other fluffy-textured material, and do not apply any oil or grease or butter to the burn.

5 If the victim is conscious, treat for SHOCK until the ambulance arrives.

Scalds are caused by heat from liquids such as water, steam, fat, tar.

1 As far as possible, remove the heat source causing the damage.

2 If any very hot clothing comes off easily, remove it; if not, leave it. Then flood the area with cold water for at least ten minutes or until the pain goes.

3 Remove jewellery, socks and shoes etc. near to the affected area before the tissues have time to swell.

4 Treat for SHOCK while waiting for medical help.

ELECTRIC SHOCK
Domestic voltage (electric fires etc)

1 Switch off the power supply if you possibly can.

2 If you can't switch off the power and the victim is still in contact, insulate yourself by standing on something dry and wrap your hand in thick newspaper or several layers of dry fabric.

3 Knock or pull the patient away from contact with the current.

4 Check that he is still breathing, if not give ARTIFICIAL RESPIRATION (see page 291).

5 Treat for BURNS until help arrives.

High voltage burns, from overhead electric cables, railway lines etc.

You can do NOTHING to help until you are certain that the power has been cut off. Keep away – at least 25 metres from the accident – and keep others away too. Once power is off, treat as for domestic electric shock and burns.

FRACTURES
Signs of a limb fracture include deformity of the part compared to the other side, pain when touched or a movement is attempted, swelling and loss of use.

Treatment Control any bleeding by applying pressure above and below but not on the suspected fracture. Immobilise by bandaging an arm to the body or a leg to the other leg.

Signs of a skull fracture include drowsiness or unconsciousness, slow breathing and pulse, pupils of unequal size, twitching muscles, bleeding from nose or ear.

Bandage a fractured arm against the patient's body to support it

Treatment Until help arrives do not move the patient unless absolutely unavoidable and under no circumstances give anything to eat or drink.

Signs of a collar bone fracture include swelling or deformity over the site of the fracture and the arm on the injured side will be partly helpless.

Treatment Allow the casualty to support the elbow of the affected side with the other hand until you can get him to a doctor or hospital.

HEART ATTACK
Symptoms Severe cramp-like pains in the centre of the chest, at the front and behind the breast bone. Pain may also spread up into the neck and jaw, or to the shoulder and down one or both arms. The victim will look grey and may sweat with the pain. He may also be breathless and even become unconscious. In a severe attack his heart may stop.

Treatment
1 Make the patient rest with his head and shoulders propped up. Loosen any tight clothing; open the windows if he is in a stuffy place.
2 If his breathing stops give the 'kiss of life', see 'Artificial respiration'.
3 When you telephone for help, explain that you think the patient has had a heart attack; some ambulances are specially equipped.
4 Do not allow the patient to move until the ambulance arrives, even if the pain is comparatively mild.

POISONING
Check that the patient is breathing and that his heart is beating. If not, give ARTIFICIAL RESPIRATION (page 291).

If the patient is conscious, try and discover the name and amount of the poison. If the poison has caused burning of the mouth or lips give him water or milk to dilute any poison remaining in the stomach. Keep any vomited matter for the doctor to see. If breathing place in the recovery position. Otherwise start artificial respiration straight away.

SHOCK
Symptoms Pale appearance, cold, sweaty skin, pulse and breathing rapid and shallow. Shock may develop even if a person has at first seemed in good condition. If not treated he is likely to lapse into unconsciousness and may die.

Treatment
1 Make the patient lie down and raise his legs so they are higher than the level of his head. Turn his head to one side.
2 If he is likely to vomit, place him in the recovery position.
3 Loosen any tight clothing, especially round the neck and waist.
4 Cover him with a blanket or coat, but do not give him a hot water bottle.
5 Do not give *anything* to eat or drink.

UNCONSCIOUSNESS (and the Recovery Position)
If a patient is breathing but unconscious and it seems safe to move him, he is best placed in the recovery position:
1 Lie him on his side to face the side you are standing. Then bring the upper arm forward so that his hand is on the ground in front of him at right angles to his body. Bend the elbow of his arm.
2 Bend the knee of the uppermost leg so this too rests on the ground in front.
3 Pull up his chin to maintain a clear air passage. If possible, arrange a slight head down tip so that any fluid or vomit will drain outwards rather than into the lungs.

DAY-TO-DAY FIRST AID
Animal bites If skin is unbroken, treat with a

Recovery position

cold compress. If skin is broken, bathe with soap and water, cover with a clean dressing and see the doctor.

Blisters Do not prick. Cover with a dry dressing.

Bruises and black eyes Apply a cold compress as soon as possible.

Choking If a small child is choking, up-end him and pat him between the shoulder blades with your hand. If the object is not dislodged, take him to hospital at once. Do not give anything to eat or drink in the meantime.

In the case of an adult, strike him three or four sharp blows between the shoulder blades. After clearing the object give artificial respiration if necessary.

Cuts Stop the bleeding (see page 291) and clean the cut thoroughly by holding it under the cold tap. If the cut is too big to be covered by a ready-made adhesive dressing, cover it with a small pad of gauze held in place by two or three strips of sticking plaster running across the wound (but check

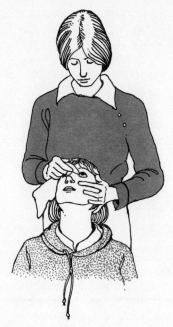

Working from behind the patient, you are best placed to remove a foreign body from the eye without causing damage

Three or four sharp slaps between the shoulders will dislodge most blockages

that the casualty is not allergic to sticking plaster first; if necessary use a bandage to secure the dressing). For large, deep or dirty cuts get medical help. Tetanus protection may be necessary.

Foreign bodies
In the eye Sit the patient facing the light and stand behind him with his head tilted back against you. Tell him to look at the ceiling and pull the lower lid down and away from the surface of the eye. With the corner of a clean handkerchief dipped in water wipe the foreign body towards the corner of the eye by the nose – but do not wipe across the pupil or the iris – and lift it out.

In the ear or nose Do not attempt to remove. Go to the doctor.

Faintness Make the patient sit with his head between his knees. If someone has fainted loosen any tight clothing and see that he has plenty of fresh air. When he comes round do not let him get up too suddenly or he may faint again. Once he has fully recovered, give him a drink of water.

Grazes Clean well and cover with a light gauze

dressing. When changing the dressing you may need to soak it off if it has stuck.

Jellyfish stings See under 'Stings'.

Nose bleeds Apply a cold water pad to the bridge of the nose and pinch the nostrils together for ten minutes to allow a clot to form. If bleeding persists, go to hospital. Make the patient sit upright and see he keeps holding his nose.

Splinters and thorns Sterilize a sewing needle by holding it in a flame until it is red hot, or by keeping it in steadily boiling water for five minutes, then allow it to cool but do not wipe off any soot. Use the needle to loosen the splinter enough to squeeze it out, or so it can be pinched out with a pair of tweezers.

Stings Use calamine lotion on jellyfish and nettle stings. Contrary to common belief both wasp and bee stings are acid, so swab the sting with an alkaline solution made from a teaspoonful of bicarbonate soda in a small cup of water or use a proprietary aerosol product for sting relief. A bee often leaves its poison sac in the skin, so do not squeeze the stung area; scrape the surface of the skin gently to ease out the sting without pressing.

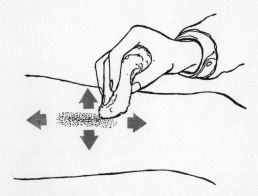

When cleaning a wound always wipe away from the centre, not over it

For a sting in the mouth or throat give ice cubes to suck or sips of cold water to counteract swelling. If there is any likelihood of suffocation get the casualty to a doctor quickly.

Sunburn The discomfort of minor sunburn can be eased by a tepid bath or by applying cool, wet cloths to the skin provided it isn't broken. Severe sunburn needs medical attention.

Index

303